SPIES & ESPIONAGE

A DIRECTORY

Chester G. Hearn

SPIES &
ESPIONAGE

A DIRECTORY

THUNDER BAY
P·R·E·S·S

San Diego, California

Thunder Bay Press
An imprint of the Advantage Publishers Group
5880 Oberlin Drive, San Diego, CA 92121-4794
www.thunderbaybooks.com

All notations of errors or omissions should be addressed to Thunder Bay Press, Editorial Department, at the above address. All other correspondence (author enquiries, permissions) concerning the content of this book should be addressed to BlueRed Press, 82 Elms Road, Clapham, London SW4 9EW, jbryant@blueredpress.com.

ISBN 13: 978-1-59223-508-7
ISBN 10: 1-59223-508-5

Library of Congress Cataloging-in-Publication Data available on request.

Printed in China
1 2 3 4 5   10 09 08 07 06

CONTENTS

INTRODUCTION

Spies are timeless, and espionage is an ever-evolving science. Four thousand years ago, warring Greeks employed spies to infiltrate the enemy's army to learn their secrets. They had no radios, cell phones, or satellites to communicate their observations, so they improvised. A Greek general and his spy used two earthen jars, each with a tiny hole of exactly the same size, plugged near the bottom. Each jar contained an identical float holding an upright arm that projected above the jar. The vertical arm contained spaced symbols, each signifying one of many possible messages the spy could communicate to his general.

The general on the hill kept one jar and the spy in the enemy's camp kept the other. When the spy determined the enemy's intentions, he hoisted a signal flag by day or a fire by night, giving notice when the plugs were to be simultaneously pulled from the jars. As the water trickled from the spy's jar, and the upright arm on the float dropped to the symbol of the desired message, the spy signaled the general to replug the jar. The general then compared the symbol to his list of prepared messages. The process could be repeated and several messages sent, but the general had no recourse to intelligence not on the message list!

From biblical times to the modern era, monarchs, dictators, warlords, politicians, generals, and even well-organized intelligence agencies have relied upon the individual spy to gather secret information. Some spies worked at the trade out of patriotism or support of a cause and expected no compensation. They were the exceptions. Most spies worked at the trade because it paid extremely well. When Karl Louis Schulmeister, who spied for Napoleon during the early nineteenth century, asked to be awarded the coveted Legion of Honor for military services,

Bonaparte stiffly replied, "gold is the only suitable reward for spies."

Some of the more interesting spies were double agents. In pre-Communist Russia, Yevno Philopovich Azev was one of the most ruthless double-dealing spymasters. He spied for the czarist government and at the same time spied for Communist organizations conspiring to overthrow the czar. Azev became very wealthy by recruiting one band of assassins to

Below: Yevgeny Maksimovich Primakov, former head of the KGB (now the SVR) and Russia's first post-Soviet spymaster, recently described modern intelligence activities: "We must use analytical methods, synthesize information. This is scientific work."

murder revolutionaries and another band of assassins to murder czarist officials. Then, to cover his bloody handiwork, he exposed the assassins and collected additional rewards.

During World War II, safecracker Eddie "Zigzag" Chapman came off the streets of London to become one of the shrewdest double agents to ever serve Great Britain. Every spectacular mission he performed for the Germans, including supposedly blowing up a British aircraft plant, was a charade, a setup, or a fake. Chapman's motives were different than most spies. He did it to expunge his criminal record in Great Britain, but he also collected fat fees from the Germans for stunts he never committed.

Alfred Redl, Austrian director of espionage, spied for Germany, Russia, and anyone who would pay him. Using Redl's own handwritten instructions for identifying spies, one of his colleagues' caught him, and Redl committed suicide.

There were also spies who were poorly trained and oblivious to the safeguards necessary to protect their lives. George Washington sent Nathan Hale to spy on the British, and because Hale knew nothing about spying, he lost his life on a British scaffold. During World War II, British intelligence sent Noor Inayat Khan, a timid and poorly trained woman, to France as a radio operator for the French underground. The Gestapo caught Inayat Khan and disposed of her at Dachau. During World War I the French executed Mata Hari as a German spy, but she never stole any secrets; Mata Hari suffered the great misfortune of having a German lover in intelligence that put her on the payroll in exchange for sexual favors, not for divulging French secrets.

Espionage began evolving in the sixteenth century, first as an art and later as a science. Its history is filled with gaps. The greatest spies may remain unknown because they were never caught. During the early seventeenth century, Cardinal Richelieu built a French espionage network composed of tens of thousands of spies, including spies who spied on spies. The only other network of equal size may have been Japanese colonel Kenji Doihara's organization in China prior to, and during, World War II. Doihara's network relied upon opium-dependent Chinese and foreign prostitutes who received their daily ration of food and opium only if they extracted intelligence from their customers.

Below: Little has changed in Russia. President Vladimir Putin (left) and former KGB chief Yevgeny Primakov (right) visit the World Trade Center after Putin's announcement of a "massive" escalation in intelligence-gathering efforts in the United States and Western Europe.

The Russian espionage system began evolving in the nineteenth century, when the Okhrana secret police came into existence to protect the czar from assassins and attacks on the government. In 1917, when the Bolsheviks took control of Russia, they wiped out the Okhrana and formed the Cheka, the Soviet secret state police and intelligence organization. Through the years, the Cheka evolved into the KGB, which, during the cold war, may have become the only other network on earth that hired as may spies as Richelieu or Doihara.

Some of the most successful espionage operations were self-contained units operating with a small number of dedicated spies, reporting to a single spymaster. During the American Revolution, Benjamin Tallmadge's Culper Ring operated with six men, most of whom used aliases. Nobody discovered the names of the spies and their couriers for more than a hundred years.

During the cold war, the Portland Spy Ring in England consisted of four spies working exclusively for one Soviet agent, Gordon Lonesdale. Without Lonesdale, the Soviets would have remained far behind in the development of underwater weapons.

During World War II the Soviets operated two tightly knit rings against the Nazis. One became known as the Black Orchestra, the other the Red Orchestra. Neither orchestra had anything to do with music, although Black Orchestra radio operators communicated a modest amount of intelligence by broadcasting coded musical compositions. The Black Orchestra included senior German officers who opposed Hitler and later plotted his assassination. They were not Communists, but the group passed intelligence to Joseph Stalin through Rudolf Roessler's "Lucy" spy ring in Switzerland, which was financially supported by Moscow. The Red Orchestra played no music, but their transmitters were called "music boxes" and their operators "musicians." The Red Orchestra also had high-placed spies in the German government and in German-occupied territory that fed intelligence to Moscow.

Much of what we know about spies comes from their own published accounts, which cannot always be trusted for accuracy. Except in the Soviet Union, most World War II and cold war spies were not executed, but merely served prison sentences. Once paroled, they wrote memoirs, often with the help of professional writers who knew how to make a good story even better.

Espionage came of age during and after World War II. Radio communication, telephones, modern photographic equipment, microdots, special invisible inks, cipher codes, recording machines, and electronic bugs all gave way to computers, floppy disks, CDs, cell phones, surveillance cameras, and satellites.

A perception exists that following the collapse of the Soviet Union and the beginning of perestroika, spies became unemployed. After the capture and trial of Aldrich Ames and Jonathan Pollard in 1985, spies became a virtually forgotten threat in today's society, but they are still out there.

Former KGB head (1991–1996) and later foreign minister Yevgeny M. Primakov admitted a lapse in espionage after the Soviet collapse in 1991 but also acknowledged stepping up the program in 1994. During the administrations of Ronald Reagan and George H. W. Bush, the U.S. government approved the development of weapons technology far beyond Russia's capability, which meant that the KGB had to get back to the business of stealing secrets. The administration of President Clinton helped pave the way for secrets theft by authorizing Jamie Gorelick, Attorney General Janet Reno's deputy, to issue an order building a wall between CIA operations and the FBI. The imposed disconnect between the two agencies simply opened the way for Russia, China, and other foreign espionage agents to infiltrate the U.S. government, its weapons research centers, and satellite communications companies, and remain undetected and at large indefinitely. Gorelick's single-page directive probably set back counterintelligence efforts in the United States 10–20 years.

From before 1161 BC, through World War II and the cold war, and up to the present day, the CIA, FBI, KGB, MI6, Mossad, and other agencies have spied on each other's countries, their own countries, their own spies, and other peoples' spies. Is it any wonder that this old art, and new science, is so fascinating?

ABEL, RUDOLF IVANOVICH (1902–1971)

Soviet spy Rudolf Ivanovich might have died an old man in the United States had his finely tuned operation not been corrupted by a careless subordinate.

Colonel Rudolf Ivonovich Abel came close to winning high honors for becoming the top spymaster in the United States for the KGB (Soviet intelligence). From 1948 to 1957, he operated a successful network of spies out of his small, rented photography studio in New York. During those years he shuttled some of America's most carefully guarded secrets to the KGB. Suspicions were first aroused when the FBI heard of a newspaper boy who had accidentally been given a hollow nickel containing microfilm, but it wasn't until several years later that Abel and his espionage activities were more fully revealed.

Though born in czarist Russia in 1902, Abel never saw much of his native country as a youth because in 1903 his family emigrated to Great Britain. Abel's father moved the family to Scotland, and young Rudolf grew up speaking English with a perfect Scottish accent. When, in 1921, the family moved back to Russia to support the revolution, 18-year-old Abel's lingual fluencies included English, Russian, German, Polish, and Yiddish.

```
----DOSSIER--------
Name: Rudolf Ivanovich Abel
Code Name: Mark
Birth/Death: 1902-1971
Nationality: Russian
Occupation: Language Expert
Involvement: Soviet Spy in
the United States
Outcome: Died of Natural
Causes in Moscow
```

Experiments in Espionage

The NKVD, the Soviet intelligence forerunner to the KGB, hired Abel as a language instructor. When World War II erupted, 38-year-old Abel served with distinction as an intelligence officer on the German front and won several

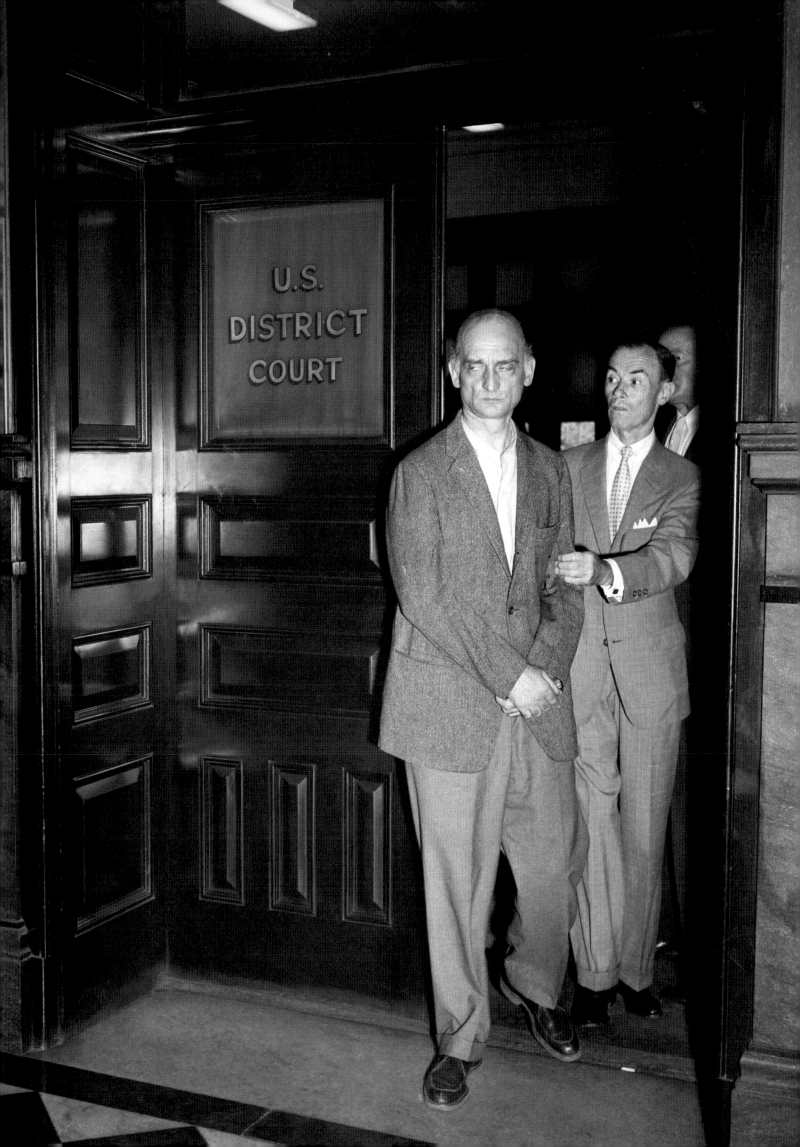

Above: Rudolf Abel at the U.S. District Court in Brooklyn, New York, after his arraignment. Following his trial, Abel appealed his convictions, claiming that rights guaranteed to him under the Constitution and laws of the United States had been violated. A five-to-four decision handed down by the Supreme Court on March 28, 1960, upheld the original convictions.

and UN political policies that could have strategic impact on the Kremlin.

In addition to language skills, Abel had developed proficiency in engineering, chemistry, nuclear physics, radio technology, and photography. He also learned the jewelers' trade and became expert at photographing documents, reducing them to microdots, and embedding the miniature dot in watches, rings, bracelets, cuff links, and hollowed-out screws. He built his own powerful shortwave radio transmitter from commercial components, and began sending and receiving coded information with Moscow. His messages came and went, usually at random times and places during the night to deceive the U.S. tracking devices in the field searching for such transmissions.

The Photographic Studio of Emil Goldfus

Abel fit perfectly into postwar New York. Through the local Communist Party he obtained a new identity as Emil R. Goldfus, and a birth certificate to prove that he had been born in New York City. The real Goldfus had died 40 years earlier at the age of two months. Being a small, slightly built, inauspicious Jewish photographer who dabbled in painting and music, Abel, a.k.a. Goldfus, passed as a bohemian artist with average skills and a pleasant demeanor no one would ever particularly notice or remember. His superiors instructed him to have no contact with the Soviet embassy in Washington, with any of the consulates in America, or with any other clandestine agency other than his own.

Abel spent most of his first year traveling through the United States solidifying his network. Later, in 1949, he settled into a slum-area hotel in

commendations. Later in the war, he impersonated a German officer and penetrated the Abwehr (German intelligence), where he skillfully extracted information on troop dispositions, enabling the Soviet army to prepare and execute effective counterstrokes. Western allies never learned of Abel's existence.

New York: A Wonderful Place to Hide

The onset of the cold war brought Abel to New York, as resident director of a network of spies whose objective was to uncover America's military secrets, particularly underwater detection devices, nuclear armaments, and rocket technology. As a secondary objective, the KGB asked Abel to keep close watch on U.S.

Manhattan and rented a small photographer's studio in Brooklyn. As an artist and photographer, nobody questioned his irregular working hours and frequent disappearances. He never met his agents at his studio and usually made a point to receive information or relay instructions in busy public areas such as parks and railway stations. In lieu of personal contact with agents, he established a number of drop zones using mailboxes, hollowed-out trees, loosened slabs of concrete, and containers with false bottoms.

The Assistant from Hell

Abel's spy network expanded so rapidly that he soon experienced difficulty attending to it. When he asked for a deputy, the KGB sent him Reino Hayhanen, who had formerly been the Soviet's top spy in Finland. Hayhanen arrived in New York with a new identity, Eugene Nicolai Maki, who had actually been born in Enaville, Idaho, but was presumed dead or beyond reach. Hayhanen floated about New York for a year before he received orders in 1954 to

Left: Torn extract from a message used by Abel. Abel also made use of hollowed-out nickels for sending and receiving messages. The "r" of the word "Trust" had a tiny hole, in which a needle could be inserted to open the nickel and obtain its contents. He also made use of hollowed-out nails that were used like the nickels, except the nails could hold microfilm.

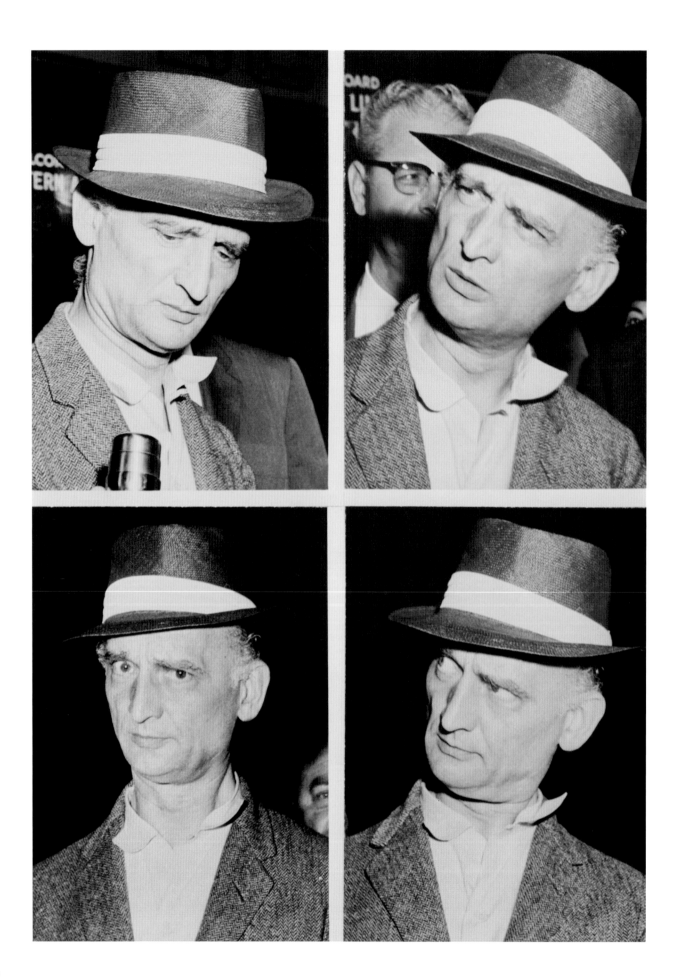

contact Abel at a certain time, on a certain day, in a Manhattan park. Abel soon discovered that Hayhanen was careless, poorly prepared, inept at most everything, but he nonetheless tried to get his deputy established and trained to collect and transmit intelligence.

By 1955 Abel showed signs of exhaustion from the constant pressure. The KGB recalled him to Moscow for six months of rest and recuperation, which the spymaster gratefully accepted. When he returned to New York in 1956, he discovered that Hayhanen had allowed his carefully constructed network to disintegrate. Abel checked his drop points and found messages several months old. He also discovered that his deputy's radio transmissions were routinely repeated from the same location, often using wrong radio bands. Six months without supervision had turned Hayhanen into a drunken philanderer, and Abel's efforts to bring him back into line failed. Hayhanen had spent most of the money Moscow forwarded to support the network on debauchery and prostitutes.

In 1957, Abel ran out of patience and demanded that Moscow recall his deputy. When orders came, Hayhanen dug up $5,000 he had hidden and went to Paris instead. He feared that he would be executed if he returned to Moscow, so after spending all his money, he went to the American embassy in Paris and begged for asylum. In exchange, he offered the name of the Soviet spymaster in the United States, for whom he worked. Officials from the Central Intelligence Agency at first suspected that Hayhanen was delusional, and psychiatrists confirmed that he was an unstable alcoholic. Nevertheless, the CIA returned the informant to the United States and began checking out his story. They found enough information to focus their efforts on Abel.

Saved by a Spy Plane

By then, Moscow knew that Hayhanen had defected and ordered Abel to leave New York immediately. The spymaster spent two months in Florida, and learning from his agents that his studio did not appear to be under surveillance, he returned. He registered at the Latham Hotel in Manhattan, under the name of Martin Collins, and the FBI immediately arrested him. Charged with espionage, Abel admitted to nothing, despite a mountain of evidence that included lists and photographs of Soviet spies, a shortwave transmitter, photographic equipment, and dozens of microdots buried in tiny pockets drilled into jewelry, pencils, coins, and other articles.

The courts found Abel guilty of espionage and sentenced him to 45 years in jail. After his trial, his defense attorney James Donovan said, "Who knows but that at some later date an American might not fall into Russian hands charged with similar offenses. If Colonel Abel is then still alive, maybe it will be possible to effect an exchange of prisoners."

Abel never spoke of his espionage activities during his years in confinement. On February 10, 1962, he was exchanged for downed U-2 pilot Gary Francis Powers. Abel spent the rest of his life living quietly in Moscow and died on November 16, 1971, as unremarkably as he had tried to live.

Opposite: Four studies of Col. Rudolf Ivanovich Abel, the Soviet spy who headed the largest Soviet spy ring ever to operate in the United States. He is shown arriving at Newark airport in New Jersey, where he was flown in from jail in Edinburgh, Texas. The following morning he was arraigned on a three-count espionage charge.

NOTES

Abel's deputy Reino Hayhanen not only solved the case of the hollow nickel for the FBI, he identified his fellow agent, Abel, and testified against him at his trial.

AKASHI, BARON MOTOJIRO (1860–1919)

Colonel Motojiro Akashi became one of Japan's most famous spies, double-dealing Russian revolutionaries at a time when his country had imperialistic designs on the Far East.

Born in the 1860s to a poor Japanese family, Motojiro Akashi would never have had the opportunity for an education had he not turned to politics—he would likely have spent his years, as impoverished youths did, in a life of crime. However, Akashi was outspoken and this brought him into the Black Dragon Society, a secret right-wing political organization that recruited thousands of youngsters from gangs roaming Japanese cities.

The Cult of the Black Dragons

The Black Dragon Society had been formed in 1901 by Ryochei Uchida, and consisted of several secret societies bent on controlling Japanese politics and the armed forces. The organization advocated an ambitious military objective: to conquer China, Manchuria, and Siberia. Akashi fit in well in the society, having espoused the fervent belief that Japan's future depended upon expansion into the Asian continent.

```
----DOSSIER--------
Name: Motojiro Akashi
Code Name: None
Birth/Death: 1860-1919
Nationality: Japanese
Occupation: Army Officer
Involvement: Spied Against
Czarist Russia
Outcome: Died of Natural
Causes
```

As a member of the Black Dragons, Akashi swore allegiance to the society, which had little regard for either the emperor or the government. Uchida sent him to military school to learn the art of warfare. After Akashi graduated, he joined the Japanese army as an officer, bonding with other Black Dragon offi-

In 1906, after the Russo-Japanese War, Akashi went into Central Asia in an effort to provoke non-European anti-Russian insurrections in the eastern regions of the czar's empire.

cers, and soon rose to the rank of colonel. He took particular interest in army intelligence and became fascinated with espionage. So, in the autumn of 1901, and at Uchida's insistence, the Japanese War Office dispatched Akashi to France, Switzerland, and Sweden as military attaché. Mitsuru Toyama, one of the most dangerous men in Japanese history, already had several Black Dragon agents posted around the world to learn whether Western nations would come to the aid of Czar Nicholas II if Japan attacked Russia.

"As you are probably aware," said Toyama to Akashi, "there is much dissatisfaction with the regime in Russia. For many years . . . revolutionary societies have been formed and have operated in secret to bring about the overthrow of the Tsar. If we made contact with some of those revolutionaries, I think that, in return for offers of money and materials which would help them carry out their activities, we could obtain from them information regarding the policies and military strength in east and central Asia . . ."

The Russian Conspiracy

After Colonel Akashi conferred with the embassies in France, Switzerland, and Sweden, he informed the Japanese War Office that European powers did not really care what happened to Russia. He then went to St. Petersburg and immediately contacted two known revolutionaries, Father Georgi Gapon of the Russian Orthodox Church, and Yevno Azev, one of the most ruthless activists in Moscow. The three men discussed ways of how Japan could help the revolutionary cause.

Akashi also befriended Abdur Rashid Ibraham, who published a Tartar newspaper called *Ulfet*. As advisor to the Russian government on Muslim affairs, Ibraham knew a great deal more about czarist troop and naval dispositions in Asiatic Russia.

Meanwhile, Akashi continued to increase Japan's network of spies across Europe. He forwarded all his collected intelligence in a weekly diplomatic pouch to Japan. When the Japanese navy attacked the czarist warships at Port Arthur without first declaring war, the commander of the Japanese fleet knew exactly when and how to defeat Russia's eastern squadron. The Japanese surprise came with all the guile of the Pearl Harbor attack launched four decades later. Much of the credit for the destruction of Russia's capital ships at Port Arthur can be attributed to Colonel Akashi's intelligence gathering.

After the Russo-Japanese war became official, Ibraham worked closely with

Akashi never knew that Azev was an assassin and a double agent, working both for and against the czarist regime.

> Akashi was promoted to governor general of Taiwan, under Japanese rule, where he died and became the only governor to be buried in Taiwan.

Colonel Akashi in organizing Muslim resistance in the Russian rear.

During the same period of time, Azev took Akashi to Stockholm, Sweden, to express his views before a meeting of the Russian Socialist Congress. Akashi was fortunate to be in Stockholm when the Japanese navy attacked the Russian fleet at Port Arthur. As the first shots were being fired on the other side of the world, Akashi told the revolutionary attendees, "I am authorized by my superiors to inform you that Japan is prepared to supply arms for revolutionary uprising in St. Petersburg, Odessa, and Kiev."

Abetting the Russian Revolution

Akashi returned to Japan during the Russo-Japanese War, but he later returned to St. Petersburg, this time as military attaché. He renewed his relationship with Father Gapon and Azev, loaned them money, and urged their followers to take stronger revolutionary measures against the czar. He mingled with high-ranking Russian generals and admirals and soon knew as much about Russian military and naval dispositions as the czar's senior officers. Despite his close working relationship with the Russian Socialist Revolutionary Party, Akashi never discovered that Azev

was a double agent and a master spy working for Okhrana, the secret police dedicated to the protection of Nicholas II and the czarist dynasty. Father Gapon also belonged to the Okhrana, and, with Azev, reported all of Akashi's activities to the secret police.

Of the many men Akashi befriended in achieving his objectives, the only person completely on his side turned out to be Ibraham, and their relationship continued for many years.

To Create an Empire

During World War I (1914–1918), Akashi became assistant chief to the Japanese general staff. Collarborating with General Sadao Araki, he urged the Japanese government to accept a plan for establishing an autonomous Mongol empire. Using the scheme as a launching platform, Akashi and Araki plotted to organize and direct the Japanese occupation of Siberia. The proposal never reached fruition, but Akashi did succeed in planning and executing the capture of German possessions on the Chinese coast. This encouraged the Black Dragon Society to increase its efforts to occupy Chinese Manchuria and Siberia.

Akashi eventually died in 1919 of natural causes, but the fruits of his espionage and planning schemes survived. In 1931 Japan invaded Manchuria and a few years later moved their forces into China, remaining there until the end of World War II.

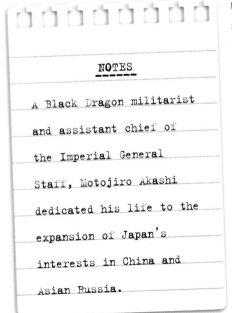

NOTES

A Black Dragon militarist and assistant chief of the Imperial General Staff, Motojiro Akashi dedicated his life to the expansion of Japan's interests in China and Asian Russia.

ALBANI, ALLESANDRO (1692–1779)

Allesandro Albani lived during the days when the Vatican stretched its controlling influence over the monarchies of Europe, a time when cardinals became involved in acts of espionage on behalf of the Roman Catholic Church.

Born in Urbino, Italy, on October 15, 1692, Allesandro Albani was the youngest son of Orazio Albani, the brother of Pope Clement XI. After Clement's election to the throne, Orazio Albani moved his family to Rome to take advantage of the entitlements accorded to relatives of the Pope. Clement, being an ardent patron and collector of art and antiquities, infused the same passion into young Allesandro, who became one of the most distinguished collectors of fine art and Roman antiquities in Europe.

```
----DOSSIER--------
Name: Allesandro Albani
Code Name: None
Birth/Death: 1692-1779
Nationality: Italian
Occupation: Cardinal
Involvement: Spy for the
Roman Catholic Church
Outcome: Died of Natural
Causes
```

To Foil the Jacobites

Mentored by Clement, Albani rose quickly in the papal hierarchy. He commanded a regiment in the Pope's Vatican army before taking ecclesiastical orders in 1712. Six years later he became Clement XI's domestic chaplain and later the Pope's Secretary of the Memorials. Clement developed full confidence in Albani and entrusted him with personal and political matters that he was unwilling to share with the representatives from the Holy Roman Emperor.

In 1720, Clement appointed Albani to the papal diplomatic corps and sent him to Vienna. The assignment caused consternation in Great Britain because George I, who ruled under the recent Protestant succession, believed that

Clement intended to use Albani to stir up intrigues between the Austrian Hapsburgs and French Bourbons, to take advantage of unstable political and religious conditions in England and return a Catholic king to the throne.

The driving issue in European politics at the time was the Jacobite movement, which evolved in 1688 when James II lost the British throne to William III during the Glorious Revolution. In 1715 James' son, who by descent had now become the "Old Pretender," failed to regain the throne and moved to Rome. There he became the instigator of constant intrigues with the Jacobites, who considered him James III, the rightful king of England, Scotland, and Ireland. Clement had always championed the Jacobite cause and in particular the Stuart dynasty, which had attempted but failed to reestablish the Catholic religion in England.

Spies in the Vatican

Albani had just begun his diplomatic assignment when, on March 19, 1721, Clement XI died and Innocent XIII became pope. With Clement gone, Albani's political fortunes suffered a reversal, but Innocent XIII bolstered the affable diplomat's career by making him a cardinal. In 1724 Innocent died unexpectedly, and Benedict XIII became Pope. The sudden papal turnover and Vatican instability worried the British.

Into this period of papal uncertainty came Philip von Stosch, a British spy paid to report on Jacobite activities. Cardinal Albani was also spying on the Jacobites on behalf of Pope Benedict, but for diametrically opposite reasons. Stosch happened to be an established art collector who shared Albani's passion for antiquities. The two men became great friends, neither aware until later that the other was a spy.

Stosch's mission was to report to the British government the plots and plans in Rome to return the Old Pretender to the British throne, along with suggesting measures to prevent that from happening. Albani's mission was to find a way to sustain the Stuart dynasty by returning James III to the throne and shepherding the British back to Catholicism. Because the Vatican protected the Old Pretender's exiled court, Albani collected a substantial amount of intelligence regarding the schemes of the Jacobites. Stosch tried to pry as much information as possible from Albani, who in turn refused to betray Pope Benedict's allegiance to the Stuarts.

Even Cardinals Can Revolt

Because of Albani's relationship with Stosch, rumors began to circulate in the Vatican that the cardinal could not be trusted. Albani sensed he had been betrayed when Benedict denied him the elevated post of Prefect of the Signatures. The rejection drove Albani into Stosch's camp, and he decided to defy the pope and became a willing spy for the British. Albani's falling out with the Pope came at

The pope instructed Albani to bring Catholicism back to England by supporting the two "Pretenders," but the cardinal directed his efforts toward doing the opposite.

Horace Mann, a British spymaster in Italy having common interests with the cardinal, induced Albani to pressure the pope into suppressing the Jacobite royal title.

a good time for England's Protestant government. Stosch's cover had been blown, but nobody suspected Albani.

Through his relationship with Stosch, Albani developed a friendship with two new British agents who also happened to be collectors of antiques and rare paintings. George Bubb Dodington (1691–1762) visited Rome in August 1732 and was able to enlist Albani into the service of the English government as an anti-Jacobite spy. This, of course, provided Albani with money to buy even more antiques. In 1737, the British government also assigned Horace Mann to a diplomatic post in Florence for the sole purpose of putting him in contact with Albani. The two men met seldom but corresponded secretly and frequently using coded messages.

The cardinal's interest in art also put him in contact with many wealthy British families traveling the continent. They came to Albani because of his vast collection of Roman antiquities and Renaissance paintings. From them he learned considerably more about sprawling Jacobite activities in Western Europe. This enabled Albani to follow the Old Pretender's whereabouts as he moved through Europe, ostensibly to raise money for an army to invade England, overthrow the government, and restore his crown.

Espionage work appealed to the cardinal. He established a network of spies in Jacobite circles and, in 1744, learned that James's son, Charles Edward (a.k.a.

Bonnie Prince Charlie, a.k.a. the Young Pretender) had disappeared from sight and was gathering troops to land in Scotland with a considerable army the following spring. It was a secret message from Albani to Mann that warned the British of the 1734 clan uprising, led by Bonnie Prince Charlie, and enabled the government to crush the rebellion. Informed by Mann, the English government organized a force to meet the prince after he came ashore. In 1745 the Young Pretender landed his troops in Scotland, raised the Jacobite flag, and marched south. The English army, waiting patiently at Culloden, stoutly repulsed the invaders. The defeat of the Jacobite rebellion can be directly traced to the information supplied by Albani.

Bonnie Prince Charlie retreated to Europe and spent the rest of his life in disillusionment and idleness. Cardinal Albani's venture in espionage enabled him to retrieve his lost influence and, when the Old Pretender died in 1766, he became instrumental in persuading the Vatican to suppress the royal title sought by the Jacobites. Albani never completely gave up the spy business, but he gradually returned to his obligations as a cardinal and spent the rest of his life immersed in his massive art collection.

NOTES

While a cardinal and a spy for the pope, Alessandro Albani amassed one of the finest art and Roman antiquities collections in Europe, and used it to collect intelligence from the Jacobites.

ALFRED THE GREAT (849–899)

Alfred the Great may have been the only monarch to spy for himself. Had he failed, the United Kingdom today might well be part of the Danish empire.

One would not expect Alfred the Great, King of Wessex, to function as his own spy, but in the ninth century, military operations were much different than they are today.

In AD 407, when the Romans withdrew from Britain, they left the country without a government, without unity, and without protection. During the next 200 years the British Isles became the target for any seafaring country or band of pirates seeking plunder, women, or shelter. Many of the intruders found the gentle climate more to their liking and became permanent settlers.

Even Kings Can Spy

During the second half of the ninth century, Denmark became interested in England and soon established control over half of the island. They also wanted the other half, but found it occupied by the forces of the king of Wessex and the Saxon people.

In 877, Danish King Guthrum's powerful army invaded England a second time and had pushed Wessex's Saxons far to

```
----DOSSIER--------
Name: Alfred the Great
Code Name: None
Birth/Death: 849-899
Nationality: English
Occupation: King of Wessex
Involvement: Liberator of
England
Outcome: Died of Natural
Causes
```

the west. As winter descended, the Danes realized they would have to wait for spring before resuming military operations, and went into camp. Alfred took his men, now numbering only 50 knights, to the island of Altheney, located at the confluence of the Parret and Tone rivers in Somerset, and not many miles from where Guthrum had pitched his winter

encampment. As winter began to fall, King Alfred changed his clothes and turned to espionage.

Guthram's Winter of Frustration

Guthrum understood that as long as Alfred lived, there would be no peace for the Danish invaders. In late December, he called his generals together to discuss a winter campaign for ridding the countryside of the Wessex king.

The successful campaigns of the summer and fall convinced Guthrum that Alfred could be annihilated, but the Danes wanted to winter in comfort. Besides, argued the generals, Alfred could not have more than a handful of

warriors holding the small fort on Altheney. What harm, they asked, could a few Saxons do to the superior forces of the Danes?

Guthrum, however, had been impressed by the military skills of Alfred's small army, something the Danish generals seemed inclined to ignore because the Saxons had been beaten in every battle. The Danes were much too enchanted by the lovely, blue-eyed Saxon women who reminded them of home. Yet Guthrum called his officers into conference every day, imploring them to take to the field. The generals resisted. Drinking and whoring had become far more pleasurable than fighting in mud, rain, sleet, and snow.

Below: King Alfred, at the lowest ebb of his fortune, entered the Danish camp masquerading as an itinerant Saxon harpist. Thus disguised, he was able to overhear much of the Danish king's plans for the forthcoming campaign.

Not Every Army Should Have a Harpist

During the daily squabbles between Guthrum and his officers, a small, seemingly innocuous Saxon harpist sat in their midst, strumming soft melodies and singing nostalgic songs with his rich, deep voice. He always seemed to be present, and only when he stole away for a day or two did anyone notice his absence. He played for his food, and everyone made sure he had plenty to eat. Soldiers noticed that he put scraps into his bag and concluded that when he disappeared, it was to take bread crusts and bits of meat home to his family. Everyone looked forward to his return. Being unacquainted with the Danish tongue, he spoke little, but his kind and affable nature made him a friend to all. Likewise, Danes could not speak the Saxon language, which made it easier for the harpist to say nothing.

As the weather improved with the coming of spring, the harpist took his usual place near Guthrum's spacious tent and heard the king assertively say that, "as soon as the spring sun has hardened the winter mud, we will march against King Alfred and his 50 warriors, and destroy him once and for all." To the king's commands, the harpist modulated his strumming to add emphasis to Guthrum's words, or softened them to hear better what was being said. The time had come for action, and as the generals and captains sat at the dinner table discussing the details of their campaign, the harpist flitted in and out, listening intently to Danish plans as he moved about, always close to the speaker, and softly playing melodies that added a pleasant ambiance to the meal.

Alfred Meets Guthram, Again

One day the harpist left and never returned. The Danes missed the music, but the roads were rapidly drying and the soldiers wanted to finish the fighting and go home. The Danish king looked forward to the campaign, expecting it to be short and decisive. With Alfred of Wessex defeated, Guthrum would rule more than Denmark. He would rule an empire.

Alfred had hardly been idle; he had raised another army. As Guthrum's force moved toward Altheney, he discovered that Alfred had placed forces directly along his line of march. A smaller Saxon force struck the Danish flanks, edging the Danes toward Edington, where Alfred had positioned his main army. Guthrum became annoyed that the Saxon fools did not know when they were whipped.

When the Danish king observed a considerable Saxon force formed at Edington, he launched his carefully arranged battle plan. To his astonishment, he found every tactic skillfully parried by Alfred's Saxons. He soon realized that his Danes were being defeated, and to save what he could of his army, he laid down his arms.

Although the defeat came as an immense blow to Guthrum's expectations, his greatest shock was to come. When the king and his generals went into Alfred's camp to sue for terms, the conundrum of their defeat soon became manifest. Alfred, King of Wessex, graciously smiled and greeted them in their own tongue. Guthrum did not have to see the harp held in Alfred's left hand to know who he was.

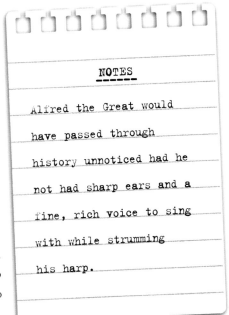

NOTES

Alfred the Great would have passed through history unnoticed had he not had sharp ears and a fine, rich voice to sing with while strumming his harp.

AMES, ALDRICH HAZEN (1941–)

Next to Benedict Arnold, no traitor ever received more public disdain than Aldrich Ames, who dug deeper into CIA secrets than any spy ever attached to the U.S. government.

Aldrich Ames is possibly the best-known American spy since Benedict Arnold defected to the British in 1780. As a top-level CIA counterintelligence officer, Ames worked in a particularly secretive branch of the U.S. government. He fed the Soviets information on spies recruited by the CIA, the FBI, and in some instances by himself, which often led to their assassination. When federal officials arrested Ames in 1994, they reluctantly admitted that he had perpetrated the greatest breach of security in CIA history.

The Most Dangerous Man in the CIA

During his nine years as a Soviet agent, Ames played a cat-and-mouse game with the CIA. He conducted more than 100 covert operations and betrayed more than 30 operatives who were spying on behalf of the CIA and other Western nations. At least 10 of the exposed operatives were Russians and Eastern Europeans working for the CIA, among them Major General Dimitri Polyakov, a Soviet GRU officer who

```
----DOSSIER--------

Name: Aldrich Hazen Ames
Code Name: Rick, Ricky
Birth/Death: 1941-
Nationality: American
Occupation: CIA Agent
Involvement: Spy for the
Soviet Union
Outcome: Remains in Prison
```

had spied for the United States for more than 20 years.

Money motivated Ames. He collected millions of dollars from the Soviets in exchange for information. He personally believed that CIA espionage operations were no more than an unimportant self-sustaining sideshow that justified his lethal acts. In 1985, when he began the

AMES, ALDRICH HAZEN
DOB 6-26-41
FILE-65A-WF-186433
FBI WMFO 2-21-94

Below: Ames's wife, Maria del Rosario Casas Ames, who was also arraigned on charges of spying for the former Soviet Union. It was in part due to Aldrich's concern at being able to maintain his wife's lavish lifestyle that he decided to become a Soviet spy.

experiment, he started by scamming Soviet agents with mainly useless information in exchange for small amounts of money. A retired KGB officer, Viktor Cherkashin, later testified that the first important secrets Ames sold were the identities of two KGB officers, stationed in the Soviet Embassy in Washington, who were serving as double agents for the United States. The FBI had recruited both men, Valery Martynov and

Sergey Motorin, and both were murdered by the Soviets.

Getting Rich the Easy Way

Had it not been for money and dissatisfaction with his early career opportunities in the CIA, Ames might never have become a double agent. At the age of 21, before receiving his degree from George Washington University, he became one of the youngest agents ever hired by the CIA.

The agency dispatched him to Ankara, in Turkey, which at the time had become one of the most spy-infested cities on the planet. Ames succumbed to the excitement and intrigues of being among spies in such exotic settings but he failed, despite having large of sums of money for the purpose, to recruit a single agent. When the CIA cut short his assignment because of his lack of results, Ames returned to Washington, arrogant and resentful.

In 1972 the CIA gave Ames another chance to become a star operative and posted him at Langley headquarters in Virginia, giving him the task of recruiting informants from the Soviet embassy. For four years Ames befriended and mingled with Russians without much success. Despite his record of poor performance, the CIA then assigned him to the task of penetrating Soviet intelligence in the United States. To get him started, the CIA handed Ames all the names and information pertaining to every Soviet spy known to be active in the country. Ames now had all the information he needed to become intimately connected with Soviet operatives who could buy his duplicitous services.

In 1980 the CIA sent Ames to the New York CIA headquarters specifically to

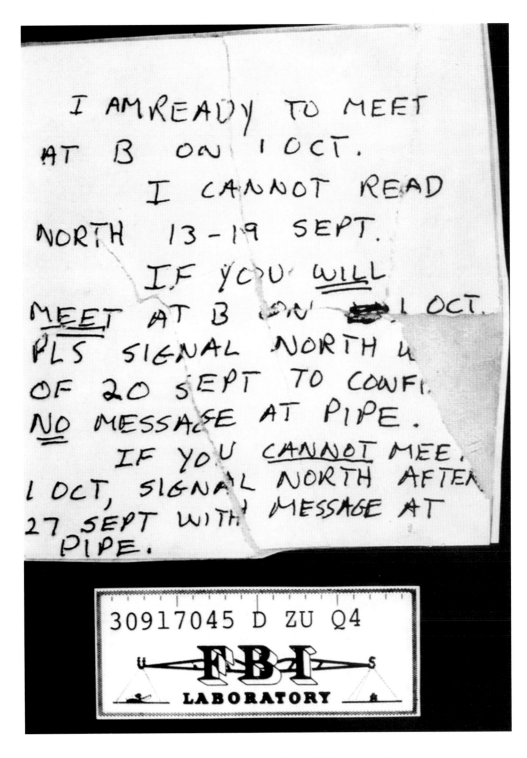

I AM READY TO MEET AT B ON 1 OCT. I CANNOT READ NORTH 13-19 SEPT. IF YOU WILL MEET AT B ON 1 OCT. PLS SIGNAL NORTH 4 OF 20 SEPT TO CONFI. NO MESSAGE AT PIPE. IF YOU CANNOT MEE. 1 OCT, SIGNAL NORTH AFTER 27 SEPT WITH MESSAGE AT PIPE.

30917045 D ZU Q4
FBI LABORATORY

Left: Handwritten note from Aldrich Ames, held as evidence by the FBI. Ames once observed that spying was in his blood. Carleton Ames, his father, had secretly worked for the CIA in Burma. In 1957, Ames got his first taste of espionage work when he joined a summer jobs program that the CIA ran exclusively for its employees' children. He spent the summer helping make the fake money used in training exercises.

recruit agents from Soviet bloc members of the United Nations. Ames did manage to get married while working in New York, although it later failed, and once again, he did not complete his assignment. Ames had simply become too well known within the company of spies.

Agent Rosario Casas

In 1985, the CIA sent Ames to Mexico City, where he met Maria del Rosario Casas, an attractive Colombian socialite working in the Colombian Embassy. Ames became romantically infatuated with her, but nevertheless recruited his

Right: Aldrich Hazen Ames is led from a U.S. Federal Courthouse in Alexandria, Virginia, on April 28, 1994, after pleading guilty to charges of spying for the former Soviet Union. This was the culmination of an intensive ten-month surveillance operation mounted by the FBI.

wife-to-be as an agent for the CIA. Rosario Casas came from an influential and wealthy upper-class Colombian family, the likes of which Ames had never experienced during his entire life. When they married in 1985, Ames earned $70,000 a year—not enough to sustain his wife's lifestyle. In that year, over concern he would never be able to provide his wife with the luxurious life she expected, he began a covert career that would make him the highest paid spy that ever

"Our Soviet espionage efforts had virtually never, or had very seldom, produced any worthwhile political or economic intelligence on the Soviet Union." —Aldrich Ames

"Espionage, for the most part, involves finding a person who knows something or has something that you can induce them secretly to give to you. That almost always involves a betrayal of trust." —Aldrich Ames

worked for the Soviet Union. Ames earned his money with the Soviets, something he failed to do for the CIA. During his nine-year stint as a double agent, Ames provided the Soviets with CIA plans to tunnel information from Russian communications sites to a building outside Moscow. He also revealed technical data, showing how Americans planned to count nuclear warheads on Soviet intercontinental missiles. He passed so much top-secret information to the Soviets that the FBI was never certain how much damage he inflicted on national security.

My dear friends:

I write this in some haste on Tues evening, 1 September. I am afraid that the signal HILL is not well-thought-out; thewooden post is often damp and mildewed -- discolored -- and thepencil mark I made on the morning of 19 August does not appear tohave been observed. After making the signal at HILL with pencil atabout 0700 on 19 August, I placed the drop at GROUND about 1600that same day. I was worried about the visibility of the signaland waited until daylight of 20 August to check to see if it hadbeen erased -- it did not appear to have been erased, and Iretrieved my package (which included documents!) later that day.Unfortunately, I left Washington for a vacation trip toCalifornia on 21 August, returning on 30 August. I will signal HILL on Weds morning, 2 September, but this timeusing chalk instead of pencil.If my package is not retrievedduring the evening of 2 September, I will return to the old, SMILE, signal site to mark it on 4 September and put my package down thatafternoon. In any case, I'll keep trying until you get it. Given the shortness of time before our next meeting, I amputtin a note on the package which I hope will cause the peoplehere to send you a telegram confirming my intent to make ourscheduled meeting on 5/6 October.Best regards, K

Left: Letter sent by Ames, regarding the difficulty he was having with a drop location. Ames communicated with his KGB contacts using "dead drops," prearranged locations where he would deposit documents for them to collect. The Soviets would then use other dead drops to leave money and instructions for Ames.

The Risk of Living Beyond One's Means

Ames had the very good fortune in 1985 of becoming head of the CIA's Soviet Counterintelligence Division, where few would raise questions about his activities. The years between 1986 and 1994 also became a period when the CIA began sending unconfirmed and often inaccurate reports gleaned from Moscow-controlled agents to the Senate Intelligence Committee and to Presidents Reagan, Bush, and Clinton. Not until later was it discovered that the same reports once thought to be authentic had been sent to the Pentagon marked "with concern as to source." During Ames's most active years as a Soviet spy, the CIA created its own credibility problem.

Right: Sergey Chuvakin the Soviet arms control expert who became Ames first handler. The deal was sealed when Ames met with Chuvakin and Viktor Cherkashin, the KGB counterintelligence chief at the Soviet Embassy in Washington, D.C. Despite the meeting being held in a "clean" room, Cherkashin didn't speak in case the room was bugged. "He took a letter out of his pocket and handed it to me," Ames said later. "It said, 'We accept your offer and are very pleased to do so.' Then it said, 'Mr. Chuvakin is not a KGB officer, but we have evaluated him and consider him reliable and mature, and he will be able to give you the money and be available to lunch with you if you care to exchange more messages.' I scribbled on the back of the note: 'Okay, thank you very much.'"

The CIA became suspicious of Ames's activities after they discovered that he owned a $40,000 red Jaguar XJ6 on his $70,000 salary. Agents began probing into Ames's finances and discovered he owned a $540,000 Cape Cod home in the exclusive suburbs of Arlington, Virginia. They also learned that he had spent another $99,000 to improve his home, and in 1992 purchased a $19,500 Honda for cash. They had yet to learn that Ames had given his wife $100,000 to buy a home in Colombia, where he soon planned to retire, and in the intervening years had invested $165,000 in securities. By then the FBI had taken charge of the case. After Ames's arrest on February 21, 1994, the FBI tracked all of his financial transactions and concluded that for his services, the Russians paid him more than $2.5 million dollars.

Under a plea bargain with federal prosecutors, Ames admitted guilt and began serving a life sentence without parole. His wife, Rosario, received a five-year sentence. In a reflective moment, Ames said, "I had come to believe that the espionage business, as carried out by the CIA . . . was and is a self-serving sham carried out by careerist bureaucrats who have managed to deceive several generations of American policymakers and the public about both the value and the necessity of their work." Ames proved his point, accurately describing himself.

His arrest in 1994 was an embarrassment to the CIA, which received much criticism over their inability to spot the high-spending mole sooner. The CIA, too, was shocked that "one of their own" could turn on them.

NOTES

CIA coworkers called him clumsy, indolent, and an ineffectual agent, but Aldrich Ames managed to sneak top secrets from under their noses and compile a fortune by acting incompetent.

ANDRÉ, MAJOR JOHN (1750–1780)

Thirty-year-old British Major John André had the great misfortune of being executed as a spy because he listened to the advice of General Benedict Arnold and changed into civilian clothes.

John André, the multi-talented son of a Swiss merchant, had settled in London. Disappointed in love, on March 4, 1771, he joined the British army. In 1774 he went to Canada as a lieutenant in the Seventh Infantry Regiment and a year later fell into the hands of the Continental Army. After being freed in a prisoner exchange, André went to Philadelphia, became a captain, and served as aide-de-camp (ADC) to General Charles Grey. There he met, and became a close friend of, Margaret "Peggy" Shippen, who later married Benedict Arnold. In Philadelphia, André proved to be an ambitious, industrious, capable, and engaging young officer who, as a pastime, enjoyed organizing and participating in Miss Shippen's dramatic performances.

```
----DOSSIER--------
Name: John André
Code Name: John Anderson
Birth/Death: 1750-1780
Nationality: British
Occupation: Military
Officer
Involvement: British Spy
Outcome: Hanged as a Spy
```

The Spy Ring

On General Grey's recommendation, André transferred to New York City in 1778 and became ADC to General Sir Henry Clinton. Sir Henry operated an extensive network of spies and entrusted André with all incoming and outgoing intelligence. In this capacity, André soon took an active interest in the intricacies of espionage, and General Clinton took notice of André's eagerness to engage in the craft.

He sent André behind the lines of the Continental Army along the Hudson River

to recruit loyalists willing to pose as patriots, infiltrate the American position, and report on what they saw. André soon had dozens of agents operating in New York, including Ann Bates, a schoolteacher from Philidelphia who regularly disguised herself as a peddler, and who had penetrated Washington's headquarters and became the most successful female spy of the war.

Though André became adept at organizing and maintaining a network of spies, he never succeeded at counterespionage. Nor did he uncover Manhattan's "Culper Ring," which also operated on Long Island, or identify the mastermind who ran the operation, Major Benjamin Tallmadge.

William Blackstone's Code Book

Not much of importance occurred through André's efforts until May 10, 1779, when loyalist courier Joseph Stansbury arrived with the startling news that an American general, Benedict Arnold, had expressed interest in switching allegiance to the British cause. Using the name "John Anderson," André immediately entered into coded correspondence with Arnold, who used alias such as Moore and Monk. They each owned a copy of William Blackstone's *Commentaries on the Laws of England* and, by using numbers that referred to pages, lines, and words, could construct and decipher messages.

In exchange for defection, Arnold wanted money and a general's rating. At first Clinton refused, mainly because Arnold at the time did not have a command. However, no deal was struck and the correspondence lapsed. In 1780 André, now a major, joined Clinton for operations against South Carolina.

Opposite: Major John André receiving a death warrant from the Continental Army after being charged as a spy for negotiating the betrayal of West Point with Benedict Arnold and hiding the incriminating papers in his boot.

Offer and Acceptance

On returning to New York, the André-Arnold correspondence resumed once more. Arnold now had something to offer: West Point, New York, where Washington had assigned him. For £20,000 and the rank of general, Arnold offered to turn the fort over to the British. This time Clinton showed interest. West Point would give him control of the lower Hudson River and serve a severe blow to Washington's efforts to sustain the revolution. Clinton agreed to let André meet secretly with Arnold, but cautioned him to stay clear of American lines and to remain in uniform to avoid being treated as a spy if caught. The major eventually ignored both warnings.

André sailed up the Hudson in the British sloop *Vulture* and, on the night of September 21, 1780, met Arnold in the

Right: Late eighteeth-century American illustration entitled "The Unfortunate Death of Major André." Unlike Arnold, who was reviled by Americans for his betrayal, André was admired for his courage. Benjamin Tallmadge, who accompanied André to the gallows, wrote, "I became so deeply attached to Major André, that I can remember no instance where my affections were so fully absorbed in any man. When I saw him swinging under the gibbet, it seemed for a time as if I could not support it. All the spectators seemed to be overwhelmed by the affecting spectacle, and many were suffused in tears."

The Unfortunate DEATH of MAJOR ANDRE
(Adjutant General to the English Army) at Head Quarters in New York, Oct.r 2 1780, who was found within the American Lines in the character of a Spy.

woods at Haverstraw. In exchange for Arnold's detailed plans of how, by his timely dispersal of American troops, West Point could be taken by assault, André agreed to the general's financial and military demands. The meeting ended late, so André imprudently accepted an invitation to go inside American lines and spend the night at a farmhouse. He discovered in the morning that the *Vulture* had been driven downriver by artillery, and at Arnold's insistence, exchanged his uniform for civilian clothes. He hid Arnold's plans in his boots and started for New York City on horseback.

The Danger of Wearing Casual Clothes

Joshua H. Smith, Arnold's Tory friend, guided André as far as the Croton River. From there the British major struggled on alone, carefully trying to avoid enemy outposts. By accident, he came upon three American militiamen at Tarrytown: John Paulding, David Williams, and Isaac van Wert. He showed General Arnold's pass, made out to John Anderson, but the militiamen were not fooled. They rifled through André's clothes and pulled the West Point plans out of his boot. André offered 100 guineas for his freedom, which merely increased his captors' suspicions. The officer in charge, Colonel John Jameson, suspected mischief and ordered the guards to escort André to Arnold's headquarters for questioning.

André and his captors had not traveled far when Major Tallmadge arrived at the outpost and learned that Arnold had provided a pass through the lines to a man named John Anderson, who was apprehended with West Point plans in his boot. Tallmadge instantly suspected Arnold of collusion and persuaded Jameson to bring "Anderson" back. Jameson felt compelled to first send a courier to Arnold explaining the detention of Anderson. When Arnold heard that André had been captured, he immediately departed from West Point and escaped down the Hudson to New York.

General Washington Proposes an Exchange

After learning of Arnold's defection and André's capture, Washington ordered that the British officer be turned over to Tallmadge for detention and held for trial before a board of American generals. André pleaded that he could not be treated as a spy because he had originally come through American lines in uniform but had been forced to change into civilian clothes after missing his ship. The board rejected the plea and found him guilty of espionage and plotting the capture of West Point while dressed as a civilian. Washington paused long enough before approving the death penalty to offer André in exchange for Arnold. Arnold still had enough honor to agree to the exchange, but Clinton refused. On October 2, 1780, André died on the scaffold.

In the aftermath of John André's execution, loyalist attorneys raised the question of whether the major could reasonably be thought of as a spy in his own country. The argument did make a good point, but not in time to save André.

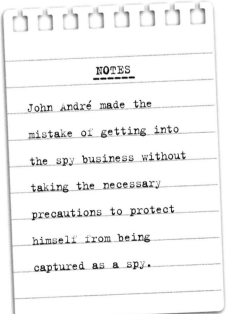

NOTES

John André made the mistake of getting into the spy business without taking the necessary precautions to protect himself from being captured as a spy.

ARMAND, MAJOR LE COMTE (?–1917)

During World War I, Major le Comte Armand became involved in a French scheme to negotiate Austria-Hungary out of further participation as Germany's ally, only to be accused by his government of committing treason.

On the eve of World War I, Count Armand was ranked as one of the wealthiest men in France, with a net worth estimated at $4 million. As the son of the former French ambassador to the Vatican, he was well connected and held a large stake in the Schneider-Creusot armament industry. He sought to follow his father as an ambassador, and it was for this driving motivation that in 1917 he agreed to perform a secret mission for the French premier, Paul Painlevé.

```
----DOSSIER--------
Name: Major le Comte Armand
Code Name: None
Birth/Death: ?-1917
Nationality: French
Occupation: Military Officer
Involvement: Secret
Negotiator for France
Outcome: Suicide
```

The French Premier's Secret Envoy

By the spring of 1917, the war-worn empire of Austria-Hungary began to disintegrate, and the new emperor, Charles (Karl), decided to conduct secret negotiations with France in an effort to exit gracefully from World War I and achieve a separate peace. Germany's powerful army completely dominated Austria-Hungary, seen as their ally, so Charles insisted that the talks be kept secret. He assigned Prince Sixte de Bourbon-Parma to negotiate a settlement, but when Charles refused to give up Trieste to Italy, the talks terminated.

At the time, France had its own problems. Mutinies mounted in the French army, and the Germans were preparing another massive spring offensive. French Premier Painlevé needed some good news to prevent further dissipation of French morale. He conferred with his ally, Lloyd George of Great Britain, who agreed that talks should be reopened with Austria. Painlevé turned to Count Armand, an intelligent young patriot who had served with distinction in combat and more recently as an agent with the Deuxième Bureau (French military intelligence). Armand made a great emissary to Austria because he understood the intelligence business and was a personal friend of Count Nicholas Rovertera, one of Emperor Charles's personal advisers.

Armand invited Rovertera to meet with him on August 7, 1917, at his spacious country home in Fribourg, Switzerland. Despite friendship, both men attempted to strike the best terms for their respective governments. The bargaining remained friendly but sharp, and Armand returned to France to report that no progress had been made.

The Ire of "the Tiger"

Shortly afterward, the Painlevé government fell and Georges Clemenceau, "the Tiger," became premier. Clemenceau instructed Armand to continue his talks with Rovertera and promised to appoint him to an unspecified ambassador's post if the talks succeeded. Refortified by the promise of an embassy, Armand contacted Rovertera, returned to Fribourg, and on February 2, 1918, resumed nego-

tiations. Rovertera proved as stubborn as before and again refused to give up Trieste. Clemenceau told Armand to reach a settlement by Easter or drop the matter. On April 3, Austria's prime minister, Ottokar Czernin, fearing that the Germans had discovered the secret negotiations, announced publicly that peace talks had been taking place between Armand and Rovertera at Clemenceau's request. To protect Austria from the wrath of Germany, Czernin stated that the talks failed not because of Charles's refusal to hand over Trieste but because Clemenceau refused to relinquish Alsace-Lorraine. Clemenceau fired back, "Count Czernin has lied!"

Because of Czernin's statement, Clemenceau suspected Armand of negotiating in bad faith, though no evidence ever surfaced to justify the French premier's suspicions. Instead of reassigning Armand to the intelligence bureau, Clemenceau sent him into the field as a staff officer to the French army corps in Orleans. Clemenceau's embarrassment continued to fester along with his unfounded suspicions, all of which he attributed to Armand.

A Man Unforgiven

Armand performed his duties in Orleans as an honorable French officer, but Clemenceau continued to suspect the young man of sabotaging the negotiations and dishonoring both him and France. One morning, as Armand

Georges Clemenceau's nickname, "the Tiger," evolved from his trait of stubborn tenacity, insisting he was right even when, later, he knew he was wrong. Clemenceau did not like to be proven wrong.

Count Ottokar Czernin's statement, which infuriated Clemenceau, and for which the latter later blamed Armand, was as follows: "Count Rovertera was . . . informed by Armand in M. Clemenceau's name, that the latter was not in a position to accept the proposed reunification on France's part, with the result that an interview between the delegates would, in the opinion of both parties, be useless at present."

returned to his quarters after making a routine inspection, he found agents from the Sûreté (the French police) searching his rooms. When he demanded an explanation, one of the agents smashed him in the face, knocked him to the floor, forcibly stripped him, and demanded the documents he was supposedly concealing that would prove his treason.

The agents found nothing and departed as secretly as they had come. Armand reported the incident to his commanding officer and requested immediate leave to go to Paris, where he intended to demand an explanation from the minister of war. Granted leave, Armand waited days to speak with the minister, who would not allow the complainant to enter the building.

While waiting for an audience, Armand received an invitation to come to the Deuxième Bureau. Expecting to have an opportunity to clear his name, he was stunned when one of his former chiefs gave him no opportunity to speak in his own defense against the charge of entering into a traitorous conspiracy with the enemy. Armand could not believe that his former friends and associates had all turned against him. No one would hear his testimony. When the room grew silent, the officer pointed to a revolver placed on a table and, before leaving the room, said, "There is the only honorable course for you."

Left in the room alone, Armand stared at the gun. His grief became overwhelming. From inside the room, a shot shattered the silence. The officer reentered the room and found Armand's body sprawled across the table. Years passed before it became known that Armand had never been disloyal to his country. When his parents questioned the government on the death of their son, they were told that he died of a virulent attack of influenza.

Woe to the man who questioned the authority of French Premier Georges Clemenceau. His wrath not only fell upon Armand, but also Captain Alfred Dreyfus, falsely charged with treason, and on Georges Picquart, who attempted to prove Dreyfus's innocence. With such a man as Clemenceau leading the French government, no man subjected to his contempt, justified or not, stood much of a chance at vindication. Dreyfus fought and won. Armand chose suicide and lost his life as well as his good reputation.

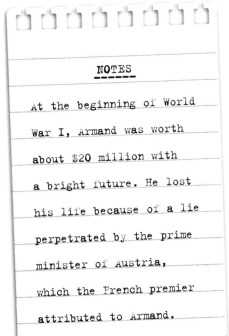

NOTES

At the beginning of World War I, Armand was worth about $20 million with a bright future. He lost his life because of a lie perpetrated by the prime minister of Austria, which the French premier attributed to Armand.

ARNOLD, GENERAL BENEDICT (1741–1801)

Benedict Arnold, one of America's greatest generals during the revolution, destroyed his life and legacy by becoming the nation's most notorious traitor and spy.

No patriot of the American Revolution, other than Benedict Arnold, ever became an outstanding general and a notorious traitor at the same time. Corrupted by his own ego, no man other than Arnold fell further from grace in American military history and in the respect of his fellow man.

The Making of a General

Born in Connecticut, Arnold served in the French and Indian War before becoming a druggist and merchant in New Haven, where he traded pork and rum. When King George's ministers imposed the "Intolerable Acts" on the colonies, Arnold stood for American rights against British oppression. In 1774, as the revolution took shape, he joined the Connecticut militia; after fighting erupted at Lexington and Concord, he went with the militia to Massachusetts to participate in the siege of British-occupied Boston.

In May 1775 Arnold became a colonel in the militia and joined Ethan Allen's "Green Mountain Boys," in which he helped capture Fort Ticonderoga on Lake

```
----DOSSIER--------
Name: Benedict Arnold
Code Name: Moore or Monk
Birth/Death: 1741-1801
Nationality: American
Occupation: Merchant,
Druggist, and Soldier
Involvement: Defector to
the British
Outcome: Died of Natural
Causes in London
```

Chaplain. The victory marked Arnold as a man who got things done. However, while he was gone, his wife died of an unspecified illness.

When George Washington decided to launch an expedition into Quebec, he gave Arnold command of the eastern wing of the army. Arnold led his men on an epic trek up the Kennebec River and

Above: American turncoat Benedict Arnold persuades Major André to conceal in his boot the papers that would enable the British to capture West Point. This ill-advised action would eventually lead to André's execution as a spy and to Arnold's unmasking as a British agent.

through the Maine wilderness to join forces with General Richard Montgomery, who commanded the army's western wing. The attempt to storm the walls of Quebec failed, Montgomery lost his life, and Arnold retreated from Canada, once again demonstrating great skill and leadership during the withdrawal.

On January 10, 1776, the Continental Congress elevated Arnold to brigadier general, which inspired him to make another strike against Quebec. The defenses of the walled city were simply too strong to penetrate. Once again Arnold returned to General Washington, only to discover that during his absence

the Continental Congress had promoted five men he viewed as his juniors to the rank of major general. Though deeply offended, Arnold put the injustice temporarily aside, marched up the Mohawk Valley, and broke the British siege of Fort Stanwix. Not long afterward, his personal valor at Saratoga led to the defeat of General John Burgoyne, who had moved south from Canada for a well-conceived military maneuver that never materialized.

In 1778 Washington showed faith in Arnold and put him in charge of Philadelphia, which the British had just evacuated. Though commissioned major general on February 17, 1777, Arnold still remained perturbed about the earlier mistake and began to nurse grudges against the Continental Congress. Part of Arnold's problem in Philadelphia stemmed from his basic nature of being a magnificent fighter but an inept governor and administrator. Because of living expenses and the worthlessness of Continental money, he soon sought a solution to his financial problems. When the Continental Congress accused him, and properly so, of getting rich by buying government flour at $5 a barrel and shipping it overseas at $28 a barrel, Arnold saw nothing wrong in the irregular transaction and demanded a court-martial.

A Tory Wife Can Turn One's Head

Meanwhile, Arnold had married Margaret "Peggy" Shippen, a loyalist friend of Major John André. Peggy strongly supported her husband's disdain for the Continental Congress and encouraged him to defect to the British. The breaking point came when the officers presiding over the court-martial found Arnold guilty of conversion. General Washington had no alternative but to follow up the military court's decision with a reprimand.

Arnold's wife, after persistent urging, put her husband in contact with Major André, the British intelligence officer who was now working for General Sir Henry Clinton in New York City. Evidence exists that she had been regularly supplying André with military intelligence coaxed from her husband. In 1779, she received £350 from Clinton and a letter thanking her "for her services, which were very meritorious."

Arnold began a covert trial correspondence with André, using aliases such as "Mr. Moore" and "Monk" as his cover; André chose "John Anderson" as his alias. A number-coded correspondence written in invisible ink passed between them. Each man used an identical copy of William Blackstone's *Commentaries on the Laws of England* as the text for reconstructing the message from a series of three numbers designating page, line, and word.

After the flour conversion episode, Washington realized that he could no longer keep Arnold in Philadelphia and in 1780 transferred him to West Point, New York, which had been recently

Below: Arnold became embittered following the reprimand he received after the guilty verdict at his court-martial and complained to General Washington: "Having . . . become a cripple in the service of my country, I little expected to meet [such] ungrateful returns."

Washington was distraught when he learned of Arnold's treachery: "Arnold is a traitor, and has fled to the British! Whom can we trust now?"

Opposite: Reproduction of a portrait painting of Benedict Arnold by the neoclassical American painter John Trumbull. Prior to his defection to the British, Arnold had been a war hero to the Americans and a trusted ally of Washington's.

fortified to provide a defensive perimeter along the Hudson River.

Treason at West Point

Washington considered West Point the "key to America" because the strong defensive network clamped a vise on Clinton's army on Manhattan Island. Despite Arnold's unauthorized business venture into flour, Washington still respected the general's military skills; otherwise he would not have trusted him with West Point. This did not mollify Arnold's feelings toward the government. Arnold offered to

defect to the British and render West Point defenseless in exchange for a payment of £20,000 and the rank of general.

Arnold's first correspondence with Major André began after the general had been removed from Philadelphia and before his assignment to West Point. At that time, it seemed to Clinton that Arnold had nothing to offer and discontinued the contact. Soon after Arnold took command of West Point, the correspondence resumed, for now Arnold had an important bargaining chip: Clinton wanted control of West Point and the Hudson River.

Right: A satirical cartoon showing Confederate president Jefferson Davis in league with both the devil and Revolutionary War traitor Benedict Arnold. Arnold and Davis stir a cauldron of "treason toddy," while the devil gloats. At the cauldron base lie two skulls marked "Libby" and "Andersonville," no doubt intended to represent Union victims of the two notorious Confederate prisons.

A Flawed Plan

On September 17, 1780, André sailed up the Hudson on the sloop *Vulture* to secretly confer with Arnold near Haverstraw. The two men met in the woods around midnight, during which André, on behalf of Clinton, agreed to Arnold's extravgant terms, and then went with the general to the home of Joshua Hett Smith, a Tory intermediary. Arnold delivered the plans of West Point and promised to disperse the garrison at a future specified time, thereby rendering it indefensible.

Meanwhile, early in the morning, the *Vulture* had came under attack from an American shore battery and had disappeared downriver. Arnold told the British major not to worry. He wrote out a pass to "John Anderson" but demanded that André change into civilian clothes. Clinton had warned his emissary to always remain in uniform, but André took Arnold's advice and made the change. He departed on horseback toward the border, dressed in civilian clothes and with the sketches of West Point stuffed in his boot.

André had the great misfortune of being stopped and searched by militia on his return to New York City. The soldiers discovered the West Point documents in André's boot, which quickly cast suspicion on the authenticity of Arnold's pass. A courier dashed off to West Point to inform Arnold that a possible spy by the name of John Anderson had been detained. The news both shocked and alerted Arnold. Arnold immediately slipped from his quarters, located the *Vulture* downriver, and escaped to New York City. General Clinton honored his agreement with Arnold; André, however, lost his life on the gallows.

The Ruined Life of a Great General

Arnold took his general's commission and formed a regiment of loyalists. He raided Virginia and devastated New London in his home state of Connecticut. After the British surrendered in 1781 at Yorktown, Arnold and his wife moved to England, where they engaged in trade. However, he was never again permitted to exercise his commission. After branding his acts of infamy into the annals of American history, Arnold passed the remainder of his years in British obscurity.

> **NOTES**
>
> For £20,000 and the rank of general, Benedict Arnold sold his life and soul to the British. He lived in London for the remainder of his life and failed in his business ventures. As an American traitor, he had lost all respect, even in England.

ASHBY, TURNER (1828–1862)

Mild-mannered Turner Ashby rode into the American Civil War undecided about the wisdom of secession. As a cavalry commander, he developed a network of spies that made it possible for General Thomas J. Jackson to win the Shenandoah Valley campaign of 1862.

Born October 23, 1828, in Fauquier County, Virginia, Turner Ashby grew up on Rose Bank, his father's plantation. The Ashby ancestry of soldiers traced back to the American Revolution. Young Turner received a rudimentary education, mostly through tutoring in the basics of reading, writing, spelling, and arithmetic. He eventually attended a small school taught by a neighbor, but he preferred hunting and horseback riding to schoolwork. Ashby never grew tall, but he was a man of great strength with jet-black hair and a rather dark complexion that could look fierce and intimidating. Ashby's constant companion was his younger brother Richard, born in 1831.

When John Brown raided the federal armory at Harpers Ferry, Virginia, in 1859, Ashby and his brother led a mounted band of friends and neighbors to the town to put down the insurrection. They arrived a few hours too late but remained on patrol as a

```
-----DOSSIER--------
Name: Turner Ashby
Code Name: None
Birth/Death: 1828-1862
Nationality: American
Occupation: Farmer
Involvement: Confederate Spy
in the American Civil War
Outcome: Killed in Battle
on June 6, 1862
```

militia company until Brown and his followers were delivered to the scaffold. Ashby lived his entire life in the area of the Shenandoah Valley and, when the Civil War began in 1861, he and his brother joined the Confederate cavalry.

"General Ashby, as a boy, was remarkable for his contempt of danger,"
wrote one of his classmates, "and his freedom from the vices common
among boys: he was never know to swear, or use profane language."

General Jackson's Horse Doctor

Ashby disapproved of secession, but when the Commonwealth of Virginia joined the Confederacy, he remained loyal to his native state. In April 1861, after Thomas J. "Stonewall" Jackson took command of a force of Virginia militia at Harpers Ferry, Ashby rode in with his brother and friends and volunteered the services of his company. Jackson immediately recognized that while Ashby knew nothing about military discipline, he knew everything about the Shenandoah Valley. Jackson's first priority was to organize the untrained volunteers into conventional army units. He formed the Seventh Virginia Cavalry under Colonel James E. B. "Jeb" Stuart and promoted Ashby to captain. Having no idea where the enemy was located, Jackson said that while he needed scouts, he also needed someone to infiltrate the Union encampment as a spy. Ashby stepped forward and volunteered.

In the late spring of 1861, Union Major General Robert Patterson's Pennsylvania Militia began assembling at Chambersburg. Ashby crossed into Pennsylvania dressed as a horse doctor, a subject of which he had considerable knowledge. He rode casually through the Union camps treating ailing horses and offering advice. He chatted with officers and asked probing questions. After a few days, Ashby crossed back into Virginia with detailed information on the size of Patterson's army, troop dispositions, and projected movements. Using Ashby's intelligence, Jackson maneuvered about the area with a much smaller force and countered every attempt of the enemy to get into the Shenandoah Valley. Had Jackson not blocked Patterson's advance, General Joseph E. Johnston's army near Winchester might never have been able to reinforce General Pierre G. T. Beauregard at Bull Run (July 21, 1861) to win the first major battle of the Civil War.

A Man of Fury

In June 1861 a Union patrol stumbled across a small scouting party led by Richard Ashby and murdered him. When

Below: Turner Ashby rides at the head of a force of men looking for co-conspirators with John Brown and the abolitionists at Harpers Ferry. During the war, Ashby and 600 of his men held up Union General Nathaniel Banks's 19,000 soldiers at a creek crossing for six days. When asked by an exasperated President Lincoln why he was delayed, Banks replied with just three words: "Ashby is here."

Ashby saw his brother's body, he flew into a rage. The usually quiet, soft-spoken leader underwent a dramatic change in how he directed his company. When dealing with the enemy, he no longer practiced moderation and at times received criticism for raiding Union camps. Nevertheless, when General Stuart took command of the Confederate cavalry, Jackson promoted Ashby to lieutenant colonel and put him in charge of the Shenandoah Valley cavalry.

Ashby's troop contained scouts and spies. The scouts worked the field in front of the enemy while the spies infiltrated the enemy's position and gathered information behind the lines. Ashby used both civilians and disguised troopers to get information.

Meanwhile, Ashby wanted revenge for his brother's death. He often broke the cavalry away from Jackson's army and took it on unauthorized raids. On March 23, 1862, while riding north with his regiment to raid a federal supply train, a superior Union force surprised and defeated him. Jackson fumed over Ashby's recklessness, but could not afford to lose his cavalry commander.

Flushing the Yankees from the Valley

During the Shenandoah Valley campaign, Jackson faced four strong Union army divisions. Each of them separately equaled or exceeded the size of his force. For more than two months, Ashby's scouts and spies consistently brought Jackson the intelligence he needed to position his forces to fight one Union army at a time, but never all together.

A crisis came on May 23, 1862, when he was forced to withdraw to Harrisonburg, Virginia. Two Union armies were advancing down the main pike to attack and drive Jackson out of the valley. Ashby had his spies posted to reconnoiter the movement of the Union column when, one evening, Belle Boyd, one of Ashby's most famous spies, arrived on a horse and found him near two tributaries of the Shenandoah River. She came from Front Royal to tell him that if Jackson moved rapidly to the north, using the Massanutten Mountain to screen his advance, he would be able strike the enemy's flank and roll up the entire column. The information Ashby obtained from Boyd was so detailed that Jackson was able to anticipate every movement of the enemy and succeeded in driving the federals out of the valley.

Ashby's intelligence work earned him a promotion to brigadier general. Union leaders, however, had become so upset with Ashby's raids and espionage that they put a price on his head, should he ever be found in disguise behind federal lines. The order was never carried out. On June 6, 1862, Ashby took part in a rearguard action. He took control of an infantry column and led a countercharge, shouting, "Forward, my brave men!" Moments later, a bullet ripped into his body and killed him instantly.

General Jackson, a man of few words, upon hearing of Ashby's death, put his face to his hands and said, "As a partisan officer I never knew his superior."

AZEV, YEVNO PHILOPOVICH (1869–1918)

Yevno Azev was one of world's most spectacular double agents. As the highest-paid spy during the waning days of czarist Russia, he was responsible for planning and performing an uncountable number of political assassinations.

Though born in Lyskovo, Russia, Yevno Azev grew up in Rostov-on-Don, where his father, a Jewish tailor, decided that business might be better in a more populous city. Azev went to school in Rostov and afterward became involved in radical left-wing politics while working as a salesman. In 1892 he expected to be arrested by the Okhrana—the Russian secret police organization dedicated to the protection of Nicholas II and the czarist dynasty—for having carelessly signed a political manifesto. So he sold his allotment of consigned goods for 850 rubles, pocketed the funds, and fled to Karlsruhe, Germany, where he enrolled as a student at the Polytechnic College.

```
----DOSSIER--------
Name: Yevno Philopovich Azev
(also Azeff)
Code Name: none
Birth/Death: 1869-1918
Nationality: Russian
Occupation: Marxist
Revolutionary
Involvement: Double Agent
Working the Czarist
Government and the
Revolutionaries
Outcome: Died in a German
Prison
```

A Grand Scheme

Azev discovered that many of his classmates belonged to the same Social Democratic Party as he. Among them were anarchists, nihilists, and terrorists, all of whom wanted to overthrow the czar. Although these were his friends, bound by common political ties, Azev desperately needed money. So to avoid starvation, he conceived an idea to

Right: Azev managed to deceive both his masters while looking after his own interests; he betrayed both the state and the revolution without bias. He was only exposed after former head of the police ministry A. A. Lopukhin met the revolutionary V. L. Burtsev.

expose his socialist comrades, never realizing that the work would open the way for him to become one of the most powerful and wealthy men in Russia.

Using an assumed name, he wrote to the Okhrana in Moscow, offering to act as an informant for 50 rubles a month. To hedge his offer, he also wrote to the Rostov-on-Don police, offering the same service. Although the Okhrana had thousands of spies operating in Russia, the agency knew nothing about the nest of anarchists at Karlsruhe. Okhrana investigators uncovered Azev's true identity, verified his claims, knew he was desperate for money, agreed to his fee, and enlisted him as a spy.

An Assassin's Balancing Act

Azev now had to play both ends against the middle: informing the Okhrana of radical socialists who were attempting to

disrupt the government and overthrow the czar, while appearing a fanatic member of the Union of Social Revolutionaries and the Socialist Revolutionary Party's Battle Organization. The Battle Organization consisted of terrorists, assassins, bomb makers, and bank robbers, dedicated to toppling the czarist government. Within a few years, Azev became the head of the Battle Organization.

Azev followed a simple formula: He would send members of his Battle Organization on missions of assassination and robbery and then inform the Okhrana who and where they were. The secret police would pick up the terrorists and execute them. On occasion, Azev would perform the nefarious work himself so as not to blow his cover with the Battle Organization. Azev's success as a double agent soon came to the attention of S. V. Zubatov, the chief of the Okhrana, who concluded, "Azev looked at everything from the point of view of personal gain and worked for the government out of no conviction but for the sake of personal profit." Indeed, Azev received excellent pay for his work. The Okhrana seeded his operation with vast funds, much of which Azev deposited in foreign banks for his own personal use.

The Demise of Father Gapon

Over the years, the spymaster had been exceptionally successful in eliminating rivals within his own organization by simply giving their names to the Okhrana.

Azev began his career in espionage for 50 rubles a month. When he escaped from Russia in 1908, he had secreted away, in foreign banks, about 2,500,000 rubles.

> Azev's assassinations included Vyacheslav Konstantinovich Plehve, the minister of the interior, because one of the czar's men wanted him removed for being "a splendid little man for little things, a stupid man for affairs of state."

He also planned the assassination of Grand Duke Sergei, the uncle of Nicolas II, and afterward identified the man who did it. Such duplicity could not continue indefinitely without someone asking questions, and the Okhrana began receiving troubling accounts about Azev's double-dealing activities. He identified the informant as Father Georgi Gapon, with whom he had recently worked on revolutionary matters but whom he now suspected of being, like himself, a double agent for the Okhrana. Azev assessed the situation accurately. Gapon had indeed informed the Okhrana that Azev had masterminded numerous unauthorized assassinations. The spymaster worked quickly. The Battle Organization kidnapped Father Gapon and hanged him in an abandoned cottage in Finland.

The Czar Assassination Plot

Azev now had to solidify his standing with the Socialist Revolutionary Party and did so by vowing to personally assassinate Nicholas II. He also had to solidify his relationship with the Okhrana and did so by turning over the names of radicals who had infiltrated the agency. When M. Gerassimov, the director of the Okhrana, learned that the Battle Organization had targeted Nicholas II, he confronted Azev, demanding to know who was behind the plot. Azev replied, "You know that I am taking every means to thwart this attempt and that I guaran-

tee to be successful. But I am unable to give you the name of my informant because he is very highly placed and only two or three people know of our relationship. Please don't press it. I must have some regard for my own safety."

Azev hatched a number of plans to assassinate Nicholas II, but because he had assigned the work to himself, nothing ever happened. He soon came under suspicion by the Socialist Revolutionary Party, and having amassed huge sums of money in foreign banks, he disappeared from Russia and enjoyed life traveling southern Europe with his mistress.

The Faithful Madame N

In 1915, during World War I, the German government arrested Azev, who had become involved in revolutionary schemes in Berlin. Instead of putting him in jail, they interned him in comfortable quarters. His mistress made regular visits, as did investigators from the German Foreign Office, but Azev swore to his last breath that he had always been a monarchist. Nobody really cared anymore. On April 24, 1918, the master spy who had caused so much political chaos in Russia died. Only one person attended the burial: Madame N, his mistress.

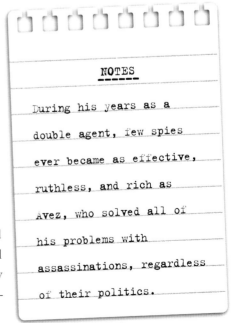

NOTES

During his years as a double agent, few spies ever became as effective, ruthless, and rich as Avez, who solved all of his problems with assassinations, regardless of their politics.

BADEN-POWELL, LORD ROBERT (1857–1941)

Robert Baden-Powell set high standards for British intelligence by his example, and when his espionage career ended, he gave the world his greatest contribution: the organization called the Boy Scouts.

Born in London, the son of an Oxford professor, Robert Baden-Powell received his public school education at Charterhouse, graduating in 1876. Instead of going to college, he joined the British army. He passed the preliminary examination with such high marks that the army excused him from the usual training, commissioned him at once, and sent him to India as an officer in the Thirteenth Hussars. He spent seven years moving from one Indian outpost to another. In 1883, when the army sent the regiment to Natal in South Africa, Baden-Powell went with it.

The Wandering Spy

In Natal, Baden-Powell carried out his first intelligence mission when assigned the task of secretly scouting the province's 600-mile frontier.

In 1887, after spending two years in England, he returned to South Africa as an intelligence officer in the renowned British Flying Column and participated in the Zulu campaign against Dinizulu.

```
----DOSSIER--------
Name: Robert Baden-Powell
Code Name: None
Birth/Death: 1857-1941
Nationality: British
Occupation: Military
Officer
Involvement: British Spy in
Europe Pre-World War I
Outcome: Died of Natural
Causes
```

Three years later, the British army sent him to Malta as military secretary to his uncle, Sir H. A. Smyth, governor of the island. The following year he became the British intelligence officer for the entire Mediterranean. He put his army uniform away and changed into civilian clothes. Posing as a bespectacled, nearsighted

butterfly collector, Baden-Powell reconnoitered the fortifications in Herzegovina, which was then part of the Austro-Hungarian Empire. He stumbled about the fields, flailing his net to amuse the guards, while closely examining the fortifications. Seating himself nearby, Baden-Powell pulled out his sketchbook and began drawing big butterflies. Into the veined wings he incorporated the exact layout of Austrian defenses.

The Kaiser's Secret

After Baden-Powell delivered the designs to London, the army sent him to Hamburg to investigate the rumor that Germany was expanding its shipbuilding capacity and adding a huge dry dock. For this assignment, Baden-Powell appeared on the site as a consulting engineer. He

pulled out his sketchbook, drew a scaled layout of the work area, and reported that Kaiser Wilhelm was indeed constructing a naval base and preparing for war. British intelligence sent Baden-Powell back to the Continent, and he spent several months traveling through Germany and Austria-Hungary assessing the kaiser's military preparations.

Baden-Powell Meets the Boers

In 1900, Baden-Powell slipped back into his army uniform and returned to South Africa. He stuffed his civilian clothes and makeup kit in a footlocker; he never knew what task would be asked of him next. He arrived at Cape Town just in time to become involved in another adventure. On October 12, 1899, the Dutch Boers went to war over British

In 1915 Baden-Powell published *My Adventures as a Spy*. Because Great Britain was involved in World War I at the time, he omitted many details for fear such knowledge could benefit the enemy.

commercial exploitation of gold and diamond fields in Transvaal and the Orange Free State. At first, the large and well-equipped Boer force won significant victories and besieged Mafeking, Kimberly, and Ladysmith.

This time, wearing his uniform, Baden-Powell led the 217-day defense of Mafeking and emerged from the Boer War a national hero. At times he infiltrated the enemy position and dispatched his findings to Lord Kitchener, who had arrived in 1900 with the British army. Kitchener eventually recaptured all the besieged cities, annexed the Boer provinces to South Africa, and bestowed enormous praise on Baden-Powell for his defense of Mafeking.

From British Intelligence to the Boy Scouts

Mansfield Cumming—who, in 1911, formally organized British intelligence (MI6)—referred to Baden-Powell as mighty eccentric but one of the most ingenious spies he had ever known. Because of his intellectual ability, Baden-Powell could make quick observations, remember everything he saw, perfectly disguise himself for any assignment, and when tracking someone, never lose his cover because he never looked the same. When Cumming took charge of British Secret Intelligence Service (SIS), Baden-Powell had already become the amateur virtuoso of British espionage. Cumming attempted to train all his operatives in Baden-Powell's techniques, but he did not often succeed.

In 1907, Baden-Powell retired from British intelligence. To his surprise, he learned that his book, *Aids to Scouting* (1899), was being used to train boys in woodcraft. Great Britain still had slum areas, a massive number of orphans, and young hoodlums. He had witnessed the same problem in every country in which he traveled. Baden-Powell believed that youngsters needed to belong to something better than street gangs. He also believed that they needed to learn discipline, survival methods, and develop self-esteem. So, in 1907, he set up an experimental camp and founded the Boy Scouts. The idea blossomed overnight and grew rapidly to become a prestigious international organization. It is for the Boy Scouts that Baden-Powell is best remembered and most honored, and it is for the Boy Scouts that he became most proud.

Baden-Powell was knighted in 1909 and raised to peerage in 1929, becoming Baron Baden-Powell of Gilwell.

BAKER, LAFAYETTE CURRY (1826–1868)

As head of the U.S. Secret Service during the Civil War, Lafayette Baker became one of the most feared and hated men in the country.

Born in New York State and raised during his teens on a poor farm in Michigan, Baker taught himself how to lie convincingly while unblinkingly staring a person straight in the eye. After a minimum amount of schooling, he rejected farming as a career and began searching for ways to get rich quick. He eventually worked his way to New York City and for a short time made a living picking pockets and fencing goods stolen by the Bowery Boys. He soon grew tired of life in New York and in 1848 decided to seek his fortune in California. By this tme, Baker had enough encounters with the law to know something about police work.

```
----DOSSIER--------
Name: Lafayette Baker
Code Name: Sam Munson
Birth/Death: 1826-1868
Nationality: American
Occupation: Con Man,
Vigilante, and Army Officer
Involvement: Spied for
the Union
Outcome: Murdered or
Committed Suicide
```

The Evolution of a Con Man

Instead of becoming a laboring nugget-seeker, working California's gold fields, Baker joined the San Francisco Vigilance Committee, the paralegal police force that patrolled the streets of the Barbary Coast. He also worked as a bouncer in Barbary saloons, which enabled him to inform on his employers and other miscreants, later helping to lynch those declared guilty.

Espionage appealed to Baker's conspiratorial nature, and when the Civil War erupted in 1861, he hurried east to offer his services as a Union spy. Baker was too forthcoming in relating his experiences as a vigilante and received a stiff rebuff from a New York cavalry colonel, who growled, "We don't enlist hangmen."

Baker then sought his fortune in the nation's capital. In Washington he wheedled his way into the office of General Winfield Scott, the army's ancient commander in chief. He tricked Scott into believing that he had lived in Richmond, Virginia, and offered to return to the Confederate capital, gather military information, and report back. Scott had no trusted operatives in Richmond at the time, so he stated what information he wanted and authorized Baker to get it. Baker said he had a perfect disguise to infiltrate Confederate lines and promised to be of immense help to the Union cause. He even demonstrated a peculiar device with a lens, which he described as a special camera. He would carry this cumbersome device, under the name of Sam Munson, and pose as photographer for the high-ranking Confederate officers. Scott explained that he could not pay much for espionage services, but Baker said he would work for expenses in

Left: General Lafayette Curry Baker, an officer and special agent with the Union army, headed up intelligence operations throughout the American Civil War. Although Baker was originally thought to have died of meningitis in 1868, it was later purported that the War Department poisoned Baker with arsenic in order to silence him, regarding the possible collusion of Stanton with Booth in the assassination of President Lincoln.

exchange for a commission in the Union army if he returned with any information.

The Tale That Never Happened

Infiltration worked both ways. Union sentries arrested Baker as a Southern spy, but Scott cleaned up the mess by telegraph and asked Baker if he really wanted to continue in the espionage business. Baker insisted he did.

After he passed through the Union lines, Confederate sentinels arrested Baker as a Northern spy. Thrown into prison in Richmond, he asserted his innocence and in his memoirs said he appealed to General Pierre G. T. Beauregard and President Jefferson Davis. According to Baker, he convinced them of his Southern sympathies by fabricating information on Union troop movements, artillery emplacements, and supply centers. Davis fell for the ploy, set Baker free, and wrote a pass allowing him to visit Southern military commands for the purpose of taking photographs.

With Davis's pass in his pocket, Baker claimed he visited every Confederate camp in General Robert E. Lee's Army of Northern Virginia. But when he stopped in Fredericksburg, he received requests from Confederate officers, whose pictures he had taken previously, and who now wanted to see them. Baker replied he had had no time to develop them. A profes-

sional photographer inspected Baker's camera and declared it a fraud. Thrown into a Fredericksburg jail as a spy, Baker claimed he escaped by using a concealed knife to chip free two loose bars. He somehow managed to get back to Washington and reported his observations and adventures to General Scott. The only part of Baker's story that was actually true was his imprisonment in Richmond, from which he escaped and spent several days hiding in shacks until he reached Union lines. Baker believed the more fantastic he made his story, the more impressed Scott would be. Scott swallowed the entire tale and made Baker a special agent with a "roving commission" signed by the equally gullible secretary of war, Edwin M. Stanton.

The Secret Service Chief

Stanton and Baker were both intriguers and slightly paranoid. The powerful secretary imagined conspiracies lurking in every shadow, and Baker made sure that Stanton had plenty to worry about. Baker, however, remained troubled by General George B. McClellan's chief of intelligence, Allan Pinkerton, who ran a legitimate detective agency. Baker set out to discredit Pinkerton and succeeded in having him dismissed after McClellan failed to press his advantage after the Battle of Antietam. Stanton had also swallowed a

In 1863, Baker began looking for officers to increase his secret service. One man, J. P. Singhi of the Fourth Maine, offered him $100 in gold for a commission. Baker replied that he had received the money, but said that he intended to only "recruit honest men, and not rogues." Baker kept the gold and refunded Singhi's money in inflated greenbacks.

Baker took great interest when the government offered a $100,000 reward for tracking down Lincoln's assassins. He made sure that he received his credit for rounding up the culprits and took most of the reward.

fictitious story that Baker had descended from a family of great patriots and convinced President Abraham Lincoln to elevate the impostor to the rank of colonel in charge of Union espionage.

The now all-powerful Lafayette Baker resorted to the same techniques practiced during his days as a vigilante. To obtain information he arrested, threatened, terrorized, moderately tortured, and blackmailed suspects. He captured Belle Boyd, the famous Confederate spy, but after a brutal interrogation, she refused to confess and was released. He also expanded the practice to include adversaries he simply disliked. Citizens were arrested in their homes and cast into prison without being charged. He routinely made false arrests, conducted illegal searches without warrants, blackmailed government officials into endorsing his practices, and pocketed large sums of money by threatening to expose profiteers.

Baker actually understood very little about espionage techniques, but he was a superb con man. He hired a few spies and put them to work in the South. For the most part, they accomplished nothing of value.

The Stain of Incompetence

Baker's most important duty involved the protection of President Lincoln, a task he virtually ignored. His so-called secret service abandoned their post for a drink at a nearby tavern the night John Wilkes

Booth fatally shot the president. Booth's gang actually lived a few blocks from Baker's office. He had no idea who shot the president until someone told him. Baker headed the pursuit of the assassins and eventually captured them with help from dozens of concerned citizens. On April 25, 1865, ten days after Lincoln's burial, Stanton made Baker a brigadier general. Soon afterward, President Andrew Johnson, who succeeded Lincoln as president, dismissed Baker for conducting espionage activities in the White House. In 1867 he published *History of the United States Secret Service*, in which he admitted this to be the case.

Baker resented being ousted by the president. Later, during Johnson's impeachment trial in the Senate, Baker presented falsified documents on behalf of the prosecution. The discovery tainted the proceedings and probably enabled Johnson to be judged not guilty.

After the trial, Baker barricaded himself in his home. He manifested signs of paranoia and claimed that a secret organization intended to kill him. True or not, in 1868 friends found him dead. Nobody could tell whether he had committed suicide or been poisoned. If a plot existed to murder Baker, it may have been the only accurate intelligence he ever gathered.

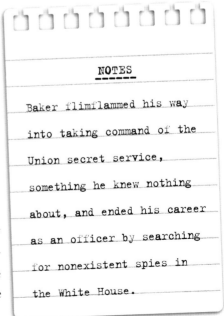

NOTES

Baker flimflammed his way into taking command of the Union secret service, something he knew nothing about, and ended his career as an officer by searching for nonexistent spies in the White House.

BANCROFT, EDWARD (1744–1821)

Double agent Edward Bancroft worked for the British government during the American Revolution. Although credited for being a superb double agent for the Crown, he might simply have been hoodwinked by Benjamin Franklin, the American who hired him.

In 1763, 19-year-old Edward Bancroft left his home in Massachusetts and went to work for Paul Wentworth of New Hampshire, the owner of a large plantation in Guiana, South America. Three years later Bancroft returned to New England but decided that he wanted to live in England. Despite having little schooling, he set out to be a scholar, a writer, and a scientist.

Ben Franklin's Spy

After moving to London in 1767, Bancroft studied medicine and became a member of the Royal College of Physicians. In recognition of his research in chemistry, he was elected to the Royal Society under the sponsorship of Benjamin Franklin, who was then the organization's representative from the colony of Pennsylvania. Franklin later introduced Bancroft to the publisher of the *Monthly Review*, and the young chemist-physician soon became the principal contributor on American affairs.

```
----DOSSIER--------
Name: Edward Bancroft
Code Name: Dr. Edwards
Birth/Death: 1744-1821
Nationality: American
Occupation: Physician and
Chemist
Involvement: Double Agent
for Great Britain and
America
Outcome: Died of Natural
Causes
```

Years before Parliament's "Intolerable Acts" created a crisis in the American colonies, Franklin had been monitoring

> To keep his cover while working for Silas Deane, Bancroft went to the
> extra trouble of asking William Eden, England's chief intelligence
> officer, to place him temporarily under false arrest.

the reaction of King George's ministers to the developing uprising in New England. He needed a trusted and highly placed colleague embedded in London to report on the Crown's reaction to growing colonial resistance, so he recruited Bancroft as his watchful spy. Franklin believed in Bancroft's patriotism to the colonies, and Bancroft enjoyed the financial emoluments emanating from a small amount of harmless undercover reporting.

Collecting Fees at Both Ends

The arrangement appeared to be working to Franklin's satisfaction. After returning home in 1775, he mentioned Bancroft's activities to Silas Deane, an American agent who was preparing to leave for Paris to recruit the aid of France. Franklin recommended that Deane hire Bancroft as his personal secretary and continue to use him as an undercover agent in England. Deane arrived in Paris in 1776 and promptly implemented Franklin's recommendations.

The strategy appeared to be working. Bancroft regularly commuted between London and Paris and provided Deane with information on troop movements, naval operations, and political proceedings. Deane forwarded the intelligence to Franklin, who found it useful, and passed it on to General George Washington. Neither Deane nor Franklin suspected that Bancroft's reports were actually long out of date and utterly useless.

Shortly after being recruited by Franklin, Bancroft disclosed the arrangement to Paul Wentworth and soon became a double agent for the British. He received for his services £1,000 per annum, twice as much as the colonists paid. In this convoluted arrangement, Bancroft reported to Wentworth and Wentworth reported to William Eden, Britain's foremost spy and intelligence officer.

In 1776, when Franklin and Arthur Lee visited Deane in Paris, Lee warned that Bancroft should be closely watched as a probable double agent. Franklin refused to believe that Bancroft could betray the American cause, so the spy continued to work as Deane's secretary.

A Spy in Action

Like all spies, Bancroft worked both sides because he loved money more than American independence or King George's empire. Because the British paid him more, Bancroft provided Wentworth with the most current details of Deane's activities in France, which included directives and intelligence coming to Deane from the colonies. Nor did Bancroft have difficulty extracting information from the French and other American agents in Paris, because Ben Franklin had credentialed him.

Bancroft's transmittals to England were written in invisible ink and placed between the lines on seemingly harmless letters signed by his pseudonym, "Dr. Edwards." He slipped the message into

In one of Franklin's 1779 letters to Arthur Lee, the wise old sage wrote: "You must not be overly concerned about Dr. Bancroft. He is a very close friend of the Tory Paul Wentworth, and what one thinks, the other does."

a "dead drop" bottle located in a hole near the roots of a tree in the gardens of the Tuileries, the Parisian royal palace. A courier from the British embassy who regularly passed through the gardens retrieved the message, replaced the bottle, and forwarded the intelligence to Wentworth. By this method, the British learned that on January 27, 1778, France had agreed to a military alliance with the colonies, before the information reached the Paris public.

The Advantage of Appearing Naive

In 1783, after Great Britain recognized the independence of the colonies, Bancroft continued to be respected as an effective American agent, although Franklin had now been warned on several occasions that his friend was a sly double agent working for the British. Franklin may not have been as deceived as Bancroft believed. Scattered evidence exists suggesting that Franklin knew of Bancroft's relationship with Wentworth as early as 1775 and specifically placed him with Deane to disseminate completely useless information to the British. Toward the end of the war, Franklin broke his silence when a

French noblewoman came to warn him of Bancroft's duplicity. Franklin calmly replied that he was not a complete fool and it was sometimes advantageous to appear naive. The only person who gained financially from this exchange was Bancroft, who pocketed £1,500 a year for passing worthless information between two employers.

The British never discovered they had been tricked by Franklin and, in 1789, sent Bancroft to Ireland to spy on a new band of revolutionaries seeking independence from the Crown (Great Britain, then at war with France, did not want to fight on two fronts). However, Bancroft then sealed a deal with France and once again became a double agent.

As Bancroft approached the age of 50, he grew weary of espionage and retired to his laboratory to work on neglected projects. He also became very successful as an importer for the dye industry. During his later years he published notable books on scientific research. Some years later he penned an indiscreet letter to the British Exchequer and mentioned his espionage service. The chancellor immediately filed the note away in the archives. When the epistle surfaced again in 1889, historians credited Bancroft as being the most successful British double agent during the American Revolution. Not until many years later did another archivist discover that wily old Ben Franklin had been using Bancroft to feed completely useless intelligence to the British.

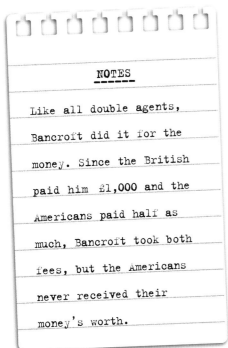

NOTES

Like all double agents, Bancroft did it for the money. Since the British paid him £1,000 and the Americans paid half as much, Bancroft took both fees, but the Americans never received their money's worth.

BATZ, BARON JEAN DE (1760–1822)

A Royalist conspirator and secret agent during the French Revolution, Jean de Batz lived a cloak-and-dagger life in constant peril. The great novel *The Scarlet Pimpernel* might very well have been inspired by the escapades of Baron Jean de Batz.

Born into French aristocracy in Gascony, Batz held the title of baron. Like other aristocrats, he joined the army. Unlike other noblemen associated with the military, he studied history and economics and published several pamphlets in an effort to reform the royal treasury's financial system. He attacked great waste in the court of King Louis XVI, urging that those funds be redirected to strengthen France's sagging economy. In 1789, when nothing happened to change the court's extravagances, Batz attended the states-general, the only quasi-legislative body in France, as a deputy of the nobility. This conference openly opposed the practices of the king and ushered in the beginning of the French Revolution.

```
----DOSSIER--------
Name: Baron Jean de Batz
Code Name: None
Birth/Death: 1760-1822
Nationality: French
Occupation: Author and
Critic
Involvement: Spy and Agent
for King Louis XVI
Outcome: Died of Natural
Causes
```

The King's Secret Agent

Batz wanted reform, not revolution. When elected to a financial post in the new national assembly—a legislative body created by the revolutionaries—he became disturbed when other members forged ahead in an attempt to overthrow Louis XVI instead concentrating on taking steps to bolster the French economy. Batz wanted no part in ousting the monarchy. He met secretly with the king and urged him to stand with the nobility against the commoners. However, the meeting ended only with Batz agreeing to serve as the king's secret agent.

Fearing riots, murder, and rape, a large number of French nobles fled France. In 1792, Batz also left the country for a year, but he circulated through Europe on behalf of the king in an attempt to rally support for the monarchy. When it became apparent that the nobility would not risk their fortunes to raise an army to sustain the king, Batz returned to Paris to oppose the homicidal revolutionaries covertly. He became the leading counter-revolutionary in the French capital, secretly gathering forces to restore most of the former functions of the government. He still wanted financial reforms, but he tabled that objective while France stumbled through social and political instability.

To Save the King and France

In 1792 revolutionaries overthrew the monarchy. They seized Louis XVI, Queen Marie Antoinette, and thousands of nobles and threw them into dungeons to await execution. Batz, a noble himself, formed an undercover ring in an effort to save the prisoners. The members of the ring used codes and passwords to communicate with each other. In the meantime, Batz engineered dozens of daring escapes. He disguised the escapees and smuggled them to the coast, where a ship waited to transport them to England. The effort did not always succeed without injury; the rescuers had to fight their way into prisons to free the prisoners and then fight through barriers and roadblocks to get them out of the city.

Batz's secret ring agreed to act together when the revolutionaries announced that, on January 21, 1793, the king would be executed. Though not a large or powerful group, Batz's volunteers agreed to free the king in open combat somewhere along the thoroughfare that the guards would have to follow to reach the guillotine. Batz placed his men in strategic locations along the route. He planned to rush the king's carriage as it approached and, during the ensuing fight, carry the monarch off to freedom.

When Batz arrived at the rendezvous, he found most of his volunteers had lost their nerve and abandoned him. He attempted to augment his force with passersby, imploring them to help save the king. When no one joined the effort,

Alexandre de Rougeville conceived the Carnation Affair, a plot to get Marie Antoinette out of the Conciergerie and out of France. The scheme involved two carnations dropped in her cell, one with a note inside. The rescue failed because Antoinette made the mistake of trusting a guard she believed loyal. Heads rolled, but Rougeville escaped capture. Batz remained in Paris to make another attempt at staging the rescue, but never obtained any support.

In 1815, after 25 years without faltering from his purpose, Batz received honors from King Louis XVIII for his lifelong loyalty to the monarchy.

he skulked among the crowd and watched the king's carriage pass. Louis went to his death, and Batz departed from the area in grief.

Batz next turned his attention to the queen, whose execution had been scheduled for October 16, 1793. Alexandre de Rougeville had already plotted the queen's rescue, the Carnation Affair, but that scheme failed. Batz had slipped among the crowd and watched in horror and dismay as Marie Antoinette ascended the platform, apologized to the executioner for accidentally stepping on his foot, and then graciously placed her head beneath the blade.

The executions angered Batz. He continued laboring to bring down the revolutionaries, and with his knowledge of finance, he tried to collapse the government by destroying the value of France's paper currency. He designed fraudulent financial schemes and enticed members of the legislature and leading revolutionaries into supporting them. He did not succeed in destroying France's economy, but did succeed in bankrupting hundreds of his enemies. His schemes were found out, a price was put on his head, and 55 of his associates were executed.

Once a Monarchist, Always a Monarchist

In 1795, Batz joined a new insurrection, the uprising of 13 Vendemaire, in Paris,

but General Napoleon Bonaparte, France's new strongman, entered the city and crushed the disturbance. Ten years later, Bonaparte became emperor.

Batz's years of undercover work began to catch up with him. When his involvement with the most recent insurrection became exposed, the police arrested him. Batz confessed to nothing and eventually won his release. Once back on the street, he resumed his efforts to restore the monarchy. He received his reward in 1814 when King Louis XVIII assumed the throne and exiled Bonaparte to the island of Elba. Bonaparte soon escaped from the island, and Louis fled from Paris. The police arrested Batz again and sent him to prison, but only for a short time.

Once again free to move, Batz organized a small group of Frenchmen who were as determined as he to undermine Bonaparte. They kept in contact with Louis XVIII and waited patiently for Bonaparte's army to be destroyed. This finally occurred in 1815 at the battle of Waterloo. Louis resumed the throne and awarded Batz a knighthood for his "heroism." Having finally accomplished his mission, at the age of 59 Batz retired in peace to his country estate at Chadieu in Gascony, where he wrote his memoirs.

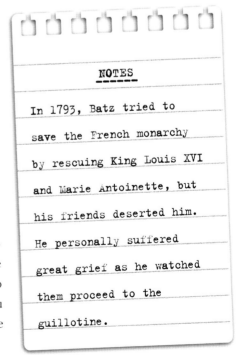

NOTES

In 1793, Batz tried to save the French monarchy by rescuing King Louis XVI and Marie Antoinette, but his friends deserted him. He personally suffered great grief as he watched them proceed to the guillotine.

BAZNA, ELYEZA (1905–1970)

An Albanian, Elyeza Bazna became involved in the business of espionage in Turkey, where he served as the personal valet of the British ambassador, Sir Hughe Knatchbull-Hugessen. His career as a spy led to the book *Operation Cicero* (1950) and the film *Five Fingers* (1952).

Born in Albania at a time when the country was still a province of the Turkish Ottoman Empire, Elyeza Bazna moved with his parents to Ankara, the capital of modern Turkey. Having had an erratic education, Bazna worked at various domestic jobs in Ankara's foreign embassies. He progressed from chauffeur to butler, and finally became a valet, serving diplomats from Yugoslavia, Germany, and the United States. His venture into espionage began in 1943, after he became the personal valet to British ambassador Sir Hughe Knatchbull-Hugessen.

The Ambassador's Valet

When Knatchbull-Hugessen arrived in Ankara in early 1943, the city had become infested with spies, much like Bern in Switzerland and Lisbon in Portugal. Being new in Ankara, he assumed that the embassy staff had insulated him against spies. But the new ambassador, by being a man of strict

----DOSSIER--------

Name: Elyeza Bazna

Code Names: Pierre, Cicero

Birth/Death: 1905–1970

Nationality: Albanian

Occupation: Chauffeur and Valet

Involvement: Spied on the British for Germany

Outcome: Died of Natural Causes

punctuality with regular habits, made himself an ideal mark for Bazna, who hoped to enhance his income by becoming an undercover operative.

Knatchbull-Hugessen wanted a neatly dressed and punctual valet and hired Bazna, an intellectually dexterous and self-taught domestic who spoke several languages fluently. Bazna soon observed that Knatchbull-Hugessen lived by the clock: breakfasting, bathing, reading the newspapers, coming and going from the office, and attending and returning from evening social affairs at exactly the same hour of the day. He also observed that the ambassador returned from the embassy each day with a black dispatch box that he kept locked in the bedroom and sometimes left there during the day. Bazna made wax impressions of the keys to the box, and those impressions turned out to be the key that opened the door to the Albanian's career in espionage. He also discovered the combination to the ambassador's safe, which contained a wealth of useful personal and confidential correspondence.

The Grand Scheme

Taking advantage of Knatchbull-Hugessen's predictable absences, Bazna opened the embassy box and began photographing top-secret documents. Having previously worked at the German embassy, he called upon the ambassador, who happened to be former German chancellor Franz von Papen. Bazna's motive was money, and lots of it, but he carried with him only a few of the many photographs already shot. Papen decided that Bazna might indeed have documents worth buying and on the night of October 26, 1943, arranged a meeting

between L. C. Moyzisch, the German intelligence officer in Ankara, and Knatchbull-Hugessen's valet.

Moyzisch met Bazna in a small, darkened room located in the German diplomatic complex. The two men studied each other. Bazna described what information he could provide and demanded $35,000 for the photographs. Moyzisch replied, "Out of the question." Bazna knew he had Moyzisch hooked and said he would deliver all the documents on rolls of film at a specific time and place, and if his demands were not met, he would sell the information to the Soviets. He gave Moyzisch until October 30 at 3:00 p.m. to make a decision and come up with the cash, otherwise the Germans would never hear from him again. As Bazna went to the door, he turned to Moyzisch and said, "You'd like to know who I am. I am the British ambassador's valet." He dropped a code name, "Pierre," and then slipped into the street. Moyzisch tried to follow, but Bazna vanished in the darkness.

In the morning Moyzisch related the visit to Papen, a man familiar with espionage. During World War I he had worked with Mata Hari and spied in the United States. Being a naturally gifted conspirator with a large staff of Abwehr spies working in the embassy, Papen replied that he could not authorize $35,000 without first examining the photographs. Nonetheless, he referred the scheme to foreign minister Joachim von

Recent documents show that the civil servants of the foreign office, suspecting Bazna to be a spy, planted a document without telling the war office, forging the signature of the foreign secretary, Anthony Eden.

Original in P.F.600,561 89a   TOP SECRET

Extract for Y Box 6351

Report on Interrogation of Walter SCHELLENBERG.

27th June - 12th July, 1945.

      SCHELLENBERG also supplied the following information which has been omitted from the general report at vthe request of the Special Agencies. No circulation whatsoever must be given by recipients to the contents of this appendix.

. . . .

II.   Additional paragraphs:

. . . .

      Para 147a: SCHELLENBERG was very anxious to know if the "CICERO" material that is, that stolen from Ambassador KNATCHBULL HUGESSEN's safe in Ankara, was real or British deception material. A wax model of the key had been sent by plane to VI F in Berlin where the key was reproduced. It fitted. SCHELLENBERG says that if the material in question was a fake then he could only take his hat off to the British for producing such convincing intelligence. At moments, especially when he once received a photograph showing a right hand thumb and a left hand thumb on it, SCHELLENBERG had his doubts. He summoned MOYCZISCH from Ankara to Berlin in order to clear the matter up. MOYCZISCH removed his doubts. In the German Foreign Office a Committee of three ministers (Gesandte) was formed in order to study the material. MOYCZISCH in Ankara, who ran the Turkish valet who stole the material from his master's safe, received the "Kriegsverdienst-kreuz" for his success. The Turkish valet received £.T.300,000. He asked to be given the later instalments in English instead of Turkish bank notes. His wish was granted and he received the rest of the money in notes faked by Amt VI F.

R.B.L./JH
9.8.45.

Ribbentrop in Berlin. Expecting the matter would be dropped, he was astonished to receive an urgent reply instructing him to pay the price and obtain the negatives immediately. Papen did not want to work with someone named "Pierre" and instructed Moyzisch to have the informant's code name changed to "Cicero."

Cicero's Deal

Promptly at 3:00 p.m., Moyzisch's telephone rang and Bazna asked, "Have you got my letters?" referring to his money. Moyzisch answered in the affirmative and departed immediately for the embassy to pick up the cash, which had just arrived in crisp, new, small denominations. He stuffed the banknotes into his pouch, returned to his office, and locked the cash in his safe.

At 10:00 p.m. Bazna, now Cicero, arrived at Moyzisch's office carrying the negatives. Moyzisch refused to hand over the money until he had developed the photographs. Bazna agreed to wait for 30 minutes—the tension increasing as the minutes ticked away slowly. As time expired, Moyzisch reappeared from the basement, content with his documents, opened the safe, and handed Bazna the money. The first documents Bazna delivered were all top-secret reports on British-American strategic planning, including details from the Casablanca conference between Churchill and Roosevelt, and a later conference in Cairo that also included China's Chiang Kai-shek.

Ribbentrop found the information so valuable that he authorized Papen and Moyzisch to continue the expensive arrangement with Cicero. Bazna routinely dipped into Knatchbull-Hugessen's dispatch box where, in addition to other sensitive documents, he also found

details of Operation Overlord, the June 1944 Allied invasion of France. In an amazing turnaround, Ribbentrop made a major mistake. He believed that Cicero's cover had been exposed and that false documents had been planted by British intelligence to deceive Germany. Quite to the contrary, Bazna never sold a bogus document to the Germans because he had none.

The Final Payoff

In 1944, Cicero's career ended abruptly when the Turkish foreign minister warned Knatchbull-Hugessen of a leak in the British embassy (ironically, Cicero had photocopied a telegram from the foreign office warning of a leak in the embassy). Soon afterward, Allied intelligence intercepted one of Papen's telegrams, decoded it, and learned of an undercover mole named Cicero. Finally, a secretary at the German embassy defected to the Allies and disclosed everything she knew about Bazna, which was considerable. Knatchbull-Hugessen fired his valet, which was to be expected, but Bazna was unprepared for his next shock: the bank informed him that most of his bank-notes were German forgeries.

Though still a young man, Bazna could no longer find work at the embassies. He wrote his autobiography, *I Was Cicero*, and though everybody had heard of Cicero by then, nobody had heard of Bazna. Like most spies, Bazna lived the rest of his life in poverty, dying penniless in 1970, still dreaming of the exciting days when he was Cicero.

Opposite: Cicero had photographed everything from the ambassador's Christmas list to private correspondence with King George VI. Sir Hughe Knatchbull-Hugessen, on discovering Cicero's espionage, declared that Bazna could not have been a spy because he was "too stupid" and spoke no English. Schellenberg and Nazi officials tried unsuccessfully to use the documents provided by Cicero as a basis from which the English code could be broken. Schellenberg was arrested in June 1945 and interrogated by MI5. Having cooperated and agreed to testify in the Nuremberg War Crimes Trial, he was able to save himself from a long-term prison sentence.

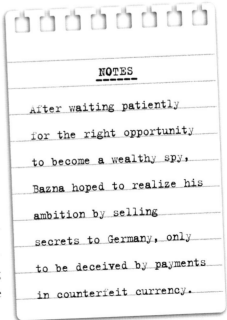

NOTES
After waiting patiently for the right opportunity to become a wealthy spy, Bazna hoped to realize his ambition by selling secrets to Germany, only to be deceived by payments in counterfeit currency.

BEAUMARCHAIS, PIERRE DE (1732–1799)

In addition to performing undercover work for King Louis XVI during the French Revolution, Pierre de Beaumarchais also wrote plays, including *The Barber of Seville* (1775) and *The Marriage of Figaro* (1784)

Born into the family of a Paris watchmaker named Caron, young Pierre decided to follow the trade of his father. While still a teenager, he invented a unique watch mechanism that fascinated an older and wealthy widow connected to the royal court. At the age of 24, he married her and assumed the aristocratic name de Beaumarchais from the title of her estate.

Living Among Royalty

The marriage gave Beaumarchais membership in the court of Versailles, where he met King Louis XV. The king admired the young man's many skills and made him the royal watchmaker and controller of the Royal Pantry. By 1759 Beaumarchais had also become an accomplished musician and a much-sought-after teacher. The king soon put the talented Beaumarchais to work instructing his daughters in music.

During idle moments, Beaumarchais devoted time to writing plays, which failed miserably. During 1764–65, while representing a Parisian financial house in Spain, he absorbed the colorful atmosphere of the cities, leading to his two greatest dramas, *The Marriage of Figaro* and *The Barber of Seville*. After two years in Spain, Beaumarchais returned to Paris as an expert in financial affairs.

----DOSSIER--------

Name: Pierre Augustin Caron de Beaumarchais

Code Name: Norac

Birth/Death: 1732–1799

Nationality: French

Occupation: Watchmaker, Musician, and Playwright

Involvement: Spy and Agent for King Louis XVI

Outcome: Died in Paris of Natural Causes

The King's Special Agent

Below: On the promise from the U.S. Congress of tobacco and other goods for resale, Beaumarchais agreed to supply arms and ammunition. The reciprocal arrangement never materialized, leaving his daughter destitute and without a dowry. Eventually Congress offered a fraction of the monies she had been anticipating, as compensation for her father's part in the demise of the British.

Enjoying the luxuries of the royal court required great sums of money to maintain the appropriate lifestyle. In 1774 a complicated scandal involving some forged financial documents brought Beaumarchais before the police. Lieutenant General of Police Sartines agreed to keep the affair quiet and give Beaumarchais an opportunity to redeem his good reputation providing that he consent to act as a spy for the French government and, indirectly, for the king.

The mission sounded simple enough— to buy off a man named Morande, an exiled former lover of Madame Du Barry, who was now the king's mistress. Morande planned on publishing an exposé of his affair, and the king wanted it stopped. Beaumarchais paid off Morande with the king's money and returned to Paris, vindicated of his crime.

Beaumarchais soon learned that once a royal secret agent, always a royal secret agent. After the death of Louis XV, Sartines discovered that the king had foolishly corresponded with the Chevalier d'Eon and revealed his ambition to invade England. When d'Eon threatened to publish the letters in England, Sartines sent Beaumarchais to buy the damaging correspondence. Using the code name "Norac" (Caron spelled backward), Beaumarchais made the exchange for cash and returned to Paris with the king's letters, again demonstrating his skills as an accomplished agent.

Convoy to the Colonies

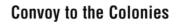

In 1776, during the American Revolution, American patriot Silas Deane came to France to engage in secret talks with the government, specifically to obtain the king's support in the war against Great Britain. Since France and England were not at war, the French foreign minister thought it best to not become directly involved with Deane and sent his middleman, Beaumarchais.

The discussions culminated in an understanding between the French foreign minister and Deane that Beaumarchais would form an import-export business called Roderique Hortalez et Cie, in Paris, as a cover for supplying arms and ammunition to the American colonies. The agreement provided that two-thirds of the capital would be supplied by the French or Spanish governments, and the balance would

"Americans, I served you with untiring zeal. I have thus far received no return for this but vexation and disappointment, and I die your creditor." —Pierre Augustin Caron de Beaumarchias

come from Beaumarchais and his friends. French aristocrats hated the British so much that they failed to see the irony of supporting a revolution against the very principles of monarchy for which they stood. Beaumarchais and his partner Hortalez realized they would incur personal debt for operating and shipping expenses, but they expected to be well compensated with the importation of American tobacco and grain.

Beaumarchais assembled a fleet of 50 ships and filled them with guns, ammunition, and clothing. He diverted the convoy through the French West Indies to disguise their true destinations, which were Charleston, South Carolina, and other ports along the American coast. The shipments arrived just in time to aid in the defeat of General John Burgoyne at Saratoga in 1777, which most historians cite as the battle that turned the tide in America's favor.

Beaumarchais and Hortalez received a shock, however, when their ships returned to France empty. Part of the problem can be traced to Deane, who did not inform the Continental Congress of his agreement with Beaumarchais, probably because he knew that there would be no commodities available to send back to France. The absence of any cargo would have thrust Beaumarchais and Hortalez into bankruptcy had the French foreign minister not appreciated the value of the firm's services in abusing the British. Beaumarchais continued to appeal to the Continental Congress for payment of his debts, but the legislature pleaded ignorance and rejected his claim.

A Matter of Unpaid Bills

By the time France declared war on Great Britain in 1778, Beaumarchais had converted his ships for commercial pursuits and began trading profitably in sugar and rum. He soon recovered enough money to sell the business and return to his first love, writing plays.

When the French Revolution broke out in 1789, Beaumarchais was arrested as a result of his lengthy relationship with the aristocracy. To secure his release from prison, he agreed to go on a secret mission to Holland and bring back a large consignment of muskets for the revolutionaries. The mission failed and Beaumarchais returned in disgrace. He managed to survive, but the revolution had ruined him financially. He died in 1799, still in debt.

Despite his deathbed pleas for money, 58 years passed before the U.S. Congress finally reconsidered the long-ignored claims made by Beaumarchais during the American Revolution. They awarded his living heirs 880,000 francs.

NOTES

Beaumarchais made a misstep by becoming involved in forgery, and to redeem himself with the court, was compelled to serve as the king's agent in resolving blackmail problems emanating from mistresses.

BENTLEY, ELIZABETH (1906–1963)

Elizabeth Bentley's membership in the Communist Party came to light in 1946, at the beginning of the cold war. Her testimony in 1948 led to the arrest of several people in the U.S. government as Soviet spies.

Prior to the outbreak of World War II, the United States grew infested with spies working for the Soviet Union. The FBI suppressed the matter from the American press when Russia became her ally. Under the direction of American Communist Party leader Earl Browder, operatives infiltrated the government, news networks, universities, Hollywood, and defense industries. By 1945 thousands of Americans, many of them unaware of the implications, had become card-carrying members of the Communist Party. The severity of the problem surfaced in 1946 when the Washington press corps broke the story of a mysterious, highly placed blond "Mata Hari" working for the federal government. The FBI had already arrested the so-called voluptuous blonde, a rather plain and pudgy 40-year-old brunette named Elizabeth Bentley, who bore no resemblance to the notorious Mata Hari.

Ms. Bentley graduated from Vassar College in 1930 and three years later received an MA from Columbia University. Like so many other naive Americans, she joined the Communist Party, immensely active at Columbia. In 1933 she traveled to Italy, witnessed Benito Mussolini's vulgar rise to power, and vowed to fight fascism.

```
-----DOSSIER--------
Name: Elizabeth Bentley
Code Name: Helen, Joan,
Mary, and Good Girl
Birth/Death: 1906-1963
Nationality: American
Occupation: Secretary
Involvement: Intermediary
for Passing U.S. Government
Secrets
Outcome: Died of Natural
Causes
```

Above: Louis Budenz, former editor of the communist *Daily Worker*, with Bentley at the Senate Investigating Committee.

For Love and Communism

During Bentley's transformation to Communism, she met and fell in love with Jacob Golos, a Russian émigré and American citizen, but also a spy on the payroll of Moscow. Golos ostensibly worked for the Society for Technical Aid to Soviet Russia, a front for Russian industrial espionage. He also headed one of the most important spy rings in Washington, and Bentley, who performed his secretarial duties, became familiar with all the workings of the network. In 1941, Golos suffered a heart attack that impaired his physical movements, and Bentley became the intermediary. When Golos died in 1944, Bentley took charge of the operation. She connected with his agents in high places and kept the net-work functioning. The spy ring that Bentley inherited consisted of 20 direct contacts in Washington, where she lived, and 30 others located elsewhere who fed the network secrets.

Revelations of an Informant

In November 1945 Bentley experienced a change of heart and went directly to the

Left: View of the Senate Committee Room where Elizabeth Bentley, repentant former Soviet spy, testified before the House Un-American Activities Committee. She testified that a former administrative assistant to the late President Roosevelt and 30 other federal employees were Soviet agents.

Left: Elizabeth Bentley, seen testifying at the microphones, stated that she had been a contact between chemical engineer Abraham Brothman and the spy Jacob Raisin, a.k.a. Joseph Golos, the chief of Soviet espionage operations in the United States.

FBI with her story. She obtained immunity in exchange for her testimony and afterward talked freely, claiming that her contacts were in the U.S. Army, Air Force, the State and Treasury departments, and the Office of Strategic Services (OSS). She also spoke of a man connected with the White House who helped place her informants at strategic information-gathering sites. While Golos lived, she collected the intelligence in Washington and passed it to him in New York, assuming it went from there to Moscow. After Golos died, Bentley claimed she passed political information over to Communist Party leader Earl Browder and military information to John Abt, a one-time government employee then living in Manhattan. Bentley's defection came as a devastating blow to Soviet espionage in the United States.

Prior to her appearance before the House Un-American Activities Committee (HUAC), Congress believed that Bentley was merely a courier for Golos. Her testimony shocked and baffled them. She implicated William W. Remington, who had worked for the War Production Board during the war and later for the Department of Commerce and the Atomic Energy Commission. She described meeting Remington on several occasions in a Washington drugstore across from Willard's Hotel to receive a packet of information in exchange for a packet of money but, as time wore on, Remington became "very nervous, very jittery, obviously scared to death" that his activities would be discovered. After Bentley's testimony, Remington not only lost his job but also his reputation.

When the HUAC demanded to know the name of the mole in the White House, Bentley blithely replied that it was Lauchlin Currie, one of President Roosevelt's closest advisers. For six years, Currie had been a White House special assistant and an overseas envoy representing the president. Bentley admitted that while she had never met Currie, she knew that he was deeply connected with former government employee George Silverman, who had passed Currie's information to Washington spymaster Nathan Gregory Silverman, the man to whom Bentley reported. She never incriminated Currie as a member of the Communist Party but simply suggested that he had been Silverman's ignorant pawn, mostly as a reult of the fact that Currie and Silverman had been classmates at Harvard.

Bentley also named Harry Dexter White, the assistant secretary of the treasury who had configured the World Bank and the International Monetary Fund. She claimed that White passed information to Silverman, Silverman gave it to her, and she forwarded it to John Abt.

The HUAC choked when Bentley openly admitted, "We knew about D-Day long before D-Day happened."

Ludwig Ullman, another member of the spy ring, worked with Silverman at the U.S. Air Force headquarters. Bentley claimed she knew all about the details of new aircraft on the drawing board in addition to where planes were being sent and for what purpose. Evidently, the information about D-Day leaked from the Air Force headquarters.

Between the HUAC investigation and her testimony to a grand jury, Bentley identified more than 30 persons who were either Communist spies or "fellow travelers" willing to supply secrets to the Washington-Manhattan espionage network. Most of the people incriminated by Bentley swore they never heard of her or participated in the acts she claimed. Bentley used many aliases when dealing with agents, usually "Helen," which would account for her name being unfamiliar to those who later testified in their own defense. But men like William Remington and others admitted to being members of the ring and corroborated much of Bentley's testimony.

As often happens in political circles, few indictments were ever brought against those Bentley incriminated. However, her testimony triggered one of the most intensive witch hunts in the history of the United States when, during the 1950s, Senator Joseph McCarthy initiated an inquisition that irreparably damaged the reputation of innocent Americans, along with the few who were guilty.

Opposite: Elizabeth Bentley is sworn in before testimony at the House Un-American Activities Committee hearing. Having become disillusioned in 1945, she took her story to the FBI; she was able to obtain immunity in exchange for her testimony and became a valued asset to the United States.

NOTES

Before Elizabeth Bentley went to the FBI in 1945 with her story, she did not know that Soviet agents were already concerned about her loyalty and were discussing a remedy "to get rid of her."

BERG, MORRIS "MOE" (1902–1972)

Most people who grew up in the 1920s and 1930s remember Moe Berg only as a professional baseball catcher. His other life as one of America's most exceptional espionage agents remained obscure until after his death.

Born in Newark, New Jersey, to Russian Jewish immigrants, Morris "Moe" Berg had three passions in life: baseball, books, and languages. He played baseball in high school and became an outstanding athlete at Princeton where, in 1923, he graduated magna cum laude with a degree in languages. He mastered German, Latin, and Greek and could usually be found sitting somewhere with a book. After Princeton, he signed with the Brooklyn Dodgers for $5,000 a year. When the season ended, Berg crossed the Atlantic to further his knowledge of languages and entered the Sorbonne.

Berg returned home to play baseball for the Reading Keys of the International League, the Dodgers' farm club. After the Keys went bankrupt in 1926, he joined the Chicago White Sox. Between seasons, he attended Columbia Law School and earned his law degree. During his 16-year career in baseball, Moe Berg played on teams with Babe Ruth, Lou Gehrig, and Jimmie Foxx. He also became a spy.

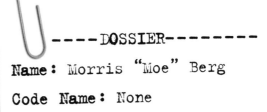

----DOSSIER--------

Name: Morris "Moe" Berg

Code Name: None

Birth/Death: 1902–1972

Nationality: American

Occupation: Professional Baseball Player

Involvement: U.S. Spy in Japan and Europe

Outcome: Died in an Accidental Fall

The Double Life of Moe Berg

In the early 1930s, the U.S. State Department contacted Berg because of his considerable linguistic skills. The government also knew that Berg had a perfect cover as a touring baseball catcher. When Berg went to Japan with the

American all-star team in 1934, he carried a message to the American consulate in Tokyo, signed by Secretary of State Cordell Hull, clarifying his mission. Berg checked into one of Tokyo's high-rise hotels—a room with a clear, panoramic view of the city. Dressed in a kimono, he stepped onto the balcony and took photographs and motion pictures of Tokyo's harbor, warships, and military installations. Between baseball games, he toured the city in tourist clothes and took pictures of Japan's weapons-manufacturing plants, which were already mass-producing arms for war with China.

On April 18, 1942, four months after the Japanese struck Pearl Harbor, Colonel James Doolittle took off from the USS *Hornet* with 16 specially modified twin-engine B-25s, and led the first bombing raids against Japan. The planning had taken months. Doolittle spent weeks

Left: Moe Berg was recruited in 1942 by the OSS (Office of Strategic Services). He served almost 10 years in this capacity. Although sometimes portrayed as a careless spy, he was able, due to his significant linguistic abilities and general ease of manner, to infiltrate many organizations to great effect.

Berg's baseball chums remembered that while the team read the sports pages, Moe read the classics.

studying targets in Tokyo to make every bomb count. The only photos and films of the city's military installations and armament facilities came from Berg. The air strike shocked the Japanese. Imperial Japanese headquarters staff scratched their heads searching for Doolittle's air base. President Roosevelt announced that the planes came from Shangri-la, the mystical city in James Hilton's novel *Lost Horizons*.

Working for "Wild Bill" Donovan

On January 7, 1942, Moe Berg hung up his catcher's mitt, retired from baseball, and went to work for the government in Nelson Rockefeller's Office of the Coordinator of Inter-American Affairs, a cover for the Office of Current Intelligence (OCI) at the CIA. Berg went on "goodwill missions" in Latin America,

but his actual task was to look into the activities of certain foreign businesses controlled by Japan. Berg's keen observations impressed General William "Wild Bill" Donovan, head of the U.S. Office of Strategic Services (OSS). In 1943 Donovan recruited Berg into the ranks of the OSS as an espionage agent. At the age of 41, Berg was still in better physical condition than many OSS agents 20 years younger.

Berg did most of his spying in Europe. In 1943 he parachuted into Yugoslavia to assess the effectiveness of partisan units fighting the Nazis. Berg made the call. He sent Donovan a report urging that the Allies support Josip Tito's guerrillas. Prime Minister Winston Churchill agreed, and Special Operations forces and weaponry began flowing to Tito.

That same year, Berg parachuted into Norway, met with underground freedom fighters, and reconnoitered the secret Nazi heavy water (deuterium oxide) plant at Rjukan. Hitler needed deuterium oxide for his atomic bomb program. Berg returned with details for an air strike. The bombers missed the plant, but Norwegian Knut Haukelid took matters into his own hands and destroyed the chemicals before the Nazis transported them from Norway. Hitler dropped the project.

In 1944 Donovan sent Berg to Switzerland, a neutral country in the center of war-torn Europe. He expected Berg to work with Allen Dulles, the OSS chief of operations in Europe. Though they collaborated on assignments, Berg did not always agree with Dulles. He continued to take most of his instructions directly from Donovan.

Using Switzerland as his base, Berg infiltrated Italy and Germany and located several atomic scientists. He spoke to a few of them during the war, identified several others, and reported their names to Donovan. As soon as the war ended, it became a diplomatic race between the United States and the Soviet Union as to which country would be the first to scoop up the names on Berg's list. Donovan's Special Operations commandos won the race, liberating top physicists and missile engineers like Werner von Braun, who, with others, helped develop America's space and nuclear weapons programs.

The Mysterious Moe Berg

After the war, the government awarded Berg the American Medal of Merit, the highest decoration given to a civilian during wartime. For reasons Berg never explained, he turned it down, perhaps because he preferred privacy to notoriety; Berg was that kind of man. There may have been another reason: Berg went to work for the CIA and NATO as a scientific adviser and continued to take espionage missions into Eastern Bloc countries. Perhaps it was better to not be well known. Berg retired in the late 1960s. An old friend remembered seeing him at the ballpark, a Dodgers hat pulled down over his forehead, reading a book between innings.

Opposite: Moe Berg, right, with Giants slugger Lefty O'Doul and Sotaro Suzuki of the Tokyo Baseball Club, en route to Japan, where Babe Ruth's American all-star team was to play an exhibition tour. Berg was able to slip away and take valuable film footage of the Tokyo skyline and munitions bases that were used to plan future raids on Tokyo.

Berg's activities as a spy remained mostly unknown to the public until the late 1970s, when Fritz Lang chronicled Moe's life in the suspense film *Cloak and Dagger*.

BERIA, LAVRENTI PAVLOVICH (1899–1953)

Lavrenti Pavlovich Beria rose from obscurity to become Joseph Stalin's personal assassin, head of the Soviet Union's secret police, and the director of the NKVD, the forerunner of the KGB.

Lavrenti Beria made the ideal Bolshevik. Born to poor Georgian peasants in the seaside resort of Merkheuli on the Black Sea, Beria never received much schooling. During World War I, the czarist regime drafted him into the army, but he deserted in 1917 to support the Russian Revolution. He returned to Georgia and in 1919 received a degree in architecture from the technical college in Baku—a degree he never used.

A Thirst for Power

Becoming a strongman for the revolutionaries appealed to Beria. He joined the Cheka, the Bolshevik secret police, whose duties were to protect revolutionaries against czarists. After a short course in police work, Beria returned to Georgia to inform on any person displaying disloyalty toward the revolution. He soon became associated with Joseph Stalin, who as head of Georgia's secret police had become a ruthless collector of intelligence. When the Bolsheviks expanded

```
----DOSSIER--------

Name: Lavrenti Pavlovich
Beria
Code Name: None
Birth/Death: 1899-1953
Nationality: Russian
Occupation: First chief of
the NKVD
Involvement: Progressed
from Murderer and Spy to
Stalin's Strongman
Outcome: Murdered in Moscow
```

into Georgia, they seized and executed every person on Beria's list.

Beria's ascent to power began with the Cheka, and later with its successor, the GPU, all of which later evolved into the

NKVD. Regardless of the transition from one name to another, they were all agencies involved in espionage, counterespionage, undercover police work, and assassination. Beria increased his influence by compromising higher-placed party officials and taking their places. He tricked his superiors by engaging prostitutes to lure them into alliances and then ruined the men's lives by creating a scandal. When tricks failed he resorted to murder, sometimes by his own hand and sometimes with help from his thugs.

Knowing the Right People

Stalin developed a deep appreciation for Beria's skills, having relied on him on occasion to liquidate political challengers. In 1921, when he found an opportunity to return the favor, he convinced Lenin to make Beria head of Soviet intelligence. When Lenin died in 1924, Beria eliminated a few more political obstacles to solidify Stalin's ascent to uncontested power. Once again, Stalin repaid Beria by making him a member of the Central Committee of the Communist Party.

Beria became Stalin's number-one assassin, but there were other liquidators in the field. Vyacheslav Menzhinsky fit neatly in the death squad because he poisoned his boss to become head of the secret police. In 1934 Stalin purged Menzhinsky and replaced him with Genrikh Yagoda. When Yagoda demonstrated too little bloodthirstiness, Stalin replaced him with Nikolai Yezhov, the first head of the NKVD and perhaps the most thoroughly evil fanatic to ever hold the post. Yezhov soon wielded more power than Stalin, who began to question whether he had made the right choice. Stalin explained his problem to Beria, whom Yezhov was, at that time, building

a case against and soon planned to arrest. Beria acted quickly. It is said that, in December 1938 he forcibly removed Yezhov from headquarters and took him to a psychiatric institute where, on the following day, attendants found the former head of the NKVD hanging from a window bar. One contemporary claimed that Beria entered Yezhov's office and personally strangled him. The truth behind his death remains unknown.

How Much Higher Can an Assassin Go?

Stalin rewarded Beria by making him head of the NKVD and a nonvoting member of the Politburo, the first chief of the

Above: Beria met Stalin in 1931 and by 1935 had become one of his most trusted aides. In 1938 he was brought to Moscow as deputy head of the NKVD, which was run by Nikolai Yezhov. The organization was to oversee the state security and to carry out prosecution of enemies of the state, which became known as the Great Purge. Beria succeeded Yezhov in 1940 to head up the NKVD.

secret police to join the powerful 10-member body. The new director tried to improve the public image of the NKVD by eliminating some of Yezhov's most despicable henchmen. He arrested five officials in the Ukraine, accused them of carrying out pointless executions, and hanged them all.

To Stalin, Beria became invaluable, despite the latter's unpleasant habit of picking up young girls on the street, forcibly taking them into his office to perform sodomy, and then retaining them for several days to be repeatedly raped. Any family member courageous enough to complain about their daughter's treatment went to jail and mysteriously disappeared. Beria eventually married one of his victims but never discontinued the sadistic practice.

In 1941 Germany invaded Soviet Russia, and Stalin named Beria deputy prime minister in charge of security behind the front lines. Beria increased his secret police force, sent them to the battlefield, and ordered them to execute any soldier who malingered or complained against the government. He also took advantage of the war to liquidate thousands of old Bolsheviks who had become politically troublesome. Beria's thugs shot some and put the others in labor camps. When the Nazi war machine pressed upon Minsk, Beria sent his henchmen into the city's political detention camp, gunned down 10,000 prisoners, blew up the compound, and burned the bodies.

The Most Feared Man in Moscow

During the war, Beria expanded the Soviet espionage service, training thousands of agents for work in the West. By 1945 the NKVD, which had become the MVD, had tens of thousands of spies on the payroll. The organization had grown so large in Soviet Russia and around the world that even Stalin began to fear the reach of Beria's power. His paranoia reached a pinnacle in 1950, when he sent an urgent message to his daughter, Svetlana, who was staying with Beria and his wife, and warned, "I don't trust Beria. He could use you as a hostage in trying to force me from my office." Svetlana arrived home safely, but her father continued to fret. In 1951, to calm his anxiety, Stalin ordered Beria to be charged as "an imperial agent," although privately he believed his old devoted liquidator intended to murder him.

Beria remained under home arrest, and before he went to trial, Stalin died. Georgi Malenkov, Stalin's successor, wanted no part of Beria, who was making every effort to work his way back to power by assassinating Malenkov. In December 1953, the Soviet supreme court tried Beria in secret and found him guilty of treason.

A number of stories arose concerning how Beria died, including a claim by Nikita Khrushchev that "Beria came into the conference room one day without his bodyguard and I shot him." Other similar, ridiculous accounts exist. The strongman of espionage and intrigue died like many of his own victims—Beria knew the drill. On December 23, 1953, guards placed him against the wall of Lubianka Prison in Moscow and he was shot by a firing squad.

Thus ended the life of one of the most brutal men in Russian history, but it did not end Soviet brutality.

Opposite: Lavrenti Beria, Vyacheslav Molotov, and Joseph Stalin carrying Mikhail Kalinin in his casket in 1946. He was laid to rest at the Kremlin Wall necropolis.

NOTES

Beria rose to power over the bodies of friends and enemies he either personally assassinated or engaged others to kill. He became so powerful that even Stalin feared him.

BLAKE, GEORGE (1922–1990)

During the cold war, George Blake, a senior officer in the British Secret Intelligence Service (MI6), spied for the KGB. He became one of the most dangerous men in the espionage business, trading information on intelligence and undercover agents to the Soviets free of charge.

Born in Rotterdam, Holland, on November 11, 1922, to a Dutch Lutheran mother and an Egyptian Jewish father, Georg Behar enjoyed all the advantages of wealth. He attended good schools and lived in comfort. His father had served in the British army during World War I, and so admired King George that he gave the monarch's name to his son. Georg's father died in 1936, leaving instructions that his son be sent to Egypt to complete his schooling. At the age of 13, Georg spent the next two years at the finest English school in Cairo.

In 1938 Behar returned to Rotterdam to finish high school, speaking English with a fine British accent. Two years later, while finishing his studies, Germany invaded the Netherlands. Because of their Jewish heritage, Behar's mother took his two sisters to England, but Georg remained behind and joined the Dutch underground resistance. Though captured by the Gestapo, Behar escaped.

----DOSSIER--------

Name: Georg Behar, a.k.a. George Blake

Code Name: None

Birth/Death: 1922–1990

Nationality: Dutch

Occupation: British Navy and MI6

Involvement: British Double Agent for the Soviets

Outcome: Died of Natural Causes in Moscow

Now a marked member of the resistance, he worked his way to France and crossed the channel to England.

The Pyongyang Betrayal

Reunited with his mother and sisters, Behar changed his name to Blake and joined the Royal Navy. The Special Operations Executive (SOE) needed men with language skills for espionage operations in German-occupied countries and inducted Blake, who offered to use his underground experience. The SOE, however, considered Blake's linguistic skills too valuable to waste with fieldwork and assigned him to a desk job in London as an interpreter. Commissioned sub-lieutenant in 1944, Blake went with the Allies to Europe on D-Day and spent the remainder of the war interpreting secret German documents and performing

Left: A portrait of double-agent George Blake, which was issued by Scotland Yard after his escape from Wormwood Scrubs Prison in England in October 1966, where he was serving a 42-year sentence—a year for every agent that he had betrayed.

Below: George Blake with
his mother on his arrival
back from Korea, where he
worked for the British
Consul in Seoul. At the
outbreak of war, he was
captured by the North
Koreans and during his
imprisonment converted
to Marxism. He attributed
his conversion not to
brainwashing but to the
treatment of the Korean
people during the war.

intelligence operations at Supreme Headquarters Allied Expeditionary Force (SHAEF).

After the war, the British Foreign office showed interest in Blake and sent him to Cambridge University to learn Russian. While there, Blake became a naturalized British citizen and, in October 1948, after completing the language course, the foreign office sent him to Seoul, South Korea, as vice-consul to the British embassy.

In June 1950 North Korean troops poured across the border, entered Seoul, captured the British diplomats, and refused to give them up. When brainwashing began, Blake said he wished to speak with someone at the Soviet embassy in Pyongyang, the capital of North Korea. Thus began the first step in Blake's long years of betrayal, about which he later claimed, "I did what I had to do for ideological reasons, never for money."

Secret Agent, but for Whom?

In 1953, the North Koreans released Blake and other members of the British embassy and sent them home via the

Below: George Blake with his mother on his arrival back from Korea, where he worked for the British Consul in Seoul. At the outbreak of war, he was captured by the North Koreans and during his imprisonment converted to Marxism. He attributed his conversion not to brainwashing but to the treatment of the Korean people during the war.

Trans-Siberian Railway. During the trip, Blake met his Soviet "handler."

After being debriefed by the foreign office, Blake requested that he rejoin MI6 so he could fulfill his ambition of becoming a British secret agent. He certainly had the credentials, and MI6 assigned him to the new "Y" section, which radio-tapped Soviets in Austria and installed bugs in the buildings that they regularly frequented.

According to Blake's own account, in October 1953 he made his first delivery, "a list of top-secret technical operations carried out by MI6 against Soviet targets with a precise indication of their nature and location."

In 1953 Blake married an MI6 secretary, the daughter of a top MI6 officer. This cemented his career with British intelligence. Blake continued to pass information to his handler in London. While working in West Germany, he disclosed the plans to build the Berlin Tunnel. He also collected useless information from his handler and turned it over to MI6, setting himself up as a bogus double agent, but all the valuable intelligence went to the enemy.

Making a Home in Moscow

For eight years, Blake operated as an undercover Soviet agent before rumors of his treason surfaced. In 1961, while studying Arabic in Lebanon, MI6 abruptly summoned him to London. Lieutenant colonel Michal Goleniewski, a defector from the Polish Intelligence Service, had supplied the CIA with information pointing to a spy buried in MI6. Investigators did their homework and tracked the infiltrator to Blake.

Blake confessed his espionage activities and went through a swift trial at the Old Bailey. Found guilty, he received a sentence of 42 years in Wormwood Scrubs Prison, "a year for each agent betrayed," he wrote. Blake later claimed he had betrayed 400 agents, but to his best recollection, he knew of none that were killed.

Prison guards expected Blake would try to escape and kept him under close watch. After four years, they stopped watching, and on October 22, 1966, Blake knocked out a loosened iron bar in his cell window. Through careful preparation, he slipped to the ground, climbed the prison wall, and descended to a waiting car driven by Sean Bourke, a member of the Irish Republican Army (IRA) and former fellow prisoner. Blake broke his wrist, but Bourke had a doctor friend who came to the safe house and set the bone. Bourke arranged for a boat to get Blake out of England. In France he had a friend drive the escapee into East Germany. MI6 believed the KGB financed Blake's escape by hiring IRA agents.

Blake settled into life in Moscow and obtained a job as an interpreter in a publishing house. He had divorced his wife while in prison and he remarried in Russia and had a son. He eventually became an associate of other British spies who sought sanctuary in Moscow, such as Guy Burgess, Harold "Kim" Philby, and Donald Maclean. In 1990, in Britain, he published his autobiography, *No Other Choice*, for which he was paid £60,000 before the British government stepped in to stop further payment.

NOTES

Captured by the North Korean army, Blake avoided brainwashing by seeking an interview with the Soviets. In exchange for his freedom, he became a Soviet spy and spent the next 10 years doing irreparable damage to British intelligence efforts.

BLUNT, ANTHONY (1907-1983)

Sir Anthony Blunt became the "fourth man" in the Cambridge Spy Ring, Great Britain's most notorious espionage case that also included Guy Burgess, Donald Maclean, and Harold "Kim" Philby.

Born in Bournmouth, the son of a clergyman from the Church of England, Anthony Blunt received opportunities for education usually reserved for England's upper class. Although he received his early education at the Marlborough public school, he became a brilliant student at Cambridge University, graduating in 1932 to become a fellow at Trinity College.

Infected by the liberal leanings of his friends, Blunt believed that the British system of democracy had failed to control the spread of economic depression, leaving the wealthy as rich as ever while the lower social classes lived in misery and poverty. In 1934 he traveled to Moscow where he first become involved with the KGB.

During his youth, Blunt's father became the British embassy's chaplain in Paris. While there, Blunt acquired an early attraction to art and this eventually became his foremost interest in life. In the mid-1930s, Blunt set his sights on a career that would both enrich his life with art and complicate his life with Marxism.

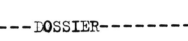

```
----DOSSIER--------
Name: Anthony Blunt
Code Name: None
Birth/Death: 1907-1983
Nationality: British
Occupation: Author and
Curator of the Queen's
Art Galleries
Involvement: Soviet Spy
Outcome: Died of Natural
Causes
```

The Genesis of the Cambridge Spy Ring

While attending Cambridge, Blunt became involved with three homosexuals, Guy Burgess, Donald Maclean, and Harold "Kim" Philby, all of whom shared common Marxist views. All four men

During 1940-1945, when Blunt was most active as a Soviet spy, he rationalized that by helping the Soviets he would also be helping Great Britain to win the war.

were fierce antifascists, and because the British government did nothing to stop Hitler from mobilizing, they placed their faith in Stalin.

In 1937, when Blunt graduated from Cambridge, he planned to work for the Soviet Union, but no KGB agent showed interest in his services. So, Blunt passed the time increasing his knowledge of art. This was suddenly interrupted in 1939 when Germany attacked Poland and the British went to war. Blunt joined the infantry, served briefly on the Continent, and in 1940 left from France with the rest of the British army.

Disillusioned with army life, Blunt joined MI5 (Military Intelligence 5, British counterespionage), where he kept surveillance on neutral missions in London, including correspondence between foreign embassies, and sometimes sat on the Joint Intelligence Committee, all of which allowed him access to secret reports. He also fell in again with Guy Burgess, who had become a British espionage officer and spy for Russia. Burgess worked through a Soviet handler in London who forwarded intelligence to Moscow. Blunt attached himself to Burgess's contact, offering himself as a counterespionage agent, and remained as such for the balance of the war.

The Retired Spy

In 1945 the war ended and Blunt resumed his study of art. Over the next 30 years he wrote several books and earned the reputation as a renowned authority on art history. His first honor came in 1945, when George VI made him surveyor of the king's pictures. In 1950 the British Academy inducted him as a fellow, and six years later Queen Elizabeth knighted him and Blunt became Sir Anthony.

During these years of international recognition, Blunt received a distressed call from Burgess, who warned that British agents were about to arrest Maclean for espionage. Realizing that he, too, could be incriminated, Blunt made a desperate call to his former Soviet contact and arranged for Burgess and Maclean to escape to Moscow. The KBG insisted Blunt come with them, but the successful art connoisseur refused, aware that London had become a much better place to live than Moscow.

The defection of Burgess and Maclean left an unanswered question. British intelligence had gathered far more information than any of the conspirators realized and suspected there had been another agent. The effort to locate this agent

In 1963 Blunt was exposed to MI5 as a spy by one of his recruitment failures, an American named Michael Straight. In exchange for all his knowledge of the KGB, Blunt was given immunity from prosecution.

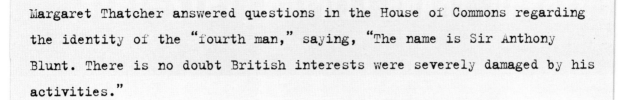

Margaret Thatcher answered questions in the House of Commons regarding the identity of the "fourth man," saying, "The name is Sir Anthony Blunt. There is no doubt British interests were severely damaged by his activities."

initially focused on Kim Philby, who had passed information to Burgess while they both worked in Washington, but British agents reported that Philby had already defected to Moscow. After Blunt helped Burgess and Maclean escape, British intelligence began looking for a fourth man.

In 1964, agents questioned Sir Anthony after they discovered his Cambridge connection with Burgess, Maclean, and Philby. Blunt secretly confessed at counterintelligence headquarters of his activities during the war in exchange for immunity, his privacy in the matter, and his freedom. He admitted to being the fourth man, passing information to the KGB for years, and arranging the escape of Burgess and Maclean. As part of his deal, he also provided information on Soviet operations in Great Britain, most of which was, by that time, out of date.

Reverses of Fortune

Believing he had relieved himself of a bothersome burden, Sir Anthony returned to his career in art, but in 1979 life suddenly turned upside down. Journalist and biographer Andrew Boyle publicly identified Blunt as the now-notorious Cambridge Spy Ring's mysterious fourth man and pointed to him as the person who engineered the escape of Burgess and Maclean. What made matters worse from the public's point of view was that British intelligence had Sir Anthony's confession but set him free. Prime Minister Margaret Thatcher tried unsuccessfully to explain the deal to Parliament, and the press demanded to know why the queen retained Sir Anthony as the keeper of the royal art galleries.

Blunt eventually gave his side of the story to the press, admitting that he chose to betray the country instead of his friends. That they were all bonded by homosexuality did not help his case. He stated that the information he gave the Soviets during the war actually harmed no one, a statement that in the 1980s could neither be proved nor disproved. Sir Anthony agreed that he had made a horrible mistake in his youth, but added that at the time, "I did not betray my conscience." On the following day, an editorial in a London newspaper shouted back, "Damn your conscience!"

Blunt's honors disintegrated overnight. The queen stripped his knighthood, Trinity College revoked his fellowship, and the British Academy expelled him. Had he gone to Moscow with his friends, life could not have become any worse. For a man who enjoyed the company of others and the great works of art, Blunt lived the balance of his life in isolation. In 1983, at the age of 72, he died a lonely man, remembered not for his great contribution to art but as the fourth member of the Cambridge Spy Ring.

Opposite: In 1979, Boyle's book *The Climate of Treason* told Blunt's story, attributing it to a character named Maurice. Following questions in Parliament, Prime Minister Margaret Thatcher revealed Blunt as the real-life "Maurice."

NOTES

Anthony Blunt had the great misfortune of retaining his connections with the Cambridge Spy Ring, not as an active spy but as an accomplice in arranging his friends' escape to Moscow.

BOSSARD, FRANK CLIFTON (1912–1978)

British agent Frank Clifton Bossard spied for the Soviet Union for many years until his cover was blown in 1965 by a KGB defector known only as "Top Hat."

The poverty of youth made Frank Clifton Bossard resentful toward the British upper class, and at an early age he came to know the misery of poverty and the value of wealth. His father, who worked as a carpenter, died before Frank was born, leaving the family penniless. Frank's mother tried to make ends meet, first by becoming a housekeeper in Lincolnshire and later by running a general store. When Frank reached the age of six, he attended a public school, but in 1923 his mother married a poor farmer and moved to the country. Frank wanted to continue school, but his stepfather could not afford the expense. So, at the age of 14 young Bossard went to work as a store clerk, lamenting his misfortune and deeply troubled over his inability to continue his education.

```
----DOSSIER--------
Name: Frank Clifton Bossard
Code Name: None
Birth/Death: 1912-1978
Nationality: British
Occupation: Royal Air Force
and MI6
Involvement: Spy for the
Soviets
Outcome: Died in Prison of
Natural Causes
```

A Quest for a Future

Though deprived of life's fundamental entitlements, Bossard developed an interest in radios and at the age of 16 built his first wireless receiver. Five years later he had saved enough money to take a course in radio technology at Norwich Technical College. There he attempted to socialize with wealthy young friends, but soon ran out of money. In 1934 he cashed a forged check to cover expenses, and spent the next six months at hard labor in jail.

After the outbreak of World War II, Bossard joined the Royal Air Force and saw action in the Middle East. Because he understood radios, the RAF transferred him into a radar unit. In 1946, when the group demobilized, Bossard had risen in rank to flight lieutenant (captain).

Bossard continued to hone his skills. After being discharged from the RAF, he lectured on radar and wireless communication at the College of Air Service at Hamble, Hampshire. The Ministry of Civil Aviation soon recognized his talents and hired him as an assistant signals officer.

Bossard performed well, and the ministry promoted him to the position of staff telecommunications officer.

Opportunity Beckons

In 1951, Bossard's life dramatically changed. He married an attractive young woman half his age, and in December accepted a position as senior officer with the Scientific and Technical Intelligence Branch in Germany. Intelligence work appealed to him, and five years later MI6, the British secret intelligence service,

Left: British aviation expert Frank Clifton Bossard, pictured in 1965, the year that he was tried on charges of selling British military secrets to the Soviets.

Above: Frank Bossard pictured with his wife. It was his infidelity with prostitutes and the heavy drinking that accompanied it, as well as his access to military secrets, that made Bossard an attractive propostion to the Soviets. They perceived that such characrer flaws would make him easy to manipulate.

recruited and hired him. MI6 attached him to the British embassy in Bonn, Germany, as an attaché with the responsibility for interviewing all the scientists, engineers, and technicians who had escaped from behind the iron curtain. Having a generous entertainment allowance at his disposal, Bossard began drinking heavily. With his defectors in tow, he entertained them—and himself—with prostitutes and strip shows. During one or more of these unauthorized trysts, he bragged of being an "undercover man."

Soviet agents took an interest in Bossard because he manifested all the personal traits they sought when recruiting spies. His position gave him access to secret documents, in particular guided missiles, and he always needed money. His habitual drinking made him unstable, and his weakness of character made him vulnerable to blackmail.

In 1961 Bossard returned to London. His heavy drinking continued but his hefty entertainment allowances stopped. His debts became so severe that he opened a small coin-collection business to

Bossard once explained that his ambition in life was to lift himself above his social station, and become involved with people better off than himself. However, his personal habits often dragged him down.

When questioned, Bossard explained how he worked: "I selected files on guided weapons, used them in my office, took them to a hotel room, and photographed suitable extracts during my lunch period. The equipment was kept in the Left Luggage office at Waterloo Station and I removed it when I needed it."

augment his income. One night while drinking in a London pub, a man who called himself Gordon took a seat beside him and opened a friendly conversation. Gordon bought the drinks that night, and for several nights to come. When Bossard complained of having no money, Gordon confessed he was a Soviet agent and offered a solution to Bossard's financial problems. Gordon advanced £250 in exchange for Bossard's commitment to photograph secret documents of interest to Russia. Bossard pocketed the money and sealed the bargain.

A Dirty Little Business

Gordon provided Bossard with nine "letterboxes," or dead drops: one a broken drain pipe on an estate, another a secluded beech tree covered with vines, and another beech tree with three trunks, all in Surrey. Bossard learned which letterbox to use by tuning into Moscow radio at 7:45 a.m. and 8:30 p.m. on the first Tuesday and Wednesday of each month. Songs specified which letterbox to use; "The Volga Boat Song," however, meant "cease operations immediately."

The arrangement continued for four years. For every packet of photographed documents Bossard delivered on guided missile systems, radar, and other secrets, he received £2,000. Instead of paying off

his debts and putting money away, he went on a spending binge. MI5 became suspicious and put Bossard under surveillance.

After following Bossard for several weeks and investigating his finances, MI5 authorized his arrest. On March 12, 1965, after Bossard checked into the Ivanhoe Hotel under an assumed name to carry out his photographing, Detective Superintendent Wise of Scotland Yard stopped the spy in the hallway, took his arm, and said, "I have reason to believe that you have committed an offense against the Official Secrets Act. Will you please accompany me back to your room?" Bossard did not resist. In checking through the spy's personal belongings, Wise uncovered photographs of secret files belonging to the Ministry of Civil Aviation, a camera used to photograph documents, a roll of film containing photographed documents, and a diary spelling out the locations of mailboxes.

On May 10, 1965, in an effort to conceal the arrest from the press, Bossard received a quick trial at the Old Bailey and was sentenced to 21 years in prison. Bossard died in 1978 of natural causes.

NOTES

Like many spies who sold out to the Soviets, Bossard became the perfect mark because of his instability, debt, and alcoholism, which eventually destroyed his health.

BOYCE, CHRISTOPHER JOHN (1953–)

American Christopher John Boyce and his friend Andrew D. Lee sold enough secrets to enable the Soviet Union to temporarily block transmissions to and from U.S. satellites positioned over Soviet Russia and Red China.

In 1975 Christopher Boyce of Palos Verdes, California, went to work at a company called TRW Defense and Space Systems Group, a high-technology aerospace contractor, building U.S. spy satellites at Redondo Beach. An unlikely candidate for classified work, Boyce got his job through his father, who was a retired FBI agent and director of security at an aircraft plant. Despite Boyce's lack of experience and record as a dropout at Loyola Marymont, TRW gave him top-secret clearances that enabled him to handle the company's most secure documents. The privilege extended to TRW's "Black Vault," the company's most secure communications center. CIA headquarters in Langley, Virginia, depended upon Black Vault operators to regularly change and update usage codes.

```
----DOSSIER--------
Name: Christopher
John Boyce
Code Name: None
Birth/Death: 1953-
Nationality: American
Occupation: Aerospace
Worker
Involvement: Spy for the
Soviets
Outcome: Currently
Serving a 130-year Prison
Sentence
```

The Genius and the Idiot

As a youth, Boyce attended a Roman Catholic School where he met his closest friend, Andrew Daulton Lee. They played on the football team together, developed common interests, raised and trained falcons, and had a disdain for the Vietnam War. They were both disillusioned with politics and commiserated

together while smoking marijuana and imbibing a number of other drugs. As feckless boys tend to do when dissastisfied with life, Lee and Boyce would make plans to change the world.

With an IQ of 142, Boyce could have moved forward with his life and become successful had he chosen a profession instead of indolence. Lee had no particular skills outside of dealing cocaine but, like Boyce, had developed an insatiable appetite for money. Boyce's $140-a-week salary fell far short of his expectations of pocket money and Lee found himself short of cash, so they shared a fool's dream—should the opportunity avail itself, they would go into the espionage business together.

Welcome to the Black Vault

Five months into his employment, the opportunity fell into Boyce's lap when he was introduced to TRW's Black Vault, where his responsibilities entailed the daily change of cipher keys to CIA satellites. TRW had two satellites in orbit, code-named Rhyolite and Argus. They were managed from the Black Vault using Signals Intelligence (SIGNET). Rhyolite hovered 18,000 miles over Russia and China, listening for the sound of missile engines, but the electronic instrumentation on board was sensitive enough to monitor and record whispered conversations from telephones on the ground. Boyce quickly grasped the importance of his job, and during a pot-smoking session with Lee he said, "You know that stuff would be worth a lot of money to a foreign power."

Twenty-one-year-old Boyce did not know where to look for a Russian agent, so he solved the problem in April 1975 by sending Lee to Mexico City. Lee landed at the airport, arranged a ride to the Soviet embassy, blandly walked up to the guard at the gate, and stated his purpose. A few minutes later the Soviet attaché conducted him into a private room. Between servings of vodka and caviar, Lee offered to sell TRW's secrets and showed the attaché a sample 12-inch paper tape used in the company's crypto machines. Imprinted on it were messages from Rhyolite. The attaché excused himself and left the room with the sample. A few minutes later he returned showing great interest and offered to buy everything that Lee could bring him. At the time, Lee did not realize that the attaché was actually KGB spymaster Boris Alexei Grishin. In parting, Grishin gave Lee $250 to cover his flight expenses and promised thousands more in the future. Boyce and Lee were now in the spy business.

Novices at Work

A Soviet handler soon contacted Lee and operations commenced in TRW's Black Vault. When Boyce learned that the KGB demanded to know the name of the person on the inside, he instructed Lee to never tell them. Boyce smuggled the secrets out of TRW and Lee carried them to Grishin in Mexico City, who paid $10,000 for every delivery of information containing ciphers. After each trip, Lee returned with the cash but gave Boyce only $3,000.

Boyce became suspicious and blew his cover with the KGB by flying to Mexico City to confer with Grishin directly. Before leaving the embassy, Boyce agreed to photograph and prepare one last bulk shipment of cryptology secrets in exchange for $75,000. The highly secret information contained TRW's next satellite network, code-named Pyramider, a new spy system that could be operated inside the Soviet Union and China.

The information would have been priceless to the Soviets, but Grishin never received it. In 1977, Lee needed some

money and decided to travel to the Soviet embassy again. The Mexican police arrested him as a terrorist suspect. During a clothing search, they found filmstrips of classified documents. The FBI arrived and began asking questions. Lee now started to panic and implicated Boyce. One hour later, FBI agents in Los Angeles picked up Boyce, who confessed to copying thousands of documents and selling them to Grishin and Russia.

Lessons in Wasted Youth

In April 1977, both men went to trial. Boyce received a 40-year sentence and Lee went to prison for life. Three years later, Boyce escaped from the maximum-security federal prison in Lompoc, California. With two buddies, he went on a bank-robbing spree in the Pacific Northwest. After separating from his partners, Boyce bought a 29-foot salmon trawler in Port Angeles, Washington. He intended to sail to the Bering Strait and take refuge in Siberia. He was warned he would never make it.

The FBI and U.S. marshals, after searching in Costa Rica, Mexico, Australia, and South Africa, located and apprehended Boyce at a Port Angeles flying school, learning to fly. Boyce is currently in prison, serving the balance of his 40-year prison term, with another 90 years added.

The escapades of Boyce and Lee became the subject of a book and movie both titled *The Falcon and the Snowman.* The titles are not without meaning: Boyce loved falconry and Lee loved cocaine.

Opposite: On January 21, 1980, Boyce escaped from the Lompoc Correctional Institute. Boyce was the first high-profile escapee that the U.S. Marshals Service had been entrusted with, and it took them 19 months and the assistance of the FBI to apprehend him. On his capture, on August 21, 1981, he still had 36 years of his sentence left to serve. Shown here on August 24, Boyce is escorted from the Seattle Courthouse by federal marshals.

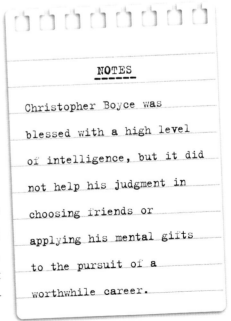

NOTES

Christopher Boyce was blessed with a high level of intelligence, but it did not help his judgment in choosing friends or applying his mental gifts to the pursuit of a worthwhile career.

BOYD, ISABELLE "BELLE" (1844–1900)

Belle Boyd became one of the first heroic Confederate spies to ride into the Civil War on horseback, voluntarily scouting enemy positions and relaying vital intelligence to the Southern army.

Although her parents named her Isabelle, she never liked the name and insisted upon being called Belle—and with good reason. At the age of 17 she had become charming, beautiful, and determined. She did exactly as she chose because her father owned a prosperous general store in Martinsburg, Virginia, and could afford her impulses. In 1860 Boyd graduated from the exclusive Mount Washington Female College in Baltimore, Maryland, and returned to her home with a liberal education, a flair for drama, and a love of horses and excitement.

Civil War Comes to the Valley

When Virginia seceded from the Union in April 1861, Boyd's father joined the Confederate Army and became a member of Colonel Thomas Jonathan Jackson's command at Harpers Ferry. For the next fourteen months, Jackson's troops were never far from Martinsburg or the Shenandoah Valley, but Union troops often occupied Martinsburg.

```
----DOSSIER--------
Name: Isabelle "Belle" Boyd
Code Name: None
Birth/Death: 1844-1900
Nationality: American
Occupation: Actress
Involvement: Spy for the
Confederacy
Outcome: Died of Natural
Causes
```

Belle Boyd could not conceal her rage when federal cavalry came to her front door and insisted on flying the Union flag from a top window. Although her mother refused to allow the men to enter, one burly trooper lowered his shoulder and crashed through the door. When he looked up, he noticed a pretty young girl walking toward him from the

Below: Boyd carried information across enemy lines, was arrested three times, and on her last prison sojourn she contracted typhus. On her release she moved to England to recuperate; while returning to the U.S., her blockade-runner was captured by a Union warship. Boyd seduced the ship's captain and then fell in love with him. He was subsequently court-martialed for having allowed her to escape.

hallway gripping a pistol in her hand. Boyd fired, the bullet tore through the trooper's head, and he died instantly. Arrested for murder, Boyd appeared before a tribunal of Union officers in her own defense. She testified that the soldier broke into her home and abused her mother, so she shot him. The trial provided Boyd with her first dramatic appearance without a script. She charmed the federal officers, who ruled that she had committed justifiable homicide and set her free.

Stonewall Jackson's Intrepid Spy

Boyd no longer feared the enemy. After returning home, she rode back and forth

through enemy lines to visit her father. She met General Jackson and offered to keep close watch over the enemy's activities. Jackson turned her over to cavalry commander Colonel Turner Ashby, who performed the general's scouting and served as the brigade's intelligence officer. The assignment, which nobody but Boyd took seriously, became a great asset during Jackson's Shenandoah campaign.

After the Battle of Bull Run in July 1861, Jackson established headquarters in Winchester, Virginia, some 30 miles south of Martinsburg. Boyd scouted the lower Shenandoah Valley, making frequent trips through the countryside. When Boyd had information to report, she saddled her horse and rode south looking for Ashby. She never wrote her notes in code, and Ashby tried, without success, to urge her to be more careful. Nor did warnings from her mother keep her from scouting back roads alone. Boyd never seemed concerned about her safety. Being a crack shot with the pistol in her jacket was all the protection she needed.

The Unbreakable Belle

In 1861, while caring for wounded soldiers after a Confederate retreat, she reported the size and direction of the enemy's march to Ashby. On returning home, Union agents arrested her as a spy. Allan Pinkerton, head of Union espionage, interrogated Boyd, who gave another dramatic performance that so charmed the detective that he said, "There is no reason to hold her," and set her free. Boyd returned home, wrote a report describing Pinkerton's interrogation methods, and carried it to Ashby.

When the spring campaign of 1862 began, Jackson's Confederates began probing Union defenses. Arrested again for being near the lines, Boyd demurely explained that she was out for her customary morning ride. Allowed to pass, she walked her horse through the federal position, once again rendezvousing with Ashby to report her observations.

When military operations shifted to the upper Shenandoah, Boyd moved from Martinsburg to Front Royal. She lived in a hotel owned by a relative, but her motive in moving was to get closer to the action. Union officers, pursuing Jackson's withdrawal up the valley, commandeered quarters in the same hotel. Boyd used the building's air vents to eavesdrop and took notes of the enemy's battle plan.

Tactical Expert

Her activities as a spy had provided her nimble mind with a quick course in tactics. She also possessed full knowledge of the local topography and recognized that if Jackson struck the enemy flank, he could cripple General Nathaniel Banks's Union Army corps. She saddled her horse at dark, hid her notes, and galloped south, looking for Ashby's scouts. She located the colonel near a tributary of the Shenandoah River and handed him the message.

Boyd instructed Ashby to tell Jackson that if he moved on Front Royal immediately, and before the federals destroyed the bridges, he would catch the enemy spread out along the main road with its flanks exposed. Jackson probably should have made Boyd his tactician. He put the army on the road, screened it between the mountains, thundered into Front Royal, recaptured the town, and cut the enemy force in half. Jackson personally thanked Boyd "for the immense service you have rendered your country today."

In 1863, after the death of Ashby, Boyd carelessly passed information to a man who promised to deliver it to a Confederate commander, but instead turned it over to the Union's secret service chief, Lafayette Baker. Baker ordered Boyd arrested and brought her to Washington for interrogation. She delivered another fine performance and told Baker nothing. Union agents failed to search her trunks, which contained incriminating notes and $25,000 in Confederate currency she had been given by intelligence operatives to buy information. Baker detained her in Washington for several weeks but, finding her unbreakable, sent her to Richmond with a warning that if he ever saw her again, he would shoot her.

Boyd received a hero's welcome in the Confederate capital and the personal thanks of President Jefferson Davis. She returned to Martinsburg, believing her days of espionage were over, but a few weeks later she received a personal request from Davis to deliver important documents to agents in England. She traveled through Canada, booked passage on a steamer, and reached London a few weeks before the war ended.

Having no war to fight, Isabelle Boyd started a new career, making her first appearance as an actress on a London stage. She returned to the United States and published a fanciful book of her memoirs, married, and spent the next decade traveling around the country performing for the public. In 1900 she died of a heart attack.

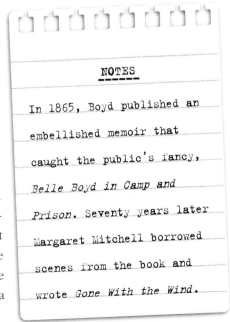

NOTES

In 1865, Boyd published an embellished memoir that caught the public's fancy, *Belle Boyd in Camp and Prison*. Seventy years later Margaret Mitchell borrowed scenes from the book and wrote *Gone With the Wind*.

BURGESS, GUY (1911–1963)

Guy Burgess became a member of the notorious Cambridge Spy Ring, which included fellow classmates Anthony Blunt, Harold "Kim" Philby, and Donald Maclean. Burgess developed into a writer and diplomat, little of which the public remembered after Scotland Yard exposed him as an undercover spy for the Soviet Union.

Born in Devonport, England, the son of an officer in the Royal Navy, Guy Burgess passed through youth with his mind set on following in his father's footsteps. Service at sea had long been a family tradition, and through his early life Burgess received constant encouragement to become a naval officer.

After a year at Eton (1924–1925), he enrolled at the naval college at Dartmouth (1925–1927), but a purported eye problem disqualified him from serving in the navy and he was unable to follow in his father's footsteps. He returned to Eton to finish his schooling and graduated in 1930.

```
----DOSSIER--------
Name: Guy Francis
de Moncy Burgess
Code Name: None
Birth/Death: 1911-1963
Nationality: British
Occupation: Journalist and
Diplomat
Involvement: Spy for the
Soviet Union
Outcome: Died in Moscow
from Alcoholism
```

The Cambridge Connection

In 1930, Burgess enrolled at Cambridge to study history, where he soon made friends with a homosexual element who fashioned themselves as the university's Communist underground. He met Anthony Blunt, with whom he shared a room, and developed close ties with Harold "Kim" Philby and Donald Maclean. The four men shared an aversion to the British political system that produced the 1930s depression and convinced each other that only the socialized system of the Soviet Union could save the oppressed. Not one of the four men had ever rubbed elbows with the working class, and their concepts of Marxism emanated mainly from their frequent bouts of intoxicated conversation. Though at the time they had no direct connection with the Soviet Union, the rise to power of Adolf Hitler in the mid-1930s and the spread of fascism in Europe convinced the quartet to take action. Burgess and Blunt began a movement on campus to convert all dedicated Cambridge Communists into secret agents for the Soviet Union's KGB. A year or two passed before the KGB actually learned of the Cambridge Spy Ring.

In 1934, a year before graduating, Burgess went to Moscow with Philby and Maclean to see the sights. Burgess came home unimpressed by the dreary city and spent most of his time drunk. He never contacted the KGB and returned to Cambridge doubtful whether Communism offered the road to the future.

Journalism and Espionage

Exactly when Burgess became a KGB spy is not known, but according to a later statement by Anthony Blunt, it began in 1935 when Burgess launched his ten-year career in journalism. After Cambridge, Burgess began a double life. He worked for the British Broadcasting Corporation (BBC) and delivered secret information to his KGB handler as he received it. His network included John Cairncross of the British Foreign Office, also a Cambridge man, who used Burgess as a conduit to funnel secrets to the Soviets.

Burgess also developed his own contacts by cultivating a friendship with Hector McNeil, the future minister of state at the Foreign Office. He also interviewed

and established a tie with Winston Churchill, soon to become prime minister. Before Germany invaded Poland, another interview put him in contact with Prime Minister Neville Chamberlain, who entrusted him with secret documents to be covertly delivered to Italian dictator Benito Mussolini and French president Edouard Daladier, in a futile effort to upset Hitler's plans and prevent war. It is uncertain whether the same information reached Moscow.

Burgess used his position as a journalist to keep connected with his Cambridge cronies. In 1937 and 1939 he met with Kim Philby for a rendezvous in France. Philby, also a journalist, divided his time

Above: Guy Burgess was one of four Cambridge spies who were recruited by Soviet intelligence, partly for their class connections, and attained high rank in the British civil and intelligence services. Burgess and a partner, Donald Maclean, defected to the Soviet Union in 1951.

between reporting on the Spanish Civil War (1936–1939) and sending intelligence to Moscow. When the civil war ended, Philby returned to England and appeared on the BBC, interviewed by his part-time lover, Guy Burgess.

In 1939 the British Secret Intelligence Service, MI6, wanted their own journalist, so they hired Burgess and assigned him to MI6, Department D. The new department, charged with intelligence gathering, initiated a vast campaign to recruit hundreds of agents. Burgess missed the visibility of broadcasting, so he hired Philby for MI6 and in 1941 went back to the BBC, where he could revive his connections with the Foreign Office and better serve his KGB handlers.

Spies in the Foreign Office

In 1944, when the British Foreign Office decided to hire a man to discreetly handle their news, Labour Minister Hector McNeil chose Burgess. McNeil knew of Burgess's homosexual activities and leftist leanings but never suspected his relationship with Moscow. He merely warned him to behave, and for six years Burgess pursued his habits outside the Foreign Office and continued to pass secrets to the Soviets.

With the exception of Blunt, who had become the queen's curator of art and a recognized scholar of art history, the other three members of the Cambridge Spy Ring stayed in close contact. When the Foreign Office sent Burgess to the British Embassy in Washington, D.C., in 1950, Philby was already there as first secretary. Somewhat to Burgess's surprise, he discovered Philby had married. The two men resumed collective espionage activities, conspiring during the evening at Philby's home. Mrs. Philby developed a deep dislike for Burgess's habitual intoxication, superior demeanor, and reputation for homosexuality. Burgess's habits also annoyed the British ambassador who, in 1951, ordered him back to London. Before Burgess departed, Philby received information that Maclean, who had also served at the embassy and was then with the British Foreign Office, was under surveillance for spying. He urged Burgess to warn Maclean immediately upon reaching London.

Burgess called Maclean, and Maclean called Blunt. Blunt was no longer a spy but still had Soviet contacts. Moscow ordered Burgess, Blunt, and Maclean to leave London immediately. Burgess and Maclean followed instructions, but Blunt had been knighted and opted to continue with his distinguished career. Philby remained at large, unaware that agents began looking into the background of Burgess. The Cambridge connection led them to Philby, the suspected "third man." Philby escaped to Moscow in 1963, the same year Burgess died of alcoholism. Agents then began searching for a fourth man, and, in 1979, arrested Blunt.

In Soviet Russia, Burgess was never happy. He did not bother to learn Russian, homosexuality was frowned upon, he often talked fondly of Britain, and ordered his suits from tailors in Saville Row, London. He continued to drink heavily and finally drank himself to death in 1963. The Soviets sent Burgess's remains back to England, where he was buried without ceremony.

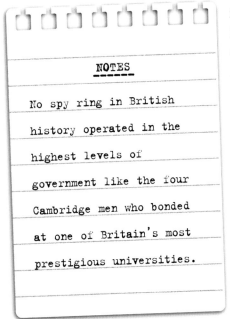

NOTES

No spy ring in British history operated in the highest levels of government like the four Cambridge men who bonded at one of Britain's most prestigious universities.

BURTON, SIR RICHARD (1821–1890)

Richard Burton started life as a linguist because he enjoyed studying languages. He became known to the world as a brilliant author, explorer, and Orientalist, but he was also the greatest amateur spy in India and Arabia.

Born in Torquay, England, Richard Burton grew up with a hypochondriac father who retired as a colonel from the army early in life so he could spend the rest of his years wandering the planet in search of the healthiest place to live, where he could extend his life to the maximum. The father's eccentricities had little effect on his son.

During his youth, Burton studied foreign languages with a passion. In 1840, when entering Oxford, he already spoke fluent French, German, Spanish, Italian, Portuguese, and modern Greek. During his two years at Oxford, he studied ancient Greek, Latin, and Arabic. He would eventually learn to speak more than 35 languages and 40 dialects.

```
----DOSSIER--------
Name: Richard Burton
Code Name: Mirza Abdullah
El Bushiri
Birth/Death: 1821-1890
Nationality: British
Occupation: Officer in the
East India Company
Involvement: British Agent
in India and Arabia
Outcome: Died of Natural
Causes
```

The Mystic Land of Sind

By 1842 Burton was tired of study and began looking for adventure. India appealed to him, and he persuaded his father to buy him a commission in the mercenary army of the East India Company. In 1843 the private trading consortium sent Burton to the province of Sind (now Pakistan), where he fell in with General Sir Charles Napier. Recognizing Burton's linguistic skills, Napier sent him into the recently captured northern provinces to learn the languages and customs of the inhabitants and identify dissident leaders. Thus began Burton's long career as a spy.

Burton quickly mastered the language and the dialects. Disguised as a native, with his skin lightly tinted with henna, his hair dyed black, and sometimes wearing a long black moustache, he moved through the villages, sifted through bazaars, and mingled with sojourners. He chose suitable clothes for each mission, such as wearing native dress when he joined work gangs digging drainage ditches and leveling canals: Napier wanted the canals surveyed, and Burton obtained the information by working on them. In the next town he might be seen in the rags of a dervish peddler, milling about a village market to observe the local tribal leader. He walked into remote areas among the hills, making notes on

customs. When he infiltrated the remote camps of tribal leaders, no one ever suspected Burton of being anything other than a down-and-out wandering Muslim. His disguises could fool anyone, including one fellow British officer who shoved him aside as he passed.

The information Burton collected exceeded the expectations of the general, especially the knowledge he obtained about the far-flung hill tribes. Napier used the intelligence to prevent disturbances and to keep tribes under control.

The Brothels of Karachi

Napier became troubled when he heard rumors about three homosexual brothels in Karachi that, he feared, were being patronized by his troops. If the dens of iniquity existed, he wanted them shut down and asked Burton to find them.

Disguised as a Persian merchant named Mirza Abdullah El Bushiri, Burton circulated through the tawdry district of Karachi. After making some inquiries, he located all three back-alley brothels, found them packed with naked men, and reported his observations to Napier. The general raided the brothels and shut them down.

A few weeks later, Napier received new orders and departed. His replacement did not like Burton. He read the spy's report on the brothels of Karachi and used it to ruin him. Severely reprimanded by the East India Company and stripped of his commission, Burton departed from India in 1849, in disgrace and poor health.

The Hajji of Mirza Abdullah El Bushiri

In 1849 Burton returned to London. After recovering his health, he explained what

Below: Burton regularly went undercover in various disguises, which enabled him to obtain information and infiltrate different cultures. In 1853, he journeyed in disguise to the then-forbidden cities of Mecca and Medina.

had happened, but his career with the East India Company was over. He spent the next three years studying Arabic dialects and the Islamic religion. Once again, at the age if 32, the urge for adventure put him back on the road, this time to Arabia.

Burton packed his disguises, again assumed the persona of Persian merchant Mirza Abdullah El Bushiri, and to "study the inner life of the Muslim," joined the annual pilgrimage to Medina and Mecca. Had Burton been discovered, he would have been beheaded. His disguise allowed him to infiltrate the holiest sanctuaries of Islam. At Mecca he received the title of Hajji and the green turban that signified his completion of the great pilgrimage. For more than a year Burton mingled among the Arabs, studying the customs of the people and their tribal leaders and, in 1854, delivered a comprehensive report to the British government.

The Greatest Work to Come

Burton could travel anywhere in the world because he either spoke the language or his vast experience enabled him to adapt. He explored Ethiopia and Somalia and went deep into the African continent searching for the source of the Nile. In 1861 the British Foreign Office put him back to work, placing him in charge of consulates in Africa and Brazil, specifically to collect intelligence. He led expeditions of exploration through the Holy Land and into Syria, creating

maps and recording observations as he traveled.

Burton retired in Trieste, his last post. He spent the next several years on a six-volume translation of *The Arabian Nights*, his life's masterpiece. By 1887 the stain of his espionage in Karachi's brothels had been long forgiven. Queen Victoria awarded Burton the title of Knight Commander of St. Michael and St. George for his services to the Crown, an honor he enjoyed briefly before he died.

Above: During his life Burton wrote and translated many books, perhaps the most famous of these was his translation of the *Kama Sutra*. Due to the stringent pornography laws of the time this was originally published through a private society known as the Kama Shastra Society.

In 1855 Burton published his experiences in Arabia, titled *Pilgrimage to Al Maginah and Meccah*, a book as brilliantly written as T. E. Lawrence's later epic on Arabia, *The Seven Pillars of Wisdom*.

CANARIS, WILHELM FRANZ (1887–1945)

Wilhelm Franz Canaris, German chief of the Abwehr during World War II, built one of the greatest espionage networks in the history of the world. In 1944, he was executed after being implicated in the unsuccessful assassination attempt of Adolf Hitler.

The youngest of three children, Wilhelm Canaris grew up near Dortmund, in Germany, where his father, an engineer, managed an iron works and provided a good living for the family. Canaris went to a public school, developed an inquisitive mind, and attracted notice because he insisted on knowing what everyone was doing and why. He grew up with the nickname "Keiker," which translates to "Snooper." The habit pushed Canaris into a life of espionage.

The Making of a Spy

On April 1, 1905, 18-year-old Canaris entered the Imperial Naval Academy at Kiel. He occupied his free time by prying into the affairs of fellow cadets and documenting their behavioral responses and eccentricities. Despite this self-imposed distraction, he ranked high in his class and went to sea as an officer.

At the outbreak of World War I, Canaris served on the light cruiser *Dresden*, part of Admiral Graf Spee's squadron that

```
----DOSSIER--------
Name: Wilhelm Franz Canaris
Code Name: Reed Rosas
Birth/Death: 1887-1945
Nationality: German
Occupation: Admiral and
Chief of Abwehr
Involvement: Anti-Hitler
Activist
Outcome: Executed by
the SS
```

suffered disaster at the hands of the British fleet off the Falkland Islands. Imprisoned on the desolate Quirquina Island, near Valparaiso in Chile, Canaris ignored the escape conspiracies of others and made his own plans. He stole a small boat and then exchanged it for a horse,

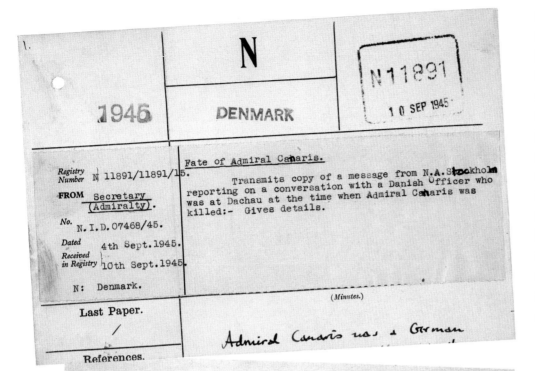

Left: Canaris was executed along with Dietrich Bonhoeffer, Major General Hans Oster, Judge Advocate General Carl Sack, and Captain Ludwig Gehre at the Flossenburg concentration camp on April 9, 1945. He went to the gallows unrepentant of his actions: "I die for my fatherland. I have a clear conscience. I only did my duty to my country when I tried to oppose the criminal folly of Hitler."

Left: Danish Colonel Lunding, former director of Danish military intelligence, was imprisoned in the cell next to Canaris. Shortly before being led naked to his execution, Canaris communicated with Lunding by tapping on the wall of his cell: "This is the end. Badly mishandled. My nose broken. I have done nothing against Germany. If you survive, please tell my wife."

and disguised himself as a Chilean named Reed Rosas. He crossed the Andes, obtained a Chilean passport from the German embassy in Buenos Aires, Argentina, and sailed to Rotterdam on a Dutch steamer. He returned to Germany a hero and received the Iron Cross.

Recruited by German intelligence, Canaris received his first espionage assignment and went to Spain to spy on Allied diplomats and military operatives. When he returned to Germany in 1916 as a captain, intelligence sent him on a mission through Switzerland and into Italy. He used his Chilean identity as Reed Rosas, but Italian police suspected him of spying and threw him in jail. He escaped and in 1917 returned to Berlin.

The Rise to Power

After the war ended, political chaos spread across Germany. Out of work, Canaris married Ericka Waag, the first and only woman in his life. He could not decide where to throw his support and

Right: In Spain in 1943, Canaris met with Stuart Menzies, chief of British intelligence. He outlined a plan for peace incorporating a cease-fire in the West and the elimination or handing over of Hitler. Unfortunately, his peace offer was rejected.

finally decided to work for the Weimar Republic. Now a family man, he recommitted to the navy and over the next 15 years rose through the ranks to admiral and chief of staff of naval operations. In 1935 Abwehr chief Konrad Patzig returned to active duty in the navy, and Admiral Erich Raeder replaced him with Canaris.

On January 1, 1935, Canaris took charge of German intelligence. He instinctively did not like Adolf Hitler, who was now in full control of the Third Reich. He loathed Heinrich Himmler, head of German internal security, and despised his henchman, Reinhard Heydrich, chief of political espionage, both of whom were attempting to infiltrate the Abwehr and fill it with their own operatives.

Having studied Hitler's two henchmen with the same deliberate scrutiny that he studied everyone, he manipulated them with friendship but at the same time worked against them. While Himmler and Heydrich believed they were making inroads into the Abwehr, Canaris balanced the relationship by expanding the secret service and inserting trusted agents into Himmler and Heydrich's operations. Himmler never discovered that Canaris had vowed to dispose of Hitler.

The Black Orchestra

In 1935 Canaris joined the Black Orchestra, a secret organization devoted to ousting Hitler. The Gestapo coined the name: "black" meant anyone opposed to Hitler, and "orchestra" referred to the coded espionage music that the organization transmitted using shortwave radios. Those who understood the codes learned of Hitler's plan to annex Austria, invade Czechoslovakia in 1938, and blitzkrieg Poland in 1939. To no avail, Black Orchestra operatives in England urged Prime Minister Neville Chamberlain to intercede and stop Hitler's aggression before it started.

During the war, Canaris became one of the most powerful men in Germany, but his influence ebbed and flowed along with Hitler's defeats and victories. At times, Himmler intercepted leaks casting suspicion on Canaris, but his agents always concluded their investigations without finding sufficient evidence. Over time, Hitler became alarmed at the growing power of the Abwehr and in early 1944 he disbanded it, claiming it was "inefficient."

The Allied invasion of France in June 1944 weakened Hitler's power. Leaders of the Black Orchestra decided the time had come to assassinate the führer. Canaris knew about the plot but was unimpressed with the planning. Major Fabian von Schlabrendorff and Colonel Caesar von Hofacker promoted the plan, and Count Claus Schenk von Stauffenberg volunteered to carry a bomb into a high-level meeting with Hitler. Before the bomb exploded, Hitler moved to another part of the conference room and survived the blast.

During the days that followed, Canaris was arrested along with dozens of other suspects. He never gave the Gestapo information on any other resistance members but, because he knew of the plot and failed to report it, he was incarcerated.

On the morning of April 9, 1945, SS guards dragged Canaris naked from his cell and hanged him before a cheering crowd of SS troops. His corpse was left to rot.

NOTES

Admiral Canaris served his country as a loyal German. He tried to rid his country of Hitler without destroying it, but the assissination plot failed.

CARRÉ, MATHILDE (1908–1971)

Sultry Mathilde Carré worked with the French underground in German-occupied Paris during World War II and became a lethal menace to those who trusted her most.

The daughter of a decorated French Army officer who wore the Legion of Honor, Mathilde-Lucie Belard moved from central France to Paris with her parents as a teenager. During the 1930s she attended the Sorbonne and later became a teacher. She married Maurice Carré, an army officer, and moved to Algeria in North Africa, where Maurice taught in a French-run military school. Her husband was killed at the beginning of World War II and Mathilde decided to return to Paris to train as a nurse.

The French Underground

During the autumn of 1940, after the Germans occupied France, Captain Roman Czerniawski (code-named Armand) recruited Carré into an important and most-secret Paris underground operation called Interallié. British Special Operations (SOE) had wanted an espionage network established in Paris and funded Czerniawski to organize and operate it. Carré became immediately attracted to Czerniawski, who had been a Polish air

```
----DOSSIER--------
Name: Mathilde Carré
Code Names: Lily, the Cat
Birth/Death: 1908-1971
Nationality: French
Occupation: Teacher, Nurse
Involvement: Spied for
France, Germany, and
England
Outcome: Died of Natural
Causes
```

force fighter pilot and a member of the Polish resistance. He gave her the code name "Lily," but she preferred being called "the Cat."

Carré soon became one of Czerniawski's hardest-working operatives. She learned codes, how to operate shortwave radio transmissions, and became an expert with invisible inks. She developed a keen eye for recognizing German army insignias, aircraft, types of tanks and artillery, and could evaluate troop movements. Most of the reports received by British intelligence came from the Cat.

Operating out of headquarters in the Rue de Baubourg St. Jacques, Interallié soon evolved into the largest and most effective underground espionage network in occupied France. Czerniawski posted spies everywhere, and many of them were attractive women plying intelligence from German soldiers. One spy, Christine Bouffet, made the mistake of soliciting Sergeant Hugo Bleicher. He knew she was a spy and had her arrested and interrogated.

Bouffet's confession led to the arrest of

Below: January 5, 1949, French double agent Mathilde Carré stands trial in Paris after allegedly betraying several resistance fighters to the Germans and destroying Franco-Polish resistance group Interallie.

MOST SECRET

SUMMARY OF TRAFFIC OF SERVICE INTEREST FROM 28.2.42 -
31.3.42.

5.3.42	London asked for information about the bombing of the Renault factory.
5.3.42	Agent reported that in the raid on 3/4.3.42 the Renault works were destroyed and that there had been a large number of civilian dead.
10.3.42	Agent reported that the Renault works had been almost completely destroyed, that 20,000 people had been thrown out of work and that it would be several months before the factory was rebuilt. Many hits had been scored on the Salmson works and as a result of great destruction at the Farman works, 20,000 had been thrown out of work. A petrol tanker on the Seine had also been bombed and sunk. As a result of the foregoing public opinion was beginning to turn against England while de Brinon had made an anti-British speech during which he had said that not only had England deserted France in her fall but that she was now bombing the civilian population. The casualties amounted to 700 killed and 2,000 wounded.
12.3.42	London asked for details of the bombing of the Matford works at Poissy and of the bombing of Bethune and district.
17.3.42	Agent reported that it had been learnt by a fisherman at Dinan that a mine-layer had laid a mine barrage between 2 and 4 degrees along the coast from North East to South West at a distance of about 15 sea miles from the islands. The fisherman had learned this in a tavern at Dinan from German sailors who had come from St. Malo and who had laid the barrage.
21.3.42	Agent reported that the Ford workshops at Poissy had been hit by ten bombs and considerably damaged with the result that 500 men were out of work. There were no casualties.
24.3.42	Agent reported that he had observed a few days before that the Germans had installed anti-aircraft guns round the Matford works.

.3.42 London asked for reports about the damage caused by the English action at St. Nazaire, an estimate of the length of time required for repairs and whether the Germans had reinforced their coastal and anti-aircraft defences and what was the number of occupying troops. London also asked for the following particulars:-

1. Exact positions of stores of munitions, fuels and lubricants, food and equipment; the like with regard to the new works, fortifications and busy junctions.

2. the Number of German troops and identification marks in order to bring the order of battle up to date.

Opposite and Left: A sample report from agents showing the surveillance being carried out in France, reports on bombing missions and damage that had been executed by the British on these raids. This report reveals the propaganda being spread by Fernand de Brinon, the third-ranking member of the Vichy regime, stating that not only had England deserted France but that they were now picking civilian targets. These reports were essential in providing up-to-date information as to the activities of the German forces, indicating where they were amassing artillery, mines, fuel, food, and munitions, and allowing Britain to decide on bombing targets or enabling them to bring their order of battle up to date.

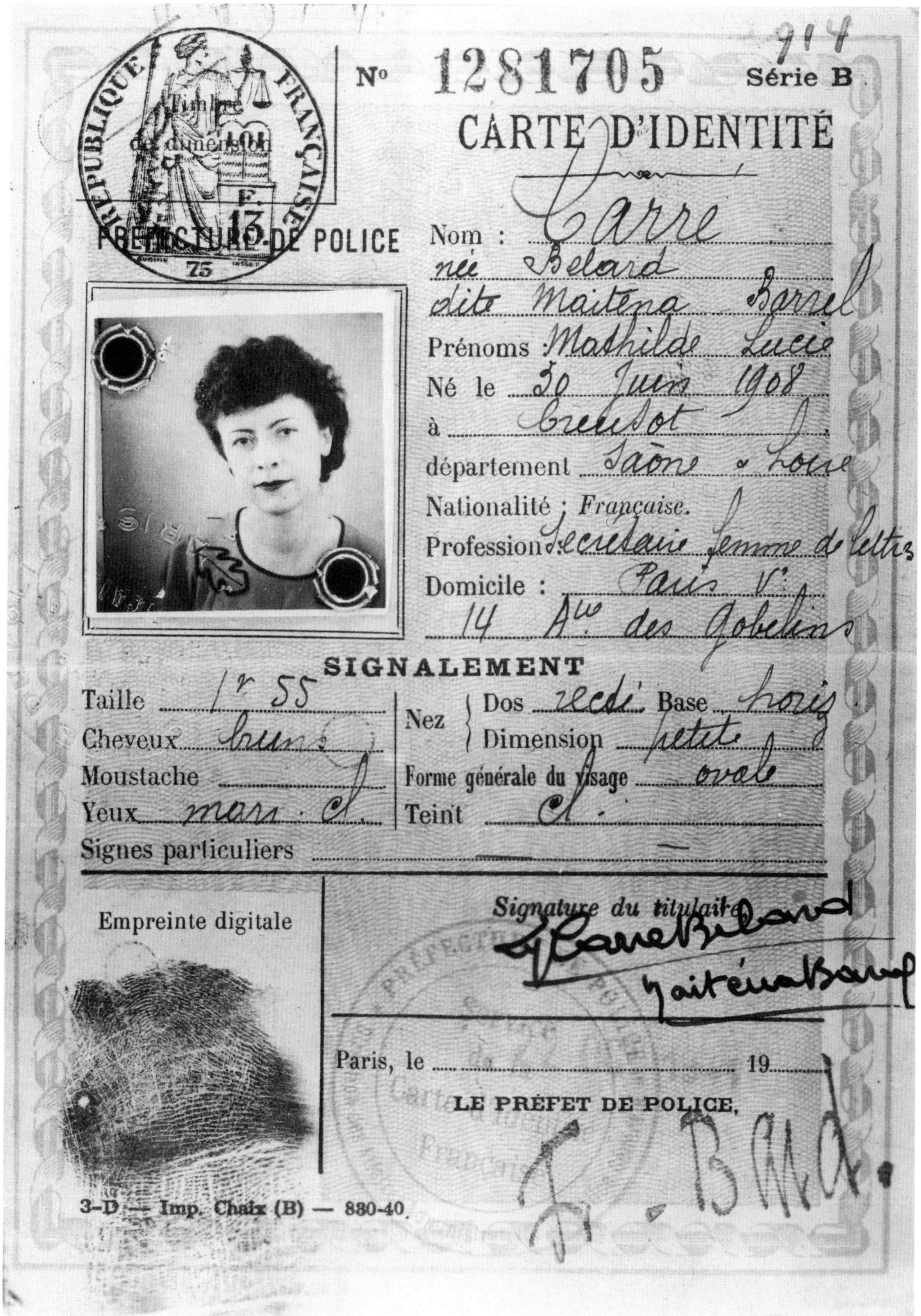

914

RÉPUBLIQUE FRANÇAISE
Timbre de dimension
F. 13
75

PRÉFECTURE DE POLICE

Nº 1281705 Série B

CARTE D'IDENTITÉ

Nom : Carré
née Belard
dite Maitena Barrel
Prénoms Mathilde Lucie
Né le 30 Juin 1908
à Creusot
département Saône et Loire
Nationalité : Française.
Profession Secrétaire femme de lettres
Domicile : Paris Vᵉ
14 Av. des Gobelins

SIGNALEMENT

Taille	1ᵐ 55	Nez — Dos	recti — Base horiz
Cheveux	bruns	Nez — Dimension	petit
Moustache		Forme générale du visage	ovale
Yeux	marr. cl.	Teint	cl.

Signes particuliers —

Empreinte digitale

Signature du titulaire
Carré Belard
Maitena Barrel

Paris, le 22 ... 19

LE PRÉFET DE POLICE,

3-D — Imp. Chaix (B) — 880-40.

her handler, which in November 1941 led to a raid on Interallié headquarters. Bleicher rounded up Czerniawski, his mistress, and the Cat. Though beaten and tortured, the Pole refused to talk. Bleicher found Carré more pliable. "You have two choices," he said. "You can either be shot or work for us as a double agent. If you cooperate, I will do what I can to save your friends. Which is it to be?" The Cat craved life and luxuries. When Bleicher offered her 60,000 francs a month, a deluxe suite at Hotel Edward VII (Abwehr headquarters), and a lavish expense account, Carré accepted the bargain and became a double agent for Germany. Within days, the Gestapo arrested all of Czerniawski's agents and destroyed the Interallié network. More than 100 French agents were cast into concentration camps, tortured for information, and executed.

The Cat Becomes a Double Agent

During the raid on Interallié headquarters, Bleicher captured four radio sets. He proposed that all the arrests remain secret and that the sets be used to send useless information to London in exchange for collecting valuable intelligence from the British. The Cat knew all the codes, transmission schedules, and security checks and became the centerpiece of the operation. The ruse worked so well that the SOE sent a message to say that a special agent was on the way to Paris to confer with Interallié, which of course no longer existed.

Bleicher never completely trusted Carré and controlled everything she did. She had become his mistress and moved with him into a spacious villa when Pierre de Vomecourt, a veteran SOE agent, arrived from London. The Cat transmitted his messages as if nothing had changed. When Vomecourt prepared to return to London, Bleicher decided to let him go so he could inform SOE that Interallié was smoothly functioning. The German received a shock, however, when Vomecourt insisted that Carré accompany him back to London so she could brief SOE on Interallié's operations.

Bleicher decided that Carré could be of immense help to Abwehr by collecting information on how the SOE operated and approved the venture. He even aided their escape, helping them to meet a British torpedo boat after their plane failed to arrive at a secret airfield. Vomecourt was no fool, having canceled the plane himself. During his time in Paris he had grown suspicious of Carré's relationship with Bleicher. While speeding across the channel, he accused her of being a double agent. The Cat broke into tears and confessed her relationship with Bleicher. When the tears stopped flowing, she offered to serve SOE as a triple agent and reveal everything she knew about Abwehr operations.

In London, Vomecourt turned Carré over to Colonel Maurice Buckmaster, a tough, experienced, and unseductable SOE interrogator. After the Cat exposed everything that she knew about Bleicher's operation, Buckmaster decided to keep her in London. He fed her completely useless information about the SOE, which she forwarded to Bleicher. The arrangement worked until Vomecourt, during another mission to France, was captured, thrown in prison, and tortured.

Opposite: Carré's identity card, released by MI5 in November 2002 to the National Archives. The release included documents detailing the MI5 case against Carré, including interrogation papers, original letters, manuscript notes about the arrest of agents in the Walenty organization, and payments made to Carré.

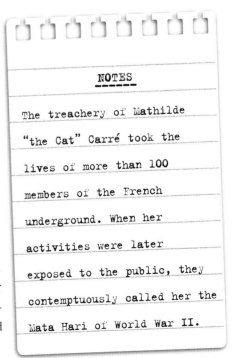

NOTES

The treachery of Mathilde "the Cat" Carré took the lives of more than 100 members of the French underground. When her activities were later exposed to the public, they contemptuously called her the Mata Hari of World War II.

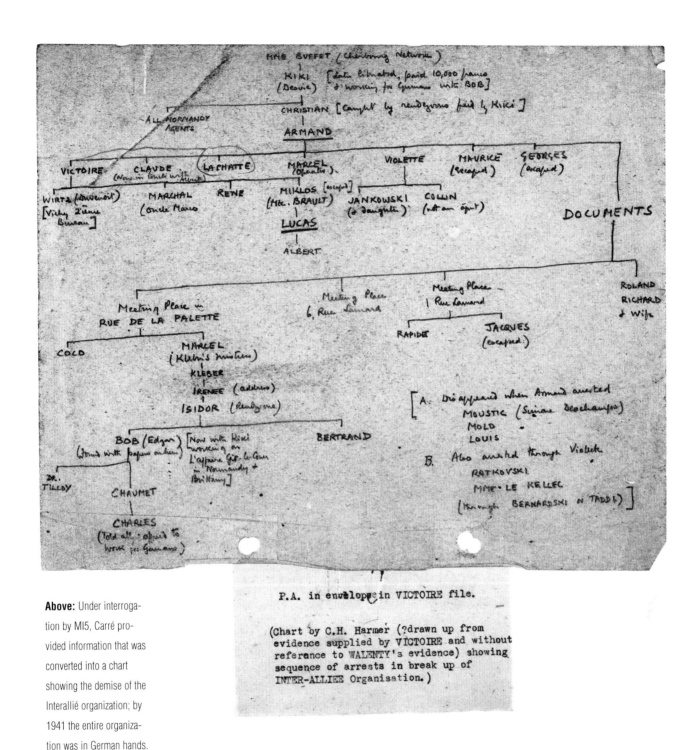

P.A. in envelope in VICTOIRE file.

(Chart by C.H. Harmer (?drawn up from evidence supplied by VICTOIRE and without reference to WALENTY's evidence) showing sequence of arrests in break up of INTER-ALLIEE Organisation.)

Above: Under interrogation by MI5, Carré provided information that was converted into a chart showing the demise of the Interallié organization; by 1941 the entire organization was in German hands.

Opposite: A copy of a report by Carré reviewing troop and tank movements and the production of tank tracks and gas masks at local factories.

Buckmaster feared that Carré had been compromised and tucked her away in a woman's prison until the war ended. In 1945 he sent her back to Paris, where authorities charged her with spying for the Germans and threw her in jail. Brought to trial in 1949, the court found the Cat guilty and sentenced her to death by guillotine. The government later commuted her sentence to life imprisonment, but in 1954 released her. She changed her name, sought sanctuary in the country, and wrote her memoirs, *I Was the Cat*. Carré had sought the high life but her instinct for self-preservation meant she died on November 28, 1971, as an obscure person hated by those who did remember her and could neither forget

5/

DEPOT D'HUILES à LONGUEAU-26-I-42-YVES"
Vaste dépots d'huiles situés entre le Dépot de la S N C F et la
véranda de la gare de LONGUEAU.

X
X X
X

PARIS-27-I-42-"CLAUDE"(xxxxxxxxxxxxxxxxxxxxxxxxxxxxxxxxxxxxxxxxxxxxxx
Voitures rencontrées pendant ces 2 derniers jours: (armée de terre)

nombreuses hippo

REMARQUES:
1° le trafic des voitures est énormément réduit.
2° les xxxxxxx éléments de la Division de PARIS
sont partis et ont été remplacés par
des éléments de la Division de
BEAUNE.

VINCENNES-24-I-42-"CLAUDE"
Plus de P.C. de Rgt.
Voitures:

PONTOISE-23-I-42-"CLAUDE"
A la caserne des Dragons arrivées de nouvelles recrues et dans la cour
de la caserne une soixantaine de chars légers,allemands.
Nouveau panneau:

MAISON LAFFITTE-25-I-42-"CLAUDE"
Sous le marché couvert 7 chars SOMUA
I2 " RENAULT
Il n'ya plus dans cette localité que I20 tous jeunes soldats des troupes
blindées.
Voitures:

X
X X
X

VI-INDUSTRIE
ROUEN-26-I-42-"EMILE"
La Société Electro Cables fabrique des masques à gaz en grosse
quantité.
PARIS-26-I-42-"CLAUDE"
A l'Usine TALBOT la production quotidienne des chaines pour tanks
est passée de I à 7.

VICTOIRE/

CHAMBERS, WHITTAKER (1901–1961)

Whittaker Chambers, an American journalist and senior editor of *Time* magazine, lived a complicated life, balancing his undercover life between spying for the Soviet Union and informing the FBI of KGB spies operating in the United States.

Born in Philadelphia, the son of a journalist, Whittaker Chambers grew up in Lynbrook, on Long Island. His father deserted the family in 1908 and disappeared for three years, leaving his mother virtually penniless. Young Whittaker worked hard during those years to help the family survive.

In 1919, Chambers managed to graduate from high school and in 1920 entered Columbia University. Two years later, Columbia expelled him for writing a blasphemous play. For three years he aimlessly kicked about, living in a vacuum of discontent. Opportunity knocked in 1925.

Chambers joined New York's Communist Party and earned a living as editor of the *Daily Worker*. His life changed in 1931 when he married Esther Shemitz, a steadfast Communist, who introduced him to an underground Soviet cell involved in espionage. In 1934, under orders from his handlers, Chambers moved to Baltimore to act as a courier named Karl. He transported photographs and classified documents from Communist spies in the government to a Soviet handler in New York. Chambers's handler introduced him to Harold Ware, head of a Communist underground cell that included Alger Hiss.

----DOSSIER--------

Name: Whittaker Chambers

Code Names: George Crosley, Karl

Birth/Death: 1901–1961

Nationality: American

Occupation: Journalist

Involvement: Double Agent for U.S. and the Soviet Union

Outcome: Died of Natural Causes

The Disillusioned Spy

By the mid-1930s, Chambers developed a dislike for Joseph Stalin's brutal tactics in Russia. He broke from the Communist Party and in 1937 went to work for *Time* magazine as a journalist. In 1939, when the Soviet Union signed a nonaggression pact with Nazi Germany, Chambers decided to tell the federal government everything he knew about communist operations in America. He went to

Right: Whittaker Chambers (left), pictured looking over a news account with Richard Nixon (center) and Robert Stripling (right), the chief investigator for the House Committee on Un-American Activities. It was Stripling who ordered a subpoena for Chambers to submit to HUAC any evidence he had regarding Alger Hiss. Chambers gave committee investigators the film of government documents that would come to be known as the "Pumpkin Papers."

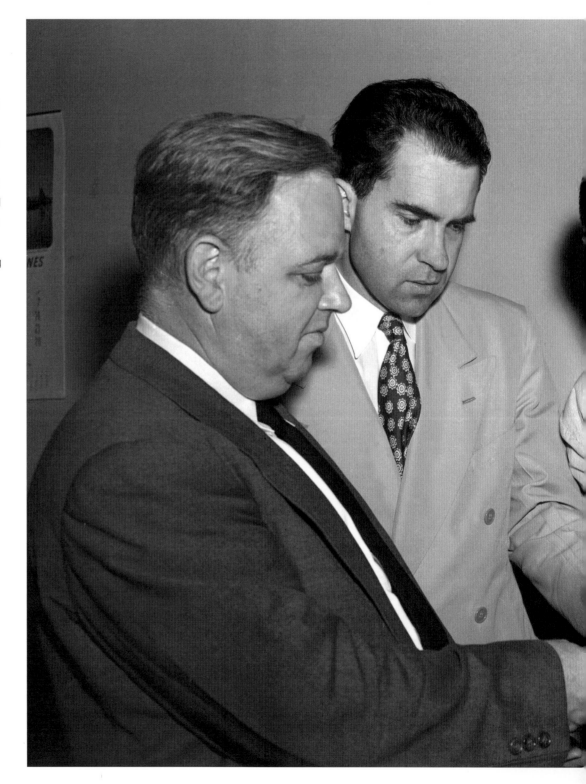

Assistant Secretary of State Adolf Berle and informed him that Alger Hiss, Berle's own indispensable aide, had been a communist spy since 1935. Berle ridiculed the charge. Chambers returned to New York, but he kept an eye on Hiss's activities, which

were considerable. A brilliant lawyer, Hiss continued his career inside the government, becoming a member of the delegation that accompanied President Roosevelt to the Yalta Conference. He later served a term as the first Secretary General of the United Nations.

Targeting Alger Hiss

Few people in the United States watched Alger Hiss more intently than Chambers. In 1948 Chambers shocked the nation when he voluntarily appeared before the House Committee on Un-American Activities and disclosed what he knew about Hiss. He described how, in the 1930s, Hiss brought confidential documents home from the State Department for his wife, Priscilla, to retype and deliver to a man known as "Karl." Chambers admitted to being Karl, Hiss's courier. Chambers backed up his testimony by entering into evidence films of documents, four notes in Hiss's handwriting, and 65 documents copied on Priscilla's typewriter.

On August 5, 1948, Hiss appeared before the committee, denied the accusations, and demanded that Chambers confront him. Before staging a session that could turn into a circus, a committee met with Chambers in New York to verify his statements. He astonished them with intricate details from memory, such as the pet names Hiss used when addressing Priscilla, the old Ford that Hiss had donated to the Communist Party, the family's cocker spaniel, and how Hiss had sent his stepson Timmy Hobson to a cheaper school so he could donate more money to the American Communist Party. Investigators located the old typewriter, which Hiss's wife had years ago given to their handyman Ira Lockey, and con-

Right: Whittaker Chambers in the subway station entrance to federal court for his testimony in the trial of Alger Hiss. Chambers emphatically identified Hiss in court as the man he first met in the late spring or early summer of 1934. He took the stand as the star government witness in the perjury trial of Hiss.

Opposite: Communist subversive papers of Harry Dexter White, found among Whittaker Chambers's Pumpkin Papers. Elizabeth Bentley had implicated White in the House Committee on Un-American Activities hearing. While White denied being a Soviet agent, Chambers testified that he was the least productive of his contacts.

firmed that the keystrokes matched the typing on the documents. Confronted by the committee, Hiss admitted that he may have met a man in the 1930s by the name of George Crosley (Chambers's code name). By then the committee had substantiated most of Chambers's accusations and further found that Hiss had with-

drawn $400 from his account on the day that Chambers claimed to have borrowed that amount.

The investigation moved too slowly for Chambers, so he repeated his accusations against Hiss on the radio program *Meet the Press*. Hiss sued his accuser for slander, but Chambers went to court well

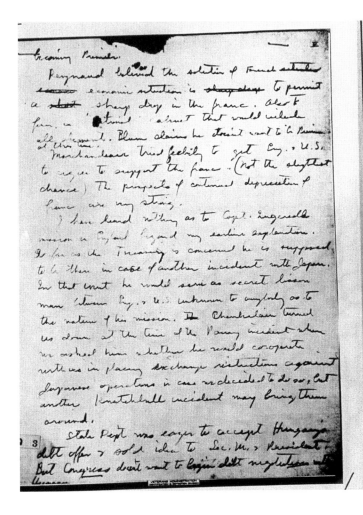

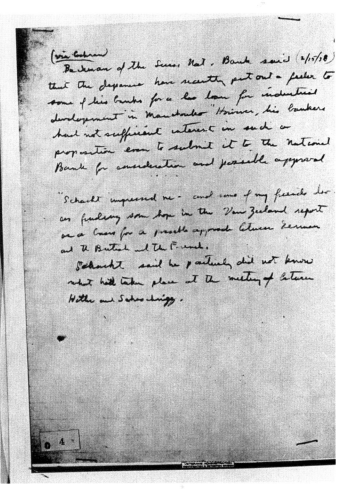

prepared. During the trial, which began on December 15, 1948, Chambers produced rolls of microfilm he had hidden in a hollowed-out pumpkin on his northern Maryland farm, which went into evidence as the "Pumpkin Papers." The grand jury indicted Hiss for perjury, not because he spied for the Soviets, but because he lied about knowing Chambers. Hiss's court trial ended in a hung jury—eight to four for conviction. A second trial followed on January 20, 1950, and this time Hiss went to jail for five years.

Never Any Winners

The Chambers-Hiss affair did neither man any good. Chambers succeeded in incriminating Hiss as a former Soviet spy, but he also incriminated himself. Hiss went to jail for perjury and in 1980 wrote a 250-page brief in an effort to overturn his conviction. The Federal District Court turned down the appeal.

Chambers suffered from depression for much of the remainder of his life. Several times he contemplated suicide. He bolstered his life by turning to religion, which gave him the stamina and purpose to write his memoirs. On July 9, 1961, Whittaker Chambers died of natural causes. Twenty-three years later, President Ronald Reagan posthumously awarded Chambers America's highest civilian honor, the Medal of Freedom.

NOTES

Whittaker Chambers spent much of his adult life trying to expose Alger Hiss for Communist connections, but also succeeded in destroying his own life in the process.

CHAPMAN, EDDIE (1908–1997)

Eddie Chapman may have been among the greatest con men who ever lived, and as a British double agent he consistently hoodwinked the German Abwehr.

Eddie Chapman grew up in Sunderland without many opportunities in life. During his childhood he picked pockets and became a petty thief. As an adult he became a professional safecracker, and one of England's best. By the age of 30, he had learned how to break into safes thought to be impenetrable and carried off sacks filled with cash and jewels. Now on the run from Scotland Yard, Chapman pocketed his stash and went into hiding on the Channel island of Jersey. In 1939 detectives tracked him down and threw him in jail. When the Germans occupied Jersey in 1940, they found Chapman locked in a cell.

```
----DOSSIER--------
Name: Eddie Chapman
Code Names: Fritz, Zigzag
Birth/Death: 1908-1997
Nationality: British
Occupation: Petty Thief and
Safecracker
Involvement: British Double
Agent in England
Outcome: Disappeared
briefly, died of old age.
```

Conning the Abwehr

Interviewed by the Abwehr, Chapman grasped the opportunity to line his pockets with German marks and spun a yarn about the miserable childhood that compelled him to become a thief. He wanted vengeance against his native country for spoiling his life and offered to spy for the Abwehr, providing it paid well. Agents checked Chapman's background and decided he was telling the truth. They had to look no further than Chapman's own press clippings, which included news stories about his escapades as a burglar and safecracker. That Chapman understood explosives and knew how to blow open safes appealed to the Abwehr, which at the time was running a campaign to recruit saboteurs. So the Abwehr hauled Chapman off to Paris, put him in spy school, and trained him in sabotage.

"I'll Gut the Damned Place"

Captain Stephen Grunen, Chapman's supervisor, thought he observed enormous potential in the safecracker and gave him an impossible task: to blow up England's de Haviland Aircraft Works in Hatfield, north of London. When the Abwehr questioned the wisdom of authorizing the high-risk and virtually impossible assignment, Chapman merely said, "I'll gut the damned place." The Abwehr feared they had trained a lunatic, but Grunen insisted that Chapman had

Below: During the 1920s and 1930s, Chapman formed the "Gelignite Gang," a team of safecrackers who were the first to make use of this newly discovered explosive.

Right and Opposite:

Operation Damp Squib was a complex scheme devised by MI5 to reinforce Chapman's credentials with his German handlers. The plan involved a fake bomb explosion on the *City of Lancaster* (the ship that took Chapman to Lisbon) and circulating rumors that Chapman had been responsible for the explosion.

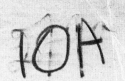

PLAN DAMP SQUIB 1.

1.   It is hoped that ZIGZAG's bomb will arrive in the U.K. before the CITY OF LANCASTER so that its form and functions can be confirmed.

2.   Commander Montagu, N.I.D., should be requested by Colonel Robertson to try and arrange that the CITY OF LANCASTER should be diverted from Liverpool or any other port to which she may be proceeding, to Manchester.

3.   When the ship arrives, she will first be boarded by the Customs, who will have been informed about the plan. Mr Reed will board the ship with the Customs officials, either disguised as a Customs official or in some other way if this is not convenient.

4.   He will contact the master and will obtain his approval for another of the Customs officials to plant a bomb (which will be provided by B.1.C) in one of the ship's bunkers, not the one from which coal would normally be taken at that time. The rest of the plan is based on the assumption that the master agrees.

5.   The bomb will be brought on board in an attache case by Mr Reed, and having obtained the master's approval he will pass the attache case to Customs official X.

6.   Customs official X, who will previously have been to M.I.5 head office for tuition in working the bomb, will proceed to "examine" the above-mentioned bunker for contraband. In the event of his meeting any of the crew in the bunker, he will ask them to leave while he is conducting his examination. He will then place the bomb in the bunker, start the fuse and retire, making certain that no one enters the bunker room until after the explosion. The delay will be approximately three minutes between starting the fuse and the explosion. The explosion will do no damage and will not set light to any coal that may be in the bunker, though it would be dangerous for anyone to be within 20 feet of it.

7.   Customs official X. on hearing the explosion will fall down and pretend he has hurt his arm, which will be bandaged up by the master.+

8.   The master will request assistance from the shore, and Major Macphail staff will immediately proceed to the ship and conduct a preliminary enquiry.

9.   The preliminary enquiry will cause Major Macphail to ring up head office and request a specialist investigator to be sent up.

10.   Two officers will be sent up to carry out the investigation. They will as a matter of fact be in the vicinity already, but will meet Major Macphail at the appropriate time, after the arrival of the train on which they should have arrived, at the Midland Hotel.

PTO

+The Customs official will say that he was poking the coal in the bunker when there was a hissing noise, followed by an explosion which blew him over and hurt his arm.

11.   These two officers from M.I.5. head office, together with Major Macphail's staff, will proceed on board the CITY OF LANCASTER and will carry out the most searching investigation, all members of the crew being closely interrogated both from the point of view of any of them being responsible and the possibility of a bomb having been put on board at the last port of call, or the port of call before that.

12.   All members of the crew will be sworn to secrecy.

13.   Major Macphail will arrange for the circulation of rumours locally through his underground post.

8.4.43.

Comments of R.G. 14.4.43.

(1). The Customs officer should be emerging from the bunker at the time of the explosion; this would be more readily consistent with little or no injury and a supposedly sizeable explosion in the body of the coal.

(2). Binding up a notional injury is gratuitously introducing unnecessary "fineness" of a dangerous kind.

(3). Why bind the crew to secrecy? If it had really been as is to be simulated there would be no special emphasis on secrecy. Is the Captain's permission to go through the back interrogation of the crew not just as necessary as his permission to the placing of the bomb? Presumably secrecy is just a spur to rumour spreading.

(4) Will B.1.A. report the incident?

Below: Photograph of the "coal bomb" used on the *City of Lancaster* during Operation Damp Squib. Chapman was so successful in his deception of the Germans that they awarded him the Iron Cross.

NO 55692

TRAVEL PERMIT

Valid for Travel Between Ireland and the

United Kingdom only

Subject to compliance with any re:

eire

NAME OF HOLDER *Morgan*

MAIDEN NAME

PLACE OF RESIDENCE *Irela*

ISSUED AT *Dublin*

ON *5th Decemb*

VALID FOR 12 MONTHS AFTER

THE BEARER OF THIS I

Citizen of I

Page 2

Occupation *electrical engineer*

Place of Birth *Newbridge, Co. Kildare*

Date of Birth *16th Nov. 1914*

Home Address *30 Upper Rathmines Road*

Dublin

Signature of bearer *Morgan O Bryan*

CHILDREN

Name	Age	Sex	Name	Age	Sex

Right: Fake papers issued to Chapman by the British Double Cross network. The Double Cross Committee was known as the Twenty Committee because the Roman numeral XX formed a double cross.

140

Everything Eddie Chapman did for the Abwehr was a sham, a setup, and a fake, and only a daring man with nerves of steel could have made it work.

the intellectual ability to perform the task. Grunen gave Chapman the code name "Fritz," and on the foggy night of December 20, 1942, sent him across the English Channel in a German cargo plane. Chapman dropped into a field near Welbech, buried his parachute, walked to Littleport, and took a train to London. At least part of the story was true. Chapman actually went into Welbech and called the police in Littleport to pick him up and take him to British counterintelligence, MI5.

A Stunning Report from Fritz

Chapman shared his fantastic story with a roomful of doubters at MI5. He then offered to become a double agent if England dropped all criminal charges against him. MI5 agreed to the conditions and gave Chapman a new code name, "Zigzag." The agency also agreed to make it appear that he had actually blown up the aircraft plant. To delude the Abwehr, MI5 arranged for Chapman to visit the plant so he could see the layout and learn which buildings were important and which were unimportant should the Abwehr later ask questions.

On December 23, Chapman, alias Fritz, sent his first encrypted radio message to Captain Grunen, reporting that he was "casing" the main power plant. A few days later he reported purchasing explosives and hiding them in a nearby quarry. Members of the Abwehr had long ago given up hope of the bizarre mission

succeeding and had merely written Chapman off as expendable.

Grunen still had faith in the safecracker. When he received a message from Chapman on January 27, 1943, that read: "Will attempt sabotage this even. at six o'clock," he circulated it among those who had probably wagered against the project ever succeeding. Grunen waited as the hours passed, and later that night a second message arrived: "Mission successfully accomplished."

Chapman explained how he had built two time bombs, attached them to a simple wristwatch trigger device, and set them to explode within the power plant. Grunen jumped to his feet and waved the message in the faces of his colleagues. Nobody actually believed Grunen. The following day the Luftwaffe dispatched two reconnaissance planes to overfly the aircraft works and verify the report. The planes returned with film showing two enormous holes in the roof of the power plant and photographs of debris and pieces of generators and heavy equipment scattered all over the area. MI5 carried out such a great job of preparing the area for aerial photography that it looked like a bomb had hit the plant, and the Abwehr swallowed the hoax.

The Life of a Double Agent

Chapman clearly understood that German agents in England might someday discover the de Haviland scam. He had to get to Paris to collect the £100,000

Below: Another of the many sets of false papers used by Chapman. In an assessment, an MI5 officer wrote: "The Germans came to love Chapman . . . But although he went cynically through all the forms he did not reciprocate. Chapman loved himself, loved adventure, and loved his country, probably in that order."

the Abwehr had promised to pay him for blowing up the plant, which was still operating unimpeded and at full capacity. While waiting for the Abwehr to arrange transportation out of England, he continued to feed Grunen bogus secrets provided by MI5. British intelligence had broken the Abwehr's enigma codes and were aware of what the Germans knew and did not know, so MI5 told Chapman what information to send to Grunen. In mid-February Chapman radioed Grunen that it was too dangerous to remain in

England and that he would be returning to Paris through Lisbon. When he reached Paris, the Abwehr greeted Chapman with open arms and swallowed more stories about how he hated his native country.

On June 1, 1944, Chapman slipped back into England and, with MI5 authorization, radioed the Abwehr that Allied forces were about to invade France at Normandy. MI5 knew that Hitler had already dismissed a beach assault at Normandy, and that the Abwehr would

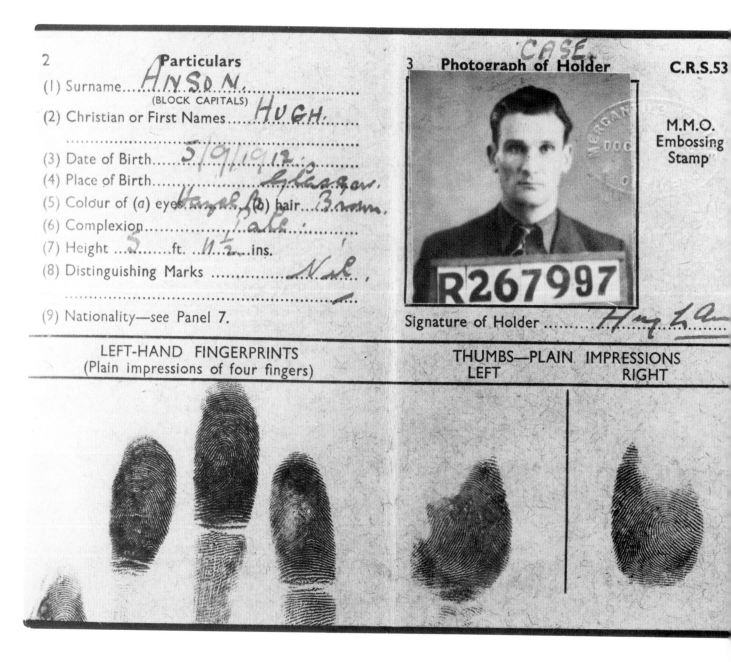

> One account suggested that MI5 expunged Chapman's criminal record and offered him a medal for his espionage work, to which he replied, "Medal be damned. You birds owe me twenty-five thousand pounds." The words sounded like something Eddie Chapman would say.

reject Chapman's intelligence for the same reason. The ruse worked. Chapman retained his veracity with the Abwehr when, on June 6, 1944, Allied forces waded ashore on Normandy.

During the summer of 1944, after an abortive attempt on Hitler's life, Heinrich Himmler's dreaded SS took over what remained of the Abwehr. In November 1944 Chapman mysteriously disappeared. For many years afterward, the Abwehr fondly remembered Chapman as one of their most outstanding agents. In the same month, the man known as Zigzag also went off the roster of MI5. Chapman had admitted to his MI5 handler that he had told his Norwegian girlfriend about his undercover work and he was therefore deemed too much of a risk to retain.

After the war, Chapman wrote an account of his adventures in espionage that was serialized in a newspaper. Once again he found himself in court, this time on a charge of breaching the Official Secrets Act. Upon hearing the evidence presented by Chapman's MI5 case officer, the judge declared that while he had no option but to find Chapman guilty as charged, he regarded him as the bravest man that he was ever likely to meet, and therefore fined him a nominal sum.

In 1966 a film was made about Chapman's life of spying, called *Triple Cross*, starring Christopher Plummer and Yul Brynner.

Particulars—continued
- Dis. A. No. .....R. 267997.....
  (To be entered in *all* cases.)
- Certificates held—
- Grade.....None..... No. .....
  (including E.D.H., Ship's Cook, Lifeboat, etc.)
- Rank or Rating if not a certificated Officer
  (if A.B. Supt. to verify and initial).
  .....Greaser.....
- National Service Registration No.
  .....MMG/12/64729.....
- Is holder an Armed Forces Reservist? .....
  (Reservists include R.N.S.R. and H.M.S. "Gordon.")

RIGHT-HAND FINGERPRINTS
(Plain impressions of four fingers)

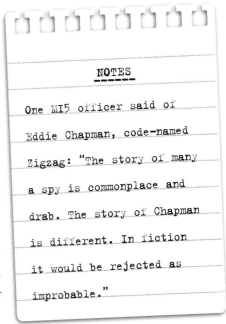

NOTES

One MI5 officer said of Eddie Chapman, code-named Zigzag: "The story of many a spy is commonplace and drab. The story of Chapman is different. In fiction it would be rejected as improbable."

COPLON, JUDITH (1922–)

Judith Coplon believed in the Soviet system without ever understanding how it worked and spent the first years of her career spying for the KGB in exchange for love and excitement.

Born in Brooklyn, New York, Judith Coplon grew up in a middle-class Jewish family. Her father's toy manufacturing business provided the family with a comfortable income and Judith with a good education. In 1938 Coplon graduated from high school and enrolled at Barnard College, a prestigious school for girls, where she studied Russia and Russian literature. Everything she read about the Soviet system impressed her and in 1943, after she graduated cum laude, all the socialist views she expressed as managing editor of the college's newspaper dropped out of sight.

The Daring Spy

Coplon did not plan on becoming a spy when she obtained her first job with the Department of Justice in New York in 1943. The FBI conducted a cursory search of Coplon's past activities and found nothing suspicious. So in 1945, when she received promotion to the department's Washington headquarters, the FBI passed her through. Coplon

```
----DOSSIER--------
Name: Judith Coplon
Code Name: None
Birth/Death: 1922-
Nationality: American
Occupation: Justice
Department Employee
Involvement: Spied for
the KGB
Outcome: Set Free on Appeal
```

worked in the foreign agents registration section, whose lists the FBI used to identify potential foreign spies. She had full access to files on foreign diplomats and agents, and among the shelves she found FBI reports on Russians.

The KGB had never been able to acquire this information until Coplon, whom they recognized as a Soviet sympathizer, arrived in Washington. After making the initial contact and obtaining her support, the KGB sent spymaster Valentin Gubitchev to New York as her special handler. He may have exceeded the KGB's expectations by also becoming her lover. Coplon made many trips to New York with secret files, ostensibly to visit her parents, but she never got farther than Gubitchev, who worked as an employee of the Soviet delegation to the United States.

To Catch a Spy

By 1948 the FBI had Coplon in their sights as a suspected courier for a Soviet spy ring. Confidential documents from her department had been spotted in the Russian embassy and reported in Moscow. J. Edgar Hoover, director of the FBI, said she should be fired immediately but counterintelligence officials wanted her watched so they could gain information about her contacts. Her boss, William E. Foley, bought the plan and Hoover reluctantly agreed to provide a surveillance team. Agents tapped her phone, bugged her apartment, and put her under 24-hour watch.

Early in 1949 the FBI prepared a bogus document signed by Hoover, and Foley made sure that Coplon noticed it. On February 18, she once again took a long weekend, traveling by train to New York. Surveillance agents followed. They tailed her up Broadway until she stopped at an intersecting street and slipped inside a doorway. Moments later, Gubitchev dashed out the door, ran down the street, and disappeared in the crowd.

In March, Foley created a second set of fictitious documents relating to the same subject. He laid them before Coplon, told her to file them, and left the room. One hour later, Coplon took a train to New York, again followed by FBI agents. This time, when she rendezvoused with

Below: Judith Coplon arrives at court to stand trial on charges of espionage.

Gubitchev, the agents closed rapidly, and after a brief chase along 16th Street and Third Avenue, apprehended both suspects. An FBI matron searched Coplon and found in her purse a sealed advertisement for nylons with an unusual bulge. Inside the advertisement was the 34-page document planted by Foley.

The agents obtained arrest warrants for the 27-year-old Coplon and charged her with espionage and treason and charged the 32-year-old Gubitchev with espionage. Gubitchev claimed diplomatic immunity through the Soviet embassy, but UN officials ruled the Russian was an employee and not entitled to immunity.

The FBI lied under oath about bugging and failed to get a warrant to search her purse, leading to an overturned verdict.

In June 1949, during the trial in Washington, Coplon hired the bombastic Archie Palmer, a clever defense lawyer who could twist facts, misstate evidence, and completely confuse a jury with his antics. When Coplon took the stand in her own defense, she attempted to sell herself to the jury as a trusted and loyal government worker who would never deliver confidential documents to a Soviet spy. She implied that the FBI must have planted the documents to catch Gubitchev, with whom she had unsuspectingly fallen in love after meeting him at a Manhattan art museum. She also testified that Foley had given her the spurious correspondence to analyze over the weekend, and it was not unusual for her to take documents home. The only person in the courtroom who believed Coplon's testimony was her mother, who sat through the trial squeezing a wet handkerchief. Though two million words had been entered into testimony, the jury promptly returned a verdict of guilty. Judge Albert Reeves agreed and sentenced Coplon to 10 years in prison. Palmer consoled her, saying, "It's only a verdict, Judy."

The FBI Strikes Out

After one trial ended, another began. Palmer took Coplon to New York to stand trial with Gubitchev for conspiracy. The Manhattan jury listened to testimony from 77 FBI agents involved in the case. Two of the agents described their surveillance methods, which included phone records and wiretaps. One agent admitted seeing the records before the FBI destroyed them. Another agent admitted that he was unfamiliar with the 12-year-old Supreme Court decision prohibiting wiretapped evidence in federal trials. Despite the argument over wiretaps and destroyed evidence, the jury found Coplon guilty. She received a 15-year sentence for conspiracy, and Gubitchev went back to Moscow.

Coplon never spent a day in prison on either count. In 1952 Palmer convinced an appeals court that the evidence against Coplon had been illegally obtained by the FBI and involved illegal wiretaps, nor had the FBI obtained arrest warrants, without which they could not legally have searched Coplon's purse. Hoover damaged the government's case by refusing to turn evidence over to Palmer prior to the trial because it might expose the department's operations. The appeals court overturned the lower courts. The blundered case reflected directly on Hoover and discredited the FBI.

After the trial, Coplon married Albert Socolov, a 41-year-old attorney who had been working for the firm handling her defense case. She continues to live in the United States; she and her husband have four children.

Opposite: Judith Coplon, a former employee for the Justice Department accused of spying for the Soviets, stands with her attorney Archibald Palmer (right) as he speaks with reporters in federal court in Manhattan.

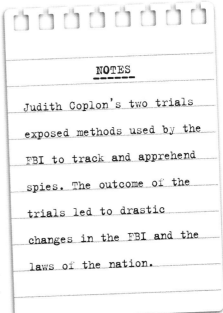

NOTES

Judith Coplon's two trials exposed methods used by the FBI to track and apprehend spies. The outcome of the trials led to drastic changes in the FBI and the laws of the nation.

CRABB, LIONEL PHILLIP KENNETH (1910–1956)

"Buster" Crabb sought adventure and danger on the seas and had to settle for becoming a frogman. Forty years after his mysterious disappearance in 1956, a retired Russian naval officer explained how Great Britain's foremost frogman died.

Born in London, Lionel Crabb came from a poor, working-class family. He received little education before going to work himself. Like many English youths, he wanted to be a navy man. Being too young to enlist, he fulfilled his ambition by joining the British merchant marine. His voyages took him into ports from the Atlantic to the Pacific. During the early 1930s, he spent time in Singapore and eventually went to China. During the Japanese invasion of Manchuria and Shanghai, Crabb became a spy for Morris "Two-Gun" Cohen, who ran Chiang Kai-shek's intelligence service during the Japanese intervention. Crabb enjoyed the adventure and danger in spying, but he still wanted to be a navy man.

```
----DOSSIER--------
Name: Lionel Phillip
Kenneth "Buster" Crabb
Code Name: None
Birth/Death: 1910-1956
Nationality: British
Occupation: Merchant
Sailor, Businessman,
Photographer
Involvement: British
Frogman and Spy
Outcome: Presumed Murdered
in Portsmouth Harbour
```

Finding a Niche in the Royal Navy

In 1939, when World War II erupted in Poland, Crabb rejoined the merchant marine as a gunner on freighters running the gauntlet of German U-boats in the Atlantic. Returning to England in 1940, he attempted once more to enlist in the Royal Navy, but was rejected because of

After retiring from the Royal Navy, Crabb acted as a consultant for the film *Cockleshell Heroes*, a job he disliked because it was about the marines and not the navy.

poor eyesight. A year later he tried again, this time volunteering as an underwater bomb disposal expert, a job so hazardous no one else wanted it.

Commissioned in 1941, Crabb served in a frogman unit in the Mediterranean. He worked in the harbor at Gibraltar, clearing delayed-action limpet mines from the hulls of British warships. He also battled beneath the waves with Italian frogmen who were attaching mines to British ships or serving as "human torpedoes." On occasion, he swam into Italy's ports and attached charges to Italian ships and naval installations. When the Allied offensive began, he blew up obstructions so supply ships could enter Italian ports. After Italy surrendered to the Allies in 1943, Italian frogmen, as a demonstration of respect, refused to surrender to anybody other than Lieutenant Commander Crabb of the Royal Navy.

Once a Frogman, Always a Frogman

In 1948, Crabb reluctantly accepted his discharge from the navy. He had never been a good swimmer or a particularly powerful frogman. For his heroic wartime service, the British government awarded him the George Medal and the Order of the Empire. Crabb was not ready to retire. The government eventually granted his wish and put him back in the Royal Navy, where British intelligence (MI6) used him for covert undersea missions.

When the new Soviet cruiser *Sverdlov* arrived in Portsmouth Harbour in honor of Queen Elizabeth's coronation, MI6 wanted to know how the ship could maneuver so well with two screws. Crabb took the assignment, ran the ship's hull from bow to stern, made observations on the cruiser's underwater sonar equipment, and found it surprisingly similar to the British design. The discovery should not have come as a great surprise to MI6 because Soviet spy Gordon Lonsdale had been sending British underwater detection secrets to Moscow since 1954.

The Final Call to Duty

In 1955, at the age of 45, Crabb left the navy for good. He found a few underwater jobs as a civilian, but over the course of a single year fell out of shape. In 1956 he received a call. MI6 hired Crabb for a secret project that coincided with the state visit of Soviet premier Nicolai Bulganin and party chairman Nikita Khrushchev, who were on the way to meet with prime minister Anthony Eden. The Soviet leaders were expected to arrive at Portsmouth Harbour on the *Ordzhonikidze*, a Soviet cruiser of modern design, great speed, easy maneuverability, and accompanied by the destroyers *Sovershenny* and *Smotryashchy*. The *Ordzhonikidze* tied up at a jetty in Portsmouth Harbour and waited while the two Soviet leaders departed for London.

MI6 engaged MI5 and the British Admiralty in Crabb's undercover, under-

Above: Crabb (right), being readied to investigate an object in the sea in 1953. The Admiralty disclosed that Crabb was "missing, presumed dead" after an underwater exercise on April 19, 1956.

"shiny, snouted figure in the rubber suit of a navy frogman [who] . . . with a kick of his long black flippers . . . dove down into the dark, dirty waters of the historic English Port." "Buster" Crabb never returned from his mission.

The Headless, Handless Body

On June 9, 1957, 14 months after Crabb's disappearance and 10 miles from Portsmouth Harbour, fishermen found a headless, handless corpse floating off Pilsey Island. Authorities assumed it was Crabb, but they were unable to identify the remains. When the House of Commons demanded an explanation regarding Crabb's disappearance, Anthony Eden said that it would be in the best interest of the public to not discuss the disappearance of the commander and stated that the government had no knowledge of Crabb's activities.

In 1996 an Israeli journalist interviewed Joseph Zverkin, who had been with the Soviet naval intelligence. Zverkin claimed that a Russian lieutenant observed a frogman swimming near the cruiser, shot him in the head with a sniper's rifle, and watched him sink. Stories about Crabb's disappearance continue to surface. In April 2006, a media report speculated that the headless body was not Crabb. One theory suggests that Crabb planned to defect to the Soviets and MI6 ordered his liquidation. Another theorist claimed that the Soviets had kidnapped Crabb. To this day, his death remains a mystery.

water operation. The frogman submerged in the harbor, swam underwater to the cruiser, and began carrying out his mission from below the waterline. At 7:30 a.m. on April 19, 1956, Soviet sailors standing at the rail of the *Ordzhonikidze* noticed an object come to the surface beside the ship and then disappear. One observer described the sighting as a

In 1963, KGB defector Anatoli Golitsin admitted that Soviet naval intelligence knew that an attempt would be made by a diver to inspect the *Ordzhonikidze* and had posted snipers to watch for him.

CUSHMAN, PAULINE (1833–1893)

Pauline Cushman set out in life to become a famous actress. Her best performances occurred during the Civil War when she disguised herself as a man to spy on the Confederate Army of Tennessee.

Born on June 10, 1833, Pauline Cushman began life in New Orleans as Harriet Wood. She grew up in the frontier village of Grand Rapids, Michigan, where her father ran a trading post for Indians.

At the age of 18, she ran off to New York to become an actress, using the name Pauline Cushman. She met Thomas Placide, who gave her minor parts in light comedies. Placide put the show on the road, traveling south and entertaining in Kentucky and Tennessee. When the ensemble reached New Orleans, Placide gave Cushman her first featured part. She was an instant success.

----DOSSIER--------

Name: Pauline Cushman (née Harriet Wood)

Code Name: None

Birth/Death: 1833–1893

Nationality: American

Occupation: Actress

Involvement: Union Spy in the Civil War

Outcome: Found Dead of a Morphine Overdose

A Call to Arms

While performing shows in New Orleans, Cushman married actor Charles Dickenson. With the Civil War developing, Dickenson left the show and volunteered as a musician in the Union army. A few months later, he died of dysentery.

Returning to the stage to earn a living, Cushman appeared in Union-held Louisville. Two paroled Confederate officers bribed her to make a toast to Confederate president Jefferson Davis during one of her performances. She did, but not until after reporting the incident to Union authorities. During the conversation, the provost marshal asked Cushman if she would like to be a spy.

When she answered in the affirmative, he told her to go ahead and give the toast because a public expression of secessionist loyalty would give her an entrée into Confederate camps. Not many in the audience appreciated the toast, but it launched Cushman's new career.

A Spy in the Enemy's Midst

In March 1863, Cushman began following General Braxton Bragg's Confederate army through Kentucky and into Tennessee. She became the darling of Southern troops, gathering information of value and carrying it through the lines to federal scouts. Confederate officers spoke freely and she listened, later making notes on paper. Officers became suspicious when she periodically left camp and headed in the direction of the Union Army of the Cumberland. When Confederate soldiers stopped and searched her, they found Bragg's battle plans stuffed inside a boot. The general ordered her tried by military court-martial. Found guilty of espionage, the court sentenced her to be hanged. Before the provost marshal could carry out the sentence, Union troops overran Shelbyville, Tennessee, and set her free.

Having narrowly escaped death, she might have resumed her stage career in a safe and populous Northern city. But, when approached by William Truesdale from the Union military police, she agreed to slip behind Confederate lines at Nashville and report on Bragg's movements. After mingling among Confederate officers, a scout from General Nathan Bedford Forrest's cavalry recognized her. Captured again, Cushman faced Bragg for a second time. Confederate officers applauded her persistency, but Bragg ordered her hanged before she got away again. Before the execution could commence, Major General Gordon Granger's Union army division turned Bragg's flank and saved Cushman from the gallows. When Union troops told Granger that he had rescued a notorious federal spy, the general looked at the actress, shook his head doubtfully, and said, "On your way,

Early in the war, Pauline Cushman performed a special task for the Union provost marshal by going into St. Louis undercover and ferreting out Confederate spies operating in the city.

you willful, naughty girl." Cushman smiled, and informed Granger of everything she knew about Bragg's plans, which eventually evolved into a Union victory at Stones River, Tennessee, in December 1863.

The Willful, Naughty Girl

Whatever compelled Cushman to continue spying on Bragg's army had to involve more than excitement or patriotism, but she never said. Because she could no longer prowl the Confederate camp without being recognized, Cushman cut her hair, slipped into the clothes of a Confederate soldier, and continued spying for the Union. The grueling missions finally took their toll. She crawled back to federal lines completely exhausted. General William S. Rosecrans sent her to the hospital, where he often visited her to express his thanks for her services.

When Cushman recovered, she accepted an invitation from President Abraham Lincoln to stop at the White House. He presented her with an honorary major's commission and made arrangements with the quartermaster department to furnish her with a resplendent uniform to go with her rank.

The Spy of the Cumberland

Once again in full health, Cushman went back to the other profession she loved— acting. She portrayed herself as "the Spy of the Cumberland" and wore her major's uniform for every appearance.

Cushman never became a famous actress, though for two decades she was a popular performer. She married a second time, divorced, and separated from a third husband. Her years as a spy took a toll on her body: the long, hard months of sleeping in the rain and marching in the mud brought on arthritis and rheumatism. Forced to give up the stage, Cushman retired to San Francisco and attempted to earn a living as a seamstress, but her hands and fingers soon stopped working. She slipped into obscurity and retired to a small room. Cushman tried to control the pain with small doses of morphine but could not suppress it. On December 2, 1893, the landlord found her dead of an intentional overdose.

When news spread of her death, hundreds of donations provided her a fine casket to be buried in. A hundred veterans from the San Francisco Grand Army of the Republic buried her with military honors in their private cemetery.

Opposite: Having decided to pursue her career on the stage, she changed her name from Harriet Wood to Pauline Cushman. When requested to toast Jefferson Davis in a theatrical performance, she duly informed the incident to a Union officer; this became her opening into espionage for the Union army.

The marker provided by the San Francisco Grand Army of the Republic reads: "Pauline Cushman, Federal Spy and Scout of the Cumberland."

DEFOE, DANIEL (1660–1731)

Daniel Defoe failed to succeed in business and finance, went bankrupt, and to survive, engaged in spying. He became so adept at espionage that today the British rate him as England's "Father of the Secret Service."

Born and raised in London in a Presbyterian family, Daniel Defoe was not permitted by law to attend the better schools controlled by the Church of England. He received a good education, however, in one of the "dissenting academies" founded by Presbyterians. At the age of 23, he opened a small mercantile business and attempted to make a living. In 1684 he married Mary Tuffley and that same year made the mistake of joining the rebellion led by the Duke of Monmouth. After narrowly escaping capture and execution, he traveled though Europe, in exile, until he felt it safe to return. In 1692 his business failed, partly due to financial commitments made on behalf of Monmouth. He suffered bankruptcy and served a term in debtor's prison.

```
----DOSSIER--------
Name: Daniel Defoe
Code Names: Andrew Moreton,
Alexander Goldsmith,
Claude Builot
Birth/Death: 1660-1731
Nationality: British
Occupation: Novelist and
Journalist
Involvement: British Spy
Against the Jacobites
Outcome: Possibly Murdered
in a Cheap Boarding House
```

From Satire to Espionage

Set free and penniless, Defoe turned to writing. He wrote and published widely read satirical pamphlets on politics and religion, including a pamphlet called *The True-Born Englishman*, which became the best-selling poem ever at that time. Another poem, *The Shortest Way with Dissenters* (1703), offended Queen Anne,

While traveling in disguise, Defoe passed himself off as a shipbuilder, a promoter of a glass factory, a salt producer, a woolen merchant from Aberdeen, and a fish merchant from Glasgow.

who ordered Defoe fined, pilloried, and thrown in jail. Again, he found himself in financial difficulties but this time he had six children and a wife to support.

After his second unpleasant experience with the British government, he decided to join it. Having no special employment skills apart from writing popular satires, he decided to try his hand at espionage.

Through his amusing popular pamphlets, Defoe had connected with Robert Harley, the young speaker of the House of Commons. Writing from jail in 1703, he asked Harley to intercede on his behalf with Queen Anne. He promised to travel throughout England, secretly search for political conspiracies against the Crown, and report to Harley what he found. The proposal appealed to the ambitious speaker—Harley would have a personal spy to ferret out political enemies. Defoe could also infiltrate the Jacobites, who were conspiring to return the "Old Pretender," who styled himself James III, to the British throne lost by his father.

Father of the Secret Service

Harley took the scheme to the queen, and she pardoned Defoe. Defoe's complicated proposal to Harley involved going through England, county by county, recruiting a network of spies who would list all the influential men in the district and report their political persuasions. He also promised to devote special attention to the morality of magistrates and clergymen. Defoe also planned to eventually plant a similar operation in Scotland. His agents would submit their reports to him, and he would summarize them for Harley. "I firmly believe," Defoe said to Harley, "this journey may be the foundation of such an intelligence as never was in England."

In 1704, funded by Harley and others, Defoe launched the project. He journeyed through southern England on horseback recruiting agents and implementing a secret reporting system. He pretended to be a merchant, using the alias Alexander Goldsmith or Claude Guilot. To authenticate his disguise, he actually bought and sold a few goods.

In a remarkably short period of time, Defoe built a vast network of intelligence spies who regularly sent him reports on opponents of the government. Before sending reports to Harley, he inserted emendations to add clarity and interpretation, which in later years became the foundation for all intelligence gathering.

Even Defoe's son-in-law seemed unaware of his father-in-law's espionage activities when he noted in a short obituary, "A few days ago died Daniel Defoe Senior, a person well known for his numerous writings."

According to Earl Cowper, "Defoe loved tricks . . . from an inward satisfaction he took in applauding his own cunning. If any man was ever born under the necessity of becoming a knave, he was."

With help from Defoe's network, Harley became secretary of state.

In 1706, Harley sent Defoe into Glasgow as an undercover agent to talk with influential citizens and solicit their support for unifying Scotland with England. Defoe worked diligently. He sent unsigned letters to London weekly, guiding Harley's efforts to steer the negotiations. In 1707 the parliaments of Scotland and England joined to create the kingdom of Great Britain. Three years later Harley received his reward by becoming head of the British government, and in 1711, the queen dubbed him Earl of Oxford.

The Counterfeit Jacobite

In 1714, Harley fell from power when Queen Anne died and George I arrived from Hanover, Germany, to become king. Though Harley had fallen from power, the new government continued to employ Defoe as a spy. The Jacobites were attempting to place Charles Stuart—"the Young Pretender"—on the throne. King George used spies on the Continent to keep watch on the Jacobites, and he brought his practice with him to England.

In 1715, Defoe received a new assignment: to infiltrate the Jacobite underworld. Using his journalistic skills, Defoe became senior editor of a Jacobite newspaper, the *Weekly Journal*. He wrote marvelously ingenious editorials, making ambiguous comments designed to wreck the Jacobite movement without attracting the notice of the publisher. That it succeeded was a tribute to Defoe's ability to write an editorial that meant the opposite of what it said.

Eventually, Defoe was tired of spying and working for a journal in whose cause he had no interest. In 1719, after publishing the novel *Robinson Crusoe*, he left the *Weekly Journal* to devote the rest of his life to writing novels. He pioneered the style of social realism and *Captain Jack* and *Moll Flanders* and other novels soon followed.

When he died in 1731, Defoe had published more than 500 pamphlets and books and his works had earned a place among the great classics of the world. However, Defoe had become so popular as a novelist that nobody ever knew about his career as a spy. In his later life, after he stopped writing, his family never saw him again. It took time before biographers began unearthing Defoe's past.

The creator of England's secret service died in 1731, aged 71, penniless, in a cheap boarding house in Ropemaker's Alley, in the parish of St. Giles-in-Cripplegate, London. The reported nature of his death varied from "lethargy" to suggestions that revenge-seeking Jacobites had hunted him down and murdered him.

NOTES

Toward the end of his life, Defoe once again went deeply into debt, and in order to avoid paying his creditors or being arrested, he went into hiding.

DELILAH (CIRCA 1161 BC)

Delilah established a standard for the modern femme fatale spy, proving that no matter how resistant a masculine opponent, an attractive woman's physical attributes can tear down a man's defenses.

Biblical spies are common in both the Old and New Testaments, but Delilah came on the scene in the twelfth century BC as the first femme fatale. She grew up in Philistia, along the shore of the eastern Mediterranean, a land which today stretches from Gaza to Jaffa.

Nobody knows when she was born or the year she died, but in 1161 BC she left her mark on biblical history at a time when early Israelites were attempting to break from Philistine oppression.

A Man Named Samson

In the book of Judges, Jehovah (God) gave the Israelites Samson, who was born to a barren Hebrew woman for a very specific purpose in life—to throw off the yoke of the Philistines. As the boy grew, he performed great feats of strength. He killed an adult lion with his hands, and as he grew to manhood, he began directing that strength against the Philistines. Yet, when he reached the age of marriage, he informed his parents that he had chosen as his wife a Philistine woman. This did not please his family. They did not know that Jehovah had ordained the marriage and tried to dissuade their son from pursuing such madness. Samson remained adamant, and his father, Manoah, finally consented.

```
----DOSSIER--------
Name: Delilah
Code Name: None
Birth/Death: Circa 1161 BC
Nationality: Philistine
Occupation: None
Involvement: Infiltrated
Israel
Outcome: Died When Samson
Destroyed the Temple
```

The Philistines might also have objected, because people of different religious beliefs did not marry. But like some of the Israelite elders, they recognized political advantages in the alliance and approved the wedding.

Samson's Riddle

At the wedding feast, Samson challenged one of the Philistines to a riddle. If they solved it in seven days, he would give them 30 sets of clothing. If the Philistine failed, they would give Samson 30 sets of clothing. The Philistines eventually realized they could not solve the riddle, so they threatened Samson's wife, warning they would harm her family if she failed to pry the answer from her husband.

His wife plied Samson with sexual pleasure, learned the secret of the riddle, and conveyed it to the Philistines. When the Philistines returned on the appointed day with the correct solution, Samson flew into a rage. He killed 30 Philistines, tore off their clothing to pay the wager, deserted his wife, and returned to his father's dwelling.

Samson's Revenge

Over time, Samson's temper cooled and he decided to make amends with his wife. When he arrived at his father-in-law's house, he learned that his wife had been sold as a concubine to his best friend. Samson refused to be consoled by accepting his wife's lovely younger sister, Delilah, in exchange and departed in a rage.

Seeking vengeance, Samson caught three foxes, attached lighted torches to their tails, and stampeded them through Philistine vineyards, olive groves, and ripe fields of grain. In reprisal, the Philistines murdered Samson's wife and her father. Beset by another fit of rage, Samson repaid the treachery by killing dozens of Philistines.

The Philistines wanted no more trouble from Samson and sent 3,000 men into Judah to take him prisoner. Fearing a bru-

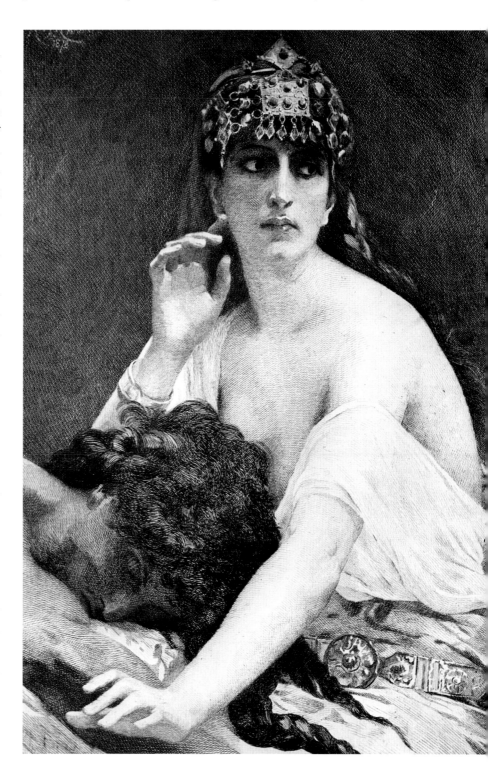

Below: Samson rests his head in Delilah's lap. Original artwork: from a painting by Alexandre Cabanel (1823–1889).

tal bloodbath, Judean elders pleaded with Samson, and he agreed to be bound with rope and turned over to the enemy.

Finding Samson helpless during the march to the kingdom of Dan, a dwarf jester taunted him with the jawbone of an ass. Furious, Samson broke his bonds, rose up in anger, picked up the jawbone, and with it killed a thousand Philistines. The others fled.

Samson now understood, though he may have experienced periods of doubt, that Jehovah really meant for him to free Israel from the Philistines.

Delilah the Delightful

Even though they were frustrated by another failure, the Philistines were at least observant enough to recognize Samson's one fault—his weakness for feminine beauty. Unaware of the source of Samson's great strength, they decided that the sensuous body of a beautiful woman might be more effective in subduing the powerful man than the Philistine army. So they turned once again to Delilah, who had grown even more beautiful than before, and promised her 1,100 pieces of silver for finding the secret to Samson's strength.

Delilah established a camp near Samson's home, and he soon paid her a visit. Attracted by her beauty, he quickly succumbed to her physical charms. Samson, who had become a wise Judean judge, suspected Delilah of being a spy. He parried many of her attempts to learn the secret of his strength by providing her with false answers. Samson could have ended the relationship, but Delilah's sensuous charms overpowered his better judgment.

Like all deeply infatuated targets of spies, Samson believed in his own ability to enjoy Delilah's charms without revealing his secrets. Delilah, however, continued to probe, and Samson grew overconfident and reckless. He knew what she wanted and toyed with her, and he did not expect her to believe him when, jokingly, told her that his strength came from his hair. Samson belonged to the Nazarite sect, who never cut their hair, and there were quite a few of them in the neighborhood, but Delilah thought trimming it worth a try.

One night while Samson lay in a drunken stupor, Delilah took her scissors and cropped Samson's hair. She beckoned Philistine soldiers to come quickly. They found Samson weak and took him back to Philistia as their prisoner.

Samson's Final Curtain

For the sexual submission of her body, Delilah received her reward of 1,100 pieces of silver and became the celebrated heroine of the Philistines. She watched as the soldiers blinded Samson, and was present when they carried him to the great Philistine temple to be mocked.

Unable to see, Samson placed his hands between two pillars to steady himself. Slowly at first, he felt strength trickling into his arms. Samson pushed outward against the pillars, and in a sudden surge of power, tore them from their bases and toppled the temple, killing himself, the watchful Delilah, and thousands of those who had gathered to witness his disgrace.

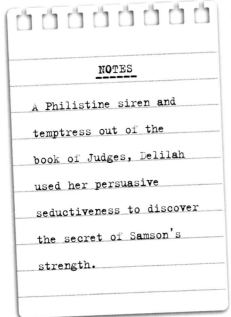

NOTES

A Philistine siren and temptress out of the book of Judges, Delilah used her persuasive seductiveness to discover the secret of Samson's strength.

D'EON, CHEVALIER CHARLES (1728–1810)

Chevalier d'Eon's eccentric mother gave her son the middle names Geneviève and Louise because she wanted a daughter. When d'Eon became a spy during the French Revolution, he wore the disguise of a woman and easily passed for one.

Perhaps no mother was ever more distressed than Madame d'Eon when, in 1728, she gave birth to a son instead of a daughter. After naming him Charles, she gave him two middle names of feminine gender, Geneviève and Louise. He later changed the latter of these two names to Louis.

Charles could never decide which sex he preferred because, from the ages of four through to seven, his eccentric mother dressed him as a girl. For the rest of his life, d'Eon owned two wardrobes, alternating between menswear and fashionable ladies' attire. Being slim with soft features and beardless, he could pass for either a man or a woman.

D'Eon adapted well to masculine pursuits, though he ignored the family's tradition of seeking high rank in the king's army. He became an excellent swordsman, studied law, and joined the bar when most men his age were just beginning their studies. He also wrote a masterful thesis on the finances of Louis XIV, which brought him to the attention of Louis XV.

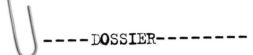

----DOSSIER--------

Name: Chevalier Charles Geneviève Louise d'Eon

Code Name: Lia de Beaumont

Birth/Death: 1728–1810

Nationality: French

Occupation: Lawyer

Involvement: Spy for King Louis XV

Outcome: Died of Natural Causes

The King's Secret

When Louis XV discovered d'Eon's habit of wearing women's clothing, he decided to try the young man as a spy and recruited him into the King's Secret, a

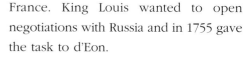

Below: A picture taken from *The London Magazine*, published in 1777, of the Chevalier d'Eon dressed partly as a man and partly as a woman.

small group of agents who reported directly to the Crown. At the time, Louis needed an emissary to travel to St. Petersburg, Russia, and gain the confidence of Russian Empress Elizabeth, whose pro-British foreign minister was negotiating with England, and who refused to talk with France.

The British wanted thousands of Russian mercenaries to help protect George II's home province of Hanover, which the foreign minister said France and Prussia were plotting to invade. English envoys were so persistent with Elizabeth, who actually wanted the half million pounds offered for her troops, that she refused to speak to anyone from

France. King Louis wanted to open negotiations with Russia and in 1755 gave the task to d'Eon.

D'Eon believed that a woman stood a better chance of penetrating political barriers than a man. He packed his dresses and gowns and traveled as Mlle. Lia de Beaumont, accompanied by a fictitious fur trader named Douglass. D'Eon arrived at the St. Petersburg palace and so charmed the empress that she consented to a private interview.

Once inside, d'Eon threw off his disguise, stated his purpose as the envoy of King Louis, and presented her with a letter written by the king, proposing a secret agreement between France and Russia. Elizabeth was fascinated by both d'Eon's disguise and the king's proposal, and later entered into a secret alliance with France and agreed not to help George II. After d'Eon arranged the pact, Louis recalled his agent-envoy to France and rewarded him with a substantial annuity and a commission in the royal dragoons. Henceforth, d'Eon became Louis's favorite spy.

The King's Undercover Transvestite

In 1763 Louis sent d'Eon to England, this time as a man, and instructed him to secretly uncover what terms the British would accept for ending the Seven Years' War. D'Eon accomplished his mission possibly with a change to women's wear as he lifted secret documents from a drunken British officer in the service of the Duke of Bedford. The papers disclosed a willingness on the part of England to negotiate a settlement, and Louis struck a deal with England.

As soon as the war ended, the king sent d'Eon back to England to secretly extract details from high-ranking British officers on the strength of the armed forces, coastal defenses, and anything else that might be valuable to France if the king decided to send an invading army across the channel. D'Eon obtained documents, probed unsuspecting officers and politicians with questions, and kept coded records for delivery to the king. Miffed by not being chosen as the next ambassador to England, the king assuaged the wound by naming d'Eon minister plenipotentiary, thus giving him the title of chevalier.

The chevalier continued the practice of cross-dressing. When he appeared publicly in fancy gowns, wigs, and makeup in England, people openly speculated on his gender. Those who ridiculed his costumes received a challenge. D'Eon had become an excellent swordsman, and his challengers paid a bloody price for their comments.

The Dress Code of Louis XVI

The French spy remained in England until 1774, when Louis XV died. Louis XVI ordered d'Eon home. Angered by the recall, he refused to obey unless he received a large endowment and protection against his enemies in France; otherwise he would divulge to the British all the secret correspondence collected for Louis XV. This France could not afford, so the king dispatched Pierre Augustin Caron de Beaumarchais to England to retrieve the documents in exchange for the king's promise to meet d'Eon's terms.

When the chevalier returned to France, the king kept his bargain, but he set forth a condition: d'Eon must live out his life dressed as a woman. Years later, neighbors reported seeing d'Eon riding about

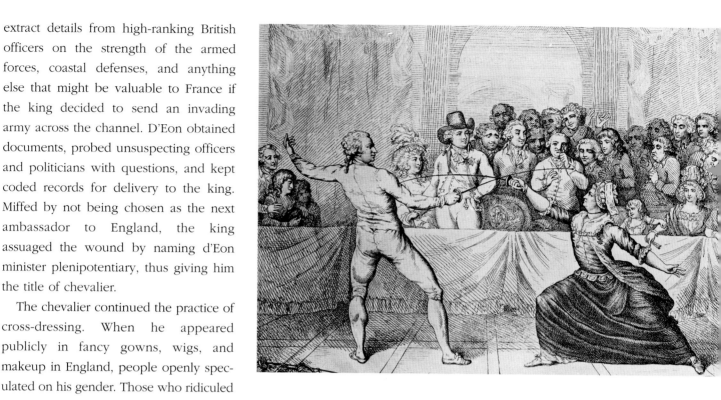

his estate dressed in his old dragoons uniform. French authorities warned him to never do it again.

Dissappointed in France, and having lost all his money during the French Revolution, d'Eon returned to England and made a new life as a fencing instructor. He considered England "a country more free than Holland and well worthy of being visited by a man of thought and lover of liberty." His well-attended fencing class was the only one in England where the talented teacher wore women's clothes.

When the chevalier died in 1810, several English gentlemen insisted upon settling long-standing wagers over his true gender. Most of them lost their bets when the coroner reported that Chevalier Charles Geneviève Louise d'Eon was neither a lady nor a hermaphrodite but, indeed, a man.

Above: The Chevalier d'Eon, pictured in a fencing match with the famous fencer, the Chevalier de Saint Georges.

NOTES

His mother knew at his birth, but d'Eon never married and the issue of his gender remained a matter of public speculation for 81 years. After he died, a coroner ended the mystery.

DOIHARA, KENJI (1883–1948)

Kenji Doihara deeply believed in the slogan "Asia for the Asians." More accurately, he meant Asia for the Japanese, and in the early 1900s he installed a vast network of spies throughout the Far East to promote that goal.

Born in Tokyo to an ancestral family of samurais—a military class of Japanese warriors—Kenji Doihara's military education began the day he became cognitive. To become a samurai, a man must receive training in the aristocratic art of Bushido; a Japanese military officer could not advance rapidly through the ranks if he were not Bushido.

As Doihara passed through his teens, he became brutally ambitious for a military career. His devious mind settled on a plan: Using his skills as an amateur photographer, he forced his sister to pose naked. He developed the photos, choosing only those most sexually provocative, and sent them to Prince Kotohito Kanin, a married and lecherous predator who preyed on young girls. Kanin replied that he would welcome Doihara's sister into his household as a concubine.

Kenji Doihara sealed the deal, and in exchange for his sister, he obtained the rank of major in the Imperial Japanese Army.

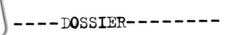

```
----DOSSIER--------
Name: Kenji Doihara
Code Name: Lawrence of
Manchuria
Birth/Death: 1883-1948
Nationality: Japanese
Occupation: Samurai
Military Officer
Involvement: Spymaster in
China and Manchuria
Outcome: Hanged as a War
Criminal
```

The Quest for Asia Begins

In 1904 Japanese intelligence sent Doihara to Peking as adjutant to the military attaché at the Japanese embassy. There General Sigeru Honjo introduced him to the black art of espionage.

Doihara secretly opened dozens of brothels and opium dens throughout China and recruited hundreds of spies and drug addicts. As he had callously used his sister to acquire his commission, he ruthlessly used prostitutes to gather intelligence against officials who tried to keep China unified. Such men were Doihara's enemies.

Unlike other operatives, Doihara learned Chinese dialects and traveled about the provinces disguised as a peddler. Through his sordid network, he learned the weaknesses of local authorities and the names of those who supported breaking from the central government and declaring independence. He also dealt with warlords, bribing them with money and prostitutes in exchange for their promise to keep China divided.

By 1911 nobody understood the frailties of China better than Doihara. He

Left: Kenji Doihara smoking a cigarette. Doihara's ruthless nature was evident throughout his life. From his callous use of his sister to achieve his first military commission through to his cold-blooded treatment of the prostitutes that he used to spread opium addiction, Doihara would stop at nothing to achieve his aims.

urged Japan to invade the weak and sparsely populated northeastern province of Manchuria, which he said could be easily attacked from Japanese-held Korea. Manchuria could provide the launching platform for the invasion of China. Doihara's superiors were impressed, so they sent him into Manchuria. He made inroads with the warlords to such an extent that during World War I Japanese politicians referred to Doihara as "Lawrence of Manchuria." Doihara, however, was not at all like T. E. Lawrence of Arabia. The ruthless, calculating spymaster was out to devastate China in ways that would subordinate the nation to Japanese rule.

During a diplomatic visit to Manchuria in October 1916, Prince Kanin arrived in the provincial capital of Mukden. Doihara met the prince and, along with other Japanese officers, urged him to seize the city. Kanin was about to give the order when Japanese prime minister Masatake Terauchi cautioned the prince to wait because of unsettled political conditions in Russia. Terauchi did not want to waste military resources on China if eastern Siberia could be grabbed.

The Russian Revolution

Doihara remained in Manchuria to manage his Chinese espionage network, now officially called the Special Service Organ. When 200,000 White Russians spilled into Manchuria to escape the bloody Bolshevik revolution, he trained the Russian women as spies, addicted them to opium, paid them

enough to survive, and expanded his brothel and opium den business.

By the mid-1920s, Doihara had more than 80,000 Chinese and White Russian spies operating in the Far East. The men became assassins, saboteurs, and riot organizers; the women worked in brothels. When Chiang Kai-shek took control of the Chinese government, he did too little to stop Japanese infiltration. In 1926 Chang Tso-lin, who ruled Manchuria, became so annoyed at Chiang's pacification policies that he sent troops from Manchuria to lay siege on Peking in protest. Chang Tso-lin never realized that his troops contained thousands of Doihara's spies, who were there to overthrow the Chinese government.

While Chang dallied at Peking, Doihara brought Japanese military reinforcements into Manchuria. He now laid plans to get rid of Chang. In June 1928 he learned that Chang would be returning to Mukden by rail; he issued instructions to his agents, and they blew up the train. In Tokyo, Emperor Hirohito opened the doors of the royal palace and feasted all the espionage officers involved in the plot and made Doihara a colonel.

The Mayor of Mukden

In 1931, Doihara created the "Mukden Incident," which began when his spies detonated explosives along the Japanese-controlled South Manchurian Railroad. The dynamite had been set back from the tracks to send up rocks and debris but not damage the railway. Nonetheless, Doihara used the incident to order a full-scale attack against the Chinese. By noon the next day, Japanese troops completely overpowered Chinese forces, and Doihara appointed himself mayor of Mukden. Although General Sigeru Honjo

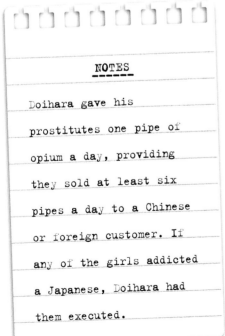

NOTES

Doihara gave his prostitutes one pipe of opium a day, providing they sold at least six pipes a day to a Chinese or foreign customer. If any of the girls addicted a Japanese, Doihara had them executed.

commanded the army, Doihara ran Manchuria much as he wanted and added several thousand new agents, both Chinese and European, to the vast network already in China. After the Japanese moved into northern China, one reporter observed that "mass graves beside the garbage dumps outside all major cities were kept open for the daily disposal of overdose victims cleared from the streets each morning."

Doihara's operations in Manchuria paved the way for Japan to invade China. He used his agents to attack Japanese commercial interests throughout China solely as an excuse for bringing on the war. The success of his tactics encouraged Emperor Hirohito to withdraw from the League of Nations in 1933. Japanese forces promptly moved into Jehol and Mongolia. Doihara followed. He recruited more agents, created more internal dissention, and bred lethal warfare between warlords.

By 1941 Doihara, now an air force major general, sat in the highest councils of Japan. When Hideki Tojo deliberated over bombing Pearl Harbor, Doihara encouraged him to launch the infamous attack. Doihara now had his war, one that stretched from Burma east to the Aleutian Atoll and south to the Solomon Islands. When his war record came to light after Japan surrendered in August 1945, American authorities jailed him. Found guilty of war crimes, on December 23, 1948, Doihara climbed the scaffold with Tojo and six others and became the only spymaster in World War II to be executed by the Allies for crimes against humanity.

Left: Kenji Doihara standing in the dock at the Tokyo War Crimes Trials, hearing his death sentence passed by the court. Doihara was one of 25 Japanese politicians and generals put on trial for "Class A" crimes against peace by the Allies. Led by Sir William Webb of Australia, the judges would eventually pass the death sentence on 14 of the 25. Doihara's sentence was carried out on December 23, 1948, when he was hanged for his actions.

DREYFUS, ALFRED (1859–1935)

The French army falsely accused Captain Alfred Dreyfus of spying in a case that resulted in an atrocious miscarriage of justice and a public distrust of the French army that still exists.

Born in Mulhouse, Alsace, to wealthy French Jewish parents engaged in the manufacturing business, Alfred Dreyfus had every advantage in life. He attended the best French schools and dreamed of becoming a soldier. After the Franco-Prussian War, when Germany annexed Alsace in 1871, the family moved to Paris. Dreyfus entered École Polytechnique, the French military school, and joined the army. He specialized in artillery, graduated in 1880 with an outstanding record, and was assigned to the Fourteenth Regiment of Artillery with the rank of lieutenant. In 1889 he married Lucie Hadomard and started a family of two children. Dreyfus lived better than most officers because he received a financial supplement from his father's business.

Anti-Semitism and the French Army

Promoted to captain in 1893, Dreyfus underwent intensive training after being nominated to the army staff college. A

```
----DOSSIER--------
Name: Alfred Dreyfus
Code Name: None
Birth/Death: 1859-1935
Nationality: French
Occupation: French Military
Officer
Involvement: Accused of
Spying for Germany
Outcome: Died of Natural
Causes
```

number of his colleagues, in particular Major Hubert Henry, disliked Dreyfus because he was rich and a Jew. Other aristocrats among the officers' corps considered him overly ambitious in a "vulgar bourgeois manner." Dreyfus graduated third in his class. Other staff members ignored the remark, and after Dreyfus served the customary year's probation, the French army assigned him to the Deuxième Bureau (military intelligence) of the general staff in Paris. For Dreyfus, being a wealthy Jewish captain serving in military intelligence among a small group of anti-Semitic officers was a recipe for personal disaster.

The Wastebasket of Maximilian von Schwartzkoppen

In 1894, soon after joining the Deuxième Bureau, Dreyfus was suddenly arrested and charged with high treason. The evidence supporting the charge was a torn note offering to sell information on French military fortifications and new weapons to the Germans. The note came from a French spy named Bastian, who served as a maid in the German embassy. Bastian claimed she had plucked the note from the wastebasket beside the desk of Lieutenant Colonel Maximilian von Schwartzkoppen, the German embassy's military attaché. Another German memo that she claimed to have found referred to "that scoundrel D." Major Henry, also of the Deuxième Bureau, put the four pieces of the torn note before the general staff, swore it was in Dreyfus's handwriting, and claimed the "scoundrel D" must be he.

Summoned before senior staff officers, Dreyfus found himself confronted by Major Armand du Paty de Clam, supposedly a handwriting expert. At the request of the general staff, Dreyfus penned a few lines, which Paty de Clam declared identical to the note allegedly lifted from Schwartzkoppen's wastebasket. After being incarcerated for treason, Dreyfus received repeated visits from Paty de Clam, who tried, unsuccessfully, to obtain from him a confession of guilt. Like Major Henry, Paty de Clam was a committed anti-Semite, anxious to believe the worst about a Jewish officer.

Welcome to Devil's Island

Appearing for court-martial before a privately assembled military tribunal on December 19, 1894, Dreyfus attempted to provide evidence of his innocence. Under the guise of "protecting national security," the court denied the admission of evidence and forbade cross-examination. For four days General Auguste Mercier, an admitted anti-Semite, manipulated the court and the evidence to prove Dreyfus's guilt. Marched before French troops for ceremonial degradation, General Darras removed the stripes from Dreyfus's uniform and broke his sword. Returned to

Below: Alfred Dreyfus with his wife and family. The Dreyfus affair had a huge impact on France. It brought together moderate republicans, radicals, and socialists and led to a strengthening of the republic. The Radical Party managed to pass the legislation separating the church and state in France in 1905 partly by emphasizing the role played by the Catholic leadership in the Dreyfus case.

Above: Dreyfus, far right, before the Council of War at Rennes. Even after exoneration, Dreyfus remained a hate figure for the French. While attending the relocation of Zola's remains to the Pantheon in 1908, he was shot and lightly wounded by a right-wing journalist.

jail, Dreyfus waited in disgrace until the next ship sailed for Devil's Island, the miserable, insect-infested penal colony located off the coast of French Guiana in South America.

From 1895 to 1899 Dreyfus suffered alone in a small stone hut with barred windows, constantly watched by armed guards posted at the door. Once a day, the guards led him outside to walk in a half-acre treeless dust bowl. When not ill with fever or indigestion from rotten

food, he studied English, forever wondering if he would ever see France again.

Colonel Picquart's Inquest

In 1896 the Statistics Section of the Deuxième Bureau intercepted an incriminating note from a German intelligence officer to Major Ferdinand Esterhazy of the French general staff. An ensuing investigation proved that Esterhazy was

"Dreyfus," shouted General Darras in a public forum, "you are unworthy to wear the uniform! In the name of the French people, we deprive you of your rank!"

the spy, not Dreyfus. The general staff suppressed the evidence.

One Frenchman, Deuxième Bureau chief Lieutenant Colonel Georges Picquart, became troubled by the entire Dreyfus affair. Defying orders to not inspect the court's documents, he matched the handwriting on the note that condemned Dreyfus to the handwriting of Esterhazy. He went to the general staff and accused Major Henry of having immediately recognized the handwriting of his friend Esterhazy, and to save him, accused Dreyfus. The thunderbolt stirred the generals into an even greater concealment. They hurled the evidence into Picquart's face and told him to shut up. The colonel stubbornly warned that if the information ever became public, it would tarnish the French general staff. Picquart suffered the penalty for being honest and was sent out of the country to a meaningless post. A panicky Major Henry proceeded to create more forged documents to disprove Picquart's evidence.

The French Army vs. the French Public

Mathieu Dreyfus stepped into the battle and initiated a campaign to exonerate his brother. He publicized Picquart's discoveries and named Esterhazy as the spy. Caught in their deceit, the general staff brought Esterhazy to trial and a rigged court-martial acquitted him. The flagrant cover-up infuriated Émile Zola, the lead-

ing French journalist of the day. On January 13, 1898, he publicly and fearlessly denounced the military caste system that protected its own corrupt members, and the French government that backed the general staff. Zola could have been imprisoned for writing his eye-opening exposé, *J'Accuse*, but the general staff went only halfway, charging Zola with libel and striking his name from the Legion of Honor. The militarists degraded Zola the same way they had degraded Dreyfus and forced him to move to England to protect his family.

France's greatest writers stepped into the battle and nagged the government until Dreyfus was brought to France and retried. Major Henry realized that he would be exposed and instead slit his throat. Esterhazy fled to England and years later admitted to being the spy. The general staff, however, remained characteristically stubborn and shocked the world by convicting Dreyfus again, this time "with extenuating circumstances." The public knew Dreyfus was innocent, and to mollify critics, French president Emile Loubet pardoned Dreyfus with an equivocating decree. Dreyfus refused to be appeased and demanded complete vindication. In 1906 the French court of appeals reversed the military tribunal, cleared Dreyfus of all charges of treason and espionage, and ordered that he be returned to the army. The government elevated Dreyfus to the rank of major and awarded him the Cross of the Cavalier of the Legion of Honor.

During World War I, Dreyfus served with distinction, rose in rank to lieutenant colonel, and was named an Officer of the Legion of Honor.

DUKES, PAUL (1889–1967)

Paul Dukes, a musician who loved opera, also loved intrigue, and the combination of his two loves put him to work as a British spy during the Russian Revolution.

Born in London, the son of a clergyman in the Church of England, Paul Dukes developed an interest in music at an early age. He graduated from Charterhouse in Surrey in 1909 and went to St. Petersburg, Russia, to study music at the conservatory attached to the famous Marinsky Theatre. He planned to make music his life and soon earned a post as assistant to conductor Albert Coates at the opera house. He also became proficient in the Russian language.

Agent ST-25

Dukes's life changed in 1915 when he accepted a position with the Anglo-Russian Commission as the king's messenger. The organization was based in St. Petersburg, where they coordinated the joint military and political efforts of the two countries after World War I began. Dukes's passport listed him as a diplomatic courier, but his actual responsibilities entailed monitoring and reporting on what was being said in the Russian press.

Dukes must have made a good impression because in 1917, the year of the

```
----DOSSIER--------
Name: Paul Dukes
Code Name: Agent ST-25
Birth/Death: 1889-1967
Nationality: British
Occupation: Musician
and Conductor
Involvement: Spy for Great
Britain in Russia
Outcome: Died of Natural
Causes
```

Russian Revolution, the British foreign office provided him with a "roving commission" without explaining his duties. His assignment became clearer in 1918 when British Intelligence (MI6) tagged him as Agent ST-25, officially making him a British spy. Delighted with his new role, Dukes returned to London for training under British spymaster

Commander Mansfield Cumming, an expert with invisible inks and codes. Finding Dukes an amazingly rapid learner, Cumming sent him back to Russia as MI6's embedded spymaster.

The Man Who Wasn't There

Dukes was a master of disguise and traveled through Russia, using aliases and forged identification papers to conceal his movements. He despised the tactics of Bolshevik communists and urged the British to support the White Russian monarchists. Dukes became so adept at espionage that MI6 placed him charge of all British agents in Russia.

Dukes established close contact with the leaders of the White Russian army and supported them with money and intelligence. Using gold supplied by Cumming, Dukes expanded his network, financing sabotage and insurrection operations against Bolshevik installations. However, most of the paper money that Cumming sent was too poorly counterfeited to use, and when Dukes needed money, he drew loans from Russian banks using disguises and aliases and then quickly vanished.

Dukes concentrated his efforts on rescuing politicians and influential Russians thrown into Bolshevik prison camps. He saved hundreds of lives by launching armed attacks on the compounds, spiriting the prisoners to Helsinki, Finland, and delivering them to Lieutenant Augustus Agar of the Royal Navy. Agar commanded a squadron of specially modified torpedo boats that he used for transporting Dukes's refugees to safety. During one rendezvous, Dukes gave the British skipper detailed information on the location of the Russian fleet. Agar loaded his boats with torpedoes and, in a hazardous sortie into the Russian harbor, sank a cruiser and a battleship.

In 1919, wearing all new disguises, Dukes joined the Communist Party and the Red Army. Once on the inside, he obtained or forged an internal passport giving him the credentials of an officer in the Cheka, the Bolshevik secret police. He then infiltrated the Cominterm, where he gathered secret political and military information straight from Lenin and Trotsky. He found every level of government infested with spies and double agents and knew he could trust no one.

When Dukes learned that Cheka spies had discovered the location of the White Russian headquarters, he sent a warning but it arrived too late. On the night of August 28, 1919, Cheka police raided the organization and seized N. N. Shchepkin, the political leader, and Admiral Kolchak, the military leader. The Cheka rounded up more than a thousand White Russian agents and executed the leaders.

Discovery and Escape

Counterintelligence agents became aware of Dukes's presence and the nature of his activities. The secret police constantly watched for him. By using different

When Dukes joined the Communist Party, he used the alias Comrade Piotrovsky, but the Cheka never a found a man of that name who bore a resemblance to his photograph.

After relating his story to the Latvian press, Dukes admitted his mistake, saying, "Long before I reached London, I realized that Red Russia was closed to me, perhaps forever."

names and different disguises, by moving from place to place and never sleeping twice in the same house, Dukes avoided capture. Such good fortune could not last forever. Disguised and holding forged passports, he escaped to Helsinki but found Lieutenant Agar gone. To avoid spies, he crossed over mountains and through swamps to Lake Luban and escaped by foot into Latvia.

Filthy and exhausted, Dukes contacted White Russian friends. They gave him a bath and fresh clothes but indiscriminately blew his cover by relating his brilliant escape to the Latvian press.

With his undercover career in Russia finished, Dukes connected with Agar in Latvia and returned to Great Britain. Cumming was delighted to find both men safe and in good health. Enthused and proud of their accomplishments, he arranged for them to meet King George V. The king listened intently, fascinated by the adventures of Dukes and Agar. When the interview ended, George awarded the Victoria Cross to Agar. Dukes could not receive the medal because he was a civilian. His award came in 1920 when George V made Dukes a knight, the only British agent to ever receive knighthood as a reward for espionage.

For two years, Dukes had sent regular reports back to London without ever being detected, but his efforts did not prevent the Communists from tightening their grip on Russia.

Once a Spy, Always a Spy

Twenty years later, on the eve of World War II, Dukes walked into MI6 and offered his services. British intelligence had lost contact with Alfred Obry, a wealthy Czech businessman, and because Dukes was available, they sent him into Germany to search for the man. MI6 had learned through agents that Obry had last been seen in Berlin, where he had gone to protest demands by the Nazis that he sign over all his vast industrial and commercial enterprises to Germany. At first MI6 believed Obry may have fled under a false passport, but too much time had passed since the last contact.

Dukes assumed that Obry would have taken a train from Berlin to Czechoslovakia and meticulously backtracked his probable route of travel. While searching local newspapers, he discovered that the mutilated body of Friedrich Schweiger, supposedly a tailor from Prague, had been found lying alongside the railroad. He persuaded German authorities that they should exhume the body, which friends identified as Obry. Dukes returned to MI6, where his exploits as a spy finally faded into the annals of espionage.

NOTES

Sir Paul Dukes went on to write two books about his adventures, *Red Dusk and the Morrow* (1932), and *The Story of "ST-25": Adventure and Romance in the Secret Intelligence Service in Red Russia* (1939).

EASTERN JEWEL (1906-1948)

A Chinese-born Tartar princess and a real-life dragon lady, Eastern Jewel became corrupted early in life by the Japanese culture and grew up committed to the Bushido code of military conquest.

Eastern Jewel's ancestry traces back to Nurhachi, founder of the Manchu dynasty in 1616. Her father, Prince Su, promised his daughter to Naniwa Kawashima, his Japanese military adviser. Kawashima took Eastern Jewel as a baby and raised her as his own daughter.

Kawashima sent her to Japan to be educated, and when she reached the age of eight, her adoptive father renamed her Yoshiko Kawashima. As part of her Bushido training, Eastern Jewel learned judo and fencing.

In 1921, Prince Su died. His wife, a concubine with no official standing, committed traditional suicide. The news of the deaths of her mother and father brought no tears to the eyes of 15-year-old Eastern Jewel, who had very little interest in her Chinese heritage—by this time, she worshipped all things Japanese.

Despite her young age, Eastern Jewel claimed to have been seduced by Kawashima's aged father. After a heated affair with Kawashima himself, she seduced several young Japanese officers

```
----DOSSIER--------
Name: Eastern Jewel
Code Name: None
Birth/Death: 1906-1948
Nationality: Chinese
Occupation: Manchu Princess
Involvement: Chinese Spy
for Japan
Outcome: Beheaded by the
Japanese
```

and fell in love with Lieutenant Yamaga. He was the first man to reject her advances but the falling-out only increased her insatiable appetite for seduction, and she used her charm, good looks, and wealth to attract many lovers.

An Arranged Marriage

At the age of 21, Eastern Jewel acceded to her deceased father's wish that she marry Mongol Prince Kanjurjab, an ineffectual youth who she deserted after only four months, claiming that she never allowed him to touch her. She departed from Mongolia, circulated through southern China, and in 1928 returned to Japan. Eastern Jewel continued to socialize with men, luring one member of the Japanese Diet to Shanghai and then dumping him when he finally ran out of money.

While in Shanghai at a New Year's party, Eastern Jewel met Major Ryuichi Tanaka, local head of the Japanese intelligence service. At first, Tanaka resisted involvement with a Chinese woman, especially as she was a princess and he, as he claimed, a mere commoner. Jewel borrowed enough money from him to downgrade herself to his level and she eventually seduced him. Men found it extremely difficult to resist Eastern Jewel because she was pretty, petite, and had a fetish for men's clothing, especially uniforms. Tanaka also had a fetish. He liked her boots.

The Emergence of the Dragon Lady

To keep Eastern Jewel available for personal pleasure, Tanaka put her on the payroll of Japanese intelligence as a spy. He also sent her to school to learn English under the pretext of preparing her for espionage assignments. Those missions began in the fall of 1931 when Tanaka received orders to create disturbances in Shanghai to screen the Japanese takeover of Manchuria. Colonel Kenji Doihara, in charge of Japanese espionage, wanted much more. He wanted Tanaka to start a war with China.

Using $10,000 provided by Tanaka, Eastern Jewel hired gangs of Chinese thugs to break into Japanese homes and businesses in Shanghai, create bedlam, and undermine the confidence of the residents. She engaged enough hoodlums to keep the police at bay. The sackings continued and the Imperial Japanese Navy was able to sail into the harbor under the pretext of protecting national interests. Marines came ashore, took control of the city, and stayed.

Because Eastern Jewel had succeeded so well with her first mission, Colonel Doihara assigned her to another. He had designs of overthrowing Manchuria and wanted to install the deposed boy emperor, Henry Pu-Yi, the last of the Manchu sovereigns, as a puppet ruler. This meant that Pu-Yi would have to move from Tientsin to Mukden and, because Eastern Jewel was also Manchu and they were friends, Doihara believed that Pu-Yi would trust her.

Eastern Jewel flew from Shanghai to Tientsin and immediately called upon Pu-Yi and his opium-addicted wife, Elizabeth. Using spies posing as assassins,

In his book, *A History of Japanese Secret Service*, Richard Deacon describes Jewel as "half tom-boy and half heroine, and with this passion for dressing up as a male."

Doihara once thought Eastern Jewel was a boy. When she refused to tell him, he undressed her with the point of his sword, saying, "If you will not tell me who you are, let's see what you are."

Eastern Jewel terrorized Pu-Yi and said he must flee to Mukden or be killed. Pu-Yi appealed to Doihara for protection, but the colonel merely carried out a phony investigation and worried the young man more by identifying the would-be assassin as a warlord who despised Manchus. When Pu-Yi balked at leaving his palatial home, Eastern Jewel increased the pressure by putting snakes in the young man's bed and planting bombs in his fruit basket. Pu-Yi crumbled and in March of 1932 Doihara smuggled or kidnapped Pu-Yi into Mukden and seated him on the provincial throne.

Delighted with Eastern Jewel's performance, Imperial Japanese Headquarters permitted her to wear the uniform of an officer and gave her the rank of commander.

The Quest for Wealth and Power

The turning point in Eastern Jewel's fortunes began the day she flew over Shanghai and laughed at the damage done by Japanese bombers. Thousands of her countrymen lay slaughtered on the ground. After landing, she walked through the area with Japanese officers, stepping over bodies of women and children, and quite delighted in the carnage. No Chinese who witnessed her glee would ever forget Eastern Jewel.

During the war she moved to Peking and set herself up as a Japanese informant. Instead of informing, she bribed wealthy Chinese merchants by threatening to turn them over to Colonel Yamaga for collaborating with Chiang Kai-shek. She split the money with Yamaga until he demanded a greater percentage of the spoils. Eastern Jewel flew to Tokyo and falsely informed the Imperial General Headquarters that Yamaga opposed General Tojo's war plans. The generals believed her and dismissed Yamaga from the army.

With Yamaga gone, Eastern Jewel did as she pleased, including indulging in ever-more-exotic sex practices with both men and women. Her desire was insatiable, but she became a bloated syphilitic. When nobody wanted her anymore, she preyed on children and used actors and sing-song girls for entertainment.

When the war ended in 1945, Chiang Kai-shek returned to power and Eastern Jewel went into hiding. She could no longer afford a luxurious life and took refuge in a hovel. Betrayed by a former lover, in 1948 the government arrested, tried, and convicted her as a war criminal. Her offense was that she rode in Japanese airplanes over bombed-out villages and laughed.

Denied the military honor of a firing squad, Eastern Jewel suffered the indignity of being beheaded.

NOTES

Eastern Jewel, while operating as a spy, may have done more than any other operative in China to bring on World War II in the Far East.

EDMONDS, SARAH EMMA (1842–1898)

Canadian-born Emma Edmonds dreamed of becoming a missionary. Instead, the Civil War changed her life and she became a spy and a soldier in a man's army.

Born on a poor farm in New Brunswick, Canada, Emma Edmonds faithfully read her Bible every day, attended church regularly, and dreamed of becoming a missionary in some far-off land. Most of her education came from Christian training. Her father resented that she was girl and treated her badly through most of her youth, so Emma tried to behave like a boy.

In 1856, Emma fled to Rhode Island to escape a marriage arranged by her father. Penniless and wearing boy's clothes, she took refuge in a Christian community, using the alias Franklin Thompson. In 1860, while still posing as a young man, she obtained a job as a salesman, selling Bibles and religious tracts in a territory that stretched from New England to the upper Midwest. In those days, there were no traveling saleswomen, and Edmonds never would have received the job had they known her true, female identity. In late 1860, Edmond's employer transferred her to Flint, Michigan, where militia companies began organizing in 1861.

```
-----DOSSIER--------
Name: Sarah Emma Edmonds
Code Names: Franklin
Thompson, Bridget O'Shea,
Charles Mayberry, Cuff
Birth/Death: 1842-1898
Nationality: Canadian
Occupation: Traveling
Bible Salesperson
Involvement: Spy for
the Union
Outcome: Died of Natural
Causes
```

Outbreak of the Civil War

After four attempts at joining the Union army, Emma Edmonds enlisted as Private

Franklin Thompson, male nurse in the Second Michigan Infantry. She despised slavery, admitted to being an abolitionist, and believed in the Union cause. Private Thompson did not become concerned about concealing her sex until July, when the regiment reported to Washington, D.C., for operations against Confederate forces at Bull Run. Though unsuspecting comrades joked about her small stature, Edmonds would carry out her duties as a field nurse for two years before lodging problems caused by illness threatened to expose her gender.

Left: It took Edmonds four attempts to enlist in the Union army; luckily, at the time, the medical exam consisted only of a list of questions—no physical exam was required.

do it, Edmonds studied all she could find on weaponry, tactics, and local geography. After an interview with McClellan's staff, Private Thompson got the job.

McClellan wanted Yorktown's defenses reconnoitered, and Edmonds insisted she could do it. Using burned cork to darken her skin, she posed as a black man named Cuff, stole across Confederate lines, and became pressed into labor as a slave. After the first day, her hands were so blistered from shoveling dirt that the officer in charge put her in the kitchen. She learned that the Confederate force was weak and that many of the guns were not guns at all but logs painted black, known as "Quaker guns." She sketched the defenses and tucked the paper in her shoes. A few nights later she slipped through Confederate pickets and escaped into Union lines. McClellan digested the intelligence, thanked Private Thompson, and sent her back to her regiment. A few days later, Union forces captured Yorktown.

Two months passed before McClellan summoned her again, this time to infiltrate enemy lines during the Seven Days campaign. This tme, she dressed as a fat peddler woman named Bridget O'Shea and meandered through Confederate camps selling her wares. Having completed the mission, she jumped on a horse and headed for the Union lines. Though wounded in the arm, she made it back to headquarters with the intelligence McClellan wanted.

On another occasion in August 1862, Edmonds disguised herself as a "black

Above: An appeal to the War Department led to the following statement: "That Franklin Thompson and Mrs. Sarah E. E. Seeley are one and the same person is . . . beyond a doubt."

From Nurse to Spy

In 1862, during General George B. McClellan's Peninsular Campaign, Edmonds volunteered to work undercover after one of the army's best spies was apprehended and executed. She wanted the job, and to prove she could

Emma Edmonds became the only woman to serve in the Civil War as a man and receive a soldier's pension.

Edmonds was possibly the only spy in history who was both transvestite and transracial.

mammy" and went behind enemy lines as a laundress. One day, when cleaning the uniform of one of the officers, some papers fell from the pocket. Of course, the laundress pocketed them and returned to the Union lines to hand over the information.

Operations in the West

When Edmonds's Michigan regiment went with General Ambrose Burnside's Ninth Corps to Kentucky, Private Thompson tagged along with her nurse's kit. Well aware of Edmonds's success as a spy, Burnside gave her the alias Charles Mayberry and asked her to circulate through Louisville and try to find out who belonged to the city's Confederate spy ring. Edmonds returned a week later and gave a list of names to the general.

Private Thompson next found herself on the Mississippi, working under the command of General Ulysses S. Grant in a Union hospital near Vicksburg. She worked grueling hours and finally became ill with malaria. She didn't want to expose her identity by admitting herself to the hospital, and had to think long and hard how to cure herself without giving herself away.

Shaking with fever, Private Thompson left camp, became a woman again, and checked herself into a hospital in Cairo, Illinois. She was about to change back into uniform once more when she saw her name, Private Thompson, posted on a list of deserters.

Will the Real Emma Please Step Forward?

With the last of her funds, Edmonds bought a train ticket to Washington. As a woman again, she worked to the end of the war as a nurse. After eleven successful missions as a spy, she knew her life as Franklin Thompson, along with all her other aliases, had come to an end.

In 1867, Edmonds returned to Canada, dressed as a sprightly young woman, and soon fell in love and married Linus Seelye. He eventually took her back to the United States, where she raised three sons. One of them enlisted in the army "just as Mama did."

Edmonds fretted over being branded a deserter and, after being urged by friends, petitioned the War Department. On March 28, 1884, the House of Representatives validated "Mrs. Seelye's" case. On July 5, she received, by special act of Congress, an honorable discharge made out to Emma Edmonds, alias Franklin Thompson, plus a bonus and a pension of $12 a month.

Emma Edmonds Seelye lived the rest of her life in La Porte, Texas, where she died on September 5, 1889. She was the only female member of the Union organization of veterans formed after the Civil War—the Grand Army of the Republic.

NOTES

After the war, Edmonds wrote her memoirs, *Nurse and Spy in the Union Army*, which sold thousands of copies. She donated all her royalties to the war relief fund.

Eric Erickson performed undercover work in Germany during World War II so convincingly that his friends in the United States and Sweden believed he had turned traitor.

Born to a poor, working-class family in Brooklyn, New York, Eric Erickson resolved at an early age to work hard and become successful. When poverty cut his high school education short, he went to Texas and labored in the oil fields as a pipeline walker. He saved money, finished school, and in 1917, at the age of 28, he entered Cornell University. World War I interrupted his education, but when the fighting ended he returned to Cornell, became a football star, and graduated with a degree in engineering.

Erickson returned to work for Standard Oil and, after spending a number of years in Shanghai, was sent to Stockholm, Sweden. He made good friends, opened his own business as a petroleum importer, renounced his American citizenship, and in 1936 became a Swede.

The Career Within a Career

Erickson's life began to change in 1939, when U.S. ambassador to Moscow Laurence Steinhardt arrived in Stockholm

----DOSSIER--------

Name: Eric Erickson

Code Name: None

Birth/Death: 1889–1960

Nationality: American

Occupation: Petroleum Engineer

Involvement: U.S. Spy during World War II

Outcome: Died of Natural Causes

and invited Erickson to dinner. Steinhardt's conversation focused on Erickson's business relationships with German oil importers, many of who belonged to the Nazi Party. Because of Hitler's mobilization for war, Steinhardt knew that Germany would need oil. He also knew that Sweden's neutrality would enable Erickson to come and go in Germany. He explained that Hitler had engineers working on a secret process to develop synthetic oil and asked Erickson if he would spy for the American Office of Strategic Services (OSS). Though under no patriotic obligation, Erickson agreed. After receiving only 38 hours of espionage instruction from the OSS in Stockholm, Erickson made arrangements to contact the Nazis.

He fully understood that working with Nazis would stain his reputation. The only people outside the OSS that knew his purpose were his young new wife and Prince Carl Bernadotte, the Swedish king's nephew. Bernadotte frequently traveled to Germany on diplomatic matters and used the visits to introduce Erickson to Nazi oil industrialists. Posing as a friend of fascism, Erickson cemented strong relationships with Hitler's cronies and during the war made countless trips into Germany. Though shunned as a collaborationist by the Swedes, he turned invaluable information on the German oil industry over to the OSS. Although Erickson ostensibly worked for the OSS, he also reported clandestinely to British intelligence (MI6), which had a common interest with the United States in locating and destroying any major Nazi oil installations.

Erickson put himself at great risk. Gestapo agents tenaciously tracked him every time he entered the country. He met once too often with a trusted woman, who had been under surveillance as a possible spy. One evening when they were together, the Gestapo came to the door and arrested them. Taken to Gestapo headquarters and separated for interrogation, they both told the same previously prepared story—that she was a high-priced prostitute and he was her customer. The Gestapo believed Erickson's story and released him, but they accused the woman of spying, took her outside, and shot her.

The Oil Refinery Caper

In 1943, as Allied forces accelerated the bombing of Germany, the OSS and Britain's MI6 asked Erickson to help locate the enemy's oil refineries. Erickson concocted a scheme that the Germans could not refuse: He went directly to Heinrich Himmler, head of the Gestapo and the German SS, and offered to build a refinery in Sweden, one safe from Allied bombs and with enough capacity to deliver all the oil the Wehrmacht needed. Erickson not only fooled Himmler, the most feared man in Germany, he also fooled Walter Schellenberg, head of Nazi counterespionage. To mollify any suspicions they might have, he admitted being listed on the Allied blacklist as a traitor, but Himmler and Schellenberg already knew that.

Himmler showed great interest in the project, so Erickson went back to Sweden to put together a proposal. He returned a few weeks later with detailed drawings of the proposed Swedish refinery, showing

Although Erickson officially worked for the OSS, he also reported to British intelligence, revealing the locations of major Nazi oil installations.

By 1943, Heinrich Himmler was in charge of virtually everything and everyone inside German-held territories. That Erickson fooled Hitler's brutal and cunning deputy demonstrates his outstanding ability as a spy.

projected costs and output calculations. Himmler was hooked.

Erickson explained that he had a technical problem to resolve before he could break ground. He needed to visit Germany's oil refineries and to speak with petroleum engineers in order to install the most efficient processing equipment to meet Germany's fuel requirements. Himmler agreed. He gave Erickson a top-level Gestapo pass and a signed order from Hitler authorizing automobiles and unlimited gas coupons.

Recognized

Before leaving on tour, Erickson had a potential setback when he accidentally encountered a Nazi oil executive whom he thought had died. Erickson smiled and offered the man a drink. While they sat together in a *gasthaus*, the Nazi narrowed his eyes and said, "I am very curious to hear how one day you're working hand in glove with the god-damned Jews and the next day you're hooked up with our side against your own people." Erickson merely smiled and replied that he was always a businessman first and had been supporting the Nazis for years. The German still looked doubtful, so Erickson showed him Himmler's authorization. The

man gave Erickson a quizzical look, excused himself, and abruptly left.

Erickson followed the Nazi and watched him pull up near a phone booth. He parked to the other side of the road and got out of the car. Opening the long blade of a penknife in his coat, Erickson pulled open the door of the phone booth and killed the man.

Oil Crisis

With the threat removed, Erickson spent the next two months inspecting every oil refinery in Germany and the Balkans. He passed the information to OSS and MI6, and one by one, Germany's oil refineries came under air attack. By 1945, the Wehrmacht and the Luftwaffe began running out of fuel. Tanks stalled on the battlefield and fighter planes remained grounded for lack of aviation gas. In 1945, when more than 300,000 German troops surrendered in the Ruhr Valley, they blamed their capitulation on the inability to obtain fuel.

After the war, Erickson returned to Sweden to repair his tarnished image. General Dwight D. Eisenhower made it clear that he attributed the destruction of Germany's oil industry to one man, Eric Erickson. When the story broke, the American Swede enjoyed a sudden surge of popularity. Without recognition from Eisenhower, Erickson might have lived the balance of his life a traitor, but instead he became an international hero.

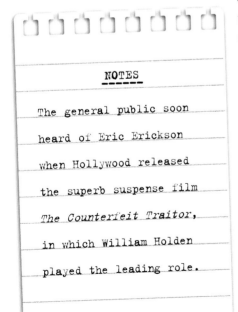

NOTES

The general public soon heard of Eric Erickson when Hollywood released the superb suspense film *The Counterfeit Traitor*, in which William Holden played the leading role.

FARNSWORTH, JOHN S. (1893–?)

A brilliant and charming man, John Farnsworth needed money to sustain his lifestyle, so he became a spy for the Japanese during the interval of peace between the two great wars.

John Farnsworth came from a middle-class family in Cincinnati, Ohio, where he graduated from high school at the top of his class. He aspired to become a navy officer and, in 1911, he secured an appointment to the U.S. Naval Academy at Annapolis, Maryland. In 1915, he graduated near the top of his class.

During World War I he served on a destroyer and after the war returned to Annapolis to study aeronautical engineering. In 1923, because of rapidly developing technology in airplanes and aircraft carriers, he spent a year taking an advanced course at the Massachusetts Institute of Technology in Cambridge. The navy promoted Farnsworth to lieutenant commander and transferred him to the Pensacola naval air base to teach flying.

Living High on an Officer's Salary

In 1926 the navy assigned Farnsworth to the air base at Norfolk, Virginia, where he commanded a squadron of fighters. He met and married a high society girl, accustomed to an expensive home, country clubs, late-night parties, and a luxurious life. Getting deeper into debt, Farnsworth borrowed money from an enlisted man and, when pressed to repay the debt, he refused. The sailor

```
----DOSSIER--------
Name: John Semer Farnsworth
Code Name: None
Birth/Death: 1893–?
Nationality: American
Occupation: U.S. Naval
Officer
Involvement: Spied for the
Japanese
Outcome: Disappeared After
Release from Prison
```

complained, and in 1927 Farnsworth received a dishonorable discharge for borrowing money from an enlisted man. His wife filed for divorce, and Farnsworth resumed drinking. No shipping line or aviation firm would hire him because of his military record. When he applied for work with foreign countries, all but Japan flatly turned him down.

Getting Back at the Navy

During an interview in Washington, D.C., Farnsworth learned that the Japanese had no interest in him as a technical adviser but could offer him employment in another capacity: If he would obtain technical information on America's new naval vessels and deliver it to Commander Yoshiashi Ichimiya at the Japanese Embassy in Washington, he would be paid well for his services. Farnsworth asked for more specifics, and his interviewer replied that Japan needed top-secret information on the navy's new aircraft carriers, advanced communications systems, weaponry, and the configuration and capabilities of the navy's newest planes. Farnsworth said he could get the information from friends in the service and walked away from the interview loaded with cash. He immediately obtained a fashionable suite at Washington's New Willard, remarried, and resumed his affair with nightclubs.

With unlimited funds, Farnsworth began traveling up and down the East Coast. He visited old friends on the pretext of recruiting their help so he could return to the navy. What he really wanted were navy secrets. In 1930, with the world at peace, espionage was not a dangerous profession; the penalty for being caught amounted to a few years in prison. Farnsworth operated openly. Sometimes he "borrowed" files from the offices of his friends, took them to a commercial operation for copying, and told the firm he was a navy man and needed the documents in a hurry.

In 1927, American intelligence discovered that Emperor Hirohito had approved a military plan to invade China. Intelligence also learned that Japan would only issue visas for travel in the United States to spies. Farnsworth had once been observed in the company of a Japanese attaché, but only briefly. At the time, the FBI agent watching Ichimiya considered the meeting accidental but noted it in his report.

In 1934 the Office of Naval Intelligence (ONI) grew curious about Farnsworth's activities when Captain William Puleston

Below: John S. Farnsworth, left, talking to a reporter before his arraignment in Washington, D.C., in March 1937. He was sentenced for conspiring to sell American fleet secrets to the Japanese and received a sentence of 4–12 years.

read a routine report from Lieutenant Commander Leslie Gehres. Gehres mentioned that a highly classified booklet, *The Service of Information and Security*, had disappeared from his office during a recent visit by Farnsworth. He went on to say that, after an extensive search of the office, he called Farnsworth, who admitted he had picked up the booklet accidentally and promptly returned it.

The information jogged Puleston's curiosity. He looked into Farnsworth's background, discovered the dishonorable discharge and divorce, learned of his difficulty in finding work, yet noticed that he lived luxuriously at the Willard. Puleston made inquiries and learned that Farnsworth spent most of his time at the bar, always carried a fat roll of $100 bills, but had no money in his bank account and a second marriage in trouble. This was inconsistent with Gehres's statement that Farnsworth was still looking for a job. Puleston recalled a recent incident between another ex-navy man and the attaché at the Japanese Embassy. He probed Ichimiya's bank records and discovered that a lot of extra money flowing into the embassy account was being withdrawn in large quantities of $100 bills.

The Hunters and the Hunted

Being understaffed at ONI, Puleston turned the case and his findings over to the FBI. Agents dogged Farnsworth for two years without learning how he kept himself in money. He seldom left the hotel except to visit friends in the navy, and he never ran out of $100 bills.

Remembering the accidental meeting between Farnsworth and Ichimiya, the FBI began watching the attaché's hotel. They also followed Farnsworth to the home of Lieutenant Commander James E. Mather in Annapolis. After Farnsworth left, the agents knocked on the door and spoke with the Mathers, who said that Farnsworth appeared to be unstrung and under pressure to get information about the USS *Baddlitt*, a recently commissioned destroyer.

When Farnsworth returned to Washington, he discovered that Ichimiya had been recalled and replaced by Commander Akira Yamaki. He also noticed in the newspapers that an ex-navy man named Harry Thompson had been arrested on the West Coast on charges of spying for the Japanese and sent to prison for 15 years. Stunned by the sentence, he felt a desperate impulse to speak with Yamaki. Farnsworth waited until late before slipping into the night. Agents watched as he walked swiftly toward Yamaki's hotel and entered through the back entrance. They now had their man but wanted more evidence.

In late 1936 the FBI accumulated enough incriminating material to arrest Farnsworth on charges of espionage. Believing he was about to be arrested for espionage, he tried to preempt the FBI by selling a phony story for $20,000 to journalist Fulton Lewis, Jr. He told Lewis that he had pretended to be a spy for the Japanese in the hope that his efforts might lead to reinstatement in the navy. Lewis refused to buy the story.

On February 23, 1937, Farnsworth was sentenced to 4–12 years in federal prison. Once released, he vanished, never to be seen again.

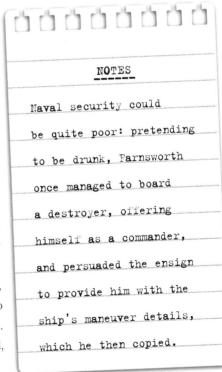

NOTES

Naval security could be quite poor: pretending to be drunk, Farnsworth once managed to board a destroyer, offering himself as a commander, and persuaded the ensign to provide him with the ship's maneuver details, which he then copied.

FOOTE, ALEXANDER (1905–1958)

During World War II, Alexander Foote spied on Germany for the Soviets and became the conduit for collecting and passing some of the Wehrmacht's most carefully guarded secrets to Moscow.

Born in 1905 to a poor, working-class family in Liverpool, England, Alexander Foote never knew if there would be food on the table. He wore secondhand clothes, quit school at an early age, and drifted from one menial job to another. Disaffected by a hopeless lifestyle, he became involved with left-wing political groups but never joined the British Communist Party. During the early 1930s, he volunteered for the RAF and then deserted. He joined a pro-Communist British battalion in the International Brigade, which was fighting General Francisco Franco's effort to overthrow and replace the legal government of Spain with a fascist government. A few months before the Spanish Civil War ended in 1939, Foote took leave and returned to England.

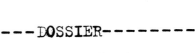

```
-----DOSSIER--------
Name: Alexander Foote
Code Names: Jim, Major
Granatov
Birth/Death: 1905-1958
Nationality: British
Occupation: British Soldier
Involvement: British Spy
for the Soviets
Outcome: Died of Natural
Causes
```

The Woman Named Sonia

In mid-1939, soon after arriving in London, Foote fell in with a Soviet agent who informed him that he had been chosen for a dangerous mission abroad.

Without asking for particulars, Foote agreed to do it. The agent handed him travel fare, gave him passwords, and told him to go at once to Geneva, Switzerland. After he arrived, he was to go to the post office, where he would meet a woman.

Foote followed instructions and waited outside Geneva's main post office until a woman walked up and exchanged passwords. Over coffee in a nearby café, she identified herself as Ursula-Maria Hamburger and told Foote he must use her code name, "Sonia." Her real name was Ruth Kuczynski, and she was the German-Jewish daughter of an economist who had fled to England to escape from the Nazis.

After several days and more meetings, she handed Foote a packet of coded instructions, expense money, and sent him on a three-month mission to Munich to spy on German politicians. He returned on schedule and delivered a packet of intelligence to Sonia, who

Left: Foote was the only British agent in the Rote Drei Soviet spy ring, and even after he had defected to the British, he was approached by Jean Pierre Vigier, a fellow member, for a meeting. It was thought that Russia didn't realize that his cover had, in fact, been blown.

APPENDIX B.

FOOTE's STATEMENT ON HIS CODE.

1. The code used by me for all my communications with MOSCOW was handed to me towards the end of 1940 by SONIA and was based on the word FINGER as follows:-

00 F	3 I	6 N	40 G	8 E	9 R
1 A	03 B	06 C	41 D	44 H	47 J
01 K	04 L	07 M	7 O	45 P	48 Q
2 S	5 T	08 U	42 V	46 W	49 X
02 Y	05 Z	09 Signal	43 .		

2. As will be seen, all letters not forming part of the word "FINGER", follow in sequence in horizontal lines. The letters A, S, T, N, O, E, R take the single numbers 1 to 9, 4 being excluded. All numbers run vertically starting from the top left hand corner. The signal (09) denotes change from text to numbers in the message (as below). All numbers being written in triplicate.

JI M (Key Group)		.T H	E Q U	I C K
47307	77109	43544	84808	30601
21320		64302	67861	13067
68627				

BROW	N FO	X JU	M P	SO VE
03974	66007	49470	80745	27428
43206				
46170				

R LAZ	Y D	O G .	NR .SIG	1 3
90410	50241	74143	69430	91113
			31206	
			90636	

6	.	(Key Group)	.	
33666	43434	21665	34343	77989

3. All telegrams sent by me always had JIM at the beginning of the message. All messages from MOSCOW to me were also headed JIM, but were signed "DIRECTOR".

4. The code book used by me from March 1941 to about July 1943 had formerly been that of SONIA, and was the Statistical Handbook of Foreign Trade for 1938, published by H.M. Stationary Office. From July 1943 until my arrest my code book was the Swiss Hand-Book of Trade Statistics for 1939.

5. Numbers were taken from this book and added to <u>the cyphered</u> text in order to close the message.

6. The numbers taken from the code-book always commenced at the third cypher of the numbers in the column chosen, as follows:

Third
cypher

21320 6
shown on
know what
message,

To this is
the end of
cyphered te

This group w
cyphered mes
cyphered, I
time on inst
sixth or seve

7. A key group
from the end
the last grou

8. A final group

Grou
19

These numbers

- 2 -

Col.3   Page 168

94320   7302   43671   94306
4321   3206   4302   67861
42861   43261   67801   13467

, which are added to the cyphered text as
...er that the recipient of the telegram may
...een taken from the code-book to close the
...made up as follows:-

            Col: Line:

             3   02

...hen the number of the page
...e 99, the first cypher was
...s it was always the custom
...a cable where the last one
...hed in the code-book.

...ant group, which in my case from March 1941 to
73737, together with the fifth group of the
...osing numbers as follows:-

...Page, column, line.

...Constant number

...Fifth Group etc.

...tal - Key group

...ween the first and second groups of the
...on Page 1. (For the greater part of cables
...a group as stated above, but from time to
...MOSCOW, other groups were used such as the

...tructed, except the fifth (?) group is taken
...and this completed key group is placed before
...e as shown on Page 1.

...age, column, line.

...nstant group.

...fth group from the end.

...he end of the completed cable as follows:-

... Nr: Date
...56   2

...he first group of the telegram as follows:-

+ NOTE When the cable contained more
than 99 groups, and the telegram Nr.
was higher than the same figure, the
last two cyphers of the number only
are used, and always only the last
figure of the date.

scanned it and threw it away. The mission had been a test. Foote began working in Lausanne as Sonia's radio operator. She taught him how to use codes, transmit and receive information, and perform incidental espionage missions. When the Soviets sent Sonia to England in 1940, Foote went back to Geneva to work for Hungarian Communist Sandor Alexander Rado, a careless agent who supervised the spy ring in Switzerland.

The Man They Call Jim

Because the war had become complicated by Germany's invasion of France, Rado received instructions from Moscow to stop sending intelligence by courier and to use only wireless. Rado collected information from spies in Germany and turned it over to Foote, alias Jim, for transmission to Moscow. Most of the information came from Rachel Duebendorfer, code-named Sissy, and Christian Schneider, code-named Taylor. Schneider's information came out of Germany through Rudolf Roessler, perhaps the most effective spy in World War II and the man called "Lucy." Roessler's source came from deep in the Wehrmacht. He consistently provided German military plans far in advance of their execution. American and British intelligence analysts believed the information came through Admiral Wilhelm Canaris, head of the Abwehr, who had been secretly working to undermine Hitler since 1933.

For Foote, life in Switzerland during the war went smoothly until 1943, when two Soviet agents, George and Joanna Wilmer, defected to the Germans and exposed Rado's network. Heinrich Himmler put pressure on the Swiss government to shut down Jim's transmissions. Foote operated

Opposite: Shown here are the codes that Foote used in all his transmissions. Upon his defection to the British, Foote provided full statements and instructions so that his information could be verified.

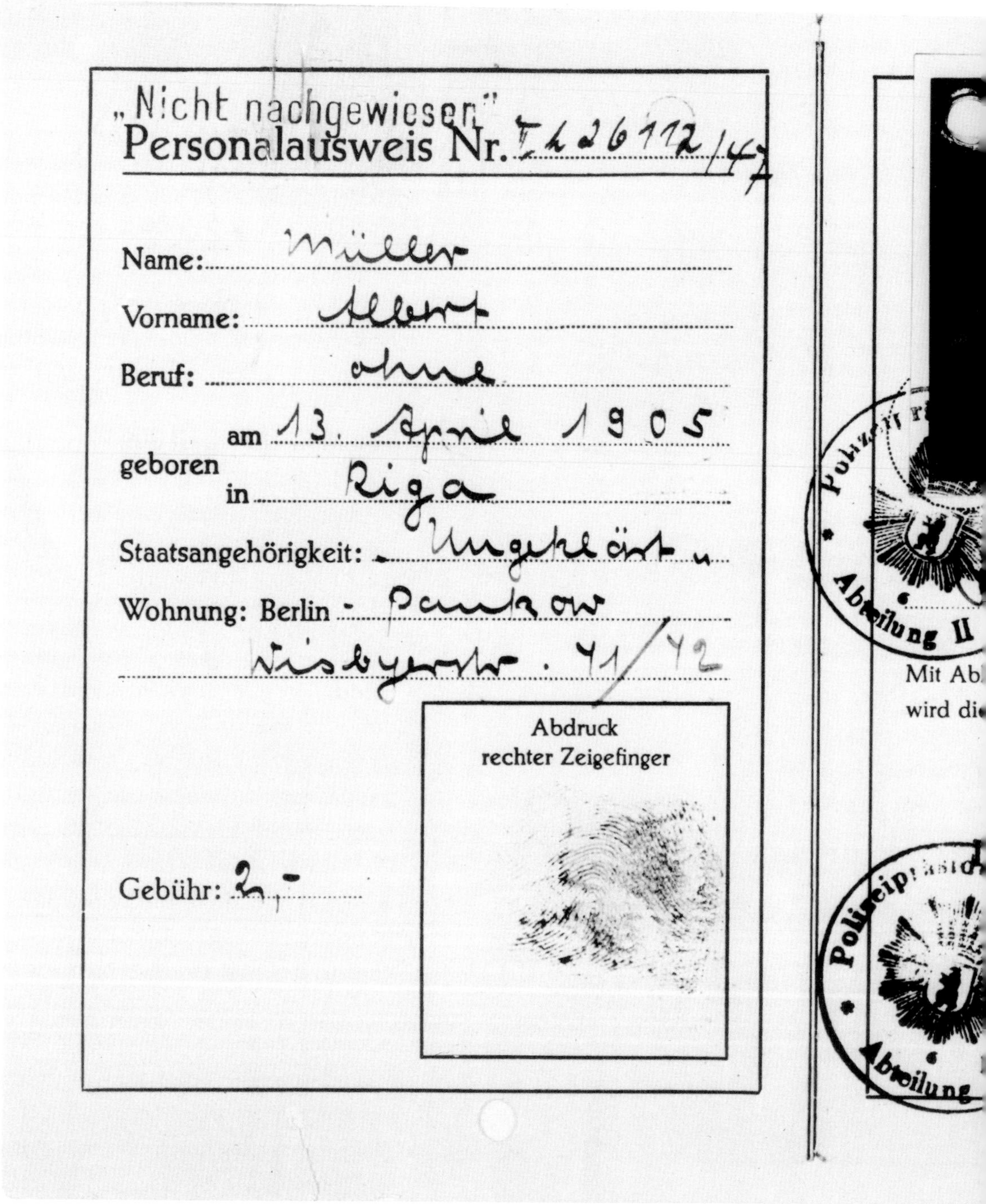

Right: A copy of Foote's false German passport. Documents were a major concern to Alexander Foote. He described many documents prepared during World War II as being in many instances "beneath contempt" and "veritable death warrants to their unhappy holders." The nature of espionage, however, made false documentation a matter of prime importance.

"Nicht nachgewiesen"
Personalausweis Nr. _____

Name: _Müller_

Vorname: _Albert_

Beruf: _ohne_

geboren am _13. April 1905_
in _Riga_

Staatsangehörigkeit: _Ungeklärt_

Wohnung: Berlin - _Pankow_
Visbyerstr. 41/42

Abdruck
rechter Zeigefinger

Gebühr: _2,-_

the wireless from his home on Chemin de Longeraie and on November 19, 1943, during his regular report, Swiss agents began pounding on his door. Instead of answering, Foote threw all his codebooks and documents in the trash, set them on fire, and destroyed his wireless set, seconds before the police broke through the door.

Interrogated for days by Swiss police, Foote said nothing. After ten months in jail, the police offered to release him in exchange for his admission that he had been working for Moscow. Foote refused to discuss the matter, but the police released him on bail in exchange for his promise to be available for trial. Foote paid a fine of 2,400 francs for his freedom, evaded surveillance, crossed the border into France, and joined Rado in Paris.

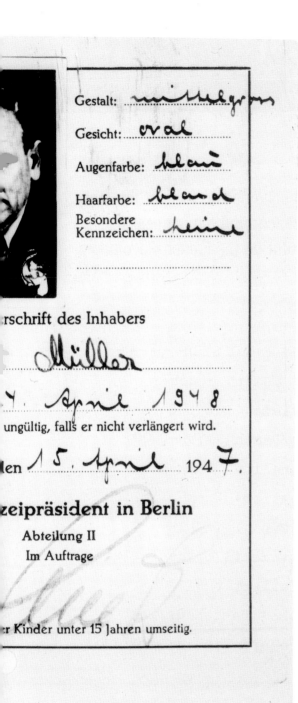

Gestalt: mittelgr...

Gesicht: oval

Augenfarbe: blau

Haarfarbe: blond

Besondere
Kennzeichen: keine

...rschrift des Inhabers

Müller

7. April 1948

ungültig, falls er nicht verlängert wird.

...en 15. April 1947.

...zeipräsident in Berlin

Abteilung II

Im Auftrage

...r Kinder unter 15 Jahren umseitig.

Revelations of a Spy

Foote arrived in Paris at a bad time. Rado's mistress, Margaret Bolli, had compromised him by unknowingly having sexual relations with an Abwehr agent who had kidnapped her. Rado contacted Moscow and received instructions to leave immediately with Foote for the Soviet capital. Because German forces controlled sections of Russia, Rado and Foote had to fly to Cairo to avoid war zones. On January 6, 1945, a Soviet warplane picked up the two passengers in Paris and flew them to Cairo. When the plane landed, Rado went into the men's room and vanished.

Foote continued on to Moscow, professed his loyalty to the Soviet cause, and asked for another assignment. The GRU did not normally put agents back into the field for five years, but in 1947 the center suddenly decided to insert a spy network into Argentina. Foote was already trained and available. The GRU gave Foote a new identity, Major Granatov, and flew him to Berlin to catch a commercial flight to Buenos Aires.

After two years in Moscow, Foote decided that his choice to move to mother Russia was a bad one. Once he reached Berlin, Foote slipped away from his Soviet aides and took a cab to the British sector. Because he had never harmed the English by spying against Germany for Russia, MI6 released him. Foote returned to England where he spent the rest of his life working in the Ministry of Agriculture and Fisheries.

After Foote's return to civilian life, the theory was put forward that he had been recruited by British intelligence in 1936 and pulled out of the RAF to become a double agent. The evidence to back this proposition is, however, inconclusive, and it is mostly believed that Foote was working for the Soviets all along.

NOTES

MI6 documents indicate that by 1947 Foote was very short of money, and sent pleading letters to the agency. MI6 helped him by enouraging him to write an account of his activities, and so in 1949 *A Handbook for Spies* was published.

FOUCHÉ, JOSEPH (1759–1820)

During the Napoleonic era, Joseph Fouché became one of the most feared and despised men in France, committing unspeakable atrocities against suspected loyalists during the French Revolution.

Born in Nantes, France, on May 31, 1759, to a seafaring family, Joseph Fouché wanted a life less harsh. His parents insisted that he dedicate his life to the Catholic Church and sent him to study with the Order of the Oratorians.

Fouché joined the order in the preliminary degrees, and then became a teacher of physics and mathematics and an inspector of schools. Such mundane work, however, never appealed to Fouché. One day he met Maximilien de Robespierre and Lazare Carnot, who talked to him of the principles of revolution and, in 1789, Fouché found his true vocation as a radical. In 1790 the order sent him to Nantes in an effort to keep him away from revolutionary ideas. However, he renounced his orders, joined the Jacobin Club, and soon assumed the chairmanship. The Jacobins noticed that people listened when Fouché talked, and in 1792 he was elected as a delegate to the National Convention in Paris, an organization dedicated to deposing the king and taking control of the government.

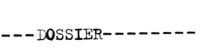

```
-----DOSSIER--------
Name: Joseph Fouché
Code Name: Duc D'Otrante
Birth/Death: 1759-1820
Nationality: French
Occupation: French Police
Minister
Involvement: Spymaster and
Revolutionist
Outcome: Banished from
France and Died in Poverty
```

A Thirst for Power

Fouché went to the National Convention to be heard and to act. When he demanded that King Louis XVI be executed, he noted the opposition and led punitive expeditions into their towns. He arrested opponents without explanation and killed them.

Fouché found that killing brought him power and on January 21, 1793, he derived immense satisfaction as he watched the guillotine remove the head of Louis XVI. By then he had already become the second-most feared man in France. The only person holding more power and influence was Fouché's sponsor and mentor Robespierre, the leader of the Reign of Terror. Robespierre, however, soon became a man in the way. Fouché led the plot to unseat the most powerful man in France and watched again with satisfaction as the guillotine decapitated his number-one rival.

Napoleon's Police Chief

After disposing of Robespierre, Fouché swung his support to Napoleon Bonaparte, France's next strongman and leader. The emperor needed somebody like Fouché to curb civil disturbance made him minister of police in 1799. To help carry out his police work, Fouché hired the dregs of society, most of whom were criminals and cutthroats, out to enrich themselves at the expense of the monarch-loving nobility and well-to-do middle class.

But Emperor Bonaparte wanted more than a police force: he wanted an intelligence network organized to spy on the public and root out dissenters. Who better to ask to put such an organization in place than his police chief?

Fouché accepted the task with enthusiasm. He contacted the men he had thrown into prison and informed them that their police records would be expunged if they agreed to work as spies. When Fouché required more spies, he compromised honest men by tricking them into committing petty crimes. Then he then gave them a choice: they could go to jail or work for him as spies.

Fouché's espionage network succeeded in driving most of the nobility out of France. Refugees left great wealth behind, much of which lined the pockets of Fouché and his lieutenants. If anyone in France protested, the guillotine settled the issue. Napoleon approved of Fouché's tactics. He was often in the field, and needed a powerful man to keep France under control.

Counterintelligence

Sometime during his second term as minister of police (1804–1810), Fouché expanded the espionage network by recruiting a new brand of spies, this time for counterintelligence work. They infiltrated the army to spy on everyone from the newest recruit to Napoleon's grand marshals. Fouché even put double agents into the army to spy on his spies. Some were Irishmen who had no love for English monarchs and had drifted into France. The system worked so well

Fouché developed the Test of Fidelity, under which his henchmen chose men who had committed crimes but had not yet been punished, and in exchange for a clean record, became spies.

> Fouché understood the nature of the people he hired as spies. He raised their performance to a level unprecedented in the history of espionage in any country up to his time.

in the army that he added double agents to his police force to spy on spies employed to watch the civilian population. Fouché trusted no one. Conscious of the tactics he used to gain power, Fouché constantly worried that somebody with his ambitions would do to him exactly what he had done to others.

Fouché stopped at nothing to gain information. He deluded the public with propaganda; he disarmed suspects with disinformation; and when bribery, coercion, kidnapping, and torture failed, he resorted to the guillotine. He maintained up-to-date files on everyone—friends and potential enemies alike—and he dutifully kept the emperor informed on political enemies. In 1809 Fouché began falling out of favor with the public but Napoleon rewarded the spymaster's fidelity and propped him up by making him Duke of Otranto.

The Plot That Failed

By 1810 Fouché could see French support slipping away from Napoleon. He began looking out for himself, and Napoleon began to hear troubling rumors about his police chief's activities. Behind Napoleon's back, Fouché secretly contacted Louis XVIII, who was in exile. He attempted to ingratiate himself with the monarch should Napoleon fall. Meanwhile, Napoleon grew suspicious, removed Fouché from the ministry of police, and sent him to Naples, Italy, as a diplomat.

In 1814, after Napoleon's abdication and exile to Elba, Fouché rushed back to Paris to seek a high post in government from Louis XVIII. Fouché received a stinging rebuff because in 1792 he had voted to execute the king's grandfather.

Napoleon escaped from Elba, raised an army, and in 1815 returned to France and seized power. Fouché once again tried to get back into police work; when he succeeded he tried to persuade Napoleon to popularize his rule. However, at the Battle of Waterloo, Napoleon lost the Hundred Days' War, his army, and his reputation. Fouché went back to Louis XVIII and urged him to exile Napoleon. He promised to hunt down Bonapartists if the king reinstated him as minister of police. This time the king consented, but the job did not last.

Royalist extremists, still unreconciled over the execution of Louis XVI and the Reign of Terror that followed, reminded the king repeatedly of Fouché's treachery. Louis relented and ordered Fouché's arrest. Tried and convicted for implication in the execution of Louis XVI, Fouché was banished from France.

Fouché wandered across Europe, carrying with him his reputation for evil and terror, until he ran out of money. On Christmas Day, 1820, the owner of a rooming house in Trieste found him dead.

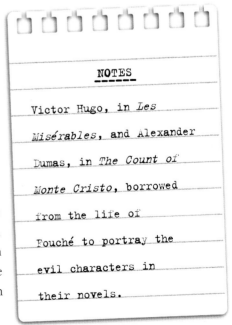

NOTES

Victor Hugo, in *Les Misérables*, and Alexander Dumas, in *The Count of Monte Cristo*, borrowed from the life of Fouché to portray the evil characters in their novels.

FUCHS, KLAUS (1911–1988)

By turning over America's atomic secrets to the Soviets in 1945, German-born British scientist Klaus Fuchs became the most damaging spy in circulation during the mid-twentieth century.

Klaus Fuchs grew up in Beerfelden, Germany, near Heidelberg, where his father, Emil Fuchs, served the local Lutheran church as pastor and ran his home like an extension of the sanctuary. The elder Fuchs despised Adolf Hitler's hostility toward the church, and he transferred that same loathing to his son. As a child, young Fuchs developed strong moral character, bringing his father's anti-Nazi predispositions with him into manhood. After entering the university at Kiel, he joined the Communist Party because he hated fascism. When Hitler became chancellor in 1933, Fuchs moved to England to complete his education. Having a brilliant mind for physics and math, he received his PhD in Bristol and his ScD in Edinburgh.

```
----DOSSIER--------
Name: Klaus Fuchs
Code Name: None
Birth/Death: 1911-1988
Nationality: German
Occupation: Physicist
Involvement: Spied for the
Soviet Union
Outcome: Imprisoned,
Released, and Died in East
Germany
```

The Making of a Spy

Throughout his postgraduate years, Fuchs continued his membership in the Communist Party. After Great Britain went to war against Germany, agents erroneously arrested Fuchs as a German spy and sent him to an internment camp in Canada. While suffering in miserable conditions among other detainees, Fuchs became vulnerable. When approached by a friendly Soviet agent, he agreed to share with Russia any secrets, should England someday hire him to work as a physicist. Meanwhile in England, officials reviewed

Name	EMIL JULIUS KLAUS FUCHS, with aliases Dr. Karl Fuchs, Klaus Fuchs, Klaus Emil Fuchs
Residence	Wormwood Scrubs Prison, England
Occupation	Research physicist
Description	
Born	12/29/11 Russelsheim, Germany
Citizenship	Naturalized British citizen
height	5'11"
Build	Thin
Complexion	Dark and sallow
Hair	Brown, receding at temples and decidedly balding
Eyes	Brown (wears glasses)
Features	Medium, high forehead given to wrinkling when in thought or study, cleanshaven. Has noticeable vein running from left eye level across temple level of hair line.

Fuchs's file, discovered the young man's anti-Nazi sentiments, and decided they had made a horrible mistake. Great Britain had a severe shortage of physicists and apologized to Fuchs. In 1942, as a consolation, the government offered him a good job working on scientific projects. Fuchs accepted the apology and the offer and returned to England. When University of Birmingham professor Rudolf Peierls, also a German refugee,

learned that his former friend was back in England, he requested Fuchs.

Peierls and others were fully engaged in atomic bomb research when Fuchs joined the team. The former detainee received security clearance and, because of the nature of the work, mandatory British citizenship. With the ink on his papers barely dry, Fuchs traveled to the Soviet Embassy in London and contacted Semion Kremer, the military attaché.

Opposite: S.O.E. file note on Fuchs. Despite providing information to the Soviets that was of considerably greater significance than what the Rosenbergs divulged, he received a far lighter sentence: 14 years imprisonment, rather than the death sentence given to the Rosenbergs.

Left: Recently released files from MI5 revealed that Fuchs was convinced that he would not be prosecuted for his espionage, even after he was unmasked as a spy, because he was indispensable to the program to build the British bomb.

Below: Klaus Fuchs, left, walks across the tarmac at Schoenefeld Airport, East Berlin, on June 23, 1959, accompanied by his nephew, Klaus Kittowski. Fuchs had recently been released from Wakefield Prison after serving nine and a half years of a 14-year sentence.

During the meeting, Fuchs promised to hand over secrets on atomic research. He morally and naively believed that because the Soviets were allies, fighting the Nazis, that they had the right to know what the United States and Great Britain were doing to develop an atomic bomb. Fuchs worked at the university for 18 months. At the end of each month, he sent a handwritten copy of his report to the Soviet Embassy.

Fuchs in America

In 1944 Fuchs transferred to New York City and joined the staff of scientists working on atomic energy at Columbia University. Before leaving London, Fuchs received instructions on how to meet his new Soviet contact. On a specific day on a specific street corner in downtown Manhattan, Fuchs connected with Harry Gold. Over the next year he turned over

TOP SECRET

Appendix B,
568 C

SUMMARY OF INFORMATION OBTAINED FROM DR. FUCHS REGARDING

HIS ESPIONAGE CONTACTS.

1. Recruitment.

FUCHS states that at the beginning of 1942 he decided voluntarily to inform the Russians of his work with the Atomic Energy research team at Birmingham University. He consulted an alien Communist friend who agreed to put him into contact with a Russian but who played no part in the subsequent meetings. The initial meeting took place in London at a house south of Hyde Park.

2. Espionage contacts.

(a) 1942 - November 1943.

FUCHS' first contact has been identified as Simon KREMER, then Secretary to the Soviet Military Attache in London. On one occasion they met at the Soviet Embassy in London. Later during this period KREMER was replaced by an unidentified woman who met FUCHS near Banbury. No more than six meetings took place during these two years.

(b) 1944 - 1945.

During this period FUCHS was in the U.S.A. Details of his activities there have been supplied to the F.B.I.

(c) 1946.

FUCHS states that he deliberately neglected the pre-arranged meeting in London.

(d) 1947 - 1949.

FUCHS states that in early 1947 he decided to resume contact with the Russians and attempted to locate the alien Communist friend (who had first introduced him) through a mutual foreign Communist acquaintance, a woman. Failing to locate him he admitted to the woman his reasons for wishing to do so and she agreed to help. Through her he met a man, probably a Russian, with whom he remained in contact until February 1949, when he made a forward rendez-vous for June 1949 which he deliberately failed to keep. That, he states, ended his contact with the Russians and he knows of no attempt on their part to re-open the liaison.

3. Rendez-vous and Methods of Making Contact.

Meetings were usually at intervals of two to three months and each rendez-vous was arranged at the previous meeting; the arrangements allowed for alternatives to meet unforeseen difficulties. Normally, therefore, all communication about meetings was oral.

/Rendez-vous

TOP SECRET

Left: File notes from Fuchs's interrogation. Fuchs's motivation to pass information to the Soviets was due to his "unswerving devotion to Communism."

hundreds of pages of handwritten notes detailing the research on how to manufacture, test, and explode a nuclear device. It may never have occurred to Fuchs that if the Allies wanted the Soviets to have the data, they would have made it available.

As the Colombia research team expanded into other uses of nuclear energy, the government transferred Fuchs to Los Alamos, New Mexico, to work on the "Manhattan Project," the actual construction of the bomb. Wherever Fuchs went, Gold followed, and when Fuchs

Right: Notes from Fuchs of his meetings where he passed information to his contacts. During his work at Harwell, he compartmentalized his life between his beliefs and his necessity for friends and personal relations. He admitted in his court statement that "the best way of expressing it seems to be to call it a controlled schizophrenia." In passing sentence at Fuchs's trial, Chief Justice Lord Goddard said: "You have betrayed the hospitality and protection given to you by this country with the grossest treachery."

TOP SECRET

Notes by FUCHS on Contacts and Meetings.

Meetings.

First Contact. London. Meetings arranged to suit my convenience. Usually week-ends. Evenings. First meeting in house. Later in street, quiet residential street, or busy bus stop. Contact left and arrived on foot, but on one occasion he had left private car in neighbouring street. Location different each time. Information consisted primarily in spare copies of my own papers, which at that time I was typing myself. In envelope or wrapped in packing paper.

Second Contact. Always country road just outside Banbury. (On one occasion she came to Birmingham and we met in cafe opposite Snow Hill Station.) Week-ends. Time arranged to suit trains from Birmingham. Usually afternoon. Information as above, though later I used original manuscript. Contact arrived and left by train.

Third Contact. New York. In street. Evening. Date arranged to suit his convenience. Place varied each time. Sometimes lonely street, sometimes busy square. Usually Manhattan. Would arrive and leave on foot. Information as above. Would walk from meeting place through streets.

Boston. Busy street, somewhat off the main centre. Mixed residential and business. Arrived and left on foot. Don't remember second place. Time between two meetings probably a day. Information: Notes written between two meetings.

Santa Fé . One meeting in quiet street along river. One in country lane just outside town. I picked him up in my car and drove along lonely country roads. Date arranged to suit him. Arrived and left Sant Fé by bus. Obviously had difficulty to arrange meetings. Informationl Notes, handwritten or typed?

Fourth Contact. London. Usually varied between two places, both pubs. Would follow him from pub and meet in side streets and stroll through streets. Arrived and left on foot. Had certainly associates near-by since he would take papers away and re-appear in a few minutes. They probably watched for me, since he used to appear always a few minutes after myself and they may have watched whether we were followed. I think they had a car to take papers away. Usually Saturday evening at my convenience. Was prepared to meet me anywhere else (Didcot, Reading), if I wished. Pressed again at last meeting that I should suggest place where we could meet more often, perhaps on Sunday morning in a place I could reach by car. Information: handwritten or typed notes, sometimes manuscripts. In envelope or package.

Contact two told me to take precautions not to be followed, such as taking several taxis in succession. I assured him I knew how to make sure and I never received any instructions thereafter from any of the contacts, but on many occasions admonitions.

arranged only   I remember only two outside meetings with No.1. One was/for purpose of handing over papers. We met on bus stop, boarded bus, took seats on top side by side and he soon left. On the second occasion he took me from the meeting place to his car and we cruised through dark streets in residential area.

Contact 2, I thought had underground experience, but since all but one of the meetings were in country it is not so easy to judge.

Contacts 3 and 4 I thought had no underground experience, an impression which was mainly due to the very obvious manner in which they looked back to see whether we were being followed.

TOP SECRET

witnessed the test explosion of the first atomic bomb at Los Alamos, the Soviets heard about it before anyone else. A few weeks later, the *Enola Gay* flew over Hiroshima and scorched the city, announcing the discovery of the A-bomb to the rest of the world.

When the news of the blast reached Los Alamos, the engineers who had been working on the Manhattan Project decided to celebrate. Fuchs volunteered to drive into Santa Fe and buy the liquor. There, he met Harry Gold at a bar and handed him all the details he had compiled on how to build the bomb and detonate it without losing years in research. Gold took the papers and Fuchs never saw him again.

The Soviet Misstep

Fuchs returned to England in 1946 and joined the staff of atomic scientists at the British research center at Harwell, where he worked for Dr. Cockroft. He could have considered his business with the Soviets finished, but he went to the Soviet Embassy and continued feeding the attaché information on thermonuclear developments. Ruth Kuczynski, alias Sonia, became his contact. In 1939 she headed the Soviet spy ring in Switzerland and had engaged Alexander Foote as her radio operator. Sonia pressed Fuchs too hard. In 1947, after the iron curtain descended, he concluded that he may have made a mistake and terminated contacts with the Soviets.

Fuchs might have remained a renowned scientist at Harwell had the FBI not initiated a massive campaign in the United States to round up Soviet agents. During the sweep in 1949, agents picked up an associate of Harry Gold, who bragged about how a brilliant British

physicist had helped the Soviets obtain the secrets to the atomic bomb. The FBI informed British counterintelligence (MI5), and Fuchs became the number-one suspect. The German physicist knew he was in trouble and unburdened himself to MI5 interrogator William Skardon. During his testimony, Fuchs told what he knew about Soviet activity in the United States. His statements led to the arrest of Harry Gold, who implicated David Greenglass, who gave up Julius and Ethel Rosenberg.

Tried and sentenced to 14 years in Wormwood Scrubs prison, Fuchs served nine years as the facility's librarian. Released in 1959, he went immediately to East Germany, where the Soviets put him in charge of nuclear research at Dresden. Nothing more was ever heard of Fuchs until 1988, when he died of natural causes.

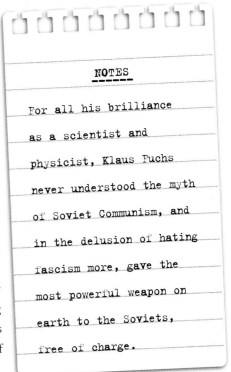

NOTES

For all his brilliance as a scientist and physicist, Klaus Fuchs never understood the myth of Soviet Communism, and in the delusion of hating fascism more, gave the most powerful weapon on earth to the Soviets, free of charge.

FURUSAWA, TAKASHI (1891–1945)

The investigation of Dr. Takashi Furusawa began with a locked briefcase containing secret U.S. documents and ended with the sneak attack on Pearl Harbor.

Little is known about the background of Dr. Takashi Furusawa other than in 1930 he opened and owned a small, private nursing home at 117 Weller Street in Los Angeles, California, which also served as his home. Nobody suspected him of any mischief until an October day in 1933, when he discovered that a young Japanese language student named Torii had been knocked down by a car and killed on a Los Angeles street.

Torii's personal documents, in addition to giving his name, revealed that he was also a lieutenant commander in the Imperial Japanese Navy. This by itself aroused no suspicion because many Japanese officers came to California to learn the English language, but a call from Dr. Furusawa stirred the curiosity of Los Angeles police.

```
----DOSSIER--------
Name: Dr. Takashi Furusawa
Code Name: None
Birth/Death: 1891-1945
Nationality: Japanese
Occupation: Physician
and Surgeon
Involvement: Spied in the
U.S. for Japan
Outcome: Died in an Air
Raid in 1945
```

The Mysterious Briefcase

When police arrived on the scene of the accident, they picked up Torii's locked briefcase and returned to the station,

intending to prepare a statement for the coroner, notify the Japanese consul, and hand over the body. Before much could be done, the police received a telephone call from Dr. Furusawa, who had heard the news on the radio and said he was a

After Mrs. Furusawa married the doctor, she founded the Los Angeles Branch of the Women's Patriotic Society of Japan with headquarters at 7425 Franklin Avenue, the official residence of the Japanese consul.

friend. Furusawa asked if Torii was carrying a briefcase, and the police answered in the affirmative. Furusawa then asked if it was locked, and the police said it was and they would turn it over to the Japanese legation in the morning.

When the police detected a noticeable sigh of relief from the caller, they began to wonder why the doctor regarded the briefcase with more importance than his colleague, Torii. The police tripped the lock on the briefcase, discovered classified documents from the U.S. government, and called the FBI.

Agents arrived with cameras, photographed the documents, but found nothing in the briefcase posing a threat to American security. They put the documents back in the briefcase, locked it, and posted agents to learn how Dr. Furusawa, a respected physician and surgeon, became involved.

The FBI began to dig into the doctor's background and discovered that he had graduated from Stanford University. While in school, he met his wife, Sachiko, who worked as a waitress in Little Tokyo, the Japanese quarter of San Francisco. Agents noted that she was a lovely, artic-ulate woman with a delightful personality and a keen mind. With a little more digging, they discovered that at the age of 15, Sachiko had married a much older man, and finding his views of life much different from hers, ran off to San Francisco.

Five years later she fell in love, divorced her husband, and married Furusawa. The happy pair now spent a considerable amount of their time with officials and military attachés at the Japanese consulate and had become active in Japanese-American social and fraternal groups.

Who Is Doctor Furusawa?

Background checks still failed to explain the doctor's interest in Torii's briefcase. The FBI looked into the doctor's nursing home and found it well-equipped and well-staffed. Although Furusawa had been in business for three years, there was no evidence he ever had a bed patient, yet many Japanese and other visitors came and went.

One day Count Hermann von Keitel, a high-ranking officer in the Abwehr,

FBI agents tracking Dr. Furusawa noted his frequent visits to an exclusive and private German nightclub on 5 East 66th Street, where he received admittance without question.

> The FBI tracked Mrs. Furusawa and noticed that when the doctor's guests re-embarked for Japan, she would carry one briefcase after another onto the ship but always return to shore empty-handed.

arrived, and during his stay dozens of Japanese came and went over a two-day span. The FBI recognized Keitel immediately, and agents also identified some of the Japanese visitors as suspected spies from the East Coast.

The FBI considered that the numerous visitors were, in fact, delivering secret documents from all over the country to either Keitel or Furusawa, or both. After further investigation, the FBI came to believe that Keitel, who had recently been employed with the German vice-consul in New York, was not only obtaining reports from Furusawa, but he was also delivering intelligence on behalf of Japanese agents operating within China.

The FBI repeatedly asked the Department of Justice for permission to arrest the Furusawas and several others for espionage. They claimed to have collected enough information to bring down the entire German-Japanese espionage network. The question went all the way to President Franklin D. Roosevelt, who merely said that if the FBI shut down Furusawa's network, another would rise in its place, and that it was better to know who the spies were than to have to search for new ones.

Frustrated, the FBI continued to watch as Mrs. Furusawa hosted a regular flow of Japanese "visitors," arriving on Japanese ships at Los Angeles. She lavishly entertained the women while her husband talked business with the men at the nursing home. In November 1941, the guests stopped arriving and the others returned to Japan.

A Sudden Quiet Descends

The FBI warned the Department of Justice of the sudden, mysterious decrease in Japanese traffic and again requested permission to reel in the Furusawas and the rest of the network. Although the request was denied, agents remained on the job.

A few weeks before December 7, 1941, the day of the Japanese sneak attack on Pearl Harbor, FBI agents watched helplessly as the Furusawas departed from the nursing home in the dead of night with all their belongings. They drove to Long Beach, where they boarded a Japanese freighter. As the ship pulled away from the dock, Furusawa appeared on the deck. He looked down at the FBI agents standing in the shadows, walked into the light where he could clearly be seen, and mockingly waved.

According to an investigation conducted after the war, Dr. Furusawa lost his life during an air raid in 1945.

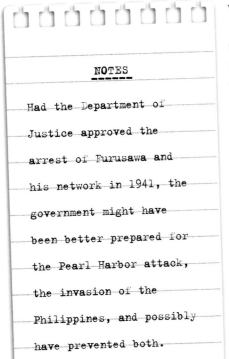

NOTES

Had the Department of Justice approved the arrest of Furusawa and his network in 1941, the government might have been better prepared for the Pearl Harbor attack, the invasion of the Philippines, and possibly have prevented both.

GIMPEL, ERICH (1910-?)

Despite being experienced, bright, and able to use his initiative, Erich Gimpel's simple assignment to cover a presidential election in the United States was thwarted by his partner's drunkenness and lack of commitment.

Born in Merseburg, Germany, Erich Gimpel became fascinated with radios at an early age. After graduating from high school, he studied high-frequency transformer technology and went into the radio business. At the age of 25 he joined Telefunken, the largest radio producer in Germany, which sent him to Peru as a technician.

As World War II approached, Gimpel returned to Germany to support Adolf Hitler's rise to power. In 1939 he enlisted with the Abwehr to become a spy and after espionage training went back to Lima, Peru, to keep the German legation informed on the arrival and departure of British shipping.

In 1942, when Peru joined the Allies, local agents interned all German spies, including Gimpel. He succeeded in being repatriated by claiming to be Swedish and eventually reached Hamburg. He found work in a radio factory, which Allied bombers promptly destroyed. So in 1943 he returned to the Abwehr and became a courier, carrying

```
----DOSSIER--------
Name: Erich Gimpel
Code Name: Edward George
Green
Birth/Death: 1910-?
Nationality: German
Occupation: Radio
Technician
Involvement: German Spy
in the United States
Outcome: Unknown
```

messages from the Wehrmacht through German-occupied France to President Francisco Franco in Madrid.

In early 1944, the Japanese wanted an increase in espionage activities in the United States, and asked Admiral Canaris of the Abwehr to provide the spies.

Canaris did nothing because he opposed Hitler and knew the war was a losing proposition. In February 1944 Hitler dismissed Canaris and turned German intelligence over to Heinrich Himmler.

Gimpel Gets a Partner

Himmler, who also headed the Gestapo and the SS, unsystematically picked two agents to gather U.S. intelligence, Gimpel and American-born William C. Colepaugh.

Colepaugh had a German-born mother who was a great supporter of her homeland, including Hitler. In 1942, after failing his courses at the Massachusetts Institute of Technology, he joined the merchant marine. In 1944, when the German vessel on which he was serving docked in Lisbon, Portugal, he jumped ship and enlisted in the Abwehr. It was there that Gimpel met Colepaugh.

As espionage operations go, Gimpel and Colepaugh's assignment was mostly created to appease the Japanese. After training in the Abwehr's spy school out-

Right: Uniformed military police escort Erich Gimpel (right foreground), and William C. Colepaugh (background) into court at Governors Island, NY, on March 3, 1945, for another trial session. Both were subsequently convicted as Nazi spies and sentenced to die by hanging.

Empire News 52A

27. Oct 1957

FROM THE PRESS SECTION.

I WAS a SPY

AS we drove through the night to Bangor, congratulating ourselves on our luck, a Boy Scout was blurting out a fantastic story to an unbelieving police sergeant —a story that should have resulted in arrest within our first half-hour in America.

I learned about it in court months later.

The Boy Scout had cycled past Billy and I as we were walking along the Ellsworth to Boston road, a few minutes before the taxi picked us up.

He was 15. He still believed in spies. We were carrying suitcases, and no one in America carries a suitcase, at any rate not on a remote country road.

We had no hats, and everyone in America wears a hat. We wore trench coats, while an American walking through a heavy snowstorm would have been wearing a thick overcoat.

To the 15-year-old boy we became objects of suspicion. He began searching for footprints and found them in the soft snow. He followed them with his torch, right back to the shore, and was rightly convinced we had come from a ship.

SAFE AT LAST

He dashed to the police station. The sergeant roared with laughter and told him to go home and get some sleep. The boy then went to the local F.B.I.

They listened in amusement then said: "There haven't been any spies here for a long time. It's only Boy Scouts who find spies. At the rate of 50 a day."

We knew nothing of all this, of course. The taxi took us to Bangor where we caught the midnight train to Portland and had breakfast in the station buffet.

I sat there repeating to myself: "My name is Edward Green. I am 35, honourably discharged from the American Navy on grounds of ill-health. I was born in Bridgeport, Connecticut . . . My name is Edward Green . . ."

When we arrived in New York we found a modest double bedroom in the Kenmore Hall Hotel on 33rd Street in Manhattan.

I was beginning to feel more secure. I was speaking fluently now and letting the devil take care of my accent.

Billy was enjoying the whisky, and the generous supply of pocket money (f . . . .)

A mystery girl gate-crashed my hide-out

● After crossing the Atlantic in a U-boat to sabotage the atom bomb project, German secret service agent Erich Gimpel has landed in America with his accomplice, renegade U.S. deserter Billy Colepaugh. As they trudge along the lonely coast road a taxi stops and picks them up.

by Erich Gimpel

industry. The . . . I drank a few more double wh . . es and went to bed.

I woke a . . . . ce.

you start lecturing me like a schoolmaster."

What was I to do? I needed him, but I couldn't chain him to me. Later, an F.B.I. man was to say to me: "You made one mistake . . . you should have given Billy a shot between the eyes as soon as you landed. . . ."

One afternoon as I walked into the hotel, the doorman stopped me: "Have you forgotten something?"

ALL GONE . . .

"I don't understand," I replied.

"BUT THE BILL HAS BEEN PAID. YOUR FRIEND SAW TO EVERYTHING. HE SAID YOU HAD ALREADY GONE." BILLY HAD FLOWN.

"What did he do with the luggage?" I asked.

"Two suitcases? He took them with him"

I gave the man a few cents and went into the street. The transmitter, revolvers, diamonds and dollars—all gone. If I didn't find Billy within the next few hours it would be all up with me.

"What would you do," I kept asking myself, "if you were in Billy's place? Leave New York, obviously. By train. One of the long-distance expresses."

I had a sudden flash of inspiration. Of course, Billy would have gone to the Grand Central Station. And he wouldn't stand on the platform with the suitcases. He'd hand them in at . . . . ce.

"I've just about had enough of your drinking!" I told Billy.

(A scene from the film "A Hatful of Rain"), found myself a bottle of whisky, and poured myself a drink.

Tomorrow I would contact "Mr. Brown," the New York businessman, whose address I had been given as a contact. The next day I might perhaps be in touch with the atomic people.

THE BLONDE

Billy? I felt sorry for him. He couldn't hold out long before the police caught him. If I found him first, I would have to shoot him. I couldn't depend on him and he had sentenced me to death first.

A light orchestra was playing on the radio. I enjoyed the music as I was enjoying the warmth, the feeling of well-being, the apartment and the whisky.

Suddenly my feeling of well-being deserted me. Footsteps were approaching the door. A key in the lock! I jumped up, I snatched my revolver and released the catch.

As my finger bent round the trigger, the door opened. It was a woman, tall, young and fair. She stood there, frightened at first, then she smiled at me: "Playing Indians?" she said.

I was on the threshold of the most ridiculous experience of my life.

Next Sunday
I go for a walk and meet trouble.

Above: After his release in 1955, Gimpel was repatriated to Germany, from where he moved to South America. In 1957, he published *Spy for Germany* in Great Britain, which was serialized in *Empire News*.

Opposite: Having arrived at Frenchman Bay, the U-boat surfaced just enough to expose its machine-gun platforms. The two spies' transport, a rubber boat, was pulled through the hatch and inflated on the bridge. Due to the weather conditions, Gimpel and Colepaugh were rowed ashore but once they landed on the beach a dog began to bark. They went back to the submarine to return with sausages.

side The Hague, Gimpel and Colepaugh were to go to America, accumulate information from newspapers and other public sources regarding the upcoming 1944 presidential campaign between President Franklin D. Roosevelt and Republican challenger Thomas E. Dewey, and transmit the commentaries back to Germany. In Germany, brighter minds than theirs would study the propaganda impact of the election campaign on Hitler's war effort. Gimpel would be in charge, handling camera and radio equipment, and Colepaugh would do the talking. Gimpel received the cover name Edward George Green,

and Colepaugh became William Charles Cauldwell.

The Abwehr's Bumbling Partnership

The two spies climbed aboard a German submarine at Kiel with $60,000 in new American currency and a pouch of diamonds to sell if they needed more money. For the Atlantic crossing, the pair wore German navy uniforms, which they traded for American-made clothes as they approached Frenchman Bay, Maine. Two German sailors paddled the pair ashore in a rubber boat during a snowstorm, dis-

Right: When arrested, Gimpel was taken to the New York FBI office where he was interviewed. During the interview he gave an account of his proposed work in the United States and explained about his equipment and how he was to carry out his mission. On instructions from the attorney general, the FBI turned both spies over to the military authorities, where they were charged with violation of the 82nd Article of War and conspiracy.

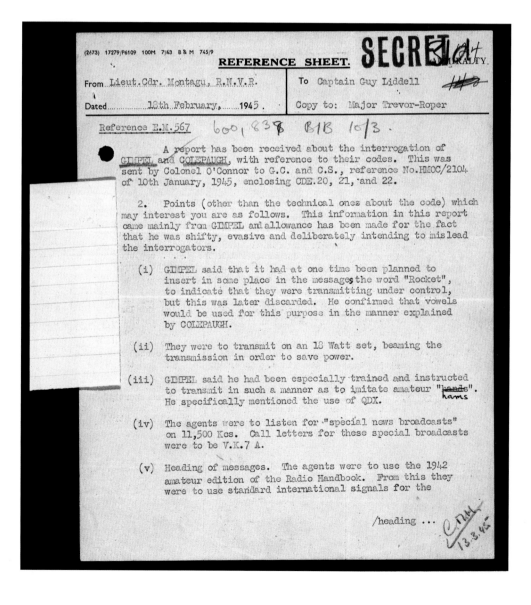

embarked them on Crabtree Point, and disappeared in the blizzard. Gimpel and Colepaugh made their way to Bangor, Maine, took a train to New York City via Boston, and settled in a hotel. After several days of enjoying the sights of the city, Gimpel suggested that they rent an inexpensive apartment and get down to business. Colepaugh argued that doing so was pointless, because the Abwehr had bungled the mission: the election was over and Roosevelt had won.

Committed to serving his country, Gimpel built a radio set and ordered Colepaugh to spy on ship activity in New York's harbor. Instead of going to the harbor, Colepaugh spent his days at movies, nightclubs, and brothels. When Gimpel demanded that Colepaugh perform his duties, the latter replied that Germany was going to lose the war and any information he collected would be useless. So why, Colepaugh asked, should he and Gimpel continue to behave like spies when they would be hanged if caught? The argument continued for several days, after which Colepaugh disappeared.

A Partnership Gone Bad

Finding it impossible to reason with Gimpel, Colepaugh visited a friend in Richmond, New York. He soon became drunk and waved a big bankroll of hundred-dollar bills. When asked where he got all the money, Colepaugh replied that he was a German spy. His friend called the FBI and agents arrived. When they arrested and questioned Colepaugh, he gave up Gimpel. The following day, agents apprehended Gimpel at a Times Square newsstand. At the time of their arrest, Gimpel and Colpaugh had been in the United States for 33 days.

THE NEW YORK TIMES, TUESDAY, JANUARY 2, 1945.

NAZI AGENTS SEIZED BY FBI

Erich Gimpel   William Colepaugh
The New York Times (FBI)

The partners faced a military tribunal on Governor's Island, New York. Throughout the trial, Gimpel said nothing. Colepaugh complained about how miserable his life had been in the United States and in Germany, and begged for clemency. The court found both men guilty of espionage and sentenced them to death by hanging. After President Roosevelt died, Harry S. Truman commuted the sentence to life in prison. Both men were later released and disappeared. In 2004 Gimpel surfaced in Brazil to celebrate his 94th birthday. Colepaugh used the business skills he learned in prison and launched a business career in Pennsylvania and now, in his mid-eighties, is retired nearby.

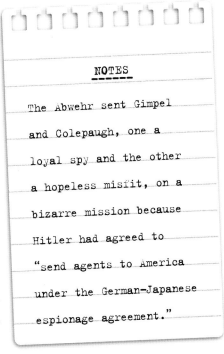

NOTES

The Abwehr sent Gimpel and Colepaugh, one a loyal spy and the other a hopeless misfit, on a bizarre mission because Hitler had agreed to "send agents to America under the German-Japanese espionage agreement."

GISKES, HERMANN J. (1896–?)

Few officers involved in counterespionage could compete with the skills of Hermann Giskes, who time and again devised the perfect strategies for ferreting out the agents of British intelligence.

Little is known of the early life of Hermann Giskes, other than he was born in the Rhineland to a Catholic family. After graduating from high school at the outbreak of World War I, he served in the German Alpine Corps. After the war he vigorously opposed the Communist coup in Germany and the establishment of a separate Rhenish Republic under French sponsorship. In 1924 he became a successful wine salesman and worked in the business for ten years. In 1934, after Adolf Hitler emerged as Germany's chancellor, Giskes rejoined the army as an officer. Three years later, the Abwehr recruited him as a spymaster, then in 1938 promoted him to major and sent him to The Hague in Holland.

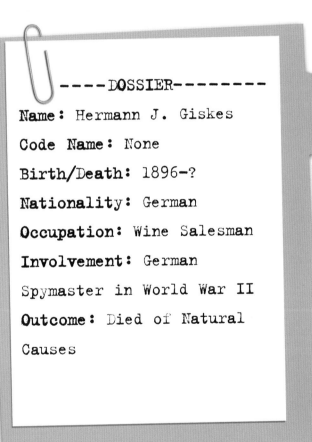

```
----DOSSIER--------
Name: Hermann J. Giskes
Code Name: None
Birth/Death: 1896-?
Nationality: German
Occupation: Wine Salesman
Involvement: German
Spymaster in World War II
Outcome: Died of Natural
Causes
```

Breaking Up British Intelligence

By 1938 The Hague had developed into one of the great international centers for espionage. British intelligence (MI6) spent 20 years building its Dutch network, and the Abwehr instructed Giskes to break it up.

In 1936 Captain Hugh Reginald Dalton, MI6's superb operative, inexplicably shot himself. Giskes wondered why and began searching for an explanation. He soon discovered that Dalton had been caught siphoning funds from an MI6 slush fund by his assistant John William Hooper. Another of Dalton's spymasters, Claude Dansey, wanted to have Hooper killed

Left: In 1941, Giskes was transferred to Abwehr IIIF—German counter-intelligence—to penetrate and break up Allied resistance, as can be seen by his quote, "Any army of occupation, irrespective of its nationality, will crush such attempts by means of the shooting of hostages and the terrorizing of the population. I have therefore decided to prevent the Allied Secret Services, by whatever means at my disposal, from supplying tons of arms and explosives to irresponsible fanatics in this country, the use of which can only mean a bloodbath for the civil population."

and his body dumped in a canal. Dalton said no. Dansey intended to carry out the scheme anyway, but Hooper temporarily disappeared. Dalton thought Hooper might go to MI6, so he killed himself.

Giskes heard the details directly from Hooper, who resurfaced in 1939 to sell his story to the Abwehr. After bleeding Hooper for the names of British spies in Holland, Giskes said he no longer needed him. Hooper still had an ace to play and claimed that he knew the name of a respected German naval engineer who had been working for MI6 for 20 years. Giskes offered 10,000 silver guilders for the information, and Hooper gave up Dr. Otto Krueger, a brilliant MI6 spy operating out of Hamburg.

SECRET

Telephone Nos.:
REGENT 6050.
WHITEHALL 6789.

BOX No. 500,
PARLIAMENT STREET B.O.,
LONDON, S.W.1.

MEMORANDUM

17th August 1945.

To: B.1.W., Mr. Wilson.

GISKES
HUNTERMANN

With reference to your P.F.601,712 and P.F.601,832
of 14.8.45, I have interrogated GISKES and HUNTERMANN on the
question you have asked with the following result:-

GISKES

GISKES states that agents with wireless sets and wireless
sets dropped for agents were, whenever possible, operated from
the locality in which it was intended that they should be used.
Agents were allowed more or less to choose their own site
within their prescribed locality.

In Belgium, he further stated, in many cases it was not
possible to operate in the locality intended and under such
circumstances messages were sent within a limit of 100 kms.,
as GISKES was firmly of the opinion that our D/F-ing was not
sufficiently accurate to record the difference.

HUNTERMANN

HUNTERMANN stated definitely that in all cases that he
knew agents with sets and sets dropped for agents were invariably
operated in the locality in which it was intended that they
should work.   He qualified this statement by saying that such
was the case up to the last six months of the war, when owing to
transport chaos and shortage of petrol and the impending advance
of the Allied armies, it was not found possible to retain the
agents in their right localities.   During this latter six months
they were withdrawn to Dreiburg, from whence they continued to send.

Lt.-Col.

Camp 020/DBS/MH

2 5 AUG 1945

MI6 had recruited Krueger in 1919 during the postwar chaos in Germany. Since then, Krueger became a successful and wealthy naval engineer for the Reichsmarine. He stole many of the German navy's top secrets and funneled the information to MI6 agents. Giskes developed an extensive résumé on Krueger and assigned six Hamburg Abwehr agents to watch Krueger night and day.

In late June 1939, the Abwehr surveillance team reported Krueger was on the move. He first traveled to the Blohm and Voss shipyards in Hamburg, ostensibly on business. From there he went to the German naval station to talk with friends about armaments for two new battle cruisers. Agents then tracked Krueger to The Hague, where he booked a room in a hotel. Listening at the door to his room one evening, they could hear a typewriter tapping, and when Krueger left the hotel around 9:00 p.m., they searched the room and found nothing. Krueger happened to be one of those rare individuals with a

Opposite and below:

The destruction of SOE's Dutch network was not only a catastrophe but a humiliation. When Hermann Giskes, the German officer in charge of Englandspiel, realized that the British would be providing no more agents for easy capture, he sent London a message mocking their failure.

FOR P.F. 601,712/GISKES, H.

EXTRACT FROM MONTHLY SUMMARY OF CURRENT CASES AT CAMPS 020 & 020R.

1st June 1945

N/C

Hermann GISKES.

Obersfleutnant Hermann GISKES @ Dr. GERHARDTS was captured in civilian clothing while hiding in the buildings at Wichl which had been used as the training-school for agents of FAK 307. After a brief preliminary interrogation in the Field he arrived at Camp 020 on the 24th May.

GISKES was put in touch with Ast Hamburg in September 1938 by Major FELDMANN. He began working for the Abwehr in January 1939 in Referat III c 1 Ast Hamburg. He was in constant liaison with ELLMANN of III F whose main preoccupation at that time was breaking down British Secret Service organisations in Holland. GISKES has given certain details of this which are under investigation. At the outbreak of war he was forming and reorganising Abwehr III sections at Ast Munster, and investigated a French Intelligence Service in Copenhagen. In June 1940 he was transferred to Ast Paris III c 2 until August 1941, being responsible for suspected spy cases in the greater Paris area and adjoining departments.

In August 1941 GISKES was transferred to III F Ast Niederlande where he had an extremely successful career in penetrating and breaking up Allied resistance organisations; in particular a large circuit of SOE wireless transmitters was operated under his direction.

In January 1944 when the III FAKs and FATs were created out of the former III F Dienststellen GISKES formed and commanded FAK 307 with its headquarters at Brussels. FAK 307 and the FATs under its control were, until the German collapse in the Ruhr, very active in training and despatching agents for a variety of missions, many of which combined penetration with espionage targets.

Preliminary investigation indicates that GISKES is providing a mass of useful and accurate information. He gives every appearance of being fully co-operative; it is apparent that he is a bitter enemy of the Gestapo and did all he could not only to save captured Allied agents from ill-treatment but also to try and have their lives spared.

Right: Having been apprehended in 1945, Giskes was interned in Camp 020 under the command of Colonel Robin Stephens. Here he fully cooperated, providing essential information on operations. Stephens was renowned for his method of interrogation, citing the tactics needed to break down a suspect: "A breaker is born and not made . . . pressure is attained by personality, tone, and rapidity of questions, a driving attack in the nature of a blast which will scare a man out of his wits."

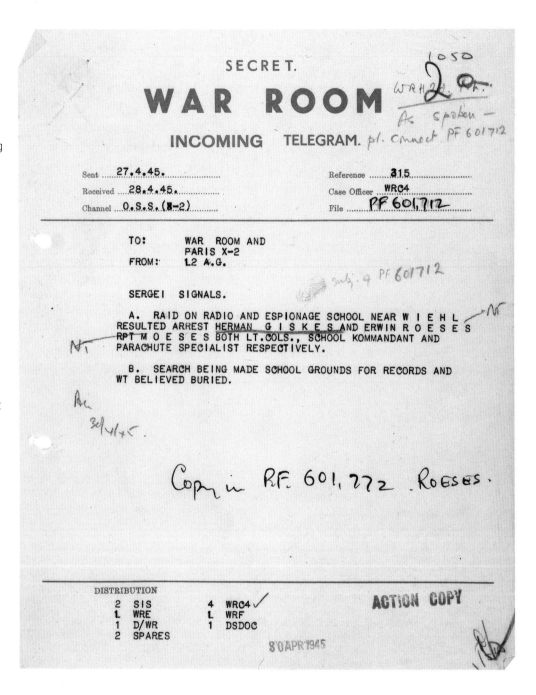

photographic memory. He typed the information he had collected from his mental bank and took the papers with him. This had been his modus operandi for 20 years.

Agents outside followed Krueger from his hotel to a villa by the sea. They watched him go inside, stay about two hours, and return to the hotel. Giskes asked who owned the villa, and local agents told him August de Fremery, a wealthy Belgian. The name meant nothing to Giskes or any other Abwehr spies. Traugott Protze, who worked with Giskes to identify the mystery man, spoke with a former British spy now working for the Nazis, who said, "Of course, it's Hendricks," meaning Captain Jan Hendricks, who had replaced Dalton as MI6's top spymaster in Holland. In July 1939, when Krueger returned to Hamburg, the Abwehr arrested him, extracted a confession, and threw him in a concentration camp from which he never returned.

Operation North Pole

Giskes performed no more major counterespionage feats until 1942, when he invented a plan to scoop up Special Operations (SOE) teams being parachuted into Holland. One of the first SOE operatives, a radio operator named Hubertus Lauwers, landed safely, moved into an apartment outside of The Hague, and began sending messages. Giskes's agents used direction-finding equipment, located Lauwers, and arrested him.

The SOE had trained Lauwers on how to behave if the Abwehr attempted to convert him to a double agent, which Giskes promptly did. The SOE also provided Lauwers with a special signal to send if this happened. Lauwers followed instructions and his next messages to London contained the secret signal, but SOE ignored it. After more transmissions from London, Lauwers realized that his signal had not been recognized, so he attempted on several occasions to slip in the word "caught." SOE remained oblivious.

Giskes enjoyed great success. As SOE agents parachuted into Holland, Abwehr agents, posing as a Dutch resistance team, intercepted them at drop points. After a friendly information-gathering debriefing, they admitted they were Abwehr agents and threw the parachutists into Haarlen Prison. After the SOE agents discovered they had been duped, Giskes converted some of them into double agents and expanded what he called Operation North Pole. He cleverly maintained the masterful deception for two years, collecting more than 500 parachuted radio sets, hundreds of Sten guns, and several tons of ammunition.

The Discovery of Oblivion

On August 29, 1943, two SOE agents, Joran B. Ubbink and Pieter Dourlein, escaped from Haarlen Prison but were unable to reach London until December. SOE could not conceal their shock and embarrassment after learning of Giskes's methods. Several months passed before SOE was able to shut down all the double agents employed by Giskes and start over again. By then, enormous damage had been done. It was appropriate that Giskes' operation was called Operation North Pole, for hundreds of British agents had been parachuted into oblivion. Giskes went on to send the message: "You are trying to make business in the Netherlands without our assistance. We think this rather unfair in view of our long and successful cooperation as your sole agent. But never mind. Whenever you will come to pay a visit to the Continent you may be assured that you will be received with the same care and result as all those you sent before. So long."

In 1945 American troops captured Giskes and removed him to prison with other Abwehr operatives. Although the Allies threatened to try him for war crimes, Dutch authorities came forward and said that Giskes never violated international law. Released in 1948, Colonel Giskes returned to Germany as perhaps the most effective counterespionage officer of the war.

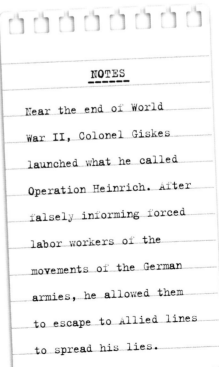

NOTES

Near the end of World War II, Colonel Giskes launched what he called Operation Heinrich. After falsely informing forced labor workers of the movements of the German armies, he allowed them to escape to Allied lines to spread his lies.

GOUZENKO, IGOR (1919–1982)

In 1943, the GRU sent Igor Gouzenko to Ottawa, Canada, as a cipher clerk in the Soviet Embassy. He found life in Canada much more compatible than life in the Soviet Union and became one of the first important Soviet intelligence officers to defect to the West.

Born outside Moscow in the town of Rogachov, Igor Gouzenko grew up in a czarist family in communist Russia. His father joined the White Russians and lost his life fighting Bolsheviks during Russia's civil war. Gouzenko attended school in Rostov-on-Don and later Verkne Spasskoye where, in 1926, his widowed mother began teaching. After joining the Communist Youth Movement, Gouzenko completed his high school education at the Komsomol.

During 1937 and 1938, Gouzenko attended the Moscow Engineering Academy and studied art and architecture. In 1939 the NKVD (later the KGB) recruited Gouzenko after his graduation and trained him as a cipher and code clerk. When Germany invaded Russia in 1941, the GRU sent Gouzenko to military intelligence school. He served on the front lines, earned a lieutenant's commission in the Red Army, and in 1943 was detached to serve as a cipher clerk in the Soviet Embassy in Ottawa, Canada.

----DOSSIER--------

Name: Igor Gouzenko

Code Name: None

Birth/Death: 1919–1982

Nationality: Russian

Occupation: Cipher Clerk for NKVD

Involvement: Soviet Defector to Canada

Outcome: Died of Natural Causes in Canada

Although ostensibly working for the Soviet Embassy, Gouzenko became part of the Soviet Canadian Network espionage ring directed from Moscow. His actual mission was to spy on Canadian officials and send secrets back to the GRU, and for two years he did. Shortly after Gouzenko reached Ottawa, his pregnant wife, Svetlana, arrived.

The Gentle Feel of Freedom

They settled into a comfortable apartment and enjoyed living with their young son in the first free country of their life. Gouzenko was amazed at the liberties enjoyed by civilians, and over time he and Svetlana grew to despise the ruthless and dictatorial regime in their homeland.

For two years they grew more and more attached to Canada.

On September 5, 1945, just three days after the official end of World War II, Gouzenko stuffed his briefcase with documents that would expose the Soviet-Canadian network and took them to the local newspaper. The editors listened to Gouzenko's amazing story without believing it. They looked at his documents and doubted their authenticity. Still convinced that the Soviets were

Below: Colonel Nicolai Zabotin (left) was head of the Ottawan spy ring; he had been sent to Canada in June 1943 to gather information on the atomic bomb project. Following Gouzenko's defection, Moscow openly declared that he had been spying. He was sent to a labor camp with his family.

est officials authorize what he considered one of the most disturbing aspects of the situation. He was Louis Stephen St. Laurent, then Minister of Justice, and now Secretary of State for External Affairs—the Canadian counterpart of our Secretary of State. Mr. St. Laurent observed, "What appalled us was the revelation that persons the Canadian Government had trusted had any other loyalty than the loyalty to the institutions for which we were all fighting. We still find it difficult to understand attitudes such as that of Dr. Allan Nunn May (the British scientist, secretly a communist, who gave the Russians samples of uranium) who set his own judgment above that of the constituted authorities as to what could and what could not be revealed."

been sent to Ottawa as cipher clerk for the Soviet military attaché. Gouzenko enjoys good literature and music, and, in general, seems bent toward a quiet cultural life. After two years in Canada, he said he was cured of communism. "No lying propaganda can stand up against facts," he declared.

On the evening of September 5, 1945, Gouzenko left the Soviet Embassy forever. Others, in recent years, have made similar breaks. Gouzenko, however, did something that none of the others has done; he carried out all the damning, incriminating documents he could safely abstract. They have resulted in the abrupt departure from Canada of all the key Russian personnel involved and the conviction to date of ten non-Russian defendants.

sibly in Canada as second secretary of the embassy. Louis Budenz, a former key communist in the United States, recently testified before the House Un-American Activities Committee in Washington that a similar NKVD secret-police ring existed in the United States.

There also was a political system, the intelligence link with the Moscow Comintern, which, if the Canadian report and other indications are correct, is far from dissolved—Soviet announcements to the contrary. Then there was an embryonic naval intelligence system, which was in process of organization when the spy story broke. And, for good measure, the commercial counselor's office, headed by Ivan I. Krotov, apparently *(Continued on Page 85)*

The swashbuckling Col. Nicolai Zabotin, Russian military attaché, got caught—and was recalled to Moscow pronto.

Puzzle man of the drama. Prof. Raymond Boyer *(left)*, of famous McGill University, has money, prestige, charm. An expert on explosives, he had many secrets. His trial impends.

The Royal Canadian Air Force to the Rescue

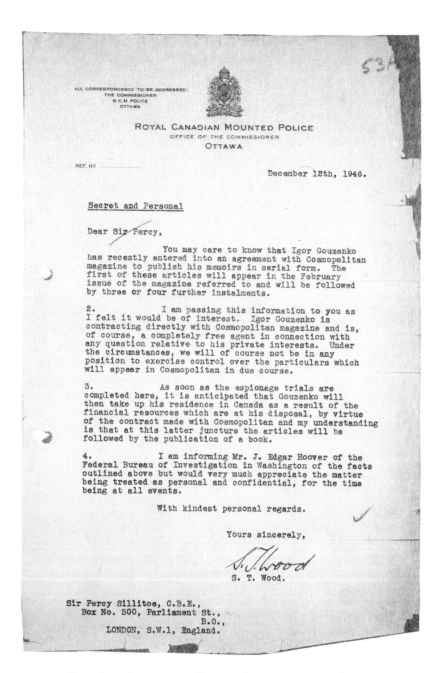

ALL CORRESPONDENCE TO BE ADDRESSED;
THE COMMISSIONER
R C M POLICE
OTTAWA

ROYAL CANADIAN MOUNTED POLICE
OFFICE OF THE COMMISSIONER
OTTAWA

REF. Nº

December 12th, 1946.

<u>Secret and Personal</u>

Dear Sir Percy,

You may care to know that Igor Gouzenko has recently entered into an agreement with Cosmopolitan magazine to publish his memoirs in serial form. The first of these articles will appear in the February issue of the magazine referred to and will be followed by three or four further instalments.

2. I am passing this information to you as I felt it would be of interest. Igor Gouzenko is contracting directly with Cosmopolitan magazine and is, of course, a completely free agent in connection with any question relative to his private interests. Under the circumstances, we will of course not be in any position to exercise control over the particulars which will appear in Cosmopolitan in due course.

3. As soon as the espionage trials are completed here, it is anticipated that Gouzenko will then take up his residence in Canada as a result of the financial resources which are at his disposal, by virtue of the contract made with Cosmopolitan and my understanding is that at this latter juncture the articles will be followed by the publication of a book.

4. I am informing Mr. J. Edgar Hoover of the Federal Bureau of Investigation in Washington of the facts outlined above but would very much appreciate the matter being treated as personal and confidential, for the time being at all events.

With kindest personal regards.

Yours sincerely,

S. T. Wood

S. T. Wood.

Sir Percy Sillitoe, C.B.E.,
Box No. 500, Parliament St.,
B.O.,
LONDON, S.W.1, England.

Above: Gouzenko serialized his memoir, *This Was My Choice*, in *Cosmopolitan* magazine and later released it as a book. Gouzenko was issued a new identity and given police protection; he very rarely appeared in public, but when he did he always wore a protective mask.

allies and not enemies, the newspaper editors showed the GRU spy the door.

Gouzenko returned to the apartment, deeply concerned that the Soviet Embassy would discover that the files were missing. The following morning, in a state of virtual panic, he contacted the Canadian State Department, but nobody there believed him, either. Now desperate and concerned for his wife, who was pregnant with a second child, Gouzenko once more tried the newspaper, but no one would talk to him.

Gouzenko returned to the apartment discouraged and deeply aggrieved. He locked the door and turned off the lights, waiting in the dark with his wife and son. Somebody knocked on the door, but he would not answer. A man called his name and he recognized the voice of the embassy chauffeur. After the man walked away, Gouzenko slipped onto the balcony and got the attention of his neighbor, Sergeant Main of the Royal Canadian Air Force. He explained his predicament and asked for help. Main brought Gouzenko's family to his apartment and contacted the police.

In the morning, Main returned to the apartment with two officers. Gouzenko repeated his story, and the officers promised to keep the building under surveillance. Around midnight, Main heard banging on a door and watched four men break into Gouzenko's apartment. He ran to a window and signaled to a policeman watching from the street. Moments later, several policemen appeared in the hallway and caught four men in the act of ransacking Gouzenko's apartment, all with passports identifying them as employees of the Soviet Embassy. An inspector arrived from the police department and instructed the ransackers to wait while he contacted the Royal Mounted Police. The four thugs brushed him aside and left.

On September 8, the Soviet Embassy contacted the Canadian Department of External Affairs and lodged a complaint against the police department for roughly handling four employees protected with diplomatic immunity. To explain the break-in, the embassy accused Gouzenko of stealing funds and demanded that he be turned over immediately, with all his papers. Meanwhile, Gouzenko met with the Royal Mounted Police and provided them with samples of his files. After a cursory inspection, the Mounties claimed that the papers exposed the greatest spy plot ever perpetrated on Canada. Agents moved Gouzenko and his family from the apartment, put them under protective custody, sent them to a secret location, and gave them different names.

The Royal Mounted Police issued arrest warrants for dozens of Soviet spies. Gouzenko had neatly listed their names and addresses on index cards with comments about each agent's behavioral patterns. The Canadian-Soviet network espionage ring reached into the United States and Great Britain with links to Soviet espionage activities throughout Europe.

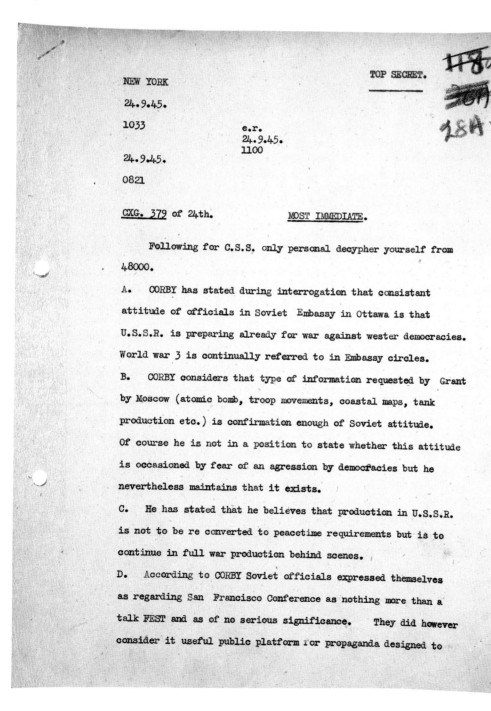

Left: After living in Canada for over two years, it became clear to Gouzenko that the Soviet government had created a false picture of life in democratic countries: "Having imposed its communist regime on the people, the government of the Soviet Union asserts that the Russian people have, as it were, their own particular understanding of freedom and democracy, different from that which prevails among the peoples of the western democracies. This is a lie. The Russian people have the same understanding of freedom as all the peoples of the world. However, the Russian people cannot realize their dream of freedom and a democratic government on account of cruel terror and persecution."

Right: Igor Gouzenko wears a hood to conceal his face during an interview with Associated Press writer Saul Pett in Canada on April 29, 1954. Gouzenko continued to lead a life with two identities, both of which were known only to his wife and a handful of Canadian officials.

NOTES

In 1948, Igor Gouzenko's memoirs about his defection became the basis for the suspense film *The Iron Curtain*.

After the arrest of Colonel Nicolai Zabotin, the GRU spymaster in Ottawa, other Canadian heads began to fall, among them Fred Rose, a member of Parliament, and Dr. Alan Nunn May, an atomic scientist. May's involvement in America's atomic energy project inadvertently led to the arrest of Klaus Fuchs in England, who gave up Harry Gold. Gold gave up David Greenglass, who in turn gave up Julius and Ethel Rosenberg.

What shocked the West the most was the extent of Moscow's control of Communist parties around the world. Gouzenko's defection served as a wake-up call to every free nation that Joseph Stalin intended to dominate the world with his Soviet brand of communism.

Gouzenko probably had no idea that his defection also marked the beginning of the cold war.

On October 10, 1945, as part of a statement, Gouzenko said, "Having arrived in Canada two years ago, I was surprised during the first days by the complete freedom of the individual which exists in Canada but does not exist in Russia. The false representations about the democratic countries who are increasingly propagated in Russia were dissipated daily, as no lying propaganda can stand up against facts . . . I am glad that I found the strength within myself to take this step and to warn Canada and the other democratic countries of the danger which hangs over them."

GREENGLASS, DAVID (1922-?)

David Greenglass became the central figure in the most controversial spy case in America, which involved his wife, his sister, his brother-in-law, the Soviets, the FBI, and the atomic bomb.

David Greenglass, the son of Russian Jewish parents, grew up on the crowded lower east side of New York City. His sister Ethel married Julius Rosenberg, a fatal mix for everyone who eventually became involved. A rather lethargic student, Greenglass joined the Young Communist League for excitement, and there he met his wife, 19-year-old Ruth Printz. He attended the Polytechnic Institute of Brooklyn and failed the majority of his courses. He transferred to New York's Pratt Institute, quit, and in 1943 joined the U.S. Army. His letters home to Ruth validated his longing for the better world promised by socialism.

```
------DOSSIER--------
Name: David Greenglass
Code Name: None
Birth/Death: 1922-?
Nationality: American
Occupation: Machine
Operator
Involvement: U.S. Spy for
the Soviets
Outcome: Served 10 Years
in Prison and Disappeared
```

The Los Alamos Machine Operator

After Greenglass completed basic training, the army gave him machine shop training and sent him to an ordnance depot to repair tanks and other vehicles. During his spare time, Greenglass continued to read books on socialism. His letters home extolled Soviet leaders for being "farsighted and intelligent" and "real geniuses." Fellow mechanics knew of Greenglass's political convictions, but no one really cared because Russia was an important ally.

In July 1944 the army transferred six machinists to Oak Ridge, Tennessee, to work on the Manhattan Project, America's secret A-bomb program. When one of the machinists went absent without leave, the army replaced him with Greenglass. The Oak Ridge facility was not on a map, nor did Greenglass know he was working on an A-bomb. His transfer into the bowels of America's most closely guarded secret came to the attention of brother-in-law Julius Rosenberg, who headed a Soviet spy ring controlled by Anatoli Yakovlev, the Soviet general consul in New York. Rosenberg's espionage efforts took a favorable leap forward when he learned that the army transferred Greenglass to Los Alamos, where the bomb was to be assembled and tested.

In 1943, when Greenglass learned that his sister and Rosenberg were Soviet spies, he offered to collaborate with them after the war, but as soon as he walked into Los Alamos, he contacted his brother-in-law for instructions. Rosenberg wrote back, informing the naive Greenglass that it would be unfair for America to not share atomic technology with the Soviet Union. Greenglass, who did little thinking of his own, agreed.

In November 1944 Greenglass took a furlough and met his wife in New Mexico. She handed him a list of information requested by Rosenberg, including the size of the Los Alamos facility, employ-

Right: David Greenglass, left, handcuffed and accompanied by a U.S. marshal, arriving at the federal courthouse in New York City on July 31, 1950. Greenglass is in for questioning by U.S. attorney Irving H. Saypol in connection with spy conspiracy charges.

ment levels, names of the top scientists, and whatever he could learn about Robert Oppenheimer, the head atomic research scientist in America. Greenglass agreed to help, and his wife returned to New York with an optimistic report for Rosenberg.

Yakovlev dispatched Harry Gold, a Communist courier, to New Mexico to set up regular information-gathering meetings with Greenglass. Gold happened to be the same courier handling Klaus Fuchs, the British scientist on the project. From later testimony, it appeared that Rosenberg also used Ruth Greenglass as a courier. The information Greenglass provided to the Rosenbergs included different types of lens molds, the amount of plutonium used in making the bomb, and a sketch of the bomb dropped on Nagasaki.

A Busted Relationship

In 1946 Greenglass received his honorable discharge from the army and went into the spy business as Julius Rosenberg's partner; the partnership depended upon Greenglass's willingness to take orders from a determined and intellectually superior coconspirator. His next shock occurred with the outset of the cold war, when the Soviets suddenly became enemies of the West. This baffled and irritated Greenglass, and led to the dissolution of the partnership in 1949. By then, Greenglass was already remorseful and afraid of being apprehended.

The end came quickly when the British arrested Klaus Fuchs, who implicated Gold. On June 15, 1950, the FBI apprehended Greenglass for passing atomic secrets to Gold. Under interrogation, Greenglass implicated his partner and on July 17, 1950, the FBI arrested Julius Rosenberg. When agents questioned Ruth Greenglass to see how she fit into the

Left: David Greenglass, accused of passing atomic secrets to Harry Gold, who was indicted on charges of passing information from the convicted British spy Klaus Fuchs to the Russian intelligence service. Greenglass's arrest followed only a few hours after the seizure of chemist Alfred Dean Slack, and he was given similar charges in connection with Gold.

scheme, Ruth pleaded innocence but incriminated Ethel, her sister-in-law.

During the trial, Greenglass gave incriminating evidence against the Rosenbergs. Observers never understood why, on the second day of his testimony, Greenglass provided such damaging evidence against his sister. It was later thought that Ethel was implicated in activities that were actually carried out by Ruth. Ethel might have received a lighter sentence; instead, on June 19, 1953, the Rosenbergs were put to death by electric chair.

Greenglass had made a deal with the FBI. In return for pleading guilty to conspiracy to commit espionage, he received a sentence of 15 years but served only 10. The jury set Ruth Greenglass free.

When released from prison, David Greenglass changed his name to escape the vengeance of the nation and melted into the landscape of America.

NOTES

On the day Greenglass left prison, reporters asked him why he gave up his sister. After 10 years to think about the question, he said that it was more important to protect a wife than a sister.

GREENHOW, ROSE O'NEALE (1817–1864)

Rose O'Neale Greenhow became the Confederacy's most daring and determined espionage agent. Operating in Washington, she dazzled scores of Union officers with her feminine charms while feeding vital intelligence to the South.

Born in Montgomery County, Maryland, Rose O'Neale lived a genteel plantation life, enjoying the graceful ambiance of the antebellum South. She learned to behave like a Southern lady but could handle a horse better than most men. In the early 1830s, she went to live with her maiden aunt, who operated the exclusive Congressional Boarding House in Washington. Personable, intelligent, and beautiful, O'Neale made a marvelous hostess at receptions, balls, and banquets. She soon became the favorite of politicians, both young and old. In 1835, she married a much older man, Dr. Robert Greenhow, a quiet physician and historian who worked long hours in the State Department.

The Washington Belle

Rose Greenhow soon became the capital's hostess of choice. She entertained practically every important politician that came to Washington, especially those that came from the South. She met Senator Jefferson Davis of Mississippi, who in 1862 became the president of the Confederacy. She also met senators John C. Calhoun and Robert Barnwell Rhett of South Carolina, both determined secessionists. From them she learned about states' rights and the reasons why

```
----DOSSIER--------
Name: Rose O'Neale Greenhow
Code Name: None
Birth/Death: 1817-1864
Nationality: American
Occupation: Socialite
Involvement: Confederate Spy
Outcome: Accidentally
Drowned
```

Southerners and Northerners should have separate governments. She knew Senator James Buchanan, a bachelor from Pennsylvania who in 1857 became president and some say influenced his hands-off policy toward the South's right to secede.

In that year, Greenhow's near-perfect life suffered a tragic turn. During a trip to San Francisco with her husband and two youngest daughters, Gertrude and Rose, Dr. Greenhow took a tumble down a grating and died. She filed a suit against the city and received a tidy settlement but then, after returning to Washington, Gertrude died of a mysterious illness. Greenhow, now with only Rose to keep her company (her other two daughters were married), wore black for the rest of her life.

The Importance of Political Connections

Greenhow began spying before the Civil War. From 1857 to 1861, she kept in close contact with President Buchanan, who affectionately signed his letters to her, "your ancient and devoted friend." She befriended Senator William H. Seward, a moving force in the upcoming 1860 presidential nomination. As a multitalented Washington socialite, she mingled with politicians and military officers at banquets and soirees throughout the city.

Greenhow became adept at differentiating fact from gossip. In the chaotic days of Southern secession, she understood what was happening between the North and the South. Before Captain Thomas Jordan resigned from the U.S. Army to join the Southern army, he organized a Confederate spy ring in Washington, and when he left the city he turned the network over to Greenhow.

The Washington Spy Network

During the spring of 1861, thousands of office seekers and military personnel flooded Washington. Greenhow's entertainment business picked up with the flow, and so did the number of loose-lipped Unionists. Her spies collected the intelligence; she interpreted the information and sent the data through couriers to the Confederate capital at Richmond, Virginia.

Not every message went to Richmond. In June 1861, Greenhow learned that Brigadier General Irwin McDowell's Union army intended to attack General Pierre G. T. Beauregard's Confederate forces at Manassas (Bull Run). During the days prior to McDowell's attack, she sent three important messages directly to

Above: Greenhow was imprisoned from August 1861 until May 1862; her youngest daughter, Rose, was allowed to stay with her. She was still successful in passing messages while in prison using ingenious methods, one of which involved hiding a message in the bun of the hair of one of her women visitors.

Beauregard. Betty Duvall carried the coded information in her black hair, held in place with a comb. The first note informed Beauregard that McDowell would begin his movement on July 16; the second note described the Union army's line of march; and the third warned Beauregard that another federal force intended to cut the Manassas Gap Railroad to prevent Southern reinforcements from coming from the Shenandoah Valley. The intelligence enabled Beauregard to take appropriate defensive measures, bring timely reinforcements from the valley, strike McDowell's flank, and rout the Union army. After the battle, Beauregard sent a note to Greenhow expressing his gratitude.

McDowell returned to Washington, his reputation damaged, and was replaced by Major General George B. McClellan.

Arrest and Release

McClellan was a great organizer but not a particularly good fighter. He built the Army of the Potomac into an impressive fighting force. He also added a secret service unit led by Allan Pinkerton, proprietor of the Pinkerton Detective Agency. The outfit had two objectives: to collect information on the enemy and to catch Confederate spies.

Pinkerton soon had Rose Greenhow in his sights and posted agents to watch her home. He found it odd that a woman of her reputation as a Southern sympathizer would receive so many visits from Union officers. On the night of August 21,

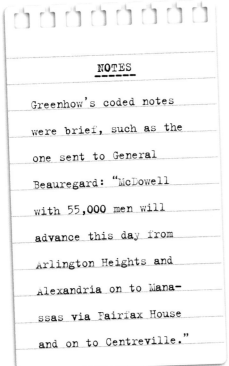

NOTES

Greenhow's coded notes were brief, such as the one sent to General Beauregard: "McDowell with 55,000 men will advance this day from Arlington Heights and Alexandria on to Manassas via Fairfax House and on to Centreville."

1861, Pinkerton watched her house with his men. When a light went on, they crossed the street. Pinkerton stood on the shoulders of one of his detectives and peered through the window. He heard someone knock at the front door, and waited. Moments later, a Union officer entered Greenhow's parlor, handed her a map, and began discussing artillery emplacements. Pinkerton waited for the man to leave. He and an agent chased the officer up the street, but they both slipped and the man got away.

Pinkerton waited until he had collected enough evidence to arrest Greenhow for spying. He picked her up on August 23, searched her home, and caught the man who had escaped two days before. On August 30, he put her in prison by government decree. In May 1862, after holding her for nine months, she was sent to Richmond with her nine-year-old daughter and told not to come back.

The Last Mission

In July 1862 Jefferson Davis engaged Greenhow as his personal courier to Great Britain and France. She put her daughter in a French convent school and enjoyed the fellowship of Southerners canvassing Europeans for support. In 1864 she embarked on a British blockade-runner, weighted down with a packet of important dispatches for the president and $2,000 in gold. On the night of September 30, her ship went aground off the Cape Fear River in North Carolina. Worried that she might be captured by Union blockaders, Greenhow tried to reach shore in a ship's boat. The boat capsized. A few days later a search party found her body washed up along the shore, dragged down by the weight of a pouch of gold tied to her wrist.

HALE, NATHAN (1755–1776)

If Nathan Hale was not the first American spy, he certainly became among the most remembered when he sacrificed his life for a cause in which he deeply believed.

The son of a Connecticut farmer, Nathan Hale enjoyed an excellent start in life and went on to graduate from Yale in 1773. That same year, men disguised as Indians threw a cargo of tea into Boston Harbor and called it the Boston Tea Party. Hale applauded his countrymen's effort to snub their noses at the king's laws, but at that time his main interest was beginning a career as a teacher in New London, Connecticut. One of Hale's contemporaries described him as blue-eyed, taller than average, plump but very agile, with a sharp and piercing voice.

Hale's teaching career ended in the spring of 1775 following a skirmish between British regulars and Colonial militia at Lexington and Concord, Massachusetts. He finished the school year and, in July, joined the Seventh Connecticut Militia as a lieutenant. The regiment participated in General George Washington's siege of Boston. When his unit joined the Continental Army, Hale became a captain in Major Thomas Knowlton's 20th Infantry Regiment, known as Knowlton's Rangers.

----DOSSIER--------

Name: Nathan Hale

Code Name: None

Birth/Death: 1755-1776

Nationality: American

Occupation: Schoolteacher

Involvement: American Spy in the Revolution

Outcome: Hanged by the British

Espionage 101

On March 17, 1776, British general William Howe evacuated Boston and later landed on Long Island, New York. The Continental Army followed and took possession of Manhattan Island. Washington began looking for someone

Above: September 22, 1776: British soldiers preparing to hang the American patriot and spy Nathan Hale. However poorly equipped he may have been to be a successful spy, Hale's patriotism and bravery were never in doubt and have left a legacy that continues to this day.

willing to infiltrate the British camp, and asked Knowlton for volunteers. On May 15, Hale had led a group of sailors on a mission that captured a British supply ship from under the shadow of the HMS *Asia*. He had enjoyed the excitement and adventure, and immediately volunteered for the mission, though he knew little about spying. However, Washington was equally inept when it came to the finer points of espionage and merely told Hale to go over to Long Island, determine the British strength, observe their movements, and let him know. The mission was important because Washington expected a fight.

Friends tried but failed to dissuade Hale from taking the assignment. William

Hull, a schoolmate who became a general in the war, reported after the revolution that he had suggested to Hale that spying was seldom thought of as a noble part of the military and that capture and subsequent death was often inglorious. To this, Hale merely replied, "I wish to be useful, and every kind of service necessary to the public good becomes honorable by becoming necessary."

Anxious to be on his way, Hale shed his uniform, changed into civilian clothes, and sailed to Long Island in a small boat. To curious Long Islanders and British scouts who asked his business, Hale replied that he was a schoolteacher. He did not pass scrutiny easily. In addition to being a noticeably tall man, he also car-

Left: This statue by Frederick William MacMonnies, entitled *Nathan Hale: Civic Virtue*, stands in a New York fountain and is one of numerous monuments to America's first spy. Hale is still revered as a patriotic hero; indeed, following the efforts of the Nathan Hale Chapter of the Sons of the American Revolution, an act of the general assembly declared Nathan Hale to be the official state hero of Connecticut.

ried suspicious scars on his face, the result of a recent gunpowder explosion. People would remember seeing him a second time.

Hale dallied around British camps. He had been on reconnaissance trips before the British took the island and may have already had some contacts there. He made sketches of the enemy's position, took notes on the location of their artillery and supply dumps, and began backtracking to Manhattan, but he waited too long. In September the British army moved toward Manhattan, and Hale, having lost his sailboat, had no recourse but to follow.

On September 16, 1776, Washington struck the British front at Harlem Heights. Hale watched the battle from behind British lines, and when General Howe began deploying 5,000 troops held in reserve, Hale could do nothing to warn the Continentals. Fortunately, Washington had anticipated a renewed attack and at 2:00 p.m. ordered a withdrawal.

Hale soon found himself farther from the Continental Army than before, but he still attempted to work around the British front to deliver promised intelligence to Washington. Hale, however, did not think to throw away the now-useless sketches. The inevitable happened on September 21 when a British patrol stripped Hale and looked in his shoes.

Exactly what led to Hale's capture remains a mystery. Some historians claim that Hale either admitted to being a spy or was simply searched and discovered. Other historians believe that Hale confided his mission to his Tory cousin Samuel Hale, who lived on Long Island and happened to be Howe's deputy commissioner of prisoners.

Either way, Hale naively thought that since he carried no weapon and wore civilian clothes, he could not be classed as a combatant and would therefore be immune from military punishment. Unaware that there were penalties for spies, it must have come as quite a shock when General Howe dispensed with a hearing and ordered Hale hanged the following morning.

Words from Joseph Addison

While waiting for execution, Hale occupied a tent with Captain John Montressor, chief engineer for the British army. Montressor decided that Hale acted out of ignorance and should not go the gallows and mentioned it to the British provost, Marshal Cunningham. Cunningham thought it strange that Hale did not plead for his life or offer to exchange information about the Continental Army to save his life.

With only one day to live, Hale used it to write letters to Knowlton (whom he did not know had been killed in battle) and other friends. He asked Cunningham to pass the notes through the lines. The provost marshal took the letters out of the tent, tore them up, and threw the scraps into a fire. When a soldier asked why he did so, Cunningham snorted, "The rebels ought not to know that they had a man in their army who could die with such firmness."

On September 22, Hale went to the scaffold at Artillary Park without a whimper. When asked for any last words, Hale said, "I only regret that I have but one life to lose for my country." Montressor recognized the words from the English play *Cato*, written by Joseph Addison, and he also knew that Hale had put the quote into one of his letters. Hale's body was left to hang for two days as a warning to other rebels.

A few days later, Montressor crossed through the Continental lines and informed Washington that Hale had been executed for spying. When Washington asked whether Hale had anything to say, Montresor quoted the patriot's words from Addison's play.

Hale's words would become the battle cry of America that would endure for hundreds of years to come.

Opposite: Illustration of Nathan Hale spying on the British disguised as a Dutch schoolmaster. While early accounts tend to point the finger of suspicion at Hale's cousin Samuel as his possible betrayer, more recently a contemporary account written by a loyalist shopkeeper, Consider Tiffany, has suggested a different story. Tiffany claims that it was in fact Major Robert Rogers who captured Hale by convincing him that he was a fellow patriot spy, thereby duping Hale into revealing his true identity and purpose.

NOTES

"A Child I sot much by but he is gone," said Deacon Richard Hale on the death of his son Nathan. In 1779, he created a monument for Nathan in the cemetry at Coventry.

As early as 1941 Adolf Hitler had designs on producing an atomic bomb. Knut Haukelid risked his life to make sure that never happened.

Very little is known about Knut Haukelid's early life other than that he was the fraternal twin brother of Sigrid Gurie, the Norwegian actress. He came on the scene during World War II as a leader of the Norwegian underground and then disappeared. What he accomplished as a spy in the Norwegian resistance may well have changed the outcome of the war.

The Water at Norsk Hydro

Before the war, in the valley near the town of Rjukan, Norway's hydroelectric authority built a facility to produce deuterium oxide, commonly known as heavy water. Buried in a barren, sparsely populated, mountainous region, barely anyone in Norway pictured the center as anything other than a remotely located power plant. The Germans, however, knew the plant was working on a process to extract deuterium oxide, and in 1942 British intelligence (MI6) learned of the operation from Norwegians. Prime Minister Winston Churchill immediately called his cabinet

```
----DOSSIER--------
Name: Knut Haukelid
Code Name: None
Birth/Death: 1917-1994
Nationality: Norwegian
Occupation: Engineer
Involvement: Norwegian
Resistance Fighter
Outcome: Unknown
```

together and made the decision to send 30 specially trained engineer troops from Special Operations Executive (SOE) into Norway to destroy the facility.

In 1942 nobody in the world had yet mastered the complicated process of making an atomic bomb. Deuterium oxide happened to be one of the many possible substances required to make the bomb. When word reached London that Adolf Hitler had taken keen interest in Norsk Hydro's heavy water project and had demanded 10,000 pounds annually, the Rjukan plant became an object of special interest to MI6.

The British enjoyed a stroke of fortune when, in January 1942, SOE operatives in Norway made contact with Professor Leif Tronstad, who knew everything about the complicated processing equipment in the Rjukan plant and provided a layout showing where everything was located. A few weeks later, Einar Skinnarland arrived in England and drew a plan of the entire Rjukan area and provided the names of the local engineers who could be trusted. The SOE gave Skinnarland a quick course in espionage and commando operations and, on March 28, inserted him into Norway to pave the way for four specially trained agents. The operation was code-named Grouse. The agents were to be dropped during the April moon period, but the operation was aborted because of unsuitable weather.

Below: When the Germans invaded Norway in April 1940, Knut was working for his father's engineering firm, Haukelid og Five. He managed to evaded the Nazis and became a lieutenant in Kompani Linge (the most successful Norwegian resistance group of World War II).

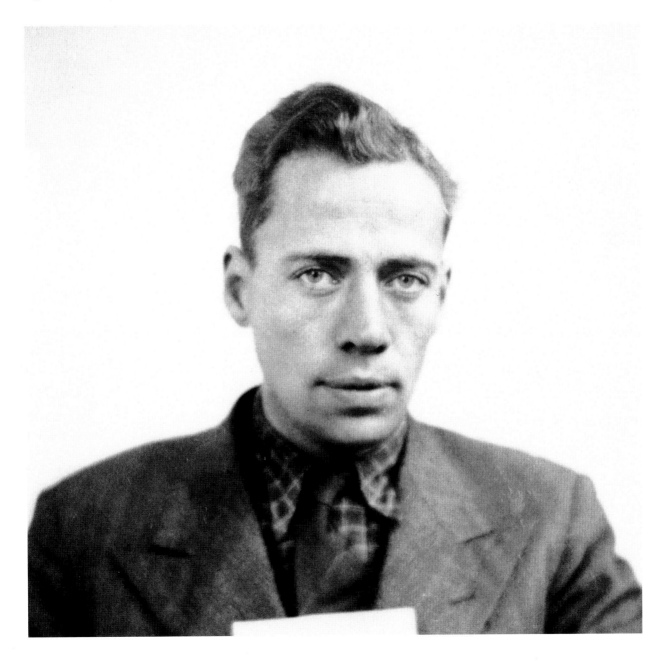

14 A

TEL. No.:
GROSVENOR 4060.

TOP SECRET

F.1868/161

MINISTRY OF ECONOMIC WARFARE,
BERKELEY SQUARE HOUSE,
BERKELEY SQUARE,
LONDON, W. 1.

30th June, 1944.

My dear General,

Thank you very much for your letter (DDMO/BM/155)
of the 28th June in which you tell me that the following awards
have been approved by The King:-

Fenrik Knut Haukelid, M.C.	D.S.O.
Sjt Einar Skinnarland	D.C.M.
Engineer Alf Larsen	M.B.E. (Civil)
Gunnar Syverstad	B.E.M.

I confirm that arrangements have been made for
the insignia for presentation to Engineer Larsen and
Gunnar Syverstad to be sent to me direct.   I will inform
you of the date and place of presentation of these awards and
of those to Fenrik Haukelid and Sjt Skinnarland in due course.

Yours very sincerely,

Major-General J.N.Kennedy, C.B., M.C.,

WAR OFFICE, S.W.1.

Churchill then released the 30 specially trained SOE troops, who were to be flown in on two gliders. After blowing up the plant, the men were to escape by foot into Sweden. Both gliders crashed, killing or injuring most of the crew, and the rest were picked up by German patrols. Because the troopers' packs contained civilian clothes, SS officers ordered the prisoners shot as spies.

Operation Gunnerside

The SOE organized a new plan, Operation Gunnerside, this time with Captain Knut Haukelid in charge. Four SOE operatives from Operation Grouse had already been dropped into Norway in October. The plan was to drop Haukelid and another four men, join forces with the Grouse team, and blow up the hydro plant. After two false starts, Haukelid's team parachuted near Rjukan and rendezvoused with Grouse. Haukelid divided the nine men into two teams, one to set the explosives and the other to provide covering fire, if necessary. The operation went smoothly, but the explosion sounded weak. Nevertheless, the facility went dead and Haukelid believed his men had put the heavy water installation permanently out of business. He remained in Norway and the other eight men to skied to Sweden.

In July 1943, Haukelid noticed the plant was back in production. He notified the SOE, and a few days later British and American bombers swooped through the valley but failed to hit the processing plant. The SOE had begun to organize another airdrop when Haukelid learned that the Nazis planned to move the plant and all the heavy water to Germany. He told SOE that he had a plan and to not send more men.

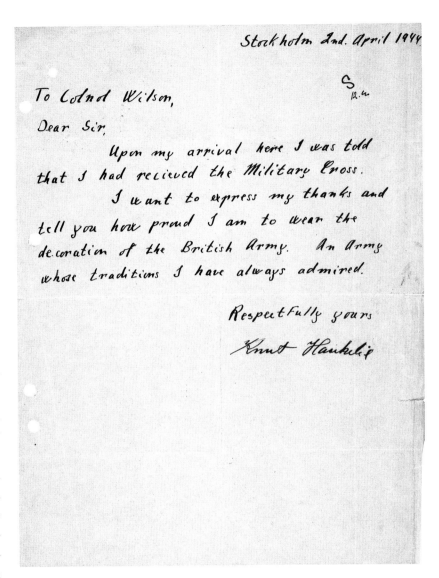

The Tinnsjö Ferry Caper

Lake Tinnsjö lay a few miles east of Rjukan, with a railroad spur connecting the town with the lake. A Lake Tinnsjö train ferry picked up people, cargo, and rail cars and hauled everything to Larvik, where the Germans would have cargo ships waiting.

Dressed as a workman, Haukelid reconnoitered the ferry and laid his plans. Learning that the Germans planned to make the transfer of the barrels early on the morning on February 20, 1944, he and his companion bribed the night watchman to let them onboard as stow-

Opposite and above: War Office correspondence regarding the awards for Haukelid and his team, opposite, and a handwritten letter of thanks from Haukelid, above. As well as the Military Cross he was awarded by the British, Haukelid also received military honors from four other nations, including the Medal of Freedom with Silver Palm from the United States.

HAUKELID, K.

SPECIAL TRAINING SCHOOLS,
ROOM 98,
HORSE GUARDS,
WHITEHALL, S.W.1.

DECLARATION

I declare that I will never disclose to anyone any information which I have acquired or may at any future time acquire as the result of my connection with this Department, unless such disclosure is necessary for my work for the Department.

In particular I declare that except under the conditions aforementioned, I will in no circumstances give away any information concerning :—

1. The name, alias description, identity, location or duties of any past, present or future member of this Department.

2. The name, alias description, identity, location or duties of any member of the staff, or any persons working with this Department, either as a member of the forces or as a civilian.

3. The nature, methods, objects or subjects of instruction of this Department.

4. The location or name of any establishment of this Department.

5. The past, present or future location, movement or employment, either potential or factual, of myself, any other member of or any person working with this Department.

I declare moreover that I understand that I am personally responsible for any disclosure of such information I may make and that disciplinary proceedings under the Official Secrets Acts 1911 and 1920, the Treachery Act 1940, or the Defence (General) Regulations 1939 may be taken against me if I at any time or in any way contravene the terms of this declaration.

Signature...................................

Witness...................................

Date....22/5/42.

KNUT HAUKELIED

Opposite: Official Secrets Act declaration signed by Haukelid. He would later downplay the bravery of his own actions: "We were armed and could hide in the mountains if we were discovered. It was worse for the people in Rjukan who helped us. They had families and homes and farms to take care of. They and their families had to live in fear of what could happen if they were found out."

Left: February 22, 1949, Captain Knut Haukelid reenacting his role in the 1943 sabotage of the Rjukan heavy water plant for the Norwegian documentary *The Fight for Heavy Water*. The film featured many of the original heroes who had destroyed the plant.

aways. The watchman conducted them to the very bottom of the boat and went back to his post. Haukelid and an assistant placed the charges and set timers to go off at 11:00 a.m. By Haukelid's calculations, at that hour the ferry would be over the deepest part of the lake.

Having arranged the 19 pounds of plastic explosives and two alarm clock fuses to blow an 11-foot hole in the bottom of the ferry, the two men withdrew, explaining to the watchman that they had left some articles behind at Rjukan. In the morning, the ferry pushed off on time and blew up over the deepest part of the lake as planned. It is claimed that some

barrels floated and later reappeared in Germany, but the action was enough to make Hitler abandon the heavy water project and with it his designs on creating nuclear weapons.

Haukelid disappeared after the explosion. Many years later, he resurfaced and published the book *Skiis Against the Atom*. Over the years, he met presidents and appeared on televeision, but mostly spent time with his wife and children.

NOTES

The story of Haukelid and his heroic Norwegian resistance fighters surfaced many years later when Hollywood released the film *The Heroes of Telemark*.

HISS, ALGER (1904–1996)

Alger Hiss shielded his relationship with the Soviet Union for most of his life and the facts never became irrefutably clear until the year of his death.

Born in Baltimore, Maryland, in 1904, Alger Hiss enjoyed a pleasant childhood despite being only three years old when his father committed suicide. The tragedy made no lasting impression on Hiss, who appeared to have led a perfectly normal life while attending Baltimore's public schools. In 1921 he graduated from the Powder Point Academy in Duxbury, Massachusetts, and in 1922 enrolled at Johns Hopkins University. He continued on to Harvard Law School, graduated in 1929, and that year married Priscilla Fansler Hobson, a divorcée with a son. Before entering his own law practice in the early 1930s, he served as a law clerk for Supreme Court justice Oliver Wendell Holmes.

```
----DOSSIER--------
Name: Alger Hiss
Code Name: None
Birth/Death: 1904-1996
Nationality: American
Occupation: Lawyer for
U.S. Government
Involvement: Spied for
the Soviet Union
Outcome: Died of Natural
Causes
```

Upwardly Mobile

In 1933 Hiss started working for the United States government in different capacities. During the years between 1933 and 1935, he became consul for the Agricultural Adjustment Administration and also served with the Nye Committee during the investigation of the arms industry. In 1935 he moved to the Department of Justice, and then to the Department of State. While with the latter, he also served as executive secretary of the Dumbarton Oaks Conference, which in 1944 founded the United Nations; the following year he became the UN's first

secretary-general. He also attended the 1945 Yalta conference as chief aide to Secretary of State Edward R. Stettinius when Roosevelt, Churchill, and Stalin agreed on geopolitical arrangements after World War II ended. Despite his notable career as one of America's highest-placed officials, Hiss's secret life soon began to unravel.

Whittaker Chambers

In 1939, *Time* journalist Whittaker Chambers met with assistant secretary of state Adolf Berle and accused Hiss of being a Communist spy, adding that Hiss's wife, Priscilla, and brother, Donald, were also spies. Chambers confessed that he knew this because he and his wife had

Right: Ex–State Department official Alger Hiss taking the stand during House Un-American Activities Committee hearings, where he denied the charges that he was ever a Communist.

also once been members of the same Communist underground network. Berle did nothing because he considered the accusation too absurd to be true.

A few months later, William C. Bullitt, the American ambassador in Paris, warned Stanley Hornbeck, Hiss's superior in the State Department, that French intelligence possessed information implicating both Alger and Donald Hiss in Soviet espionage activities. Hornbeck questioned Hiss, who denied the allegation. Though inclined to drop the matter, Hornbeck decided that, to preserve Hiss's reputation from further assaults, he would have the FBI perform a routine investigation. In 1944 the FBI interviewed Hiss, who once again said that he had no involvement with Russia and no sympathy with Communists.

Deny, Deny, Deny

In 1945 Igor Gouzenko, a cipher clerk in the Soviet Embassy in Ottawa, defected to the Canadian government. He turned over a bundle of documents proving the existence of a vast spy network in Canada and the United States. He also stated that an assistant to the U.S. Secretary of State in Washington was a member of that ring. He did not know the name of the man, but the FBI had no difficulty pinpointing Hiss. Agents from the FBI kept Hiss under surveillance, but the investigation produced nothing incriminating.

In 1946 James Byrnes became the new secretary of state and, troubled by rumors of his assistant's loyalty, asked Hiss privately if he ever had Communist ties. Hiss said no, but soon afterward he resigned

Left: Richard M. Nixon, left, and John E. Rankins, center, pictured on December 1, 1948, during the testimony in which Whittaker Chambers accused Alger Hiss of securing important U.S. documents that were turned over to a Soviet agent.

from the State Department to become president of the Carnegie Endowment for International Peace in New York City. John Foster Dulles, chairman of the Carnegie Board, took Hiss aside and raised the same question. Hiss assured him that all the rumors were false.

The Troublesome Whittaker Chambers

Called before the House Un-American Activities Committee in 1948, Whittaker Chambers admitted that in the 1930s he had been a Communist agent and had worked with Alger Hiss as a courier. At first the panel doubted the allegations, but they began to listen as Chambers recalled vivid details of Hiss's personal life. He described Hiss's home and claimed to have stayed there many times. He also recalled Hiss's personal habits and hobbies and testified how in 1936 Hiss had donated an old car to the Communist Party. More damaging still, he explained how Hiss brought documents home from the State Department for his wife Priscilla to copy on her typewriter so

Right: Prosecution lawyer Thomas F. Murphy during the trial, standing in front of the Woodstock 230009 typewriter that he claimed Alger Hiss used to copy state documents. At the conclusion of his second trial, Hiss stated, "I want only to add that I am confident that in the future the full facts of how Whittaker Chambers was able to carry out forgery by typewriter will be disclosed."

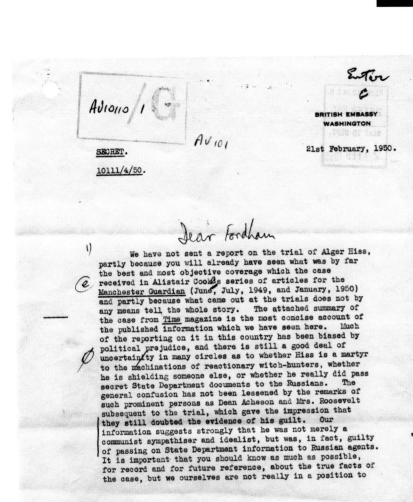

AJ10110/1 G

AV101

SECRET.

10111/4/50.

BRITISH EMBASSY
WASHINGTON

21st February, 1950.

Dear Fordham

We have not sent a report on the trial of Alger Hiss, partly because you will already have seen what was by far the best and most objective coverage which the case received in Alistair Cooke's series of articles for the Manchester Guardian (June, July, 1949, and January, 1950) and partly because what came out at the trials does not by any means tell the whole story. The attached summary of the case from Time magazine is the most concise account of the published information which we have seen here. Much of the reporting on it in this country has been biased by political prejudice, and there is still a good deal of uncertainty in many circles as to whether Hiss is a martyr to the machinations of reactionary witch-hunters, whether he is shielding someone else, or whether he really did pass secret State Department documents to the Russians. The general confusion has not been lessened by the remarks of such prominent persons as Dean Acheson and Mrs. Roosevelt subsequent to the trial, which gave the impression that they still doubted the evidence of his guilt. Our information suggests strongly that he was not merely a communist sympathiser and idealist, but was, in fact, guilty of passing on State Department information to Russian agents. It is important that you should know as much as possible, for record and for future reference, about the true facts of the case, but we ourselves are not really in a position to

A.S. Fordham, Esq.,
American Department,
Foreign Office,
London, S.W.1.

provide/

- 2 -

provide them as we are not in possession of the full details.

here is therefore asking whether they would be willing to let you have a comprehensive summary of the Hiss case. He tells us that they have all the relevant information available in London (Hiss has been an object of their attention since at least 1946), and that this includes a substantial amount of material which never emerged in court. He has also asked them to let us have a copy of whatever report is prepared for the Foreign Office.

AV1013/5

As we reported elsewhere (see our telegram No. 59 Saving of January 28th, section (a)), one of the results of the Hiss conviction was a renewal of the demand on Capitol Hill that there should be an investigation into the State Department to discover whether it was harbouring any more spies. Subsequently Senator McCarthy (R., Wisconsin) made two public speeches in which he alleged that some 300 of the Department's employees had been certified as disloyal and that its staff included 57 card-carrying communists. Senator McCarthy also cited 4 individuals by name. You may be interested to see the enclosed copy of a statement by Mr. John Peurifoy, Deputy Under-Secretary of State for Administration, which gives details of Senator McCarthy's charges and refutes them.

Yours ever,

THIS IS A COPY
THE ORIGINAL HAS BEEN RETAINED
IN THE DEPARTMENT UNDER SECTION
3(4) OF THE PUBLIC RECORDS ACT 1958

he could return the originals to the State Department in the morning. Chambers claimed he carried the documents copied by Priscilla to Communist agents in New York using as his alias, George Crosley.

Later, the House questioned Hiss, who denied that he ever knew Chambers and demanded that his accuser confront him. House members arranged a private meeting, and Chambers stared Hiss in the face and repeated everything he had told the panel and more. Backed against the wall, Hiss hazily recalled meeting a man by another name but certainly never providing him with state secrets. Chambers became annoyed when it appeared that House investigators intended to do noth-

ing, so he appeared on the radio program *Meet the Press* and said, "Alger Hiss was a Communist and may be now." Hiss sued for slander.

The Inquest and Trial

The House turned the allegations over to the Department of Justice, and both Chambers and Hiss gave testimony before a grand jury. The jury indicted Hiss on two counts of perjury—one for denying that he met Chambers in 1938, and the other for testifying under oath that he had never handed Chambers any classified documents from the State Department.

Above: A letter from the British Embassy in Washington to the American Department of the British Foreign Office. The document demonstrates the divide that the Hiss case caused in America as well as pointing out that at that time, the British had also suspected Hiss of spying for the Soviets.

Right: Alger Hiss and his wife leave New York Federal Court 21 in January 1950 after hearing Hiss's sentence of five years imprisonment for two counts of perjury. His condemnation was due to the then-investigator Richard Nixon, who became president in 1968 and was very much involved in the anti-Communist campaign instigated by John Parnell Thomas and Senator Joseph McCarthy.

During the federal court trial in 1949, Chambers produced four papers in Hiss's handwriting, photographs of State Department documents, 65 typewritten sheets from Priscilla's typewriter, and a bundle of papers that he had hidden in a hollowed-out pumpkin. Mostly due to Hiss's reputation as a longtime servant of the government, the first trial ended in a hung jury. In a second trial, conducted in 1950, the jury convicted Hiss, and he spent the next four years in the federal prison at Lewisburg, Pennsylvania.

In the 1980s Hiss attempted to vindicate himself by accusing the FBI of illegally wiretapping his phone and falsely attempting to frame him. The effort failed but created another controversy: liberals believed him and conservatives did not. In 1996, evidence surfaced through the deciphered Venona texts (Soviet intelligence messages between Moscow and other cities in the 1940s) that a high-ranking agent in the State Department codenamed "Ales" had flown to Moscow after the Yalta conference. The only American on that flight was Hiss.

The debate about Hiss's guilt continutes, with many journalists and historians questioning the veracity of the information contained in the Venona texts.

Below: Alger Hiss, center, with his wife Isabel, left, and son Tony, on October 29, 1992, at a news conference following a statement by Dmitri Volkogonov, a high-ranking Russian general with access to military intelligence archives who declared that Hiss had never spied for the Soviets. Volkogonov later admitted he had made only a cursory check of Soviet records.

HOWARD, EDWARD LEE (1952–2002)

During the mid-1980s, ex-CIA caseworker Edward Lee Howard virtually destroyed U.S. covert operations in the Soviet Union and Eastern Europe by selling out the agency's spy network to support his drinking and drug habits.

Edward Lee Howard grew up in Alamogordo, New Mexico, near the site of the first atomic bomb explosion. His father worked for the U.S. Air Force as a missile specialist at nearby Hollomon Air Force Base. His mother descended from a Hispanic-American family from New Mexico. Howard received his education wherever the Air Force based his father.

In 1972 he graduated from the University of Texas and, to avoid the Vietnam War, took a job with Exxon in Ireland. He became disinterested with the work and in 1975 joined the Peace Corps, went to Colombia, and there met his wife, Mary, another Peace Corps volunteer.

Two years later he resigned from the Peace Corps, earned a master's degree in business administration, and became a loan officer in Peru. Tiring of Peru, he returned to the United States in 1979 and sent his résumé to the CIA. By then Howard had become a heavy-drinking adventurer who used marijuana, cocaine, LSD, and other illegal substances.

```
----DOSSIER--------
Name: Edward Lee Howard
Code Name: Robert
Birth/Death: 1952-2002
Nationality: American
Occupation: Peace Corps
Volunteer
Involvement: American Spy
for the Soviet Union
Outcome: Defected to Russia
```

The CIA did not look closely at Howard's personal habits but were more impressed by his education, overseas experience, and expertise with firearms. He was recruited and sent to the Farm, the CIA's training camp, from where he graduated as an intelligence officer.

The CIA's Moscow Man

Howard was an officer with diplomatic immunity in the CIA's Soviet/Eastern European (SE) division, which ran all of the agency's espionage operations in the Soviet Union and its satellites. The CIA briefed him on all its operations behind the iron curtain and gave him the names of all the agents working in Moscow. Meanwhile, as part of his pre-Moscow training, Howard received hands-on experience in the United States, function-ing as a case officer spying on Soviet agents who were spying on America. Also, as part of the preparation for send-ing Howard abroad, the CIA trained his wife as a support worker for the American Embassy in Moscow.

On the eve of flying the Howards to Moscow, the CIA discovered that their new agent had a drinking problem. They subjected him to a polygraph test and dis-covered that he also had a drug problem and a theft problem. Under pressure from the CIA, Howard resigned.

Left: Edward Lee Howard strolling along the Arbat, a pedestrian walkway in Moscow popular for people watching, on March 22, 1995. As relations between the East and West thawed, Howard became worried that the CIA would come after him. In the David Wise book *The Spy Who Got Away*, Howard was quoted as saying, "I have to worry that the agency might try to kidnap me. It wouldn't take much: a hypodermic needle, throw me in the trunk of the car, and it's only two hours to the [Austrian] border."

For Revenge and Money

After departing from the agency, Howard went to work as an economic analyst for the New Mexico State Legislature and the New Mexico State Hospital. In July 1985 he bumped into an ex-CIA employee at a bar and, after a night of hard drinking, mentioned that he had been selling secrets to the Soviets. Word of the conversation funneled back to the CIA, which at first took no action.

During the same period, the CIA met with a recent Soviet defector, Vitaly Yurchenko, who spoke of a man code-named Robert who had visited Austria in 1984, met with Soviet officials, and in exchange for a large amount of cash, sold information on secret CIA operations in the Soviet Union. Yurchenko did not know the man but remembered him as a person who had been specially trained to go to Moscow as an operative but had resigned.

The CIA immediately associated "Robert" with Edward Lee Howard. Yurchenko's information also explained why the CIA's SE division in Moscow had lately suffered so many setbacks. During the same period of time, many of the agency's operations elsewhere in Russia and Eastern Europe had also been unaccountably blown.

The problem began when Paul M. Stambaugh, an undercover CIA agent and first secretary to the American Embassy in Moscow, was arrested along with A. G. Tolkachev, a Soviet missile and avionics expert. Stambaugh was expelled for espionage and Tolkachev was executed for treason. The expulsion of Stambaugh and the execution of Tolkachev created a ripple affect. After Howard made a second trip to Europe, the Soviets arrested and expelled Michael Sellers, the second secretary in the American Embassy in Moscow, and Eric Sites, the military attaché. After a number of undercover double agents lost their lives during the sweep, the CIA concluded that the informant had to be Howard.

In September 1985 the FBI put Howard under surveillance and obtained authorization for wiretaps. They confronted him a few days later, but Howard refused to talk. On September 21, Howard and his wife started driving toward Santa Fe, New Mexico, and the FBI followed. At some point during the trip, Howard jumped out of the car, leaving an inflated and disguised dummy (called a jack-in-the-box) in his seat while his wife drove on with the car. Two days later, the FBI issued a warrant for Howard's arrest, but by then he was headed to Moscow by way of New York, Copenhagen, and Helsinki. KGB agents met him at Helsinki, stashed him in the trunk of an embassy car, and crossed into the Soviet Union. Under questioning, Howard's wife later confessed that her husband had a secret bank account in Switzerland. The FBI checked and found a balance of $150,000.

In August 1986 Howard resurfaced in Moscow with political asylum, citizenship, a comfortable apartment, a country retreat, and an ample salary. He later appeared on television, claiming he had never done anything wrong. After perestroika, he set up a consulting company in Moscow for U.S. firms wishing to establish business relationships in Russia. He died in 2002 at the age of 50.

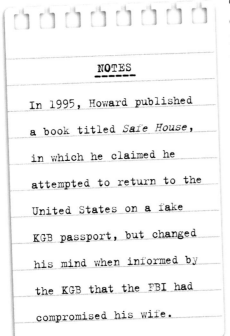

NOTES

In 1995, Howard published a book titled *Safe House*, in which he claimed he attempted to return to the United States on a fake KGB passport, but changed his mind when informed by the KGB that the FBI had compromised his wife.

KATZ, OTTO (1900–1952)

Otto Katz enjoyed many opportunities in life, but his early failures as a playwright drove him into the Russian Cheka, where he became a power-crazed assassin.

Born in 1900, the son of a wealthy textile manufacturer in Prague, Czechoslovakia, Otto Katz received the best education money could buy. He studied literature and became a friend of Franz Kafka. The relationship inspired him to become a great writer, a career for which he had excessive ambition and dedication but not enough talent.

He convinced his father, Louis Katznellenbogen, to back his plays and his mother, German actress Tilla Durieux, to perform in them. Neither his mother's acting nor his father's money could keep the productions from failing. The Katznellenbogens lost two million marks in the boundless abyss of their son's theatrical endeavors. Katz's vanity productions stopped when his father retired, and the Katznellenbogens lost the rest of the family fortune during the post–World War I inflation crisis, created by the inept Weimar Republic government.

In 1928 Katz was penniless. Communist friends arranged for him to look for a job in Moscow, the new land of opportunity.

```
----DOSSIER--------
Name: Otto Katz
(Katznellenbogen)
Code Name: André Simone
Birth/Death: 1900-1952
Nationality:
Czechoslovakian
Occupation: Playwright
Involvement: Cheka Agent
for Bolsheviks
Outcome: Hanged
```

Looking for Work

Katz's associates suggested that he consider intelligence work, so he visited the Cheka, Russia's internal security police force, which was in the process of expanding operations throughout Europe. Katz agreed to become a spy

Right: In the 2001 book *The Girls: Sappho Goes to Hollywood*, Diana McLellan posits an undocumented marriage between Katz and the movie star Marlene Dietrich. She also claims that Katz was the inspiration for Victor Laszlo in *Casablanca*. While neither of these claims can be fully substantiated, Katz was certainly moving in the right circles in Hollywood at this time.

and, after a short course in espionage, the Cheka sent him to Berlin to keep Willie Muzenberg, the wealthy Jewish leader of the German Communist Party, under surveillance.

Most of Muzenberg's wealth came from his publishing business, which printed all the party's newspapers, magazines, and pamphlets and distributed them throughout Germany. The Cheka wanted Muzenberg watched because they disapproved of his wealth and the manner in which he obtained it. They also disapproved of his predisposition to publish his own sentiments, which did not always coincide with those of Joseph Stalin. Katz expected to keep watch on Muzenberg in Berlin, but when Adolf Hitler came to power in 1933, Muzenberg feared arrest and fled to Paris. By going to France, Muzenberg lost control of the German Communist Party and no longer needed to be watched.

Katz obtained a new assignment, serving as a courier between the Communist network in Spain and Moscow. This required frequent visits through Paris, and the NKVD (formerly the Cheka) instructed Katz to investigate Muzen-

berg's activities. The ex-publisher appeared to be doing little more than living off his money.

In 1940, when the Nazis invaded Germany, the French arrested Muzenberg and threw him in an internment camp. Stalin began to worry what Muzenberg might say under interrogation. The NKVD contacted Katz and instructed him to rescue Muzenberg. With help from French Communists, Katz bribed the guards at the internment compound and freed Muzenberg and two others. On the way

Below: IBy 1948 Katz had come to the attention of the British Secret Service, who were aware of some, if not all, of his undercover activities for the Soviets as well as his use of the alias André Simone.

81

EXTRACT.

for File No.: P.F.41,664.   Name: KATZ. Otto.

in File No.: P.F.47,638. Link Volume.   Serial: 5b.   Receipt Date: 21.

riginal from: Foreign Office.   Under Ref.: CZB/139/51.   Dated: 14.6.

xtracted on: 4.7.51.   by: C.J.P.   Section: R.5.

Extract from Report re R.KATZ by the Eastern European Section ,
Foreign Office research Dept forwarded to the Foreign Office Lo
mentioning Otto KATZ.

S E C R E T.

. . . .

A further point of interest is that Otto KATZ, alias Andre
editor and diplomatic correspondent of Rudé Pravo, the official
Communist organ, and a Soviet intelligence agent, spent the war
Mexico and other Latin American countries. There is a possible
between Rolf (or Rudolf) KATZ and Otto KATZ in the post- war co
if Communist activities in the South American continent.

. . . .

4342

2nd October, 1948

Otto KATZ alias Andre SIMONE

Reference your enquiry:

This man, who is of Austrian
origin, is about 53 years old. He is a well-known
Communist and has been a member of the Party for
many years, having been first a member of the
Austrian C.P. and then later he joined the Czech
C.P. He is a journalist, a writer and a reporter.
Before the war he was connected with Willy
MUENZENBERG's publishing business and was on the
editorial staff of his "Welt am Abend" and "Arbeiter
Illustrierte Zeitung". He also contributed
regularly to other organs of the Communist Party.
He went to France in 1938, to the U.K. in 1939,
to Mexico in 1940 and to France again and
Czechoslovakia in 1946. He is a regular contributor
to the ideological organ of the K.P.C., "Tvorba"
(Creation), which is a Communist weekly in Prague
intended for the Party officials. KATZ is
vehemently opposed to the Western outlook and
was closely connected with the Comintern before
the war and with the Cominform at the present
time. He is undoubtedly a dangerous person.

USE WITH

CAUTION

> Upon arrest, Katz knew what kind of treatment he would receive and immediately offered a confession. He was tortured anyway.

back to the city, Katz looped a rope around Muzenberg's neck and strung him from a tree. The other two men returned to Paris with Katz. The execution bore all the earmarks of SMERSH, the Soviet assassination division of the NKVD with roots tracing back to the Cheka. Sometime during 1935 and 1940, Katz had become a special agent of SMERSH.

Unwelcome to Hollywood

Katz remained in Paris, using the cover name André Simone until the NKVD sent him to the American Embassy in Lisbon, Portugal, to obtain a visa to the United States. In 1941 Katz arrived in New York to begin a new assignment: he traveled to Hollywood to organize actors, writers, and producers into Communist cells. One of his contacts tipped off the FBI, who put Katz under surveillance. Local party activists warned Katz that he was being watched, so he fled to Mexico and made his way back to Moscow.

Back Home in Czechoslovakia

In February 1945 the Red Army "liberated" Czechoslovakia from the Nazis. Following closely behind came Colonel Otto Katz—the NKVD wanted all disloyal Communists rounded up. Over the next three years, Katz gathered hundreds of his fellow Czechs and threw them in prison, where most of them vanished permanently.

Katz set his sights on grasping more power. In 1948, he became chief of the Czech Government Information Service, a lofty title used to screen his secret police work. He coveted the title of Czech Foreign Minister, a position held by Jan Masaryk, so he falsely accused the incumbent of treason. On March 9, 1948, Katz announced that Masaryk had committed suicide, but the minister's death bore the footprints of another SMERSH execution.

The death of Masaryk put the MGB (formerly the NKVD) on notice that Katz might be exceeding his authority. They watched him for four years, observing that he sometimes obeyed Moscow's bidding and sometimes careened off course to feed his personal ambitions.

In 1952, Stalin authorized another great purge that cut to the heart of Communist leadership in Czechoslovakia. When the MGB arrested Katz, they took him into custody under his code name, André Simone, and listed his occupation as a journalist for Czechoslovakia's Communist newspaper. He received a quick trial and was convicted as an agent of "Jewish bourgeois nationalists" and hanged.

Nobody wept when the public learned that André Simone was, in reality, Otto Katz, least of all the family of Willie Muzenberg.

Opposite:

Documentation indicating the extent of Katz's extensive activities. It rightly concludes: "He is undoubtably a dangerous person."

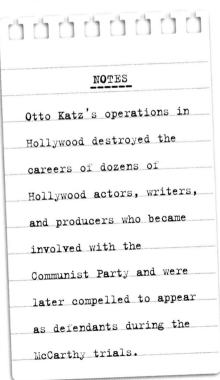

NOTES

Otto Katz's operations in Hollywood destroyed the careers of dozens of Hollywood actors, writers, and producers who became involved with the Communist Party and were later compelled to appear as defendants during the McCarthy trials.

KELL, VERNON (1873-1942)

Major General Vernon Kell built the British counterintelligence service from scratch and became the first chief of MI5, and then lost the post because Winston Churchill carried a personal grudge.

Born on November 21, 1873, in Yarmouth, England, Vernon Kell grew up in a wealthy cosmopolitan family. His mother was half Polish, so he spoke both English and Polish at a young age. Kell possessed a natural gift for languages, and between home-schooling by his mother and frequent trips to the Continent, he also mastered German, French, and Italian.

He entered Sandhurst, the equivalent of West Point in Great Britain, and graduated in 1892 with an officer's commission, after which he served in various assignments abroad as an interpreter. In 1898 Kell went to Moscow and quickly mastered the Russian language. When he returned to England, he reported to his regiment in Cork and met Constance Scott, daughter of a wealthy Cork landowner; they married on April 5, 1900. Kell spent the next two years in China, where he participated in suppressing the Boxer Rebellion—a Chinese insurrection against foreigners exploiting the country's economy.

----DOSSIER--------

Name: Major General Sir Vernon Kell

Code Name: None

Birth/Death: 1873-1942

Nationality: British

Occupation: British Army Officer

Involvement: Chief of Counterintelligence

Outcome: Dismissed from Army

The Birth of British Counterintelligence

Returning to London in 1902, Kell joined the German section of the War Office with the rank of captain. Five years later he became a member of the Committee of Imperial Defense.

In 1909 Great Britain grew concerned about German spies in England and Scotland and created the Secret Service Bureau, a counterintelligence service. Vernon Kell served as its first director. The operation began small but grew rapidly during World War I, and in 1916 became MI5 (British counterintelligence).

To learn the business of counterespionage, Kell worked with Mansfield Cumming, director of the Secret Intelligence Service (SIS, later MI6) and Reginald Hall, who ran naval intelligence. Kell also engaged Basil Thompson of the Metropolitan Police and Patrick Quinn, chief of Scotland Yard's Special Branch, because MI5 had no authority to make arrests.

Changing the Rules of Counterespionage

Between 1909 and 1914, Kell's small force of counterespionage agents identified and tracked German spies without making arrests. In 1911, Kell's agents made an accidental but ultimately essential discovery. One of the agents overheard a conversation on a train regarding the receipt of a strange letter.

Agent Stanley Clarke approached the owner of the letter, a hotel proprietor, and asked if he could see the mysterious missive. It transpired that the letter was from a senior member of German intelligence, who was part of a spy ring that had a number of drop points to pass information. After much surveillance, the ring was cracked. However, the discovery of the letter led Kell to ask Home Secretary Winston Churchill that the law be modified to enable MI5 agents to open private mail without special warrants. Churchill obliged, and the interception of correspondence involving suspected spies became a part of Kell's counterespionage tactics.

When Great Britain declared war on Germany in 1914, MI5 had dossiers, correspondence, and surveillance evidence compiled on scores of spies and apprehended the entire network in one sweep.

Below: Sir Vernon George Waldegrave Kell, during the time that he served on the intelligence staff in Tientsin. During the Boxer Rebellion he was also the foreign correspondent for the *Daily Telegraph* newspaper.

Agents arrested Karl Ernst, who operated a barbershop used as a drop center for German operatives. In Ireland agents picked up Karl Lody, Germany's top spymaster, who had been examining British military installations in Scotland. During the war, Germany continuously fed spies into England, often using fake U.S. passports. Kell's MI5 unit routinely rounded them up, put them in prison, and occasionally recommended execution.

Successful in World War I and in the years that followed, Kell rose to the rank of major general. During the 1920s and 1930s, his MI5 unit was regarded as the world's foremost counterespionage operation. He gathered information on Communist and Nazi infiltrators, expelled diplomatic spies, and maintained vast records on suspected spies that were under surveillance.

Winston Churchill and MI5

At the outbreak of war in 1939, Winston Churchill was first lord of the Admiralty, and he was not a man of great patience. He looked to MI5 to clean enemy spies out of the British Isles. When he asked MI5 for reports and they were not immediately forthcoming, he blamed Kell. Churchill became annoyed with Kell's old-fashioned methods long before the war started and complained that MI5 had not kept pace with the German Abwehr, which at the time was being run by Wilhelm Canaris. Churchill expected MI5 to be equally capable in knowing the enemy's plans.

On October 14, 1939, one month after Great

Britain's second declaration of war against Germany, a German U-boat picked its way through the Royal Navy's antisubmarine defenses in the Orkney Islands, stole into the naval base at Scapa Flow, and fired a spread of torpedoes into the HMS *Royal Oak*. The battleship sank, taking 834 sailors to the bottom.

Furious over the loss, Churchill demanded an explanation. The navy presented an unconfirmed allegation that a German spy had provided the U-boat commander with data that enabled him to work through the antisubmarine defenses at Scapa Flow. Though the report later proved to be false, Churchill placed most of the blame on MI5.

In January 1940, an explosion at the Royal Gunpowder Factory in Churchill's Waltham Abbey district killed five people. Churchill attributed the explosion to German sabotage and blamed Kell, although Scotland Yard investigators stoutly disagreed.

The Scapa Flow Scapegoat

On May 10, 1940, Churchill replaced Neville Chamberlain as British prime minister. On May 25, still convinced that the Scapa Flow sinking and the Waltham Abbey explosion occurred because of MI5 incompetence, Churchill dismissed Kell from his post.

Whether MI5 had or had not kept pace with German intelligence was never the issue: Churchill simply disliked Kell for a slight that occurred 20 years before. In the 1920s, Churchill has asked for a report from MI5, but because he was not in the government at the time, he was not entitled to see it, and Kell denied him.

Forced into retirement, Kell moved into a small cottage in Buckinghamshire where he died on March 27, 1942.

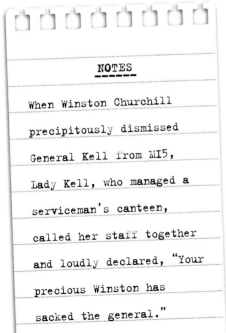

NOTES

When Winston Churchill precipitously dismissed General Kell from MI5, Lady Kell, who managed a serviceman's canteen, called her staff together and loudly declared, "Your precious Winston has sacked the general."

KHAN, NOOR INAYAT (1914–1944)

Noor Inayat Khan, a tiny wisp of a woman with the courage of a lion, kept the French underground connected with London during a period when the Abwehr believed they had shut down all radio transmissions to British intelligence.

The daughter of an Indian Sufi missionary and an American woman, Noor Inayat Khan was born in Moscow on New Year's Day 1914. Her father, a musician and a mystic, descended from Tipu Sultan ("the Tiger of Mysore"). The family had no reason to be in Moscow, but the chief of the Sufi sect of Muslims wanted to make Sufism known to the West and sent Ianyat Khan's father to Russia as an Islamic missionary. In 1915, one year after the beginning of World War I, the family fled Russia and settled in France.

While Inayat Khan went to school in Suresne on the outskirts of Paris, her father traveled around Europe peddling Sufism. He died during a visit to Delphi, and his widow decided to remain in Suresne and raise her two sons and two daughters in France. Inayat Khan finished school in Suresne, studied music in Paris, and in the mid-1930s studied child psychology at the Sorbonne. In 1937 she took two years off to study languages before applying for her license to

```
----DOSSIER--------
Name: Noor-un-Nisa
Inayat Khan
Code Names: Madeleine,
Jeanne-Marie Regnier
Birth/Death: 1914-1944
Nationality: Indian-
American
Occupation: British Women's
Auxiliary Air Force
Involvement: Allied Spy in
France During World War II
Outcome: Executed in
Dachau, Germany
```

practice psychology. In 1940 the ink had barely dried on her certificate when German Panzer divisions rumbled into

Right: Noor Inayat Khan. In Jean Overton Fuller's 1952 book *Madeleine* Captain Selwyn Jepson, who interviewed Khan when she first joined the Special Operations Executive, described her thus; "I see her very clearly as she was that first afternoon, sitting in front of me in that dingy little room, in a hard kitchen chair at the other side of a bare wooden table. Indeed, of them all—and they were many—who did not return, I find myself constantly remembering her with a curious and very personal vividness which outshines the rest. The small, still features, the dark, quiet eyes, the soft voice and the fine spirit glowing in her."

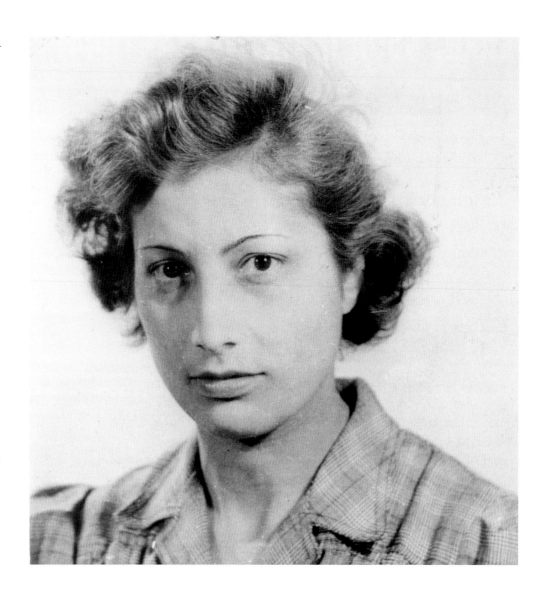

France. As the battle reached the outskirts of Paris, Inayat Khan escaped with her mother and sister to England.

From Child Psychologist to Spy

After settling in England, Inayat Khan joined the Women's Auxiliary Air Force (WAAF). She felt compelled to do more, and in late 1941 applied for a commission in intelligence. The WAAF promoted her, trained her as a signals operator, and she became the first WAAF wireless telegraphist. On February 8, 1943, Captain Selwyn Jepson of the British Special Operations Executive (SOE) recruited her out of WAAF and assigned her to the underground espionage network in France. The SOE, however, did a shoddy job of training Inayat Khan in security measures before sending her to France.

On the night of June 16, 1943, a Lysander dropped Inayat Khan near Le Mons. She was a highly intelligent woman, knew her way around the country, and spoke perfect French. No one met her at the landing field or showed her the way to Versailles. When she arrived with her shortwave radio at an apartment at 40 Rue Erlanger in Auteuil, she aroused no suspicion. Using the operational code name "Madeleine," she set up her wireless and began transmitting reports on resistance operations and supply problems to London. Allied planes soon appeared over designated drop points, parachuting crates of arms, ammunition, and supplies to the French underground.

Inayat Khan used a different code name when working directly with the French underground. Lieutenant Henri Garry, who worked for the espionage network known as Cinema, knew her only as Jeanne-Marie Regnier.

British officer Francis Suttill, code-named Prosper, commanded the Cinema unit and used the National School of Agriculture at Grignon as headquarters. From time to time, Inayat Khan could be seen pedaling her bicycle to and from the building with her messages. Suttill and Garry were even less help than the SOE in advising Inayat Khan on how to protect herself from detection.

Left: Official SOE transcripts of the codes Khan used during her radio transmissions from behind enemy lines in France.

Left: Though some of her instructors at SOE were initially unconvinced of Khan's suitability as an espionage operative, code-master Leo Marks later noted: "Her transmissions were flawless, with all their security checks intact."

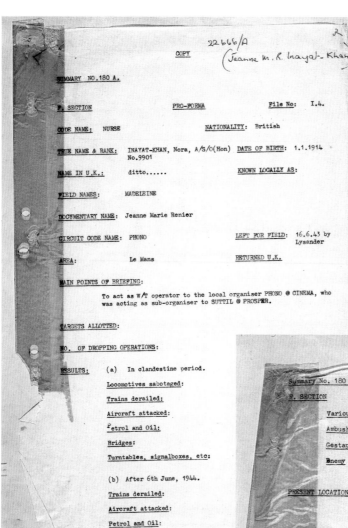

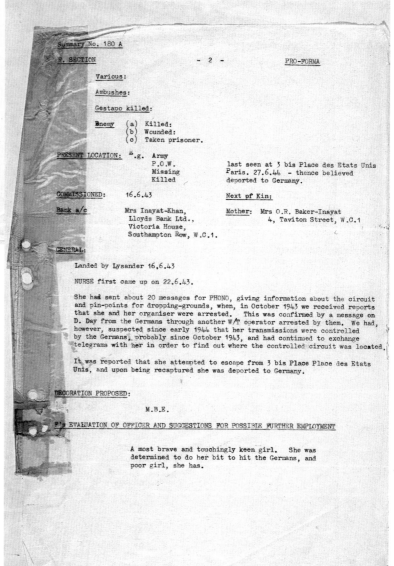

Above and Right: A citation recommending that Khan be awarded a Member of the British Empire (MBE) for her actions. Eventually Khan's indomitable courage led to her being awarded not only a posthumous MBE but also the George Cross from the British government. She was also awarded the Croix de Guerre (with Gold Star) by the French government.

A Determined Young Woman

On July 1, 1943, as Inayat Khan pedaled toward the school, she observed about 80 SS troops entering the building. She pulled her bike off the road, crept behind a hedgerow, and watched as German troops dragged underground workers from the school. When the motorcade departed, she rode back to her apartment and reported the raid to the SOE. She learned that other resistance agents had been arrested in Paris, so she warned London that Abwehr agents had infiltrated SOE operations in France.

At SOE headquarters, Colonel Buckmaster concluded that Inayat Khan must be the sole surviving operative left in the Cinema section of France and told her he would send a plane to pick her up. She refused to leave and for the next three months served as the only wireless operator in France.

Inayat Khan was a very petite, nervous, and timid person, and to remain in France under the most menacing conditions was an act of supreme courage. In London, before sending her to France, the SOE had subjected her to a series of mock Gestapo interrogations. The sessions terrified her, and she came away from the interrogation room frightened and trembling. Not eager to experience the real thing, Inayat Khan began changing lodgings after two or three transmissions and only worked the radio late at night.

For 500 Pieces of Silver

After a few months, Inayat Khan toughened up. One day, when traveling on the Metro with her transmitter, a German soldier took the seat next to her and asked what she carried in her case. She said, "Part of the machinery for a film projector." The soldier insisted upon looking inside. She opened the case and patiently waited. The soldier observed a wireless set with bulbs, nodded his head approvingly, and returned the case because he knew absolutely nothing about radio transmitters or film projectors.

On another occasion a German soldier caught her stringing an antenna in a tree. He asked what she was doing, and she said she was hanging a clothesline. He helped her place the wire in the tree and walked away. Inayat Khan's good luck

Extract from a deposition on oath of Wilhelm KRAUSS, Governor of PFORZHEIM prison, sworn before a War Crimes Investigation Unit on 6.11.46.

5. I remember that in November 1943 an English woman was delivered into Pforzheim prison. I was told that she was to be treated in accordance with regulations for "Nacht und Nebel" prisoners. (Note; "Nacht und Nebel" means Night and Fog. It was the expression used for people who "disappeared" and once in custody were kept on the lowest rations, in solitary confinement etc) and moreover, that she was to be chained hand and foot. This order was carried through.

6. After some time, I decided to remove the chains from her hands, because I felt sorry for the English girl;

7. Very shortly afterwards the Gestapo H.Q. from Karlsruhe telephoned and reprimanded me for not observing the regulations about chains which had to be strictly adhered to

changed in October 1943 when a French neighbor, in exchange for £500, told the Gestapo where they could find a wireless operator. That night, while Inayat Khan radioed London, the Gestapo caught her in the act.

Under severe interrogation, Inayat Khan said nothing and merely requested that she be shot immediately. Interrogators shoved her into a cell on the top floor of Gestapo headquarters on Avenue Foch, where she found two SOE men locked in other cells. She squeezed through the bars, released the two men, and attempted to escape during an air raid. The trio made it out of the building, but an alert guard gave the alarm and they never made it to the street.

The Gestapo transferred Inayat Khan to Pforzheim Prison in Germany, where she remained for ten months in solitary confinement. On September 13, 1944, guards moved her to Dachau, where Khan was immediately executed with three other women prisoners.

Above: Khan's bravery and defiance in the most trying of circumstances left a lasting impression on some of her captors. Hans Josef Kieffer, the chief of the Gestapo headquarters in Paris, reputedly broke down in tears when told during his postwar interrogation about her death in Dachau.

NOTES

Inayat Khan posthumously received the George Cross. The citation read: "Assistant Section Officer Inayat Khan displayed the most conspicuous courage, both moral and physical, over a period of more than twelve months."

Nikolai Khokhlov became the first SMERSH (Soviet counter-inteligence) assassin to defect to the West during the cold war.

Nikolai Khokhlov was born in Nizhnii Novgorod (now Gorki), the son of a printer who had joined the Red Army and fought for the Communists during the 1918–20 civil war. His parents divorced when he was still a child. Khokhlov's mother remarried and his stepfather took the family to Moscow. In 1938 Khokhlov entered the Komsomol (Communist youth movement). He showed promise and began rising through the Soviet system. By 1941, the third year of World War II, he was well established in the Ministry of State Security, which focused on espionage activities outside the Soviet Union. When German armies began closing on Moscow, he volunteered for service on the front line but was rejected due to bad eyesight.

----DOSSIER--------

Name: Nikolai Khokhlov

Code Names: Oberleutenant Wittgenstein, Stanislaw Lewandowski

Birth/Death: 1923–?

Nationality: Russian

Occupation: Civil Servant

Involvement: SMERSH Assassin

Outcome: Poisoned but Survived; Date of Death Unknown

Welcome to SMERSH

Khokhlov's involvement in the war began in 1941 when the Ministry of Internal Affairs (MVD) put guerrilla forces behind German lines. Posing as Oberleutenant Wittgenstein of the Secret Field Police, he assassinated Wilhelm Kube, the Nazi Gauleiter of Minsk. The Soviet counterintelligence department, SMERSH, took notice. SMERSH commander Lieutenant Colonel Pavel Sudaplatov complimented Khokhlov for the speedy execution and

ordered him to go to Ankara and assassinate Franz von Papen, the German ambassador to Turkey. Khokhlov declined the assignment because he could not speak Turkish. When the Red Army moved into Romania in 1945, Khokhlov followed, posing as a displaced person named Stanislaw Lewandowski. The MVD told him to search for OSS operatives and kill them. Khokhlov took citizenship in Romania and remained there until 1947. By then, he had become one of the MVD's top SMERSH assassins.

The Yanina Family Plan

In 1953 Colonel Lev Studnikov took control of SMERSH and ordered Khokhlov to assassinate Igor Georgi Okolovich, the director of the Society of National Unity, a powerful anti-Soviet organization headquartered in Frankfurt, Germany. The

order actually came from Prime Minister Georgi Malenkov and First Secretary Nikita Khrushchev, who considered Okolovich "the most dangerous enemy of the Soviet regime." Khokhlov visited East Berlin, hired two East Germans to act as assistants, and took them back to Moscow for SMERSH training. He also picked through an array of special SMERSH-designed weapons, including a small electric gun that looked like a pack of cigarettes but actually shot pellets filled with potassium cyanide.

While still in Moscow, Khokhlov did something he had never done before—he confided to his wife, Yanina, the details of his mission. Yanina Timashkevits was a brilliant construction engineer and a Roman Catholic. In sharing his life for the first time with Yanina, Khokhlov began to regret his work for SMERSH and asked for a transfer. Studnikov refused and

Below: Former Soviet SMERSH assassin Nikolai Khokhlov, right, talking with Georgi Okolovich, the man whose assassination he refused to carry out. The refusal led to Khokhlov's defection to the West and the disappearance of his wife and daughter.

insisted he kill Okolovich. Khokhlov knew that if he refused the mission, SMERSH would kill him, Yanina, and their one-year-old son. Yanina told her husband to take the mission but to defect to the Americans in Frankfurt instead of killing Okolovich. Khokhlov argued that doing so would be the same as signing the death warrant for the family, but Yanina insisted.

SMERSH Revealed

On February 8, 1954, Khokhlov received his orders and departed for Frankfurt. Instead of going to the Americans, he went directly to Okolovich's home, knocked on the door, and after being invited inside, said, "I am Captain Khokhlov of the MVD, and I have been ordered to kill you." Okolovich was not particularly surprised because SMERSH operatives had recently kidnapped Dr. Alexander Trushnovich, the Society of National Unity's director in Berlin. Okolovich felt much better when Khokhlov asked to be conducted to U.S. Army headquarters so he could defect. The two men departed immediately, and Khokhlov became the first of the murderous SMERSH agents to defect to the West.

When questioned by the CIA, Khokhlov revealed where his two East German assistants could be located. Both men were apprehended and happily agreed to defect to the West with Khokhlov.

Prior to Khokhlov's defection, the CIA had heard of SMERSH but only as an unsubstantiated rumor. When Khokhlov broke the story to the press, the revelation that SMERSH actually existed struck the public like a bombshell. The Soviets' sanction of government-sponsored trained assassins seemed incredible to the Western world, yet Khokhlov proved SMERSH to be all too true.

The Unspeakable Revenge of the KGB

Khokhlov feared for the safety of his family and implored U.S. officials to intervene and find a way to bring his family out of the Soviet Union. The State Department worked through the U.S. Embassy in Moscow and on June 2, 1954, they learned that the MVD (now the KGB) had arrested and imprisoned Yanina, her young son, and her 14-year-old sister. After that, nothing more was ever heard about Khokhlov's family.

Khokhlov understood what the silence meant. He then provided every detail that he could remember from his years with the MVD and SMERSH. The CIA built a file four feet thick from Khokhlov's testimony. Western intelligence agencies learned the names of hundreds of agents, where their headquarters were located, how they operated, and all about their ciphers, codes, and letter drops. Khokhlov's information virtually shut down KGB operations in Europe for more than a year.

In 1957, the KGB sent SMERSH after Khokhlov. On September 15, 1957, the assassins located him at a conference in Frankfurt. Khokhlov became seriously ill from an unknown substance, which physicians misdiagnosed as a blood disorder. He was transferred to a U.S. hospital and specialists kept him alive by intravenous feeding, massive blood transfusions, and applying new drugs. Doctors finally concluded that Soviet assassins had attempted to poison him with radioactive thallium. Khokhlov survived, assumed a new name, and disappeared to start a new life somewhere in the West.

KRIVITSKY, WALTER G. (1899-1941)

As a teenager, Walter Krivitsky joined the long list of young men who believed that a better life lay across the border in Communist Russia, and he spent most of his life supporting a cause which he came to understand was brutal, corrupt, and dangerously deceitful.

Walter Krivitsky, son of Polish Jewish parents in the province of Galicia (then part of the Hapsburg Empire), was originally born Samuel Ginsberg. At the age of 13, angry over the poverty and anti-Semitism that afflicted his family, he joined an underground political movement to overthrow the Hapsburgs. During his teens he studied the works of Karl Marx, changed his name from Ginsberg to Krivitsky to escape racial persecution, and became an avowed Communist. In 1917 he joined the Bolsheviks during the Russian revolution and obtained work with the Cheka secret police as a spy.

```
----DOSSIER--------
Name: Walter G. Krivitsky
Code Name: Dr. Martin
Lessner
Birth/Death: 1899-1941
Nationality: Polish
Occupation: Communist
Activist
Involvement: Spy for
Soviets
Outcome: Assassinated
```

Lessons in Communism

Krivitsky rose quickly in Soviet intelligence. After Lenin died, Krivitsky pledged his loyalty to Joseph Stalin. In return, Stalin sent Krivitsky to the Netherlands with the rank of general in 1935, and put him in charge of Soviet military intelligence (GRU) for western Europe. Because Holland had remained neutral in World War I, The Hague developed into the espionage center of Europe. Krivitsky set up operations in The Hague posing as Dr. Martin Lessner, an Austrian rare book dealer.

One day Ignace Reiss, also a director of Soviet intelligence in Europe, stopped at Krivitsky's office and told him about the real Stalin, a ruthless cutthroat who would stop at nothing to hold the reins of power. Reiss went on to say that Stalin intended to sign a nonintervention pact with Hitler. Because doing so bordered on treason to the Communist cause, Reiss said he must break with Stalin and the Soviet Union. Krivitsky asked Reiss where he would go, and his friend said Switzerland.

In 1937 Krivitsky moved his headquarters to Paris, where operatives informed him that SMERSH, the Soviet assassination division of the GRU, was looking for Reiss. Krivitsky said nothing but learned later that SMERSH had tracked Reiss to Switzerland and assassinated him. In late September, Krivitsky received orders to return to Moscow. He expected to be

Above: General Walter G. Krivitsky, appearing before the House Un-American Activities Committee in Washington, D.C., on October 11, 1939, where he stated that 35,000 members of the Red Army officer corps lost their lives in the 1936–37 purge in Russia.

purged out of the system and executed because of his friendship with Reiss. Krivitsky had a different plan.

Revelations of a Spy

The same day Krivitsy found out about Reiss, he walked out of his Paris office and asked the French government for asylum. After turning over all the pertinent information on Soviet intelligence operations in France, he boarded a ship for the United States. In early 1938 he met with the CIA and the FBI and provided them with a comprehensive description of GRU (now NKVD) operations in the United States—it was extensive and shocking.

British intelligence had been tracking Krivitsky ever since 1935, when he first arrived in The Hague posing as a bookseller. They also followed him to Paris, kept him under surveillance, and watched him walk into the French ministry. When Krivitsky sailed to America, British agents followed. After Krivitsky published his autobiography, lawyer and leading MI5 officer Jane Sissmore (Archer) interviewed the defector. Unfortunately, she paid little attention to his statement that a number of Cambridge students had been recruited into the NKVD (later, this turned out to be Blunt, Burgess, Maclean, and Philby), and that one of them (Philby) had been sent to Spain as a journalist to spy for the Soviets. Had Sissmore believed Krivitsky, the British may have avoided considerable embarrassment when the identities of part of the Cambridge Spy Ring became public in 1956.

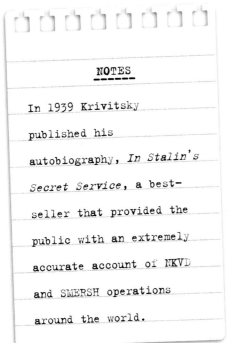

NOTES

In 1939 Krivitsky published his autobiography, *In Stalin's Secret Service*, a bestseller that provided the public with an extremely accurate account of NKVD and SMERSH operations around the world.

Krivitsky named 61 Soviet agents working in Great Britain and the British commonwealth. Six were Soviet agents working under diplomatic cover, and 18 worked under deep cover as illegals. Sixteen British subjects were paid as full-time agents of the NKVD. These included political party members, trade union officials, employees of the Foreign Office, members of MI5, and highly respected foreign correspondents employed by the British press. Those in MI5 might have been counterintelligence agents, but Krivitsky may not have known. Burgess and Philby both became journalists, but Krivitsky could not directly connect them to the foreign office or to the press.

MI5 did not pursue the unnamed agents, but Sissmore did collect enough information to identify cipher specialist Captain John Herbert King as a Soviet spy in the Foreign Office. Two MI5 agents caught up with King in a London pub and pumped him full of drinks. After becoming intoxicated, King lamented that he had become connected with the NKVD in 1935 while working as a member of the British delegation to the League of Nations in Geneva.

The agents hauled King over to the Old Bailey, where, on October 18, 1939, the court found him guilty of violating the Emergency Powers Act and sent him to prison for 10 years. If there were two other Soviet spies in the Foreign Office, as Krivitsky claimed, King did not know their names. The NKVD had a policy of removing spies about to be discovered, and this may have happened, because no more were found. Nor did the Foreign Office mention King's incarceration until after the war. He became the only Soviet spy captured in England on the strength of Krivitsky's statements. Many of the

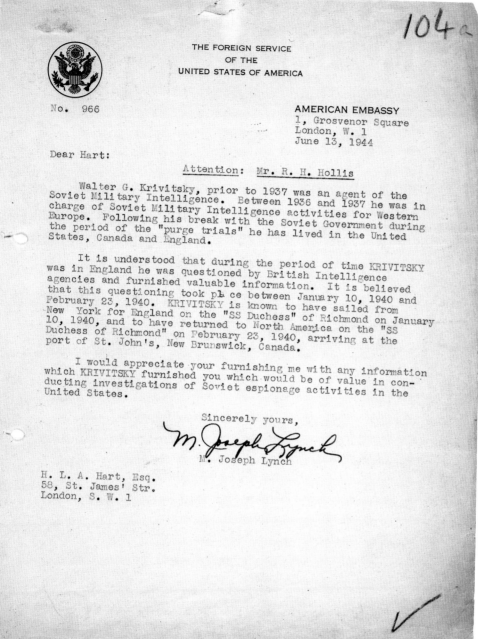

Left: Although he was interviewed numerous times by the Americans, they were still keen to find out if Krivitsky had provided the British intelligence service with any information that would further assist them in tracking down Soviet agents in the United States.

other 60 spies might have been captured had Sissmore taken Krivitsky's testimony more seriously. However, the Western governments did learn much about the brutal regime of Stalin.

A Final Word from SMERSH

After writing his autobiography, little is known of how the ex-spy enjoyed his new life in America. Krivitsky traveled to Washington, D.C., in early 1938 to begin a career in writing and make a fresh start in Virginia. Upon arriving in the capital, he settled into a room on the fifth floor of the Bellevue Hotel.

On February 9, 1941, a maid entered his room and found Krivitsky lying on the floor with a bullet in his head. His death was declared a suicide but in all probability Soviet agents had tracked him down and SMERSH did the rest.

KROGER, PETER (1910–1995) AND HELEN (1913–1992)

Peter and Helen Kroger, whose original names were Morris and Leontina Cohen, used one identity in the United States and another in Great Britain, which led to considerable confusion in tracking them down.

Morris Cohen was born in the Bronx in 1910, the son of Jewish Russian immigrants. He graduated from high school in New York and from the University of Illinois with a degree in science. In 1935 he became a member of the Communist Party.

Two years later he joined the Abraham Lincoln Brigade as Israel Altman and fought for the Communists during the Spanish civil war. While recovering from wounds, the NKVD recruited Cohen to serve as a Soviet spy in the United States.

Cohen returned to the United States and worked odd jobs for Russian-sponsored enterprises in New York until obtaining a job as a schoolteacher. In 1941 he met and married Leontina (Lona) Petka of Adams, Massachusetts, also a member of the Communist Party. She became a willing participant in her husband's party activities in New York City.

In 1942 Cohen entered the U.S. Army. Neither he nor his wife

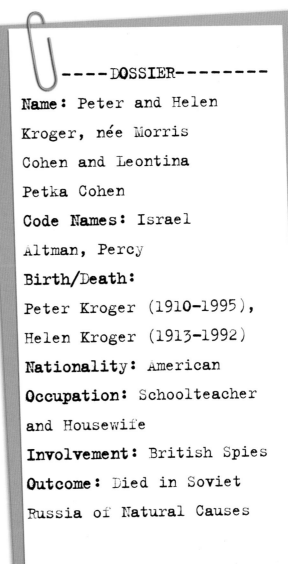

```
----DOSSIER--------
Name: Peter and Helen
Kroger, née Morris
Cohen and Leontina
Petka Cohen
Code Names: Israel
Altman, Percy
Birth/Death:
Peter Kroger (1910-1995),
Helen Kroger (1913-1992)
Nationality: American
Occupation: Schoolteacher
and Housewife
Involvement: British Spies
Outcome: Died in Soviet
Russia of Natural Causes
```

became involved in espionage activity until the beginning of the cold war.

Caught Between Two Networks

Two important Soviet espionage networks operated out of New York City in the late 1940s. Rudolf Abel, who used a small photographer's studio in Brooklyn as his cover, operated a huge network with spies in every major city of America. Julius and Ethel Rosenberg operated a much smaller network, using family members and top scientists working on the A-bomb. Cohen and his wife became involved with both networks, acting as spies for Abel and couriers for the Rosenbergs. Morris Cohen used the code name Percy while working as a mole on the Manhattan Project.

When the FBI arrested the Rosenbergs in 1950, Morris and Lona Cohen fled to New Zealand. There, assuming the names of two deceased New Zealanders and using papers provided by the ever-resourceful KGB, they became Peter and Helen Kroger.

Below: Peter Kroger puts a hand on the shoulder of his wife Helen as they board a jet at Heathrow Airport for a flight to Warsaw. The Krogers were flying to freedom after serving eight and a half years of their 20-year prison sentences.

The Portland Spy Ring

In 1954 the ex-Cohens materialized in London as the Krogers. They connected with Gordon Lonsdale, a top Russian spy posing as a Canadian businessman in England, and his Soviet spy network. They resumed the practice of espionage. The KGB had sent Lonsdale to England to learn everything he could about British underwater detection devices. For several years, Lonsdale obtained the information from British traitor Harry Houghton, a former chief petty officer in the Royal Navy and ex-employee at the top-secret Underwater Weapons Establishment at Portland, England. Houghton gathered documents and designs from his girlfriend, Ethel Gee, who still worked at the Weapons Establishment, and passed information to the KGB regarding nuclear submarines and the whereabouts of

Below: Soviet spy Peter Kroger, also known as Morris Cohen, being transferred from Wakefield Prison to Parkhurst on October 26, 1966.

Left: Spy equipment from the Lonsdale Kroger Gee case, found in the Kroger's bungalow. The breakup of the Portland spy ring began when the CIA received a series of letters signed "Sniper" from Polish intelligence officer Michal Goleniewski, who later defected. The CIA tipped off MI5 that the KGB had a spy in the British Admiralty.

secret military bases. The Krogers took over a secondhand bookstore in Ruislip, claiming to be Canadian. From there, they forwarded the information garnered from Lonsdale, Houghton, and Gee to the Soviets.

For several years, British counterintelligence (MI5) had kept what became known as the Portland Spy Ring under surveillance, gradually collecting scraps of evidence. In January 1961, Scotland Yard agents arrested Lonsdale, Houghton, and Gee. A few days later they apprehended the Krogers and searched their home. There they found a huge cache of sophisticated espionage equipment, including cipher pads, photo equipment, code books, quick-burning paper, microdots and a microdot reader, and a powerful transmitter. MI5 concluded that while Lonsdale may have been running the Portland Spy Ring, Kroger's home was the communications center.

British intelligence became curious about the Krogers and sent their finger-

prints to Washington, where the FBI identified them as Morris and Leontina Cohen. The U.S. State Department asked that the Cohens be extradited to stand trial for their involvement in the Rosenberg spy ring. The British refused. They kept the Krogers, tried them for espionage, and sent them to prison for 20 years.

The Bargaining Chip

The KGB wanted the Krogers back, fearing that after completing their 20-year sentence the pair would be sent to the United States for trial. To obtain the Krogers, the KGB had to arrange a trade, so they arrested British lecturer Gerald Brooke, who was visiting Moscow, and falsely accused him of circulating subversive literature. Brooke became the KGB's bargaining chip.

When the U.S. State Department learned of the potential deal, they argued that the Krogers—or rather the Cohens—were American citizens and could not be bartered for a British subject. If released for any reason, they would first have to be extradited to the United States. The Soviets claimed that the Krogers were Polish citizens, not Americans. The British, anxious to retrieve Brooke, accepted the Soviet argument, and in October 1969 made the trade. The Krogers remained in the Soviet Union, living on their pensions from the KGB. In the 1990s, after perestroika, they were reported as having died in 1992 (Helen), and 1995 (Peter).

Opposite: Peter and Helen Kroger seen leaving Britain for Poland in 1969. Their story was dramatized in the British television drama *Act of Betrayal* in the late 1960s and in 1983 as a stage play entitled *Pack of Lies.*

NOTES

A few years after Peter Kroger's death, the Soviet newspaper *Pravda* declared, "Thanks to Cohen, designers of the Soviet atomic bomb got piles of technical documents straight from the secret laboratories in Los Alamos."

LAWRENCE, THOMAS EDWARD (1888–1935)

T. E. Lawrence went to Arabia as a British spy. He became that and much more, rallying Bedouin Arab tribes against the Turks during World War I and becoming a legend in the process.

Born in Tremadoc, Wales, Thomas Lawrence was the second of five illegitimate sons born to Sir Thomas Chapman and Sarah Maden. His father, never able to get along with his Irish wife, had eloped with Sarah Maden to Wales and changed his name to Lawrence. After the family moved to Oxford, England, young Lawrence attended high school and went on to the university.

In 1909, after developing a keen interest in the Arab world, he traveled to Syria to work on research for his thesis. The following year he graduated from Oxford with honors in history and an interest in Middle Eastern archaeology. He joined a team of archaeologists and spent the next three years at Carchemish on the Euphrates River, digging up Hittite and Assyrian artifacts. Part of his job was to manage the local work force, a skill that would later become very useful.

After returning to Oxford in 1913, Lawrence joined a British expedition led by Captain S. F. Newcombe of British

```
-----DOSSIER--------
Name: Thomas Edward
Lawrence
Code Name: None
Birth/Death: 1888-1935
Nationality: British
Occupation: British Officer
Involvement: British Spy
in World War I
Outcome: Died in a
Motorcycle Accident
```

intelligence (MI6) and C. Leonard Woolley, ostensibly to search for the route used by Moses. The underlying purpose of the expedition was to map northern Sinai, which at the time was part of the Ottoman Empire and controlled by

Turkey. During the expedition, Lawrence became a skilled cartographer, charting unmapped desert as far as Aqaba (ancient Elath). It was also the expedition that changed Lawrence's life.

Second Lieutenant T. E. Lawrence

At the outbreak of World War I, the Turks aligned themselves with the Central Powers. In October 1914, Lawrence became a second lieutenant in MI6, spending a brief tme in the cartographic department. Because he understood and spoke Arabic dialects, the Foreign Office sent him to Cairo to interrogate prisoners. He also sketched maps of Arabia, handled communications, and performed other tasks as the British prepared to fight the Turks in the Middle East.

In 1916 the Arabs, under Emir Faisal, revolted against Turkey and looked to Great Britain for help. British intelligence sent Lawrence to act as Faisal's military adviser but also as their spymaster. Lawrence did more than advise. He led Arab raids against Turkish rail lines while collecting military intelligence for the British.

In 1917 Faisal introduced Lawrence to Ouda, a fierce Bedouin leader who bragged that he had killed 75 Arabs but never bothered to count his Turkish victims because he considered them worthless. Lawrence promised Ouda gold and spoils if he would use his Bedouins to attack Aqaba. Lawrence knew how to capture the city because he had mapped the area. All the Turkish fortifications faced the gulf, leaving the city undefended from the desert wastelands in the rear. Against specific orders, Lawrence led Ouda's Bedouins through a narrow strip of desert and on July 6, 1917, captured Aqaba. The

attack destroyed the Turkish flank and enabled British troops under the command of General Edmund H. H. Allenby to capture Jerusalem five months later.

Lawrence of Arabia

The objective of the Arab revolt was to capture Damascus, in French-controlled

Below: Lawrence served most of 1921 as a policitcal adviser to the Middle East Department in the Colonial Office. He accompanied Churchill to a conference in Cairo that established the borders between Iraq and Jordan.

Syria. To accommodate Faisal more so than General Allenby, Lawrence began staging raids to the northwest. During one of his spy excursions for Allenby, he rode a camel all the way to Damascus, reconnoitered the Turkish defenses, and rode back to Cairo with the intelligence.

A mission in November 1917 took him into Deraa disguised as a Circassian. While reconnoitering the defenses of the town, the Turks took him into custody. What happened next is uncertain, but one account suggests that the Turkish commander tried to rape him, and when he resisted, the officer pinched a fold of Lawrence's flesh together, inserted a bayonet, and twisted it. Three guards took Lawrence away and whipped him. After turning his back into a bloody mess, two guards held him down while the third man sodomized him. The following day, after being sodomized again by the commander, the guards threw him into the street. Lawrence told the Turks nothing, but after his ghastly experience in Deraa, he thirsted for revenge. He gathered together his Arabs, encountered a long line of retreating Turks, and gave the orders to slaughter them all.

Now a colonel of military intelligence and once more in good health, Lawrence learned that Allenby intended to capture the Syrian capital of Damascus. He also knew that Faisal wanted Damascus. So Lawrence went back to his Arabs, advanced several weeks ahead of the British army, and in October 1918 captured the city. When Allenby reached Damascus with French officials, he found Arabs in possession of the city and Lawrence acting as governor.

The French vociferously protested. Allenby informed Lawrence that the Arabs would not be granted complete independence, and that Great Britain and France would rule all the lands of the former Ottoman Empire. The statement contradicted what Lawrence had promised Faisal and the Arab tribal leaders. He felt compromised, mortified, and betrayed. In 1920 Faisal eventually became king of Syria, but only as a puppet to Great Britain and France.

To Set Matters Right

Lawrence resigned his commission and returned to England. He lobbied British

NOTES

In 1915, Lawrence, with C. Leonard Woolley, published his first of ten books, *The Wilderness of Zin*, an account of his experiences in the Sinai.

and French officials to grant the Arabs independence but failed. In 1919, when George V attempted to invest Lawrence with the Order of Bath, he slighted the king by refusing it.

In 1922 Lawrence accompanied Winston Churchill to Cairo for the conference that established the borders of Iraq and Jordan. He considered the measure inadequate and in 1926 published *The Seven Pillars of Wisdom*, in which he argued that the Arabs had been betrayed by the Allies and were entitled to their own land.

Out of frustration, Lawrence joined the Royal Air Force under an alias, but was almost immediately recognized and released. He then joined the Royal Tank Corps under another alias, but by then everyone knew him by sight and he was ejected again. Reacting to public uproar, the government put him back into the Royal Air Force as a colonel and sent him to India, where he served until discharged in February 1935.

In the last years of his life, Lawrence invested in several extremely fast motorcycles. Three months after he left the service, on May 13, 1935, Lawrence rounded a corner on one of his motorcycles. To avoid running into two boys on bicycles, he struck a tree. He died six days later.

Winston Churchill, one of Lawrence's greatest admirers, attended the funeral. When asked to make a comment, the future prime minister of Great Britain said that he believed Lawrence "would live forever in history." Those words were spoken several years before Hollywood produced one of the greatest epics ever filmed, *Lawrence of Arabia*.

Opposite: In 1916, taking on Arab costume, Lawrence began to work with Faisal to launch a full-scale revolt of the tribes. Lawrence described their first meeting: "I felt at first glance that this was the man I had come to Arabia to seek—the leader who would bring the Arab Revolt to full glory…"

Below: Lawrence, second from right, center row. He attended the Paris peace conference between January and May 1919 as a member of Faisal's delegtation.

LONSDALE, GORDON ARNOLD (1922–1970)

Gordon Lonsdale organized a compact spy ring in England to steal underwater detection systems from the British, and he carried out the pilfering for six years before being discovered.

Born in Moscow, seven-year-old Konon Molody moved to California in 1929 to live with his aunt, who posed as his mother. His father, a Soviet science writer, wanted his son educated in the United States. After nine years in public schools, Molody spoke English distinctly, with only a very slight Russian accent.

In 1938, at the age of 16, Molody returned to Russia and joined the Communist Youth Movement. During World War II he served in the Soviet navy, where he received training in espionage. After the war, the KGB recruited Molody and expanded his training.

The Bubblegum Man

In 1954 Molody arrived in Vancouver, Canada, with a forged passport and a false name: Gordon Arnold Lonsdale, an identity he assumed from a child born in Canada but taken to Finland, where he died. Lonsdale became the only name by which he was known.

```
----DOSSIER--------

Name: Gordon Arnold
Lonsdale
Real Name: Konon
Trofimovich Molody
Code Name: Last Act
Birth/Death: 1922-1970
Nationality: Russian
Occupation: Soldier in
World War II
Involvement: Soviet
Spymaster in England
Outcome: Died of Heart
Attack in Moscow
```

As Lonsdale, he established a new persona as a successful Canadian businessman. He remained in Canada less than a year, but long enough to sell himself to others as a man of many enterprises, which included renting juke-boxes and manufacturing bubblegum machines. Later, Lonsdale claimed that he once went to the United States and met with an agent that fits the description of Rudolf Abel, but there is no evidence he was ever in the country.

In 1955 Lonsdale arrived in England. Here his real mission for the KGB began—to ferret out secrets about Britain's underwater detection devices. Lonsdale settled into a luxurious rented apartment in Regent's Park and established several large bank accounts. He made friends and talked about plans to open an importing business and distribute amusement games in Europe. Every night he could be seen buying drinks at fashionable nightclubs with attractive women draped on his shoulder. Lonsdale was actually a philandering big-spender and a skillful con man with anti-Semite tendencies.

The Portland Spy Ring

When Lonsdale arrived in England, he had one contact: a former chief petty officer of the Royal Navy, Harry Houghton, whose girlfriend, Ethel "Bunty" Gee, worked at the Admiralty Underwater Weapons Establishment at the Portland naval base in Dorset. Houghton had performed clerical work at the British Embassy in Poland in 1951, where he became involved in black-market transactions to support his lifestyle. After being transferred back to England, he obtained a job at the underwater weapons facility, which was where his former Polish con-

tacts talked him into spying for the Soviets. Houghton, who had become an alcoholic, lost track of new developments after the base transferred him to maintenance, but his girlfriend Bunty continued to have access to confidential information and became the inside agent.

In anticipation of Lonsdale's arrival in 1954, the KGB sent Peter and Helen Kroger to England to establish a communications link with Moscow. The Krogers rented a home and filled it with sophisticated photographic equipment, a powerful transmitter, codebooks, cipher pads, a microdot reader, and other tools of the espionage trade.

Whenever Houghton and Gee collected a packet of documents, they met

Below: After his arrest, Lonsdale was taken to Scotland Yard. He did not reveal a single detail about himself and even when he came to trial at the Old Bailey, all that had been discovered about him was that he was a Russian, had a naval background, and was not the man his papers purported him to be. Lonsdale was regarded as a hero in the Soviet Union and later wrote his memoirs with the help of Kim Philby.

In 1965 Lonsdale published a book titled *Spy: Twenty Years in the Soviet Secret Service*, in which he claims to have had many "experiences" in the United States. Because the manuscript was prepared with the assistance of the KGB, and because the FBI has no record of Lonsdale, it is unlikely that he did much spying in the United States.

clandestinely with Lonsdale, usually somewhere in London, and exchanged underwater weapons secrets for cash. Lonsdale reviewed the material and took what he wanted to the Krogers' home for transmission to Moscow. Lonsdale was also the paymaster of the Krogers.

The operation functioned without discovery for six years, and many of Britain's developments on underwater weapons went swiftly from Houghton to Lonsdale to Kroger and then on to Moscow.

The Defection of Michal Golienewski

In 1960, Lieutenant Colonel Michal Golienewski of the Polish Intelligence Service defected. During a debriefing at British counterintelligence (MI5), he mentioned secrets being passed to the Soviets from the Portland underwater weapons facility. After a security check, MI5 discovered that Houghton was spending far more money than he earned. Counter-espionage agents from MI5 began shadowing Houghton, discovered his relationship with Gee, and then followed them both to their periodic meetings with Lonsdale. MI5 agents also observed an exchange of a shopping bag for a stiff envelope and turned the matter over to the Special Branch of Scotland Yard.

In 1961, while Lonsdale, Houghton, and Gee were making an exchange outside the Old Vic theater, Scotland Yard arrested the trio. The agents confiscated the shopping bag Houghton and Gee had just handed to Lonsdale. Inside they found undeveloped photographs of the 212-page *Particulars of War Vessels*, classified naval documents, detailed drawings of the navy's newest warships, and recent orders from the Admiralty. The trail led back to the Krogers, in whose home agents uncovered a complete compliment of espionage equipment.

All five spies went to trial. Lonsdale was convicted and sentenced to 25 years in prison. Houghton, Gee, and the Krogers received sentences of 20 years. Lonsdale served only three years. British diplomat Greville Wynne had been arrested for spying in Russia, and Mrs. Lonsdale arranged a trade with Mrs. Wynne. In 1964 the swap was made. In 1970 Lonsdale died of a heart attack while picking mushrooms from the small garden behind his apartment. He was buried next to another spy, Rudolf Abel.

One year later, Harry Houghton and Bunty Gee were released from prison and decided to get married.

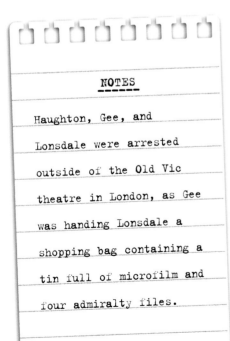

NOTES

Haughton, Gee, and Lonsdale were arrested outside of the Old Vic theatre in London, as Gee was handing Lonsdale a shopping bag containing a tin full of microfilm and four admiralty files.

MACLEAN, DONALD DUART (1913–1983)

Donald Maclean became one of the four members of the infamous Cambridge Spy Ring. The Foreign Office refused to believe that a man of Maclean's family could become a spy for the Soviets, despite condemning and conclusive evidence compiled by the CIA.

The son of a distinguished Scottish politician soon to be knighted, Donald Maclean was born in London during a time when his father served in Parliament. Pampered throughout his youth, Maclean attended Gresham's, a school composed of radical teachers who taught that the Russian Revolution opened the door to a truly utopian world. Maclean went on to Cambridge, where, along with other members of what became known as the Cambridge Five, he was recruited by the KGB.

The Patience of Moscow

When recruited, Maclean wanted to go directly to Moscow and begin a new life, but this was not how the system worked. His Soviet recruiter told him to finish his education, take advantage of his recently deceased father's good reputation, and apply for a position in the Foreign Office. Maclean followed his handler's advice. He applied for work with the diplomatic service, and during his interview admitted that he leaned toward Communism in college but had since repudiated it. Maclean got the job because his pedigree provided him with a genetic legacy for perpetual patriotism.

----DOSSIER--------

Name: Donald Duart Maclean

Code Name: None

Birth/Death: 1913–1983

Nationality: British

Occupation: British Foreign Officer

Involvement: British Spy for the Soviets

Outcome: Died of Heart Attack in Moscow

married in June 1940, and barely made it back to England before German Panzer armies overran France.

Activating a Spy

For nine years, Soviet agents kept Maclean on the hook without ever pressing him hard for secrets, mainly because he had not risen high enough in the Foreign Office to know much. Everything changed in 1944 when Maclean went to Washington, D.C., as first secretary in the British Embassy. Because he also worked in the chancery, Maclean was able to see—and select for photographing—every important document sent to the ambassador.

Maclean had left his pregnant wife in London to have the baby when he transferred to Washington. When Melinda arrived, she stayed with her mother in New York City. The arrangement worked well for Maclean because he could carry the embassy's secrets to New York without arousing suspicion. Even after Melinda moved to Washington, Maclean continued to make trips to New York. His colleagues speculated that Maclean kept a mistress there.

The Nuclear Mole

Maclean's secretarial duties included membership on the Combined Policy Committee on Atomic Development, which supervised the work on nuclear energy and the building of the atomic bomb, which was in process at Los Alamos, New Mexico. Maclean passed the minutes of every committee meeting to his handler, including Anglo-American postwar policies on atomic energy and the stockpiling of nuclear weapons. With his diplomatic pass, Maclean also had

Above: Donald Maclean. His reports to his KGB controller, along with those of Alan May Nunn and Klaus Fuchs, who provided scientific information, helped the Soviets build the atomic bomb and to estimate their nuclear arsenal's relative strength against that of the United States.

In 1935 Maclean went to work for the Foreign Office's Central Department, the unit responsible for diplomatic operations in Belgium, France, and Germany. After learning the ropes, the Foreign Office sent him to Paris, where he immediately connected with NKVD agents attached to the Soviet Embassy. Although a practicing homosexual, and more so when drunk, Maclean met Melinda Marling, the daughter of an American oil executive. They

clearance to the Atomic Energy Commission's files, which he frequently visited with specific inquiries from his handler. He also volunteered to help whenever a fellow embassy worker became ill or needed assistance, because involvement in other departments sometimes led to discovering other secrets. Twice a week Maclean packed up his stolen documents and delivered them to the Soviet Consulate in New York.

Maclean also worked with Alger Hiss on the creation and structure of the United Nations and, while doing so, he took the Soviets' concerns under consideration. As Soviet intelligence agents began filling openings at the United Nations, Maclean became increasingly besieged by demands for more information.

One of the UN's first major debates concerned the deployment of American troops in South Korea. There is no record of what Hiss may have done with the information, but Maclean kept the Soviets informed. He may have changed the outcome of the Korean War by informing Moscow that President Harry S. Truman had decided not to deploy the A-bomb.

A Spy on the Hook

In 1948 the Atomic Energy Commission complained about Maclean's constant use of department files, and the CIA canceled his pass. He came under increased suspicion when a Soviet clerk at the consulate in New York made the mistake of transmitting Maclean's stolen secrets to Moscow in simple code. James Angleton, the CIA's counterintelligence director, analyzed the intercepted message and informed British counterintelligence (MI5) that Maclean was a Soviet agent. MI5 doubted the allegation but in September 1949 Maurice Oldfield, who later became chief of the department, casually told Kim Philby, another Soviet agent in the Cambridge Spy Ring, of a probable Soviet spy in the British Embassy in Washington. Philby passed the information to the Soviets, who merely ordered Maclean to stay where he was and continue sending information. The news shocked Maclean. He began drinking heavily; in 1951 the Foreign Office recalled him.

Last Call for Moscow

The Foreign Office replaced Maclean at the British Embassy in Washington with his friend Philby, who became the new first secretary. Meanwhile, after sobering up Maclean, the Foreign Office assigned him to the American Department in London. The CIA could not believe the stupidity of the British Foreign Office. CIA agents had collected an immense amount of evidence against Maclean and put pressure on MI5 to take action.

On May 25, 1951, the very day MI5 intended to apprehend Maclean, Guy Burgess, another member of the Cambridge Spy Ring, arrived in London. He picked up Maclean, drove to Southampton, boarded a ferry to France, and both men escaped to Moscow.

Maclean soon discovered that life in Moscow was dreadful. He wrote home, admitting that he was disillusioned with Communism and wanted to see the British countryside again. He never did. He died of a heart attack at age 69 in Moscow and was cremated. Only his ashes made it back to England.

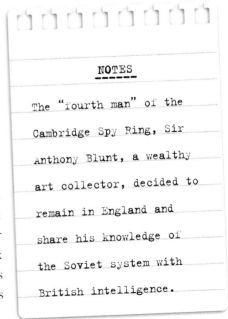

NOTES

The "fourth man" of the Cambridge Spy Ring, Sir Anthony Blunt, a wealthy art collector, decided to remain in England and share his knowledge of the Soviet system with British intelligence.

MATA HARI (1876–1917)

Corrupted early in life and victimized by a horrible marriage, Mata Hari learned how to use her body to become one of Europe's greatest entertainers, but she never learned how to become a spy.

Born in Leeuwarden, Holland, on August 7, 1876, Margaretha Gertrud Zelle should have lived a long and productive life. Her well-to-do Dutch father owned a successful men's furnishing store, and her Javanese mother provided her daughter with doting care and all the luxuries of life. When Zelle reached the age of 14, her mother died and her father sent her to a convent school for teachers. When she was 18, she was expelled for having a sexual affair with the headmaster. In 1895, after discovering she was pregnant, Zelle impulsively married Captain Rudolf MacLeod, a dashing, 40-year-old Dutch officer twice her age.

An Unfortunate Marriage

The couple moved to Banjoe-Biroe, a colonial posting in an unbearably torrid and rain-drenched climate in the Dutch East Indies. In 1896, Zelle give birth to a son, Norman, who was later poisoned by a resentful servant. A few years later she gave birth to a daughter. Meanwhile, her husband had begun to spend his time drinking and having affairs with the

```
-----DOSSIER--------

Name: Mata Hari

Code Name: H-21

Real Name: Margaretha
Gertrud Zelle

Birth/Death: 1876-1917

Nationality: Dutch

Occupation: Exotic Dancer

Involvement: Spied for
Germany and France

Outcome: Executed by
Firing Squad
```

Right: Despite the assumption in this document that the French had "ample proof" of her guilt, neither they nor the English were ever able to unearth any solid evidence that Mata Hari was spying for the Germans. This has fed the continuing fascination with her story. The question of her guilt or innocence remains one of history's great unanswered questions.

145798

M.C.O.116/1916.

The Passport Office,

British Embassy,

Madrid.

18-12-16.

ZELLE.Margaretha Geertruida. DUTCH.

Subject of M.I.5E memo No.138396/29-11-16.

This woman is at the present moment staying at the Ritz Hotel,Madrid. She is under observation by the French Bureau who will give her a visa to France as soon as she asks for it. She is in regular correspondence with her a lover,a Russian Officer on the French Front.

I am given to understand that the French have ample proof of her activities on behalf of the Enemy.

Captain.

The Secretary,

M.I.1C.War Office,

2.Whitehall Court,S.W.

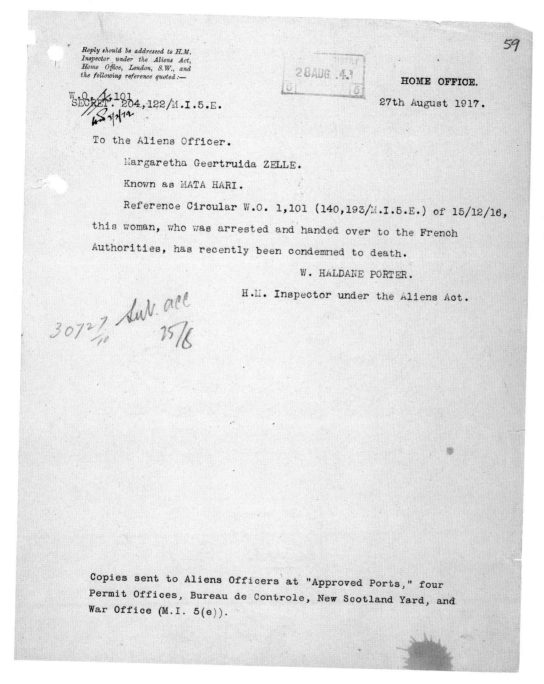

Reply should be addressed to H.M. Inspector under the Aliens Act, Home Office, London, S.W., and the following reference quoted:—

28 AUG. .4.

HOME OFFICE.

27th August 1917.

W.O. 1,101
SECRET. 204,122/M.I.5.E.

To the Aliens Officer.

Margaretha Geertruida ZELLE.

Known as MATA HARI.

Reference Circular W.O. 1,101 (140,193/M.I.5.E.) of 15/12/16, this woman, who was arrested and handed over to the French Authorities, has recently been condemned to death.

W. HALDANE PORTER.

H.M. Inspector under the Aliens Act.

Copies sent to Aliens Officers at "Approved Ports," four Permit Offices, Bureau de Controle, New Scotland Yard, and War Office (M.I. 5(e)).

Left: Only one witness for the defense appeared at Mata Hari's trial. Henry "Robert" de Marguérie was a high-ranking official in the foreign ministry and a former lover who had known Mata Hari for 14 years. De Marguérie informed the court that he had spent three days with Mata Hari not long before her arrest and that at no time had she asked him for any details regarding the war. When chief prosecutor André Mornet ridiculed this assertion, de Marguérie replied, "It may seem unlikely to you but it is the truth." Without being prompted, he continued, "Nothing has ever spoiled the good opinion that I have of this lady." Before leaving the courtroom, de Marguérie ostentatiously bowed to Mata Hari.

native girls. Zelle also had a few affairs, usually under the administration of her husband. He used her body as a means to attract wealthy men into adulterous sexual encounters so he could blackmail them. After a few sordid episodes of seducing officials to satisfy her husband's monetary demands, she returned with her daughter to the Netherlands in 1902, and four years later divorced her husband.

The Emergence of Mata Hari

In Java, the dancing girls in the Siva temples had fascinated Zelle with their mystical and erotic body movements. After collecting her divorce settlement, she placed her daughter with a relative and spent most of her money on dancing lessons. In October 1903, she went to Paris to make her reputation as an exotic dancer, but no one would hire her. She

Right: On the day of her execution, Mata Hari was led from her cell by her interrogator, Captain Pierre Bouchardon, who announced, "Have courage! Your request for clemency has been rejected by the President of the Republic. The time for expiation has come." "It's not possible!" Mata Hari shouted. "It's not possible!" As she was comforted by two nuns who had befriended her during her incarceration, Mata Hari composed herself and said firmly, "Don't be afraid, sisters. I shall know how to die."

Opposite: During her time in Java, Zelle wrote to a friend of her husband's overbearing, jealous nature: "My husband won't get me any dresses because he's afraid that I will be too beautiful. It's intolerable. Meanwhile the young lieutenants pursue me and are in love with me. It is difficult for me to behave in a way which will give my husband no cause for reproaches."

or *16th October*

"LOVELY SPY" SHOT.

MATA HARI EXECUTED BY THE FRENCH AT VINCENNES.

ROMANTIC CAREER OF INFAMY.

"Daily Express" Correspondent.

PARIS, Monday, Oct. 15.

"Mata Hari," otherwise Mlle. Marguerite Gertrude Zelle, the beautiful dancer spy, was shot at Vincennes at six o'clock this morning. She was driven from St. Lazare Prison in a motor-car,

MATA HARI.

accompanied by a doctor, a Protestant clergyman, and two detectives. She fell dead at the first volley, and was buried in the prison precincts.

Marguerite Zelle was sentenced to death by a court-martial in Paris on July 24. She appealed to the French Supreme Court, but on September 27 her appeal was rejected.

"MILADI" OF THE WAR.

WORLD'S MOST SINISTER ADVENTURESS.

The story of the career of "Mata Hari"—"Eye of the Morning"—outrivals any novel in point of dramatic interest and romance. She made her first appearance in Paris twelve years ago as a Hindu dancer, and her sinuous movements in the scantiest of drapery, the snakes which wreathed and writhed about her, and her weird beauty made her all the rage.

Her father was a subject of the Netherlands and her mother was a Javanese. Her father died when she was an infant, and in order to protect her from the dangers which beset a young girl of mixed blood in the East her mother fled from Java with her when she was three years old, and entered Burma. There further to protect her, she pledged her to celibacy and placed her in a Buddhist temple to learn dancing, as a sort of modern vestal virgin.

At twelve she was disgusted with life, and was determined to change it or end it. After a dance at a great Buddhist festival in Burma, when she was about fourteen years old, she saw a British officer—a baronet—and fell in love with him. It was her first love affair. She managed to escape from the temple, and joined him. Finally they married. Two children—a boy and a girl—were born of their union.

After a time, however, the monotonous life of a British official's wife was more than she could stand. The climax came when a maid whom she had beaten and discharged caused one of her servants to poison her infant son. The tragic events and scandal which followed her son's death are still remembered by old timers in India. She started an investigation of the killing independent of the British authorities, and, finally, in her own mind, fixed the guilt on one of her gardeners. She took a revolver and, walking into the garden where the man was working, shot him dead.

HUSHED UP.

She was arrested, but everything possible was done to suppress the news and to hush the scandal. Finally she was told that she would have to leave British India. It was just what she wanted to do. She left her home in the night, stealing her daughter from her husband. She made her way to Marseilles and thence to Holland, where she placed her daughter in a convent. Then she went straight to Paris.

Paris captivated her. She quickly became a part of the great night life of that city. She met many men. One of them was a wealthy German, who was a high official of the Berlin Government. He bought a house for her at Neuilly-sur-Seine, and furnished it in a style that was representative of truly Oriental splendour.

She was a woman eminently qualified to act as a secret agent for Germany. As a Dutch subject she was at liberty to travel anywhere, and it is quite certain that she had the facilities of obtaining information which would have been impossible for Germany to obtain elsewhere.

It was a life which would appeal to her—that of a spy. Her greatest delight was in exercising her influence to control persons with whom she came in contact, and her influence was miraculous. Her constant companion was a German woman, her maid, whom she always called Anna.

"Mata Hari" has been described as the counterpart in real life of Miladi, the beautiful spy and adventuress of Dumas' masterpiece, "The Three Musketeers." The sinister character of Dumas' great romance was not more cunning or adventurous nor played for higher stakes than Mlle. "Mata Hari." In many respects their histories should be printed in parallel columns, but for adventure, for cunning, for her great influence over the destiny of those she met, Mlle. "Mata Hari" was more powerful than Miladi.

Tall and slim, and of a strangely magnetic personality, she turned the heads of many men, and by a combination of charm and cunning, wheedled vital secrets out of them.

AN OFFICIAL SPY.

PARIS, Monday, Oct. 15.

"Mati Hari" had her duly registered number in the official German spy lists and was found to be in negotiation with leading enemy personages outside France, including notorious spy leaders. She admitted having received large sums of money since 1916 by way of remuneration for her information.—Exchange.

found work in low-life strip clubs, and by late 1904 was servicing a dozen or more men a day.

In 1905 Zelle returned to Holland to rid herself of venereal disease. She borrowed money from friends, bought a lavish wardrobe, and returned to Paris in the persona of Javanese princess Mata Hari (Eye of the Dawn). She became an overnight sensation, starring as an exotic dancer at the Oriental Studies Museum, followed by packed-house performances at the Casino de Paris, the Olympia, and the Folies-Bergère. She toured the capitals of Europe and became Europe's smoldering symbol of sex. She also became rich. During a passionate affair with Crown Prince Wilheim in Berlin, she pocketed $100,000 in diamonds and emeralds. For ten years she danced and had dozens of affairs. Then the war began.

The Exotic Spymistress

In 1912 Mata Hari considered becoming a spy as another means for making money. The year also marked her most triumphant artistic successes, but Mata Hari craved a life with more excitement, adventure, and danger. Curiously enough, neither Germany nor England took her seriously. Only former Berlin police chief Traugott von Jagow, with whom she was having an affair, recognized her potential and gave her the code name "H-21." Jagow truly loved her, and when he moved up in the ranks and became adjutant for Colonel Walther Nicolai, head of German intelligence during World War I, he paid Mata Hari 30,000 marks a night to obtain state, political, and military secrets from high-placed lovers.

While maintaining a sexual relationship with Jagow, she also had an affair with 25-year-old Captain Vadim Maslov, a Russian pilot flying for the French and the son of a Russian admiral. When Maslov suffered a wound during the summer of 1916, Mata Hari asked permission from the French government to visit him in a hospital located behind German lines. Officers at the Deuxiéme Bureau, the French intelligence service of the time, consented to the visit on the condition that she spy on the Germans, particularly the crown prince, whom

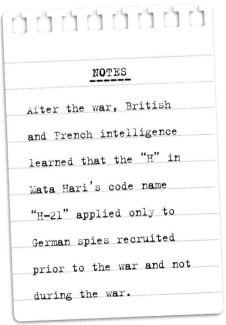

NOTES

After the war, British and French intelligence learned that the "H" in Mata Hari's code name "H-21" applied only to German spies recruited prior to the war and not during the war.

The Spy Who Never Was

she knew intimately. For her espionage services, the French agreed to pay her one million francs.

To oblige the French, Mata Hari traveled to Spain to reach neutral Holland, where she planned to cross the German border and meet the crown prince. During an interim stop at Falmouth, England, British intelligence detained her. They interrogated her, warned her to stay out of Germany, and sent her back to Spain. She had a brief affair with the German attaché in Madrid, who sent Berlin a message in simple code saying that spy "H-21" proved valuable. The British intercepted the message and advised the Deuxiéme Bureau.

On January 4, 1917, Mata Hari returned to Paris. Five weeks later, the French arrested her as a German spy. Neither the French nor British intelligence services could produce any evidence that she was a spy other than the cable from the German attaché in Spain. Investigators found invisible ink in her room, which she insisted was part of her makeup. She admitted taking money from Germans for love, but not for spying.

A French military tribunal decided Mata Hari's fate in a closed court-martial. Found guilty on charges of espionage, the French placed her before a firing squad on October 15, 1917. Mata Hari refused to be blindfolded or tied to a stake. As a 12-man firing squad stood at attention with their

Two melodramatic film classics attempted to portray the life of Mata Hari. In 1931 Greta Garbo appeared in *Mata Hari*, followed in 1964 by the French version, *Mata Hari: Agent H21*, starring Jeanne Moreau. A third version, *Mata Hari* (1985), was mainly a portrayal of her sexual affairs.

rifles, she said, "Gentlemen, I am ready," and blew them a kiss. Seconds later she lay dead. Nobody claimed Mata Hari's body. French soldiers took her remains to a Paris hospital for dissection by medical students, but memories of the legendary woman never died. They live on at the Fries Museum in Leeuwarden, the Netherlands, where she was born.

Left: When Mata Hari was detained and questioned by the British, she denied being a double agent. "I am innocent," she stated firmly. "Someone is playing with me—French counterespionage, since I am in its service, and I have acted only on its instructions."

Reply should be addressed to H.M. Inspector under the Aliens Act, Home Office, London, S.W., and the following reference quoted :—

49

HOME OFFICE.

W.O. 1,101
SECRET
140,193/M.I.5.E.

15th December 1916.

To the Aliens Officer.

ZELLE, Margaretha Geertruida

Dutch actress, professionally known as MATA HARI.

The mistress of Baron E. VAN DER CAPELLAN, a Colonel in a Dutch Hussar Regiment. At the outbreak of war left Milan, where she was engaged at the Scala Theatre, and travelled through Switzerland and Germany to Holland. She has since that time lived at Amsterdam and the Hague. She was taken off at Falmouth from a ship that put in there recently and has now been sent on from Liverpool to Spain by s.s. "Araguaga", sailing December 1st.

Height 5'5", build medium, stout, hair black, face oval, complexion olive, forehead low, eyes grey-brown, eyebrows dark, nose straight, mouth small, teeth good, chin pointed, hands well kept, feet small, age 39.

Speaks French, English, Italian, Dutch, and probably German. Handsome bold type of woman. Well dressed.

If she arrives in the United Kingdom she should be detained and a report sent to this office.

Former circulars 61207/M.O.5.E. of 9th December, 1915 and 74194/M.I.5.E. of 22nd. February, 1916 to be cancelled.

W. HALDANE PORTER.

H.M. Inspector under the Aliens Act.

Copies sent to Aliens Officers at "Approved Ports" four Permit Offices, Bureau de Controle, New Scotland Yard and War Office (M.I. 5(e)).

Opposite: Mata Hari described her dance routine: "My dance is a sacred poem in which each movement is a word and whose every word is underlined by music. The temple in which I dance can be vague or faithfully reproduced, as here today, for I am the temple. All true temple dances are religious in nature and all explain, in gestures and poses, the rules of the sacred texts."

MAUGHAM, WILLIAM SOMERSET (1874–1965)

Somerset Maugham became a spy in World War I because it provided him with an opportunity to chronicle the human pathos of war, but the experience also provided him with an opportunity to come to terms with himself.

Born in Paris, Somerset Maugham became multilingual as soon as he learned how to speak. Orphaned at the age of 10, he entered the King's School in Canterbury, England, and graduated in 1891. Undecided about what to do with his life, Maugham studied for several months at the University of Heidelberg. Still dissatisfied, he moved to London and began studying medicine at St. Thomas's Hospital.

While trying to decide on a career, he kept a copious "writer's notebook" of his observations on life. Hundreds of those pages characterized the slums of Lambeth, where he worked for several months as an obstetric clerk. Maugham's medical career changed suddenly in 1897 when he published his first novel, *Liza of Lambeth*, a bestseller written mainly for personal amusement and not for enrichment. After the royalties began to flow, Maugham decided to become a full-time writer. *Liza of Lambeth* was to change his life forever.

```
----DOSSIER--------
Name: William Somerset
Maugham
Code Name: Somerville
Birth/Death: 1874-1965
Nationality: British
Occupation: Novelist
Involvement: British Agent
in World War I
Outcome: Died of Natural
Causes in France
```

The Spy Who Wrote Novels

When World War I erupted in 1914, 41-year-old Maugham joined the ambulance service in France while still writing *Of Human Bondage*, a novel about a physician named Philip Carey who was short, clubfooted, and fixated on a conniving French prostitute. The book was about segments of his own life, for Maugham had been denied service in the British army because he, too, was short and clubfooted.

A Life of Many Experiences

Maugham became a great writer because his novels and short stories were reflections of his own intricate life. He always seemed to be searching for himself. On one hand he loved his beautiful mistress, Gwendolyn Maude Syrie Wellcome, but on the other hand he also loved a handsome young American, Gerald Haxton. If Maugham's life was not complicated enough, his mistress also became the mistress of Captain John Wallinger (later Major Sir John Wallinger), who worked in British intelligence (MI6). One evening in 1915, while the three were at dinner, Wallinger asked Maugham, because of the novelist's fluency in French and German, to join MI6 and become a spy in Switzerland. Although Maugham was under no obligation to help Wallinger, the assignment appealed to him. Being a famous writer and supposedly working on another book was the perfect cover. As a patriotic gesture, Maugham agreed to spy without pay.

Writer on Assignment

Wallinger's assignment sounded simple. Maugham agreed to go to Lucerne, contact a British agent married to a German wife, and decide whether he was a double agent working for Germany. Maugham contacted the man and convinced him to go to France. French intelligence arrested the suspected agent and

executed him as a spy. Maugham turned the experience into a short story titled "The Traitor," using a fictitious character named Ashenden as his protagonist. Maugham waited until 1928 before writing the full-blown novel *Ashenden*, which became an instant best-seller.

While in Switzerland, Maugham enjoyed the intrigue. He met with spies at

Above: When World War I broke out, Maugham served in France as a member of the British Red Cross's so-called Literary Ambulance Drivers, a group of 23 well-known writers that included Ernest Hemingway.

Published in 1915, *Of Human Bondage* became Maugham's greatest novel and a literary classic that sold more than 10 million copies. He corrected proofs for the book in a small hotel in Malo between shifts as an ambulance driver.

appointed intervals, paid them wages, recruited new spies, gave them instructions, and sent them off to Germany. He collected information and once a week he crossed into France, delivered the documents to another agent, and sometimes received new instructions from MI6. One of his contacts was an elderly woman from French Savoy who crossed Lake Geneva ostensibly to sell butter, eggs, and farm produce, but was actually an MI6 courier who operated one leg of a message relay network. Maugham performed the anchor leg. Maugham also had the unpleasant experience of being held at gunpoint by an agent who wanted more money; he later transferred the experience to one of his books.

The Retired Spy

Maugham returned to London in 1916 and found himself accused by Sir Henry Wellcome as a correspondent in adultery. Maugham admitted the affair. In May 1917, after Wellcome obtained his divorce, Maugham married Syrie Wellcome.

While settling into married life, Maugham received a call from Sir William Wiseman, who headed MI6 operations in New York. He asked Maugham to go to Russia and learn what support the Mensheviks needed to counter Bolshevik efforts and keep Russia in the war. Using the code name Somerville, Maugham arrived in Moscow as a U.S. journalist and met directly with Alexander Kerensky, the socialist leader. Kerensky hurried Maugham back to London, desperately requesting that the Allies immediately send an anti-Bolshevik army to Russia. Maugham rushed back to London and placed Kerensky's plea for men, guns, and ammunition before Lloyd George. The prime minister bluntly replied, "I can't do that." He shook Maugham's hand and excused himself for a meeting. Maugham went back to writing his novels, and on November 7, 1917, the Bolsheviks overthrew the Russian government and stepped out from the war.

In 1919 Maugham published *The Moon and Sixpence*, another marvelous story of World War I, but not so tightly woven around his own personal experiences as *Ashenden*. He moved with his wife to France, though his marriage would not last, due to his affair with another man. Maugham understood the changing temper of society, and in 1944 gave the reading public something to ponder when he published *The Razor's Edge*, a story about people who were trying to find themselves.

Maugham died on December 15, 1965, in Nice, France, a man for all ages.

NOTES

Maugham set the standard for the spy novels of the future, but neither Graham Greene, Eric Ambler, Len Deighton, nor John Le Carré were ever able to emulate the depth of *Ashenden* (1929).

MILLER, RICHARD (1937–2002)

Richard Miller always wanted to be an FBI agent. The agency assigned him to counterintelligence, where the bumbling caseworker became the first FBI agent ever convicted of spying for the Soviet Union.

Richard Miller grew up in California and during his school years excelled at nothing. He read detective magazines about G-men, watched television when Senator Joseph McCarthy began the national witch-hunt for Communists, and approved of FBI director J. Edgar Hoover's assault against subversives. Such persuasions, and little else, motivated him in 1964 to become an FBI agent.

The Return of Inspector Jacques Clouseau

Miller worked the better part of 18 years as a civil-crime case handler in Riverside, California. His record was not good. To support his family of eight children, he sold Amway products out of his FBI car, used his badge to filch candy from convenience stores, and peddled FBI files to a private investigator. A colleague described him as perpetually "unkempt, disheveled."

In 1982 the FBI transferred Miller to the Los Angeles field office and assigned him to counterintelligence, where his sloppy

```
----DOSSIER--------
Name: Richard Miller
Code Name: None
Birth/Death: 1937-2002
Nationality: American
Occupation: FBI agent
Involvement: Spy for the
Soviets
Outcome: Imprisoned for
Espionage
```

personal habits could serve as part of his cover. Miller's move to L.A. didn't improve his performance. His record showed that on one occasion he lost both his service weapon and his credentials. On another occasion, while locking up

cados. Despite Miller's shoddy performance, his supervisors usually rated him at 90 percent, the median for most agents. His good nature and affability probably kept him in the bureau.

From Russia with Money

In 1984, after serving his two-week suspension for obesity, Miller needed cash more than ever. One day he encountered a beautiful 34-year-old, dark-eyed, blond Russian émigré, Svetlana Ogorodnikova. She identified herself as a Soviet major, bluntly asked if he would like to become a spy, and promised him $65,000 in gold and cash. Miller accepted the offer and drove her to the Soviet Consulate in San Francisco to seal the deal. A surveillance team watched Ogorodnikova get out of an FBI car and walk into the consulate. In her purse she carried Miller's badge, credentials, and a classified manual with directions on how the FBI gathered intelligence as proof that she had hooked a federal agent. The surveillance team noted the incident but assumed that an officer from Los Angeles was working a case that involved the consulate.

For several years, San Francisco agents had suspected the consulate of being the center for Soviet espionage on the West Coast. After being detected while attempting to dig a tunnel under the building, the FBI resorted to conventional surveillance techniques: tapping phones and photographing people entering and leaving the consulate.

The FBI already had a file on Ogorodnikova. She first came to the bureau's attention in 1982 when agent John E. Hunt asked her to become an informant on the local community of Russian immigrants. Ogorodnikova provided Hunt with erratic bits of infor-

the FBI office, he left the key in the door. It was still there the next morning. In 1984 the Los Angeles office suspended him for two weeks because he was 60 pounds over the maximum weight allowed for an FBI man of his height. During the suspension, Miller spent time helping his wife run their avocado ranch in northern San Diego County, an enterprise that produced more debt than avo-

mation, and despite the fact she was married to a Ukrainian Jew named Nikolay Ogorodnikov, her relationship with Hunt became sexual. FBI records showed that Hunt had 55 meetings with Ogorodnikova, one of which involved a Los Angeles physician. Hunt explained that Svetlana had a rare blood disease, but he actually took her to have an abortion. When Hunt retired from the FBI in 1984, Ogorodnikova latched onto the 47-year-old Miller. When he drove Ogorodnikova to the consulate to get on the Soviet payroll, he forgot that someone might be watching.

An Affair to Forget

Not many days passed before the FBI suspected Miller of having sexual relations with Ogorodnikova. They tracked the pair, videotaped Miller's meetings with the dazzling blonde, tapped his phone calls, and checked Miller's caseload. Miller was getting his fair share of sex but demanded more money. On one occasion Ogorodnikova introduced Miller to Wolfson, the so-called KGB treasurer, who promised more cash. Undercover double agent Miller had not figured out that Wolfson, who worked as a meat packer, was also Ogorodnikova's husband. Whether Wolfson knew about his wife's extramarital relations is questionable. Svetlana evidently experienced a more compatible sexual relationship with Hunt. By her own admission, she only submitted to Miller's sexual advances "because he scared me."

Ogorodnikova gave Miller specific tasks. The Soviet Consulate wanted to know where the FBI had hidden KGB defector Major Slanislav Levchenko, and they wanted to find Victor Belenko, a Soviet pilot who had flown a MiG-25 to the West in 1976. Both men had been condemned to death by the KGB and SMERSH assassins were waiting to execute the penalty.

Welcome to Klutzdom

In September 1984, it occurred to Miller that he might be under surveillance by his own people. He approached his boss, P. Bryce Christensen, and rather clumsily explained that he had been working on his own initiative to infiltrate the KGB by becoming a double agent. He revealed his contact with Ogorodnikova and asked for Christensen's help in arranging a secret intelligence-gathering trip to Vienna for both of them. Christensen suspected that Miller had somehow spotted the FBI's surveillance team and wanted the bureau to provide money for his escape.

On October 3, the FBI arrested Miller, Svetlana, and her husband Wolfson. The Soviet spies pleaded guilty in a deal that imprisoned her for 18 years and her husband for eight years. Miller won a mistrial in November 1985 despite FBI evidence proving that he had tradecraft tools, such as photographic equipment and secret writing instruments, scattered about his apartment.

The outcome became the first espionage trial in America's history not to have ended in a conviction. Miller stood trial again three months later and was convicted of espionage. He received two life terms plus 50 years, and was fined $60,000—roughly the same amount that Ogorodnikova promised Miller for becoming a spy.

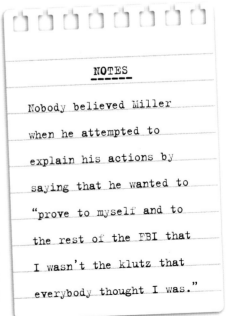

NOTES

Nobody believed Miller when he attempted to explain his actions by saying that he wanted to "prove to myself and to the rest of the FBI that I wasn't the klutz that everybody thought I was."

Opposite: Richard Miller, pictured here giving a rare interview in Los Angeles on December 7, 1989. During the course of the interview Miller admitted that sexual indiscretion led to his personal and professional downfall.

MOULIN, JEAN (1898–1943)

Jean Moulin never expected to become a hero. After the Nazis brutalized him in the early days of German occupation, Moulin left a legacy of unbreakable courage in the history of France.

Born and raised in Beziers in the south of France, Jean Moulin, the son of a scholar and professor, received an equally impressive education. He entered the University of Montpellier in 1917 but interrupted his education to serve in the French army during World War I. Returning to Montpellier in 1919, he graduated two years later with a law degree. In 1922 he obtained a post in the provincial government of French Savoy. In 1939, after rising quickly as a civil servant, he became prefect of Chartres on the eve of World War II.

The Despair of Jean Moulin

In 1940 German Panzer armies overran France and created a new collaborationist government under Marshal Henri Phillippe Pétain, a World War I hero. Many of the French disapproved of Pétain's quick capitulation and deemed him a traitor. One was 50-year-old General Charles de Gaulle, who managed to escape to England with part of his army after the fall of Dunkirk. Moulin had two choices: he could join de Gaulle or remain in France and fight the Nazis.

```
- - - - DOSSIER - - - - - - - -
Name: Jean Moulin
Code Names: Joseph-Jean
Mercier, Max, Jean Martel
Birth/Death: 1898-1943
Nationality: French
Occupation: Civil Servant
Involvement: French Spy
and Resistance Leader in
World War II
Outcome: Died as a German
Prisoner of Unknown Causes
```

Distressed by the collapse of France, Prefect Moulin became horrified when German troops goose-stepped into Chartres and shot an old woman who had cursed them. He called on German headquarters and demanded that the two soldiers who shot her be arrested for murder. A junior officer thrust a pen and a document in his face and told him to sign it. Moulin read the protocol, noted that the Germans pinned the atrocity, and others like it, on French Senegalese

Left: Moulin described his first encounter with the brutality of the Nazis: "They shoved me toward a corner where the limbless trunk of a woman lay on a table. I was projected onto human debris. It was cold and sticky, and my own bones turned to ice. In this dark corner, overcome by the nauseous odor from the bodies, I shivered feverishly.

"I realize I am now at the limits of my endurance, and if they start again tomorrow, I will end up signing. It was a terrible choice: to sign or die." Moulin chose death and attempted suicide by slashing his neck with a shard of glass.

troops. He refused to sign the document and demanded proof. The officer nodded to a soldier standing nearby who jammed the butt of his rifle into Moulin's jaw. Guards hauled Moulin out of the room,

beat him to a bloody pulp, jarred his teeth loose, and threw him into a cell with a blood-soaked Senegalese soldier in similar condition. Expecting to be beaten again, Moulin picked up a shard

Right: Operational instructions for "Rex" to be dropped back into France after one of his trips to London. Moulin had spoken of the precarious nature of his role: "I am now hunted at the same time by Vichy and the Gestapo who are not unaware of my identity, nor my activities . . . My task is becoming more and more delicate, while the difficulties increase constantly."

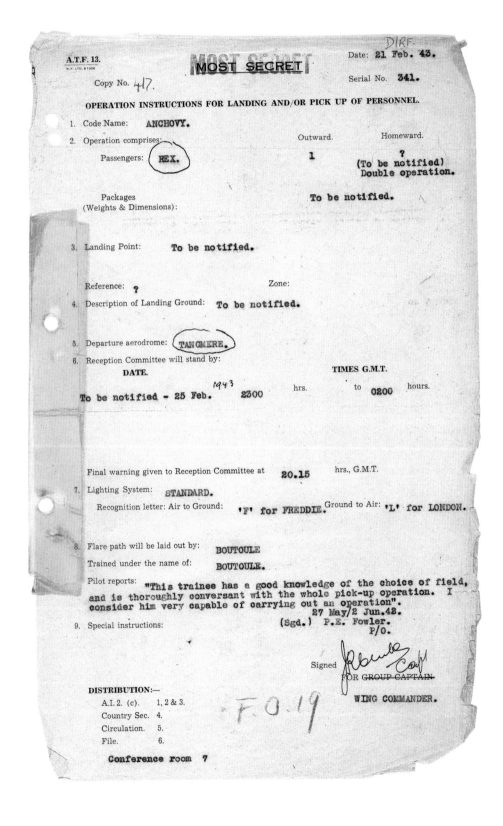

of glass and attempted to commit suicide by slitting his throat.

The Senegalese soldier hollered for help. The German officer responsible for Moulin's condition became concerned that the murder of a prefect might cause repercussions and sent him to the hospital. While recovering, Moulin received a curt note from Pétain's puppet Vichy government that he was no longer a prefect. Still unable to speak, Moulin crawled out of bed, escaped from the hospital, and went underground.

The Quest for a New Career

Moulin covered the long scar on his neck with a muffler and picked his way through France. On June 15, 1941, he reached Marseilles and began looking for a guide who could arrange his transportation to England. During the search he met Henri Frenay, a former French army officer who spoke of thousands of underground resistance fighters operating independently and without a unifying authority. Frenay suggested that Moulin go to England, speak with de Gaulle, and become that link. Moulin agreed, and instead of secretly slipping out of France, he went to the American Consulate in Marseille under a false passport, and using the alias Joseph-Jean Mercier, professor of law at New York State University, obtained clearance to Lisbon.

Moulin eventually reached London and conferred with André Dewavrin, de Gaulle's chief of intelligence. After several discussions, Dewavrin suggested that Moulin serve as de Gaulle's liaison officer between London and the resistance operations in France. Moulin finally had his interview with de Gaulle and agreed to be the general's point man in southern France (Vichy) while Dewavrin

supervised underground operations in Nazi-occupied France.

On the night of January 1, 1942, Moulin, his radio operator Joseph Manjarte, and Dewavrin's liaison officer Raymond Fassin parachuted safely down near Marseilles. After a close call with two suspicious policemen, Moulin reached Marseilles, met secretly with Freney, and from that day forward was the unifying force for the French underground in southern France.

Below: This initial assessment of Moulin by the British proved to be more than accurate. Moulin would go on to organize and inspire the resistance movement in France with such efficacy that Charles de Gaulle would later say of him, "He was the martyr of the Resistance."

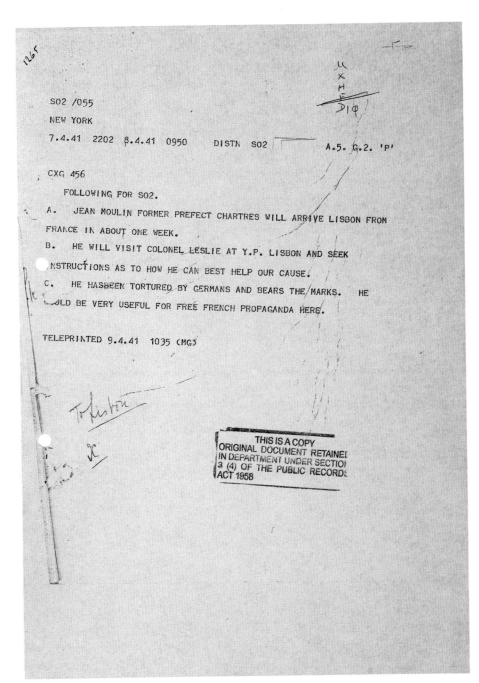

SECRET.

MOST SECRET.

COPY NO. 1/5.

AIR TRANSPORT FORM. 2.

INSTRUCTIONS FOR DEPARTURE OF AGENTS BY AIR.

1. Code Name of Operation: ROBERT   (No. of Agents 1

2. Country Section: D/RF

3. To be combined with MAINMAST A.&.B.3. Operation   (DRF Country Section)

4. Accompanying Officer from Country Section:

5. Conducting Officer from M. Section: MOB.1.

6. Preliminary Conference: (a) Place: 1, Dorset Square
                              (b) Date: 3 Nov. 41.
                              (c) Time: 1230 hrs.

   (d) At this conference Conducting Officer will meet the agent(s)
       and Accompanying Officer in order to:

       (i) Select equipment needed from the list given in Appendix A.
           Accompanying officer should also produce any other articles
           being provided by Country Section.

       (ii) Dress the agent and stow equipment, except parachute, as
            for the operation.

       (iii) Check the dropping point. Maps and if possible air
             photographs will be brought by the Conducting Officer.

       (iv) Decide on instructions to be given to the pilot as to his
            action in the event of the exact dropping point(s) not
            being located. If Reception Committee not located, return to
                                                                    base.
       (v) Check points to be reconnoitred by the agent after arrival
           for the future dropping of supplies and/or personnel.

       (vi) Ensure that the agent knows the procedure for reception
            of supplies and or personnel.

       (vii) Check Lysander picking-up points to be reconnoitred after
             arrival (for Lysander trained agents only).

       (viii) Settle any final points which may arise.

7. Date of Operation:

   (a) Operation to stand by from: 9 Nov. 41.
   (b) To be confirmed each day by MOB   to DRF by 1400   hrs.
   (c) Reception arrangements will stand by from 2100 hrs. G.M.T.
       to 0100   hrs. G.M.T. on nights. 9 Nov. onwards
       2400

8. Arrangements on day of departure:

   (a) Car provided by M. Section   will leave 1 Dorset Square
       for S.T.S.61 on 8 Nov at 1415   hrs. arriving at 1600hrs.

   (b) Conducting Officer will ensure that maps, air photographs and
       equipment given in Appendices A and B travel with the agent
       and accompanying officer. Equipment "For use in aircraft"
       will be provided at: S.T.S.61
       Accommodation
   (c) Dinner for all concerned at S.T.S.61   at   hrs.

   (d) Agent will have been searched and be completely dressed,
       including anklets, ready to leave S.T.S.61   by 1630hrs.
       from which hours the operation will be under control of: MOBL.

During his interrogation, Barbie placed a piece of paper in front of Moulin and demanded that he write down the names and locations of all French resistance leaders. Moulin's defiant answer was to draw a caricature of Barbie and hand it back to him. Barbie's response was swift and brutal—he ordered his men to cut, burn, and scald Moulin.

The Man Who Would Not Talk

After depositing 250,000 francs with Freney, Moulin began circulating. He met with underground leaders in Marseilles, Paris, Lyon, Avignon, and dozens of other cities. He organized them all into the National Council of Resistance. He did not completely discourage sabotage and ambushes, but warned that the acts would only lead to reprisals. He suggested that the resistance avoid detection and be prepared to strike the enemy when the Allies invaded France. During these encounters, Moulin continuously exposed himself to men he did not know who could be double agents working for the Nazis. His closest encounters occurred during his frequent trips back and forth from England to confer with de Gaulle, the only person to whom he reported.

On May 7, 1943, Moulin radioed de Gaulle that he feared he might soon be arrested and to send a replacement. On June 16, Clause Bouchinet arrived and met with Moulin, awestruck by the vast underground network. Five days later Moulin and local resistance leaders walked into a medical clinic in a hilly suburb of Caluire, near Lyon. Immediately, Gestapo agents led by the vicious Klaus Barbie pushed into the clinic and separated the resistance fighters from the patients. Moulin had correctly suspected that René Hardy, a trusted member of the resistance, had sold them out. Barbie knew exactly whom he had captured. He smirked broadly and called some by their code names and others by their actual names. He even staged a performance, pretending to kill Hardy while really arranging his escape.

Barbie, however, never figured out who was "Max," Moulin's code name. After torturing several resistance members, he only learned that "Max" was "Jean Martel," another of Moulin's code names. He submitted "Jean Martel" to the most horrible torture imaginable, but Moulin had been through it before and never revealed his identity.

In the morning, Barbie dragged Moulin's battered body into the open courtyard. A bystander described Moulin as hideously beaten and barely conscious. Barbie feared that the death of his prize prisoner might be attributed to him and transferred Moulin to a German jail. Moulin either died before he reached prison or soon afterward.

The good work started by Jean Moulin continued, and when the Allies liberated Paris in 1944, it was the Free French and the resistance that led the parade.

Opposite: British Secret Service briefing document for Moulin's return to France. Moulin's legacy is so strong in France that not only were his ashes reburied at the Panthéon but there are also numerous monuments and street named in his honor throughout the country.

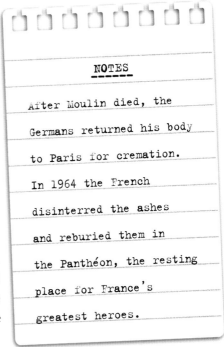

NOTES

After Moulin died, the Germans returned his body to Paris for cremation. In 1964 the French disinterred the ashes and reburied them in the Panthéon, the resting place for France's greatest heroes.

NAUJOCKS, ALFRED HELMUT (1909–)

Alfred Naujocks became one of the most dangerous and clever manipulators in the German Sicherheitsdienst (SD). Some authorities refer to him as the strategist who showed Hitler how to ease into World War II without risking reprisals.

Born in Kiel to an upper-middle-class working family, Alfred Naujocks loved his homeland and hated Communists and Jews. In 1927 he began studying engineering at the University of Kiel, but halfway through college he became interested in the Nazi Party and joined the brown-shirted Storm Troopers. A big-boned, muscular man, Naujocks had finally found his niche. He fought the Communist move-ment, often in bloody street bat-tles. Once struck on the nose with an iron bar, he wore the look of a prizefighter for the rest of his life.

The Sicherheitsdienst

In 1931 Naujocks traded in his brown shirt and joined Heinrich Himmler's fledging black-shirted Schutz Staffl (SS), ostensibly a Nazi defense unit organized to protect the interests of Hitler. After the führer became chancellor in 1933, Naujocks joined the Sicherheitsdienst (SD), the Nazi's intelli-gence department.

```
----DOSSIER--------
Name: Alfred Helmut
Naujocks
Code Name: Hans Muller
Birth/Death: 1909-
Nationality: German
Occupation: Nazi Party
Leader
Involvement:
Sicherheitsdienst Agent
Provocateur
Outcome: Disappeared
in 1945
```

In 1934 Naujocks became SD leader Reinhard Heydrich's right-hand man, bodyguard, and agent-at-large for committing sabotage and performing assassinations. Espionage activities

Left: On August 31, 1939, Naujocks led the attack on the Gleiwitz radio station in Poland. Naujocks and a small group of Germans dressed as Poles took over the radio station and broadcast a message in Polish that urged the Poles living in Silesia to strike against Germans. This was one of 21 coordinated attacks on the German-Polish border that were designed to give the impression of Polish aggression against Germany. They provided Hitler with the justification he needed to convince the Reichstag to go along with his plan to invade and "pacify" Poland.

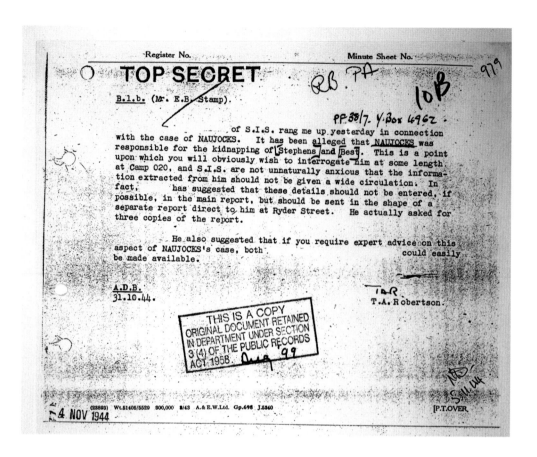

appealed to Naujocks, but he took special pleasure from hunting down Hitler's enemies and eliminating them.

One of Naujocks's odd jobs involved Otto Strasser, a recent defector from the Nazi Party who was attempting to rally right-wing opposition to Hitler. Strasser moved to Prague, Czechoslovakia, set up a clandestine radio transmitter, and used volunteers to send anti-Nazi propaganda into the heart of the Third Reich. Heydrich informed Naujocks that he wanted the "black radio" shut down and the station's chief operator, Rudolf Formis, put out of business.

On January 10, 1935, Naujocks disguised himself as a dry goods salesman and, using the name Hans Muller, entered Czechoslovakia with an SD direction finder. His voluptuous blonde girlfriend, Edith Kasbach, accompanied him. After driving around Prague with the direction finder on, Naujocks pinpointed

Strasser's black radio at the Zahori Hotel in Dobris, a small town about 15 miles southeast of the capital. He checked into the hotel with his girlfriend and took the room next to Formis. Naujocks borrowed a key for Formis's room, made a wax impression, duplicated it, and sent a one-word message—"Found"—to Heydrich, meaning he was ready to act.

Kidnap Plan

On January 23, Heydrich replied, instructing Naujocks to destroy the radio and, if possible, kidnap Formis and bring him to Germany to stand trial. That night Naujocks dropped a rope from his window to Werner Goetsch, another physically powerful SD agent who had been brought along to help in the kidnap. The pair went to Formis's door and inserted the key, but heard someone inside. Pretending to be hotel service, Naujocks knocked. When Formis opened the door, both men pushed their way inside. Formis reached for a pistol, but Naujocks fired first. The noise alerted the hotel staff, who rushed up the stairs. Naujocks placed a phosphorous charge on the transmitter, set it off, and ran from the room with Goetsch. He grabbed Kasbach, ran down the stairs, and shouted that a maniac killer was loose on the upper floor.

When Naujocks returned to Berlin, Heydrich flew into a rage over the unsuccessful kidnapping. Though he accused Naujocks of sloppy secret service work, he also knew that his man could be depended upon for countless other missions where ruthlessness and murder were the most expedient solution. As the months and years passed, Heydrich came to understand the value of having a man like Naujocks willing and able to do his dirty work.

The Methodology of Eliminating Competition

In 1936 Hitler acknowledged that the greatest threat to Europe was the spread of Communism. He worried about the Red Army and about Stalin, and he wanted to find a way to neutralize both. The SD had expanded intelligence operations into the Soviet Union and informed Heydrich that certain members of the Russian officer corps opposed Stalin's policies. Germany had similar problems, because several high-ranking officers in the Wehrmacht opposed Hitler. Heydrich conceived a plan to eliminate both problems and assigned the task to Naujocks.

Marshal Mikhail Nicolaevich Tukhachevsky, who had crushed the Kronstadt revolt in 1921, had recently

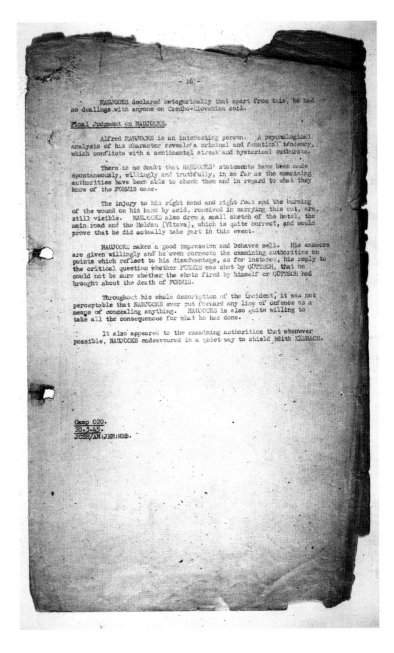

reorganized the Soviets' disjointed military system and reformed it into a modern army. Tukhachevsky and his generals had formed a cabal against Stalin and were preparing to usurp the dictator. From Heydrich's perspective, getting rid of Tukhachevsky would weaken the Red Army as well as Stalin.

Heydrich also conceived a strategy to simultaneously rid the Wehrmacht of dissenting generals, which included Admiral Wilhelm Canaris, director of the Abwehr. Heydrich did not appreciate

Above: Naujocks's personality intrigued his interrogators. Despite the ruthless and callous acts of murder that he had carried out in the service of the Nazis, he still retained a romantic streak. During his interrogations, he did his best to shield his girlfriend, Edith Kasbach, from any potential repercussions.

Right: As is noted in this preliminary interrogation report, Naujocks was happy to cooperate fully with his interrogators once he had handed himself over to the Allies—no doubt motivated by a desire to avoid his own execution. The statements that he gave proved to be of great use to the Allies during the Nuremburg Trials.

3.

COPY

		SECRET
INTERROGATOR:	CONFIDENTIAL	CASE NO: 888

FIRST UNITED STATES ARMY
Office of AC of S, G-2
Interrogation Center

MEDICAL CHECK:
M/Sgt. C. BIEVER

Date: 20 Oct 44.

SUBJECT: BONSEN, Alfred

Alias: NAUJOCKS, Alfred
Residence: 66 Ave. Cortenberg, BRUSSELS
Birth: 20 Sep 1911 in KIEL, Germany
Nationality: German
Occupation: Merchant until 1933
Party & SS Political Economic Service 1934-40
Family: Divorced Ollava LADERICH in BERLIN in 1943
Parents Richard & Therese born PAHLKE (61 & 58) in
BAD SEGEBERG (Holstein) Germany
Languages: German, little French
Education: Elementary School until the age of 14.
Orthopedic studies; auto-mechanic studies until the
age of 19.
Description: Subject is 6'1", very tall and strongly built; has
blue eyes, dark blond hair. Small nose, oval face.
No distinguishing marks claimed.

DETAILS OF ARREST: Place: Hq 205th CIC Det, MALMEDY
Date: 20 Oct 44, 1200 hrs.
Unit Making Arrest: 205 CIC Det
Person authorizing arrest: Herbert C. MARCUM, 2nd Lt Inf.
Reason for arrest: Reason given in letter of Hq V Corps,
CIC Det no. 205 to CO MIC.
Subject's comments: Subject claims he comes from VIENNA to give
information and take up connection between
Austrian Resistance movement and Col CHRISTIE
in Foreign Office, London.

IDENTITY DOCUMENTS: False German Passport on name BONSEN, Alfred

MILITARY HISTORY: For political reasons convicted and put in Penal
Co. Political friends brought him into Arty of
Div LEIBSTANDARTE AH. 1942 dismissed.

NSDAP HISTORY: Date: 1931
Party Number and Rank: around 650.000
Position: Hauptabteilungsleiter in Reichssicherheitshauptamt
Highest Position: S.S. Sturmbannführer
Other facts, organizations: Degraded in 1940 on account of dispute
with Chef der Sicherheitspolizei Reinhardt HEYDRICH.

POLICE RECORD: None.

INFORMATION SUBJECT MAY HAVE: See subject's comments and NSDAP history.

INTERROGATOR'S COMMENTS: Subject is full of information and anxious
to give it.

S E C R E T

Canaris's broad-based and powerful intelligence network because it conflicted with Heydrich's SD and Himmler's Gestapo.

Killing Two Birds with One Set of Forgeries

For the previous year, Naujocks had been working in the SD documents section. Under Heydrich's direction, he began preparing elaborate forged documents and letters showing that Tukhachevsky's officers had been conspiring with certain Wehrmacht officers to purge the Soviet Union of Stalin, and Germany of Hitler. The plot began working when Eduard Benes, president of Czechoslovakia, informed Stalin that the SD had collected documents implicating Tukhachevsky in a coup. Stalin sent NKVD representatives to Berlin with 300,000 rubles to buy the documents. Stalin obtained the forged documents, for which Heydrich received only forged rubles.

Even though Stalin doubted the authenticity of the documents, he ordered Tukhachevsky and seven top generals arrested, tried, and executed. Having tasted blood, and wanting no more threats to his premiership, Stalin ordered the 1937 purge. He liquidated or dismissed 35,000 top-ranking officers, including 90 percent of the generals and 80 percent of the colonels. Heydrich celebrated, rightfully claiming that he had severed the head of the Red Army, even though Stalin went much farther than Heydrich could have predicted.

Hitler took advantage of Stalin's extreme reaction. He claimed that the false documents were genuine and used them to cashier General Werner von Blomberg and Field Marshal Walther Brauchitsch, the two highest Wehrmacht generals who opposed his schemes for conquest. The success of the scheme made Naujocks into one of Heydrich's most trusted henchmen.

Copying the Japanese

Some historians credit Naujocks for starting World War II. Hitler wanted to find a way to grab territory without going to war, and it was Naujocks who pointed the way. An avid student of history, he suggested that Hitler follow Japan's example. The Japanese had nibbled into Manchuria and China under the ruse of acting as protectors of imperial interests while setting up puppets to do Japan's bidding.

Naujocks declared that unwarlike incursions into Austria, Czechoslovakia, and along the Polish border could be accomplished using the same strategy while at the same time allowing them to put further plans in place. Hitler adopted the strategy and Naujocks used SD operatives to create the illusion. The ruse worked until Hitler decided to end the charade and sent his armies smashing into Poland.

Naujocks spent most of the remainder of the war as a liquidator for the SD and the SS. When Germany began to collapse, he surrendered to American forces in Belgium. Held for trial as a war criminal, Naujocks tried to plea in exchange for information on SD operations. Believing that he might yet be executed, he escaped from prison and disappeared.

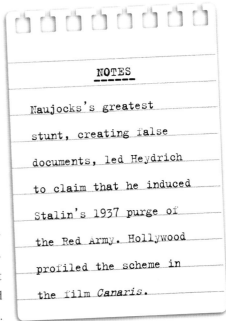

NOTES

Naujocks's greatest stunt, creating false documents, led Heydrich to claim that he induced Stalin's 1937 purge of the Red Army. Hollywood profiled the scheme in the film Canaris.

ORLOV, ALEXANDER (1895–1973)

No Soviet spymaster used more code names than Alexander Orlov. Under one alias or another, he managed to organize effective NKVD operations in virtually every country of Western Europe and the United States.

Born Leiba Lazarevich Feldbin in the Belarusian town of Bobruysk, Alexander Orlov received his early education in Jewish schools, but he eventually repudiated his religion, changed his name, and embraced Communism. During the Russian Revolution in 1917, he joined the Red Army, and as an officer, fought the White Russians during the 1918–20 civil war. In 1921 he entered the University of Moscow, completed law school in 1923, and then worked the next year as an assistant prosecutor for state security, a kangaroo court that put enemies of the state into concentration camps or before a firing squad. By the time Orlov reached the age of 30, he had become one of the most ruthless men in Russia.

Building the Soviet Network

During the Russo-Polish War of 1919–20, Orlov became involved in counterintelligence work. In 1924 the Soviet high command put him

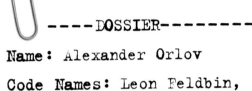

----DOSSIER--------

Name: Alexander Orlov

Code Names: Leon Feldbin, Lev Leonidovich Nikolayev, William Goldin, Alexander Berg, Igor Konstatinovich Berg, and Schwed (Swede)

Birth/Death: 1895–1973

Nationality: Russian

Occupation: Prosecuting Attorney

Involvement: Soviet Spy

Outcome: Died of Natural Causes in Cleveland, Ohio

back in the field, and in late 1925 Orlov commanded 11,000 troops responsible for policing the borders along Turkey and Persia. In 1926 he caught the eye of Felix Dzerzhinsky, the ruthless chief of the OGPU, the forerunner of the GPU, NKVD, and KGB. Dzerzhinsky put Orlov into foreign intelligence and sent him to Paris to head Russian espionage operations in France.

Using Paris as his headquarters, Orlov traveled throughout Europe for eight years, performing intelligence in every country that he visited. He recruited spies while passing himself off as a foreigner, but not a Soviet citizen. He traveled to the United States using a Soviet passport with the alias Lev Leonidovich Nikolayev, and there he picked up a fraudulent U.S. passport under the name of William Goldin, a deceased Austrian-born immigrant.

In July 1934 the newly established NKVD transferred Orlov to England to accelerate espionage activities. Orlov used his American cover as William Goldin and started a refrigerator business. Among his recruits were the four men who comprised the Cambridge Spy Ring, Guy Burgess, Donald Maclean, Kim Philby, and Anthony Blunt. In 1935, after an accidental meeting in London with an old acquaintance who recognized him, Orlov packed quickly and returned to Moscow. For one year, Orlov maintained a low profile while supervising and training NKVD agents at the Central Military School in Moscow.

The Spanish Gold Heist

In 1936 the NKVD sent Orlov to Madrid as its resident attaché, which allowed him

Below: Alexander Orlov's visa for Spain and Canada, dated 1938, the year he was involved in the Spanish treasure heist. In 1938 the Great Purge was in full swing, and Orlov watched as close associates were rounded up and shot. Having been invited to meet an unnamed NKVD chief, he decided to flee. He initially went to Paris and then on to Canada, where he defected.

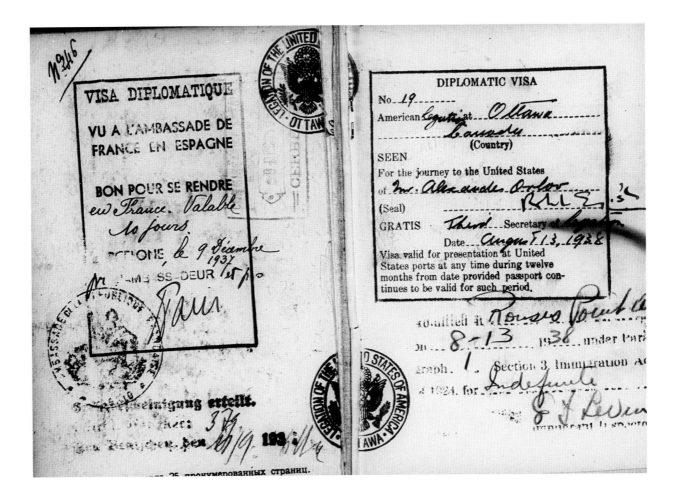

to function as the senior Soviet official in Spain. Orlov's assignment was to build a greater base of NKVD spies and act as an adviser to Communists fighting in the ranks of loyalists against Francisco Franco. While in Spain, Orlov encountered Philby, who was actually there to keep track of the progress of the war for the NKVD. Among other duties, Orlov established and supervised a spy school. The infamous Peter Kroger and his wife Helen received their espionage training at Orlov's school.

When it appeared that Franco would win control over Spain, Orlov received instructions from the NKVD to arrange for the loyalists' gold to be sent to Moscow for safekeeping, ostensibly to prevent it from falling into Franco's hands. Orlov conferred with the republican government and promised to return the gold the moment Franco was defeated. The naive republicans accepted the offer and ordered all the government's gold shipped to Cartegena. Orlov supervised the loading of hundreds of millions of dollars in gold onto a small Russian convoy of freighters waiting in the harbor to receive the shipment. He remained with the ships, accompanied the gold across the Mediterranean and through the Black Sea to Odessa, supervised its loading on a Moscow-bound train, and followed the shipment to the Soviet capital.

The Appreciation of Joseph Stalin

When the gold train reached Moscow, Stalin

thanked Orlov profusely, but the wily spy doubted the premier's sincerity. Stalin's purge was in full swing and Orlov noticed that many of his trusted agents had either disappeared or were being arrested, tried, and executed for counterrevolutionary activities. He observed that the men being purged were not only old Bolsheviks but also senior Soviet officials who had served overseas, some of whom he knew quite well.

Fearing for his life after a firing squad shot his cousin, Orlov smuggled his family out of the country with more than $30,000 of embezzled Spanish gold and took temporary refuge in Paris. Knowing he would be pursued by SMERSH, the Soviet counterintelligence agency, he defected to the Canadian Embassy. Using the alias Alexander Berg, he immigrated with his wife and 14-year-old daughter to Canada and later moved to Cleveland, Ohio. The girl, who was already ill, died in the United States.

Orlov and his wife lived almost entirely on the gold. There is also evidence that he blackmailed Stalin for more funds, threatening to expose him to the West if assassination attempts were made on his life. Orlov remained a fugitive until 1953, his presence unknown to American officials. After Stalin died in 1953, he went public and published *The Secret History of Stalin's Crimes*. A series of his articles then followed in *Life* magazine.

The FBI and the CIA spent months attempting to pry intelligence from Orlov. He told mostly half-truths in an effort to protect any agents that may have defected and, like himself, were living under assumed names in the United States. In 1973 Orlov died of natural causes and took most of his secrets to the grave.

NOTES

After Orlov's death, U.S. intelligence waited another 20 years before discovering his true identity. In 1993 John Costello and former KGB officer Oleg Tsarev published Soviet intelligence files on Schwed, Orlov's code name.

PAPEN, FRANZ VON (1879–1969)

Franz von Papen encountered many twists and turns in his life as a spymaster and a diplomat in both world wars. He served as chancellor of Germany during the rise of Hitler, and remained a conniver for most of his long life.

The son of a wealthy landowner in German Westphalia, Franz von Papen grew up an aristocrat. He entered military school in 1903, obtained his commission in the kaiser's army in 1907, and in 1913 became a member of the German general staff. The army assigned Papen to the diplomatic corps and in 1913 sent him to the German Embassy in Mexico City. Two years later, after the outbreak of World War I, new orders posted him as military attaché to the German Consulate in New York City.

The Arms Business That Never Was

Papen's career as a spy began in New York. While World War I raged between the Central Powers (Germany and Austria) and the Allies (Great Britain and France), Papen's responsibilities in the United States involved a tenuous balancing act. On one hand, Papen had to direct German agents to prevent American military supplies from reaching British and French ports. On the other hand, he had to work for the defeat of the Allies without alienating the American public against the Central Powers.

```
----DOSSIER--------
Name: Franz von Papen
Code Name: None
Birth/Death: 1879-1969
Nationality: German
Occupation: German Officer
and Diplomat
Involvement: German
Spymaster in World War I
and II
Outcome: Died of Natural
Causes
```

Under Papen's direction, German agents used funds he supplied to set up dummy armament firms in the United States, including the Bridgeport Projectile Company. The agents then hired American businessmen to front as managers. Using very attractive prices and terms, bogus sales agents booked hundreds of orders from Great Britain and France without having the means or intention of ever delivering a thing.

To jeopardize the raw material side of the armament business, Papen created different dummy firms to buy up all the gunpowder, thereby preventing it from getting into the manufacture of grenades and artillery shells being produced by legitimate firms working on orders from the Allies. They simply stored it away in large containers, never to be used.

Though successful with many of his enterprises, Papen's espionage network suffered from the incompetence of his helpers. Heinrich Albert, the commercial attaché from the New York consulate, provided money from Berlin to pay for Papen's projects. One day while traveling in New York, Albert left a briefcase filled with incriminating documents on an elevated train. An American secret agent following the attaché grabbed the briefcase and published the so-called Albert Papers in a New York newspaper.

Spies, Saboteurs, and Nincompoops

During the same period, Papen incurred another problem when Franz von Rintelen arrived from Berlin with orders to oversee sabotage in America. Rintelen told Papen that he had made a number of unique bombs and planned to place them in freighters transporting

Below: The German cabinet pictured in February1932 at the Chancellor's Office. Left to right, seated: Baron von Braun (Agriculture), Baron von Gayl (Interior), Chancellor von Papen, Foreign Minister Baron von Neurath; Standing: Dr. Gurtner, Minister of Justice, Professor Warmbold, Minister of Economy, General von Schleicher (Army).

munitions to the Allies, and also that he intended to launch a terrorist campaign in America and strike military installations. With Rintelen on the loose, Papen envisioned a quick end to his efforts to keep America out of the war.

Papen warned the Abwehr that Rintelen was reckless, and asked that he be recalled. Rintelen countered by advising Berlin that Papen was a fool. The Abwehr listened to Papen, but not until after Rintelen sabotaged several U.S. merchant ships and set off explosions at the Mare Island naval base in California. During the exchange of communications between Papen and the Abwehr, the British broke the code. Agents from Scotland Yard arrested Rintelen when the Dutch ship on which he was returning to Germany made an interim stop in England.

Taking Charge of Sabotage

With Rintelen removed, the Abwehr transferred the responsibility for supervising sabotage to Papen. He refused to put saboteurs to work in the United States but sent a gang to blow up the rails of the Canadian Pacific Railway to keep Canadian troops

Left: Papen, pictured here with Adolf Hitler on June 17, 1933, at the Berlin Train Station. During the meeting between Hitler and Papen in Cologne in January 1933, the two men reached an understanding and Papen completely committed himself to go along with Nazi policy.

Below: Hitler was initially grateful for the support that he received from Papen: "Herr von Papen, through your assistance I was appointed Chancellor of Germany and thus the Reich was saved from the abyss of Communism. I will never forget that." However, the führer's gratitude was short-lived and by the time World War II broke out he had shunted Papen to Turkey.

Opposite: Von Papen giving evidence at the Nuremberg Trials. At the first of the Nuremberg Trials Von Papen was one of three men who were found not guilty of war crimes, the other two were the German financier Dr Hjalmar Schacht and the propagandist Hans Fritzsche.

from sailing to France. British code-breakers advised the Royal Mounted Police, who prevented the saboteurs from causing any damage. The act put Papen in jeopardy. He broke American law by using the United States as a base to direct hostile activities against a friendly nation. He had also issued forged papers to German nationals who wanted to return to their homeland to fight in the war. These missteps eventually caught up with Papen, and U.S. authorities demanded his recall. Papen returned to Germany.

After the war, Papen's political career bloomed. In 1932 he became chancellor of Germany, a position for which he was

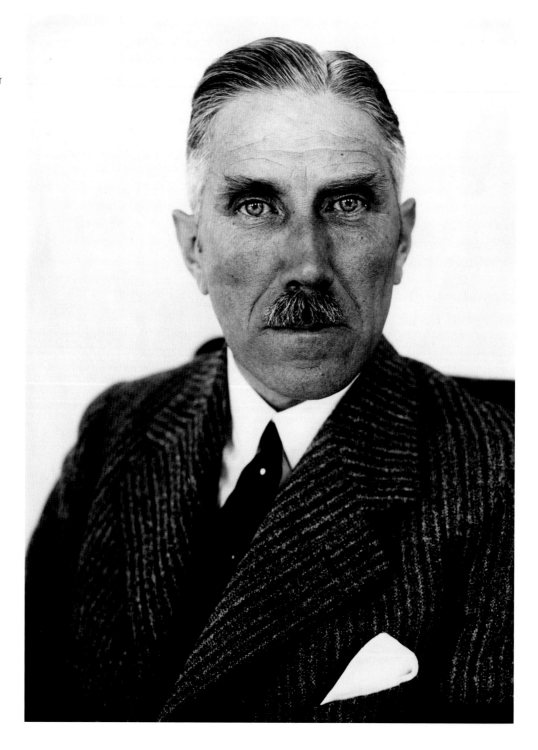

unfit. He became Hitler's ignored pawn. When Hitler began expanding the Third Reich in 1939, he wanted Papen out of the way and appointed him ambassador to Turkey, a country that in World War II remained neutral and became a haven for international spies.

From Chancellor to Cicero

Papen went back into the business of espionage and established a far-reaching spy network out of Ankara. One of his agents, Albanian-born Elyeza Bazna, code-named Cicero, became the British ambassador's valet and sold Papen the embassy's most secret documents. Bazna received thousands of British banknotes for the information, which he deposited for safekeeping in local banks. Neither Papen nor Bazna realized that the notes were counterfeits until the bank com-

plained. By then, Papen had collected all the information from Bazna, including the minutes of high-level conferences between Roosevelt and Churchill and preliminary Allied plans for the invasion of France.

Papen decided to return to Germany after the war where he was arrested and tried in 1946, at Nuremberg, for war crimes. He was found not guilty, but a German denazification court sentenced him to serve a prison term. He declared the sentence unwarranted, and after being released wrote his memoirs in an effort to absolve himself of all charges. Papen later attempted to make a return to politics but was unsuccessful.

NOTES

In 1918 Papen served briefly in Palestine to help Turkish forces put down an Arab revolt led by T. E. Lawrence. Papen returned to Germany to report another defeat.

PENKOVSKY, OLEG (1919–1963)

During World War II, Oleg Penkovsky fought for the Soviet Union
because he believed in the future of his homeland.
Not until the postwar years did he realize that the recklessness
of Soviet leadership was wrong for the world, and
become a double agent.

Born in Ordzhonikidze in the Caucasus, Oleg Penkovsky was the son of a czarist army officer who fought against the Bolsheviks during the Russian civil war. In 1937 Penkovsky graduated from Ordzhonikidze's secondary school and immediately enrolled in the Kiev Artillery School. He graduated as an officer in 1939, two years before Germany attacked the Soviet Union. During World War II, Penkovsky served with distinction in the Ukraine and in the triumphant 1944–45 Soviet campaigns in Poland and Germany. He was wounded several times and received almost a dozen Soviet decorations for his courage on the battlefield.

Penkovsky entered the Frunze Military Academy in Moscow in 1945 and graduated in 1948, after which he was assigned to the GRU, the Soviet military intelligence for the Red Army. Soon, Penkovsky worked his way up to the rank of colonel.

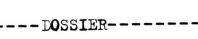

```
----DOSSIER--------
Name: Oleg Penkovsky
Code Name: Alex
Birth/Death: 1919-1963
Nationality: Russian
Occupation: Military
Intelligence
Involvement: Soviet Double
Agent for the West
Outcome: Executed by the
Soviets
```

The Disillusioned Communist

In 1955 the GRU sent Penkovsky as military attaché to the Soviet embassy in Ankara. Most of the espionage activity in

Left: Soviet colonel Oleg Vladimirovich Penkovsky hears the verdict during his Moscow trial on charges of treason and espionage in May 1963. He was found guilty and executed for leaking Russian military secrets to the West. He has been described by former Deputy Director for Intelligence Ray Cline as "the most successful CIA secret agent of the late Dulles–early McCone era."

Turkey had shut down after World War II, so Penkovsky spied on American and Turkish military installations. He found the work boring. He returned to Moscow in 1958 and received special instruction in military engineering. By then, and despite being one of the most trusted members of the GRU and the KGB, Penkovsky became progressively disillusioned by the Soviet system, questioning what he saw as Nikita Khrushchev's reckless political behavior, and fearing that the Soviet premier would provoke a nuclear war.

Foiling Nikita

In 1961 the KGB arranged for Penkovsky to lead a Soviet trade delegation to London, but the real purpose was to find

Below: The court in session on May 10, 1963, during the trial of British businessman Greville Wynne and Russian scientific worker Oleg Penkovsky, who were facing espionage charges in Moscow.

a replacement for Gordon Lonsdale, who had recently been arrested in the Portland spy case. Penkovsky made his first move when British businessman Greville Wynne arrived in Moscow to make arrangements for accommodating the Soviet delegation. When the two men met, Penkovsky surprised Wynne by informing him that he would like to talk to Western intelligence officers when he reached London. Having served in British

intelligence, Wynne arranged the meeting, which took place immediately upon Penkovsky's arrival in London.

Penkovsky spoke with officers from the CIA and MI6 and, after convincing them that he was sincere, offered to act as a double agent. To protect his cover, he passed information of minimal importance to the KGB, but the intelligence he gave the CIA and MI6 included Soviet military and political strategies, and the

Two years after Penkovsky's execution, *The Penkovsky Papers* was published under his name. It exposed Soviet intelligence and the Soviet system. Wynne said that only Penkovsky could have written the book and others agreed. Since Penkovsky was supposed to be dead, the accepted theory was that the CIA wrote the book from information provided by Penkovsky. In the spy business, one can never be certain about anything.

locations and names of Russian spies throughout the world. Over an 18-month period, Penkovsky supplied MI6 and the CIA with more than 5,000 photographs of Soviet armaments, missiles, and space satellites with detailed analyses.

When delivering information to MI6, Penkovsky used neither agents nor mailboxes. He did it all himself. He would stroll along Moscow's Tsventnoy Boulevard with a candy box under his arm and sit on a bench next to Mrs. Ruari Chisholm, whose husband served as Penkovsky's MI6 contact. She always brought her children and knew Penkovsky only as "Alex." Under the candy were rolls of microfilm, which held photographs from secret documents, taken to his small apartment at night for copying. When departing, he left the candy box for Mrs. Chisholm. Sometimes he met with Wynne, ostensibly on business, and simply handed him a dozen or more rolls of film.

One of Penkovsky's his most startling revelations occurred in 1962, during the Cuban missile crisis. He advised the CIA that, despite Khrushchev's boasting, the Soviets were actually too weak in rocket power to start a war. The knowledge aided President John Kennedy's decision to call Khrushchev's bluff and "quarantine" Cuba.

Nikita's Revenge

When Penkovsky approached Wynne with his offer, he certainly understood enough about the double agent business to know that he would eventually be discovered. The KGB knew that important secrets were being leaked, and for more than a year they searched in all the wrong places. Agents decided that the leak had to come from a high-placed, trusted official and began a feverish search for the spy. The trail led to Penkovsky and his relationship with Wynne. In 1962 the KGB picked up Penkovsky in Moscow and Wynne in Budapest, Hungary. Wynne spent nearly a year in jail before the British negotiated a trade and exchanged Gordon Lonsdale, who was in a British jail, for Wynne.

Penkovsky enjoyed no bargains. In 1963 he was tried and convicted in a show trial after prosecutors spent six months trying to pull enough evidence together to convict him of treason and espionage. According to the Russian press, Penkovsky was shot immediately after the verdict.

NOTES

In Penkovsky's letter asking for military rank and citizenship in exchange for information, he wrote, "I ask you to consider me as your soldier. Henceforth the ranks of your Armed Forces are increased by one man."

PETROV, VLADIMIR (1907–1966)

Vladimir Petrov started his career as a true believer in the Soviet system, but as the years passed he became increasingly disturbed by what he observed and defected to Australia.

Born in 1907 to peasants living in Siberia, Vladimir Shorokhov received little education before finding work as an apprentice blacksmith in 1919. Like many of his peers, he joined the Komsomol (Communist Youth Movement) and finished high school. Eventually, Shorokhov became so imbued with Communist doctrine that in 1930, when he joined the Soviet navy, he used the name Proletarsky to demonstrate his support of the proletariat.

From Proletarsky to Petrov

The navy trained Proletarsky to be a cipher expert, and they trained him well. In 1933, before he completed his mandatory four-year tour, Soviet intelligence plucked him out of the navy and assigned him to the OGPU (the Soviet secret police and intelligence forerunner of the NKVD). The OGPU needed Proletarsky's cipher skills and sent him to China to spy on the Japanese. He returned to Moscow in 1937 to work in the new NKVD cipher

```
----DOSSIER--------
Name: Vladimir Petrov
Code Name: Proletarsky
Birth/Death: 1907-1966
Nationality: Siberian
Occupation: Blacksmith
Involvement: Soviet Spy
in Australia
Outcome: Died of Natural
Causes
```

section. By 1943, Proletarsky had risen to the rank of major and was the director of his department. In this capacity he changed his name from Proletarsky to Petrov.

In 1943 the NKVD sent Petrov to Sweden to establish a spy network while serving as an attaché at the Soviet Embassy in Stockholm. After completing his mission, he returned to Moscow in 1947 and married Evdokia, also a trained cipher clerk. Petrov carried out his espionage assignments so expertly that the MVD (formerly the NKVD) decided to send him to Australia to establish a full-blown Russian spy network. In 1951 Petrov and Evdokia transferred to the Soviet Embassy in Sydney, Australia, where he would serve as third secretary and she as cipher supervisor.

A Dearth of Spies Down Under

Though well-supplied with funds, Petrov could not find many Australian government employees interested in spying. MVD boss Lavrenti Beria became increasingly critical of Petrov, and accused him of failure. Good news arrived when he learned that Beria had been arrested and executed; bad news followed when Petrov received orders to return to Moscow.

Left: After his defection, Petrov and his wife were given the names Sven and Anna Allyson, and became Australian citizens in 1956, living in suburban Melbourne. Petrov continued to assist the ASIO; the information he provided was of great value to Western intelligence. ASIO was able to identify over 500 Soviet agents and also glean information regarding the organizational structure of Soviet intelligence.

Right: Vladimir Petrov, seen leaving the court-room in Melbourne after giving evidence before the Australian Commission on Espionage, July 5, 1954. He was sent to Australia as a spy by the Russian MVD in 1951, but chose instead to defect. Petrov's life after defection was not the utopia he had imagined. For many years he lived in fear of death at the hands of a Soviet assassination squad. "No friends, no future. I wish I was dead. No one could dream of our misery."

Petrov had been implicated in Beria's plot to take control of the government after Stalin died and knew what was waiting for him. He contacted Mikhail Bialogusky, a Polish refugee he suspected was working for Australian intelligence, and the day his replacement arrived, Petrov asked for political asylum. Petrov turned over stacks of documents exposing Soviet spies throughout the world and disappeared.

Saving Evdokia

Petrov's his first concern quickly became his wife, who had become the ranking officer at the embassy. Petrov had not told

When Petrov could not recruit spies in Australia, the KGB sent P. V. Kislitsyn and later N. G. Kovaliov; both failed. The KGB blamed Petrov: "Because of the absence of [his] positive guidance."

Evdokia that he planned to defect, nor did she know that he had defected. After a few days, word of Petrov's defection made headline news, but Evdokia did not read newspapers. The KGB sent orders to agents at the embassy to arrest her immediately and put her on the first plane to Moscow. She received a phone call from her husband telling her that he had defected and to leave the embassy immediately, but agents arrested her within hours of the call.

Alerted by the press of Evdokia's arrest, an angry crowd gathered at Sydney's airport and demanded she be released. Evdokia shouted to airport police that she wanted to defect, but the two KGB agents held off the guards and shoved her so hard into a BOAC Constellation that she lost one of her high-heeled shoes and walked the rest of the way barefooted.

Australian counterespionage agents noticed that the plane's itinerary included a stop at Darwin. They made arrangements with the pilot and with local authorities to board the aircraft and remove her. Petrov was already at Darwin with Australian authorities when the plane arrived. He spoke with the KGB agents directly and ordered them to release her. When they began tugging on her, she demanded in Russian that she wanted asylum in Australia. Television crews, photographers, and news correspondents swarmed the scene. When the KGB began dragging Evdokia across the tarmac, Australian police stepped in and relieved the thugs of their SMERSH standard-issue Walther automatic pistols. Hours later the world knew of the Petrovs' defection and witnessed on television the tactics of the KGB. The Soviets broke off relations with Australia and closed the embassy. As far as the Aussies were concerned, it was good riddance.

The documents Petrov turned over to Australian authorities went back to 1952, many of which he had been expected to burn. Part of the information included a letter announcing the defection of Guy Burgess and Donald Maclean to the Soviet Union, a matter that British intelligence had been unable to verify. Another stack contained complete and severely injurious information on Soviet cryptology. After extensive debriefings before the Royal Commission investigating Soviet espionage, the Petrovs changed their name and moved to a small farm in the Australian countryside.

In 1956 Vladimir and Evdokia Petrov published *Empire of Fear*, a fascinating exposé of the brutal methods used by the KGB against dissenters in the Soviet Union and defectors abroad.

PHILBY, HAROLD "KIM" (1912–1988)

Harold "Kim" Philby met Anthony Blunt, Guy Burgess, and Donald Maclean while attending Cambridge. They all became Soviet spies, known later as the Cambridge Spy Ring.

The son of explorer and scholar St. John Philby, Harold "Kim" Philby was born in Ambala, India, where his father held a position in the Indian civil service. His parents nicknamed him Kim after the boy spy in Rudyard Kipling's novel *Kim*, never intending that their son follow in the same profession. His father sided with the colonial peoples of India, which may have had some bearing on Philby's subsequent decision to betray England.

Philby enjoyed all the advantages British life had to offer. He attended his father's school, Westminster, from 1932 to 1938, and the following year he enrolled at Cambridge to study history. At school Philby became intimately involved with Guy Burgess, Donald Maclean, and Anthony Blunt, all men who came from well-to-do homes and were disturbed by the contrast between the carefree wealthy and the suffering lower class during the economic depression of the 1930s.

All four men were intellectuals, fond of extreme ideas, and vulnerable to Communist propaganda. They believed that only the Marxist-Leninist doctrine would solve Britain's social and economic problems. Philby graduated from Cambridge in 1933 but, unlike the others, he never joined the Communist Party. However, like the others, he did become an NKVD agent.

```
----DOSSIER--------
Name: Harold Adrian Russell
"Kim" Philby
Code Name: None
Birth/Death: 1912-1988
Nationality: British
Occupation: Journalist
Involvement: British Spy
for the Soviet Union
Outcome: Died of Natural
Causes in Moscow
```

Finding His Way with Socialism

After graduation, Philby worked as a journalist in London, carefully choosing moderate publications to screen his Communist leanings and infrequent espionage assignments. Any chance of becoming a moderate vanished in 1934 when he married Austrian Communist Alice Kohlmann. They both agreed that only the Soviet Union would oppose Adolf Hitler, who in 1933 became the German chancellor and the fascist leader of a new world order.

In 1937 Philby went to Madrid during the Spanish civil war. He posed as a right-wing journalist but spied for the NKVD. While seemingly supporting General Francisco Franco's fascists, he pried secrets from cooperative commanders and shuttled the information to Soviet operatives in England. Burgess visited him in Spain, returning to London with documents for Philby's handlers.

British expeditionary force to France. When German Panzer divisions smashed through British lines, Philby returned to London during the withdrawal from Dunkirk. British military intelligence (MI6) liked Philby's coverage so well that they made him a spy, which of course delighted the Soviet Union. The NKVD now had an undercover agent in one of the few organizations on earth where they needed spies. By an odd coincidence, Philby found Burgess also working in MI6's Department D, a new and rapidly expanding unit assigned to recruit new agents for British intelligence. The two men met frequently to confer on secrets before passing them to the Soviets.

Philby led a curious life as an MI6 spy. While furnishing the Soviets with British secrets on one hand, he put MI6 agents in touch with Soviet operatives working for Sandor Rado in Switzerland. One such operative may have been Alexander Foote, who infiltrated Rado's operation as a radio operator. The Soviets approved the arrangement because anything MI6 spies did to harm the Germans helped Russia.

In 1944 Philby received a promotion to the Russian desk at MI6, where he methodically deceived his superiors by suppressing information damaging to Moscow. He frequently visited British consulates in neutral countries and near war zones, effectually keeping MI6 informed on some matters and his Soviet handlers on other matters.

But Philby's life was about to change.

Above: Collection of Soviet stamps honoring KGB heroes including notorious British defector Kim Philby (lower right).

Cambridge at MI6

In 1939, a few months before Franco took control of Spain, Philby returned to England to work at the German affairs desk for the *London Times*, a marvelous assignment for a Soviet spy. At the outbreak of World War II, he went with the

In the Heart of the USA

In 1949 the Foreign Office sent Philby to Washington, D.C., to function as a liaison between MI6 and the CIA. Philby now lived in the very core of British-American intelligence. Nothing could have pleased him more when in 1950 Burgess joined the embassy as second secretary. Burgess soon left. The Foreign Office began uncovering evidence about his past activities and recalled him to London. Meanwhile, Philby learned that Maclean was suspected of spying and urged Burgess to warn him. Burgess acted swiftly. After landing at Heathrow, he contacted Maclean, and both men packed quickly and defected to Russia.

The Burgess-Maclean defection put Philby under suspicion. British counter-intelligence (MI5) began looking into past relationships and discovered that Burgess, Maclean, and Philby had been good friends at Cambridge. MI5 also suspected Philby of tipping off Maclean and Burgess. Both MI5 and MI6 interrogated Philby, but he was clever enough to deflect the questions and remained with MI6 for more than a decade.

The Third Man Steps Out

In 1955 Marcus Lipton, a member of Parliament, named Philby as the third man in the Burgess-Maclean incident. Instead of discharging Philby, MI6 sent him to Beruit where, for eight years, he continued working as a Soviet spy. During Philby's eight years in Lebanon, MI6 continued to accumulate evidence against him. Two theories emerged, one that MI6 simply hoped to save embarrassment by coaxing Philby's defection to Moscow, the other being the difficulty of believing that men who, like themselves, came from Cambridge and Oxford, could be double agents working for the Soviets.

The first theory worked. In 1963 Philby feared he might be recalled and confronted with inconvertible evidence. He

proved to be the third man by defecting to Moscow via Odessa. The Soviets gave Philby political asylum and made him a major general in the KGB, which suited him quite well. When American and British journalists later interviewed Philby in Moscow, he bragged about how he had deceived MI6 and injured his native country.

A short time before his death, Philby told a journalist, "To betray you must first belong. I never belonged." He added, "I want to be buried in the Soviet Union, in this country, which I have considered to be my own since the 1930s."

Above: November 9, 1955: Kim Philby, the British double agent, at home during his press conference held after he had been cleared of being the "third man" in the Burgess and Maclean affair.

PINKERTON, ALLAN (1819–1884)

Allan Pinkerton liked to think of himself as the Union's greatest spymaster, but he probably helped the Army of the Potomac lose the Peninsular War by feeding Major General George B. McClellan seriously flawed intelligence.

Born in Glasgow, Scotland, the son of a police sergeant, Allan Pinkerton never received a complete education. Apprenticed to a cooper at an early age, he continued in the trade until 1842, when he emigrated to America in search of a better life. He settled in Chicago, Illinois, and later moved north to Kent County, Michigan, where he set up a cooper's shop. In 1846 Pinkerton's life changed after he discovered a band of counterfeiters, notified authorities, and helped to capture them. As a reward, Kent County made him a deputy sheriff. With his new credential as a law enforcement officer, Pinkerton moved back to rapidly growing Chicago and joined the city's police force as its first detective.

Pinkerton became so successful at hunting down criminals that in 1850 he resigned from the force and founded the Pinkerton National Detective Agency. He chose men from the ranks of Chicago's police force and personally trained them in the art of detection. Most of Pinkerton's detectives became armed guards—riding trains or protecting shipping firms from bandits and robbers. His logo, a wide-open eye inscribed with the words "We Never Sleep," attracted plenty of business. So did his reputation: Pinkerton almost always got his man.

----DOSSIER--------

Name: Allan Pinkerton

Code Name: E. J. Allen

Birth/Death: 1819–1884

Nationality: Scottish

Occupation: Cooper, Deputy Sheriff

Involvement: Union Army Spymaster

Outcome: Died of Natural Causes

The Plot to Kill the President

In 1860 the landscape of America changed suddenly. Abraham Lincoln won the national presidential election, and Southern states began seceding from the Union. When secessionists in the border state of Maryland plotted to blow up railroads and bridges, the governor asked the detective for help. Pinkerton understood the railroad business, and his success in preventing sabotage soon connected him with President-elect Lincoln.

In February 1861 Lincoln departed from his home in Springfield, Illinois, by train. He planned many short speech-making stops before rolling into Washington for his inauguration. When he arrived in New York, rumors abounded that Southern conspirators planned to kidnap or assassinate the president-elect somewhere between Philadelphia and Washington, most likely at Baltimore. Samuel Felton, president of the newly laid Philadelphia-Wilmington-Baltimore Railroad, hired Pinkerton to ensure that Lincoln reached the capital safely.

The President's Bodyguard

Using the alias E. J. Allen, Pinkerton took his two best detectives, Timothy Webster and Henry Davies, and scouted Baltimore. Davies discovered that the Baltimore police chief, a Southern sympathizer, had agreed to not interfere should an attempt be made on Lincoln's life. Pinkerton learned that an assassin had been chosen but not identified. Webster learned that another band of conspirators planned to destroy the railway line to Washington immediately after receiving word of the president-elect's death. Pinkerton

returned to Philadelphia and arranged a special night train for Lincoln. He also posted Webster and Davies at key points along the way and dozens of detectives at bridges and crossings. He conducted Lincoln to a sleeping car in the rear and posted Mrs. Kate Warne, an armed detective, in the car with him. After the train departed from Philadelphia for Baltimore, Pinkerton stood on the platform of the last car, watching for agents posted along the way to wave their lanterns, which meant "all's safe," as the train sped by. When the

Above: Portrait of Allan Pinkerton. On the facade of his detective agency's three-story Chicago headquarters was the company slogan, "We Never Sleep," accompanied by a picture of a huge black-and-white eye. The Pinkerton logo led to the use of the term "private eye."

Above: Allan Pinkerton, left, President Lincoln, center, and Major General John A. McClernand, pictured at Antietam, the site of one of the bloodiest battles in America's history.

U.S. Secret Service and asked him to send his best agents into the South and report on recruiting, troop movements, arms production, and Confederate plans. Pinkerton wore a disguise and went behind enemy lines on his own. When Major General George B. McClellan assumed command of the Army of the Potomac on July 27, 1861, he made Pinkerton his chief spymaster. Having been in the railroad business, McClellan already knew Pinkerton and trusted his judgment.

Though successful at chasing bandits and capturing safecrackers, Pinkerton knew nothing about the business of spying, and relied too heavily on panicky, misinformed civilians and runaway slaves to collect intelligence. McClellan didn't understand spying either, but he relied on Pinkerton for accurate information. During McClellan's Peninsular campaign in May–July 1862, Pinkerton consistently worried the general by overstating the size of General Robert E. Lee's opposing force. In June, Lee had fewer than 90,000 men, but Pinkerton estimated the Confederate army at 200,000. As a consequence, McClellan remained timorously on the defensive and retreated.

Furious with McClellan's pathetic performance on the Peninsula, Lincoln recalled the general from Virginia. When Confederate forces invaded Maryland in September, Lincoln reinstated the general. McClellan began tailing the Confederate army and, by the greatest stroke of good fortune, discovered Lee's plans. With a two-to-one superiority over Lee, McClellan enjoyed a marvelous opportunity to crush the Confederate army. Pinkerton, however, once again grossly overestimated the size of Lee's force, and McClellan failed to exploit his advantage during the Battle of Antietam.

train reached Baltimore, teams of horses lugged the cars to the Washington line. No incident occurred. Lincoln reached the capital safely before daybreak and personally expressed his gratitude to Pinkerton.

The General's Spymaster

When the Civil War began in April 1861, Lincoln put Pinkerton in charge of the

McClellan's career as a general soon ended, and so did Pinkerton's as head of the Secret Service. In 1862 Secretary of War Edwin M. Stanton replaced Pinkerton with Lafayette Baker, an inept charlatan with even less knowledge of espionage.

The Return of the Detective

Pinkerton returned to doing what he did best: detective work. He hired more operatives and opened branches in New York and Philadelphia. The agency made national headlines when he solved a half-million-dollar heist from the Adams Express Company and caught the thieves. Banks and railroads hired him to track down Jesse and Frank James and the Younger brothers, who had been robbing trains in Missouri and Kansas. The James brothers became so frustrated with Pinkerton's hindrance that Jesse once tracked the detective to Chicago to kill him, but failed.

Melodramatic and pompous to the end, Allan Pinkerton retired to write books about his experiences as a detective. His embellishments about his detective agency provided a dearth of material for decades of private-eye thrillers written by others. When Pinkerton died in 1884, he left his agency to his sons, William and Robert Pinkerton, who moved it into the twentieth century and started looking overseas for business.

President-elect Abraham Lincoln never outlived a modest amount of public embarrassment because Pinkerton disguised him for the trip to Washington. One senator called it "a damned piece of cowardice."

POLLARD, JONATHAN JAY (1954–)

Influenced by his father, Jonathan Pollard grew up committed to helping Israel and volunteered to become a spy to live out a delusional lifelong fantasy.

Born in South Bend, Indiana, where his father taught microbiology at Notre Dame University, Jonathan Pollard grew up with an excellent education. He believed deeply in the formation of Israel and became vicariously attached to the cause of displaced Jews who returned to the home of their ancestors to build a new nation. Pollard vowed to help the Israeli cause in any manner possible, and when he enrolled at Stanford University in 1972, he falsely claimed to have joint citizenship in the U.S. and Israel. He even tried to convince his classmates that he had fled from Czechoslovakia in 1968 because his father had been uncovered as a CIA spy. After Pollard caught everyone's attention, he falsely boasted about being a secret agent working for the Mossad. Pollard was obviously intrigued by and predisposed to espionage, but he decided to not go to Israel, though this had been his stated intention.

After dropping out of law school, Pollard applied for a job at the CIA.

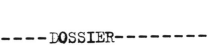

----DOSSIER--------

Name: Jonathan Jay Pollard

Code Name: Danny Cohen

Birth/Death: 1954–

Nationality: American

Occupation: U.S. Navy Research Specialist

Involvement: Spied Against U.S. for Israel

Outcome: Serving Life Sentence in Prison

The Man Who Yearned to Spy

The agency turned Pollard down because he used drugs in college. He had inserted false education and work history on his application, but nobody checked it out.

Pollard then went to the U.S. Navy, which hired him as a civilian intelligence analyst in 1979. The standard background investigation failed to look into his record, and the navy gave him top-secret security clearance. In 1982 Pollard attended high-level meetings with Israeli intelligence and came away convinced that the United States was not sharing enough information with Israel. Pollard lost his clearance when U.S. counterintelligence agents caught him meeting too frequently with the military attaché at the South African Embassy for no apparent reason. Pollard was actually trying to set up a private information service for anyone who wanted to buy classified information. In 1984 the navy restored Pollard's clearance and assigned him to a highly sensitive department concerned with satellites and CIA activities.

Soon afterward, a friend stopped at Pollard's home and mentioned that he had recently spoken with Colonel Aviem Sella, an Israeli war ace who was in New York. Pollard immediately insisted that a meeting be arranged. On May 29, 1984, Pollard met Sella in the Washington Hilton Hotel coffee shop and offered to supply U.S. secrets so Israel could strengthen its defensive capabilities. Sella suspected the possibility of a trap, but asked Pollard to bring him something. A few days later Pollard returned to New York with 48 documents. Sella studied them, concluded Pollard could be trusted, and accepted the offer.

Draining the Vault

Sella handed Pollard over to Yosef Yagur, who worked at the Israeli Consulate in New York. Yagur and Sella took Pollard and Anne Henderson, Pollard's fiancée, to Paris for a discussion with Rafael Eitan,

a veteran Israeli intelligence officer. While Pollard and Eitan spoke in private, Yagur took Henderson to a jewelry store to pick out an engagement ring. She chose a $10,000 diamond and sapphire ring. Sella purchased the ring and told Henderson to say that it came from Pollard's uncle, Joe Fisher. After Pollard closed his deal with Eitan, Sella took the couple to the airport and gave Pollard more than $10,000 in cash to enjoy his vacation in France. He also promised to put Pollard on a retainer of $1,500 a month in exchange for secrets.

After returning to the United States, Pollard began to routinely take stacks of documents, computer printouts, and photographs home. He simply stuffed them in

Below: On July 22, 2005, the federal appeals court rejected convicted spy Pollard's latest effort to reduce his sentence for selling military secrets to Israel. The court ruled that he had waited too long to try and contest his 1987 life sentence and that he had failed to make a convincing case.

Above: An Israeli calls for the release of Jonathan Pollard outside the Foreign Ministry during the U.S. Secretary of State's meeting with the Israelis on February 6, 2005, in Jerusalem.

his briefcase and walked through security without being searched. He then drove through a car wash, transferred the documents to a suitcase, and drove to a Washington apartment where Israelis copied the documents over the weekend so Pollard could return them on Monday. Yagur raised Pollard's stipend to $2,500 every month and sent him on an all-expense-paid honeymoon to Europe with a $700-per-day private compartment on the Orient Express. Fearing that Pollard might someday be caught, Yagur also set up a $30,000 Swiss bank account and provided him with a forged passport and the name Danny Cohen. By mid-1985, Pollard had delivered enough information to fill a room six feet wide and ten feet high.

```
Many of the secrets Pollard delivered to Israelis came from U.S.
Navy documents specifying the various types of weapons the Soviets
were supplying to Islamic countries.
```

The Israeli Rejection

In November 1985, Commander Jerry Agee, Pollard's commanding officer, discovered a printout missing. Because of Pollard's habitual borrowing of classified documents, Agee alerted the Naval Investigative Service (NIS). On November 18, NIS and FBI agents stopped Pollard outside the building, found secret documents in his briefcase, and brought him back to the office for questioning. Pollard succeeded in throwing off the investigators who, nonetheless, kept him under surveillance. They followed Pollard and his wife to the Israeli Embassy and watched them attempt to be admitted inside. The ambassador refused to give the Pollards asylum and turned them out. As soon as Pollard drove out of the embassy, the FBI arrested him. The following day, they apprehended his wife and charged both with espionage.

Now annoyed with his Israeli coconspirators, Pollard cooperated with the U.S. authorities. He confessed everything he knew about his Israeli handlers and created a list of the secrets he had sold. He argued that he was not spying against the United States but for Israel, a country to which he owed his Jewish heritage. Convicted, Pollard went to prison for life, and his wife drew a five-year term but only served three years.

Despite efforts by the Israeli government to lighten Pollard's sentence, he is still in prison. In 1994, attorneys representing Pollard asked President Bill Clinton to pardon Pollard. Clinton turned them down.

To this date, $2,500 a month is still being deposited in an Israeli bank account, funds Pollard may draw upon when he is freed from prison.

Below: Lawyers Eliot Lauer, right, and Jacques Semmelman, second from right, speak to the media on behalf of Jonathan Pollard, who has been campaigning for a shorter sentence. Pollard was brought to court again to find out whether he can appeal the ruling since he was sentenced to life in prison.

POWERS, GARY FRANCIS (1929–1977)

Gary Powers created an international sensation when he was forced down from a U-2 spy plane over the Soviet Union. The incident led to a show trial in Moscow featuring Nikita Khrushchev.

Born in Kentucky, the son of a shoemaker, Gary Powers went to school in his hometown of Bourdyne. In 1950 he graduated from Milligan College in Tennessee and joined the U.S. Air Force. In 1956, with the rank of captain, he transferred to the U-2 espionage program run by the Central Intelligence Agency. The CIA had recently begun flying U-2 spy planes at high altitudes over the Soviet Union in order to photograph nuclear test explosions, military war games, and other activities of potential threat to the West. As a cover story, the CIA claimed that U-2 pilots worked for the National Aeronautics and Space Administration (NASA) and were gathering scientific information.

Powers received three months of training at a secret Nevada air base before being transferred to the U-2 base at Incirlik, Turkey. For four years he flew various missions along the Turkish-Soviet border before being ordered to Pakistan, where he received a briefing for his first mission across the Soviet Union.

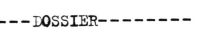

```
----DOSSIER--------
Name: Gary Francis Powers
Code Name: None
Birth/Death: 1929-1977
Nationality: American
Occupation: U.S. Air Force
Fighter Pilot
Involvement: U-2 Spy Pilot
for the United States
Outcome: Killed in a
Helicopter Crash
```

Out of the Wild Blue Yonder

On May 1, 1960, May Day for the Soviets, Powers took off from Peshawar, Pakistan, on a 3,788-mile flight that would take him 2,919 miles over the Soviet Union before landing at the American base in Bödo,

Above: August 18, 1960, Gary Francis Powers, accused of espionage over Russia in his U-2 airplane, on trial in Moscow. On the extreme left, wearing eyeglasses, is the defense counsel, Grinev.

Norway. Powers's mission was to photograph Soviet progress in the development of intercontinental ballistic missiles. Photos from an earlier flight had shown the construction of a launching compound at Tyura Tam, and President Eisenhower authorized one more flight over the area before suspending U-2 operations for a spell. However, important talks had been scheduled for May 16 in Moscow between Eisenhower, Prime Minister Harold Macmillan of Great

Britain, President Charles de Gaulle of France, and Soviet Premier Nikita Khrushchev, and Eisenhower did not want an embarrassing incident that might ruin the conference.

The CIA informed Powers that he would be flying at 68,000 feet, well above the range of Soviet aircraft or surface-to-air missiles. Over Sverdlovsk, an explosion rocked one of the U-2's engines. Unable to right the plane or use its destruct mechanism, Powers ejected him-

"We did this quite deliberately," Khrushchev declared on May 6, "because if we had given out the whole story, the Americans would have thought up another fable."

self at several thousand feet. Around 11:00 a.m., the inhabitants of a small village heard the sound of a low-flying aircraft followed by an earth-shaking crash. They peered skyward and observed a small speck parachuting to the ground. Men rushed toward the descending parachutist and arrived to find the flyer untangling himself from the parachute ropes.

They described him as medium height, stockily built, and wearing a steel-colored suit, a white helmet painted with the number 29, and brown boots. In his belt he carried a long-barreled pistol and a knife. When they asked who he was, the flyer replied in an unfamiliar language, "Gary Francis Powers."

A Tangled Web

When the U-2 failed to reach Norway on schedule, the CIA started to worry. Radio intercepts suggested that the Soviets had attempted to intercept a plane over Sverdlovsk. Assuming Powers had been killed, the CIA issued a cover story stating that a NASA weather plane making upper air studies out of Turkey had been reported overdue and missing.

On May 5 Khrushchev announced in a blistering speech that a U.S. plane had been shot down and blamed America for committing a provocative act to impede the summit conference. The U.S. State Department stuck to the CIA's weather story, suggesting that the pilot may have fallen unconscious due to a malfunction of his oxygen-supply system and, being unable to adjust his automatic pilot, accidentally violated Soviet air space.

The Americans' ploy might have worked had Khrushchev not gone on the air the following day to report the pilot alive and talking.

Aftershock

Because of the botched mission, Allen W. Dulles, director of the CIA, offered to resign, but Eisenhower refused the gesture. Khrushchev demanded an

Below: Gary Powers at his three-day open trial held at the Hall of Commons in Moscow, where he pleaded guilty to spy charges and was sentenced to 10 years by the USSR Supreme Court's Military Cases Collegium.

Below: Russian leader
Nikita Khruschev, right,
speaking to press about
shooting down the
American U-2 spy plane,
piloted by Gary Francis
Powers, flying over the
Soviet Union.

apology from Eisenhower during a European summit meeting in Paris, but the president merely admitted that he intended to do everything in his power to protect the United States from a surprise attack. When Khrushchev arrived in Paris, he refused to attend the summit conference unless the president apologized. Eisenhower canceled his trip.

Khrushchev used the U-2 incident to launch a major propaganda attack on the United States. The showplace became the Moscow trial of Gary Powers in the

Soviet Hall of Commons. Khrushchev wanted the defendant to admit that a Soviet missile had shot down the spy plane, but Powers described what everyone understood to be a jet flame-out, which is accompanied by a severe jolting explosion of gases at the aircraft's tail. To make matters more embarrassing for the Soviet government, Powers admitted to flying over Soviet territory for more than four years. During the trial, Powers's testimony actually damaged Khrushchev's leadership in the

Communist Party. Flustered and annoyed by the outcome of the trial, Khrushchev issued a warning that American bases on foreign soil would be destroyed if they allowed any more spy planes to fly over the Soviet Union.

Trial and Punishment

Powers never attempted to deny that he flew a spy plane. After listening to the reading of a long, 4,000-word indictment against him, Powers merely said, "Yes, I am guilty." Khrushchev never obtained all the propaganda he hoped to collect from the trial, and on August 19, 1960, the Soviet court sentenced Powers to a 10-year prison term.

Eighteen months later, on February 10, 1962, Powers returned to the United States in exchange for Soviet spymaster Colonel Rudolf Ivanovich Abel, who had been imprisoned in the United States. Four years later, the Kremlin ousted Khrushchev for having too many "hare-brained schemes" and for failing to get any concessions from Eisenhower or, later, from President John F. Kennedy during the Cuban missile crisis.

Gary Powers resigned from the air force in 1970 and for several years worked as a test pilot for Lockheed Aircraft Corporation. He later became a popular traffic reporter for television, watching the roads from his helicopter. On August 1, 1977, Powers died in a helicopter crash while monitoring conditions over Los Angeles. Although never recognized in his lifetme, Powers was posthumously awarded the Distinguished Flying Cross, the Department of Defense Prisoner of War Medal, and the National Defense Service Medal in a ceremony at Beale Air Force Base in northern California.

NOTES

In 1970 Gary Powers published *Operation Overflight: The U-2 Spy Pilot Tells His Story for the First Time*, which provides excellent insight into the U-2 spy flights over the Soviet Union.

PRIME, GEOFFREY (1938–)

Geoffrey Prime, a confused and corrupt man, lived a complex life as a spy, a pedophile, and a married man—until the day he confessed to his wife.

Born in Staffordshire, England, Geoffrey Prime endured an unhappy childhood because of sexual assaults from an adult relative. Though a bright and clever lad, he never fully recovered from the experience and grew up expecting little from life. He attended a technical school to learn a trade, but quit to join the Royal Air Force. Assigned to the ground crew, he applied himself and rose in the ranks to become a sergeant. While in the RAF, he took a Russian language course and was posted in West Berlin, where he intercepted Warsaw Pact military communications. Lonely and dreaming of a better life in the Soviet Union, he contacted the KGB by simply going to a Soviet checkpoint in Berlin and handing a Russian officer a note. A few days later, two KGB agents contacted him in West Berlin.

How to Spy in a Few Easy Lessons

The KGB waited for Prime's enlistment to expire because he could not be much value to the Soviets reading Warsaw Pact

```
----DOSSIER--------
Name: Geoffrey Prime
Code Name: Rowlands
Birth/Death: 1938-
Nationality: British
Occupation: Sergeant in
the Royal Air Force
Involvement: British Spy
for Soviets
Outcome: Serving 38-year
Prison Term
```

documents for the RAF. During the years of waiting, Prime kept in contact with the KGB by shortwave radio. He really wanted to spy, and the KGB suggested he get a job as a code-breaker with British Government Communications Headquarters (GCHQ) at Cheltenham, which he was able to do in 1976. At GCHQ he translated intercepted Soviet communications in the extremely secret J Division, which shared intelligence with the United States.

When the time came for Prime to take a vacation, he flew to West Berlin and slipped into East Germany to undergo espionage training. After completing the course, he received a code name, Rowlands, and a complete spy kit hidden under the false bottom of a briefcase. The contents included invisible inks and specially prepared paper for recording secret messages. Instructors also provided him with £400 to buy a short-wave radio, a tape recorder, and a camera. Prime could hardly wait to get started. After returning to Cheltenham, he immediately began photographing secret documents and sent them to East Berlin

as microdots. He also used coded short-wave broadcasts to keep his handlers informed of his progress.

Stepping Up in the World

Impressed with Prime's dedication and ability, GCHQ promoted him in November 1976 to section chief of J Division. Prime translated and processed signals received from the CIA satellite Rhyolite, the "spy in the sky" that monitored phone conversations and electronic transmissions over Red China and the Soviet Union. The CIA, working with TRW in California, was also close to completing Argus, an even more sensitive satellite.

When Prime received the news, he hurriedly contacted his handlers. At the

Below: 10th November 1982. Following Geoffrey Prime's conviction on spying charges Scotland Yard officers display the spy kit that was issued to Prime by the KGB following his training in East Germany.

KGB's request, he flew to Vienna for a meeting. When Prime arrived, he discovered that the KGB actually knew all about the project from their attaché in Mexico City, who had been buying the plans of the project from two American amateur spies, Christopher John Boyce and Andrew Daulton Lee; Boyce worked at TRW, where the satellite was being tested. Prime pocketed a small amount of money for his information and was told to go back to GCHQ and learn the exact nature of the information being communicated from the satellites. Prime immersed himself in the project. Because he was the head of the department, he had access to almost all the information flowing between the CIA and British intelligence.

Falling Down in the World

While deeply engrossed in collecting secret information for his handlers, Prime learned that Boyce and Lee had been arrested and sent to prison. He considered the KGB's offer to transfer him to Moscow before British intelligence became suspicious of his activities. Prime decided to stay at GCHQ because spying paid well. One day he precipitously quit and moved to London. He stole 500 secret documents, knowing his handlers would pay well to obtain them, and also knowing that he would need the money.

Prime, however, had an equally serious problem to address upon returning to London. For many years, he had been a predatory pedophile conducting a secret and perverted sex life preying on young girls. Though married, he kept 2,287 index cards on girls 10 to 15 years old. He knew their addresses, had their phone numbers, and sometimes called hoping to learn they were home alone. His index cards also recorded his successful and unsuccessful assaults.

Having moved back to London, he had to start all over again. In April 1981 he attacked a small girl with a knife but her screams drove him away. The girl helped a police artist draw an amazingly accurate sketch of Prime and also gave a detailed description of his car. A few days later the police knocked on Prime's door and questioned him, but he denied everything.

Rhona Prime's Last Word

The police visit unnerved Prime to such a severe degree that he confessed everything to his wife. Disgusted, Rhona Prime insisted he go to the police. Prime obliged his wife, confessed his sex crimes, but said nothing about working for the KGB. Rhona, however, intended to keep her husband off the street.

She told the police that her husband was also a Soviet agent. Scotland Yard detectives searched the apartment and found Prime's spy kit and information on how to process microdots. During the trial, the court ruled that Prime had violated the British Secrets Act by selling information "of the utmost secrecy" and sentenced him to prison for 35 years. For his sexual assaults, the court added another three years.

For five years, Prime had spied for the KGB under the very noses of British GCHQ without detection. Had his wife not notified authorities, Prime might never have been caught.

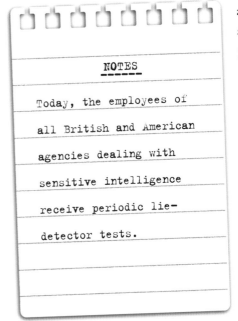

NOTES

Today, the employees of all British and American agencies dealing with sensitive intelligence receive periodic lie-detector tests.

PROFUMO, JOHN DENNIS (1915–2006)

What eventually became known as the Profumo Affair ruined the career of Prime Minister Harold Macmillan and created several years of international humiliation for the British government.

John Profumo's father, a member of the Italian aristocracy, moved to London to enjoy important social connections with the British upper class. Young John received an excellent education, graduating from Harrow School and then from Brasenose College, Oxford University. In 1940, at age 35, he became the youngest member of Parliament. In 1939, Profumo had joined the Army, became an officer, and at the outbreak of war, served in North Africa, and landed in Normandy on D-Day. In 1945, after being awarded an Order of the British Empire, he returned to civilian life as a brigadier general and went into business. Reelected to Parliament in 1950, he married actress Valerie Hobson, and during the next ten years moved up the ladder in Prime Minister Harold Macmillan's Tory government. In 1960 Profumo became secretary of state for war and a member of the Privy Council.

In January 1961, while a guest of Viscount "Bill" Astor, Profumo met Christine Keeler, a 19-year-old call girl who first delighted audiences by seduc-

```
-----DOSSIER--------
Name: John Dennis Profumo
Code Name: Bowtie
Birth/Death: 1915-2006
Nationality: Anglo-Italian
Occupation: Royal Army
Officer and Politician
Involvement: Central Figure
in British Cabinet
Espionage
Outcome: Died of a Stroke
```

tively performing onstage at the age of 16. Profumo first noticed her swimming naked in Astor's pool; he quickly succumbed to Keeler's charms and the two became involved in a steamy affair. They met secretly in the London apartment of society osteopath Dr. Stephen Ward, with whom Keeler lived platonically.

Ward knew all the "in" people, including Winston Churchill, Douglas Fairbanks Jr., and a host of other celebrities. Though Ward was known as a Communist sympathizer and a friend of Captain Yevgeni Ivanov, the naval intelligence attaché at the Soviet Embassy in London, the rela-

Below: December 12, 1952: Parliamentary Secretary to the Ministry of Civil Aviation John D. Profumo, working at his desk at Ariel House.

tionship appeared to Ward's friends to be nothing other than friendly. Profumo never suspected Ward of spying and was too captivated by Keeler's charms to consider the possibility. Although Soviet spies were being uncovered routinely by British intelligence, Profumo never thought of himself as a potential target. Nor did he know that Ward made his apartment available to Ivanov, who was also Keeler's lover.

The West Indian Incident

In 1961, MI5 observed the troublesome connection between Ward, who they watched because of his Communist connection with Ivanov, and Profumo, who had been making frequent visits to the suspected spy's apartment. The FBI had also collected information on Keeler's relationships with Ivanov, Ward, and Profumo (whom they code-named "Bowtie"). It was the early 1960s, the height of the cold war, and with the Cuban missile crisis looming, a highly connected government official involved in sexual relations in which a Soviet intelligence officer was also involved, raised questions. Keeler later admitted that Ward and Ivanov had asked her to quiz Profumo on American plans to move nuclear missiles into West Germany, but she never admitted whether or not she complied. MI5 agents took Profumo aside and warned him of the Ward-Ivanov connection. Profumo still did not know about Keeler's sexual relationship with Ivanov, but he took MI5's warning seriously and toward the end of 1961 terminated the relationship.

A year later, Keeler became involved in a love triangle with two West Indians, resulting in a knife fight in which one was seriously injured. The assailant was

FBI director J. Edgar Hoover watched the Profumo affair from abroad. He already knew that Ivanov was a GRU intelligence officer, and he also knew that Ward's circle of call girls also included Suzy Chang and Mariella Novotny, who had also serviced President John F. Kennedy.

arrested and scheduled for trial. The press became involved, performed their own investigation, and concluded that Keeler and several others were all members of a high-class call girl ring operated by Ward. Keeler told her story to the press and named Ward, Profumo, and Ivanov. The KGB immediately recalled Ivanov to Moscow, where his wife served him with divorce papers.

Bringing Down the Government

Because Keeler's scandalous statements involved a cabinet member, the press postponed any public statement until they spoke with Profumo. In an effort to stop publication, Profumo denied everything, although MI5 had a secret collection of documents, including those from the FBI, implicating Ward as a spy for Ivanov who

Below: John Profumo and his wife, Valerie Hobson, in their car two weeks after he admitted in the House of Commons that he had lied about his association with Christine Keeler.

used Keeler to ply secrets from Profumo. Keeler later admitted this was true.

Reporters approached Ward to hear his side of the story. The osteopath threatened to "bring down the government" by revealing the Profumo-Keeler affair if the press printed a single word about his involvement, but he did not mention Ivanov. Keeler had already sold the press personal love letters from Profumo. Nobody was fooling anybody anymore, but reporters still repressed the scandal.

Anxious to clear the air, the House of Commons invited Profumo to answer a few questions. On March 22, 1963, the secretary of war stood before the bar and somberly stated that he had never indulged in any indiscretions with Christine Keeler. Prime Minister Macmillan and the House of Commons accepted the statement as truthful. MI5 was not convinced—they were edgy because Soviet spy John Vassall had recently been arrested, and Kim Philby, a former high-ranking government official and the third member of the Cambridge Spy Ring, had just defected to Moscow.

Public attention now shifted to Ward, who faced prosecution for enhancing his income by running a prostitution ring. In an attempt to save himself, Ward sent a letter to Macmillan stating that Profumo had lied to the House of Commons. Once again, pressure reverted back to Profumo and it soon became unbearable. The press began to question the character of those the government's war minister chose as friends. They also wondered what Profumo might have confided to Keeler that she passed to Ivanov. Profumo could no longer appear in public without being surrounded by reporters who asked questions he did not want to answer.

Knowing he would never escape from the scandal, on June 4, 1963, he wrote a letter to the prime minister, confessing that he had lied about the affair but had never spied, and tendered his resignation.

The Consequences of Being Human

Profumo withdrew from public and, with his wife, spent the rest of his life doing charitable work. She didn't know about her husband's affair with Keeler until the scandal broke, but she never left his side.

NOTES

In 1992, Yevgeny published *The Naked Spy*, an autobiographic work that shed considerably more light on Christine Keeler, her friends, and his efforts to obtain information from Profumo.

In 1975 Queen Elizabeth awarded Profumo one of the country's highest honors for his social work, Commander of the British Empire.

Keeler went to prison for nine months, later married, and moved to north London. After many years she admitted to being asked to probe secrets from Profumo, but whether she did is still unclear. Ivanov knew she was having a relationship with Profumo, but Profumo did not know she was having an affair with Ivanov until later. A reporter for *Tass*, the Soviet news agency, admitted that Ivanov had formed connections in Tory circles, but did not mention Profumo.

Ward may have been a middleman for Ivanov. At least, the FBI thought so. Ward avoided conviction for prostitution by overdosing on sleeping pills.

After the press broke the story, Macmillan asked Lord Denning to investigate the scandal. Denning absolved the prime minister, but Macmillan's trust and support of Profumo led to the prime minister's downfall, and a month later he resigned.

On March 7, 2006, John Profumo passed away at the age of 91, after suffering a stroke. His death was much reported in the UK and, though fully vindicated, aspects of the affair remain hazy.

Opposite: Russian attaché Eugene Ivanov. London solicitor Michael Eddowes claimed Ivanov had asked Christine Keeler to obtain information from British war minister John Profumo, with whom she also associated.

Left: On June 5, 1963, Profumo resigned as Secretary of State for War after his affair with call girl Christine Keeler became public knowledge. Referring in Parliament to his previous denial of any impropriety, he stated, "To my very deep regret I have to admit that this was not true, and that I misled . . . my colleagues and the House."

RADO, SANDOR (1899–1981)

Sandor Rado operated one of the Soviets' most efficient spy networks, but the real credit belonged to the agents who worked for him.

Born Alexander Radolfi, the son of a wealthy Jewish businessman, Sandor Rado grew up and received his education in a suburb of Budapest, Hungary. While a student at the local university, he joined the Communist Party. In 1919 the party made him a commissar, and he took part in the coup that briefly took over the Hungarian government and made Russian-backed Béla Kun dictator. When nationalists drove the Communists out, Rado fled to Moscow, where he met and married Helene Jensen, also a Communist in exile. He then went to the University of Jena and became a professional cartographer and geographer.

Dora Meets Sonia and Sissy

When Rado returned to Moscow in 1931, the NKVD recruited and trained him as an espionage agent. The following year, Rado posed as a clerk in the Russian Embassy in Berlin, but his real assignment was to spy on the Nazis, who were rapidly taking over Germany. Rado

----DOSSIER--------

Name: Sandor Rado

Real Name: Alexander Radolfi

Code Names: Dora, Itgnati Kulichev

Birth/Death: 1899–1981

Nationality: Hungarian

Occupation: Clerk in Russian Embassy

Involvement: Soviet Spymaster in Europe During World War II

Outcome: Died of Natural Causes in Budapest

organized Communist gangs to rough up Hitler's brown-shirted storm troopers, leading to an increased number of street fights. When Reinhard Heydrich took over the Nazi secret police, he ordered his thugs to assassinate Rado for being a troublesome Communist and a hated Jew. The NKVD moved Rado to Paris, where he established Geopress, ostensibly a publishing house for maps and geopolitical events but actually a cover for spying on France and Germany.

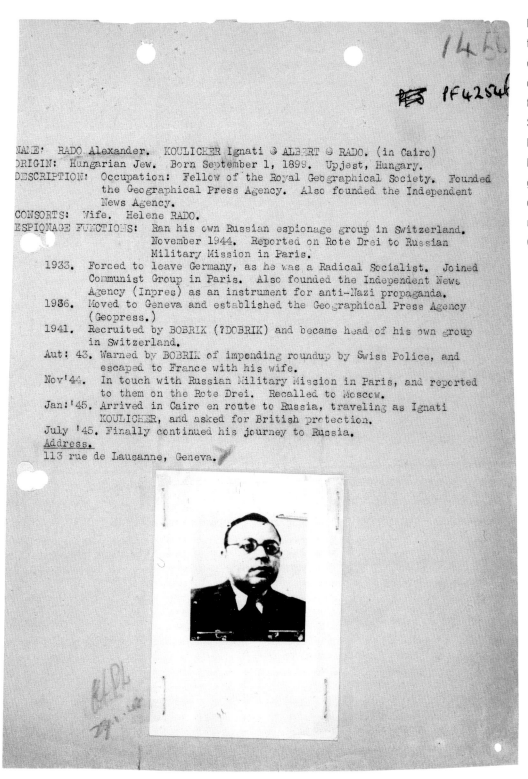

Left: British intelligence file notes on Rado briefly outlining his espionage career in World War II. As the resident director of the Swiss-based network, Rado had held the secret Red Army rank of major general. For the work carried out by this spy ring, he was awarded the Order of Lenin in 1943.

In 1936, Rado came to the notice of the GRU (Soviet intelligence for the Red Army), which sent him to Switzerland as resident director of intelligence. There he adopted the code name Dora—a mixed spelling for Rado—and began recruiting top-notch spies, one of whom was British subject Ruth Kuczynski (a.k.a. Ursula-Maria Hamburger). Using the code name Sonia, Kuczynski became one of Rado's top agents. She recruited Alexander Foote, whom neither she nor Rado ever realized was a British counterintelligence plant, and Foote became Sonia's radioman. Every secret he radioed to Moscow, he radioed to London. Kuczynski later went to England as handler for Klaus Fuchs, the atomic bomb spy.

Rado recruited Rachel Duebendorfer, who used the code name Sissy. She and Sonia fronted for Rado, who preferred running his well-balanced and efficient network from behind the scenes. During the late 1930s, Rado's operation proved to be the Soviets' best source for information on Nazi military plans and political activities.

Orchestras Without Musicians

The source of Rado's priceless information came from a man named Lucy. Only Duebendorfer (Sissy) and Christian Schneider (Taylor) knew that Lucy was Rudolf Roessler, who ranked among the two or three most accomplished spies in World War II. Roessler obtained his information directly from members of the Black Orchestra, high-ranking German officers and officials opposed to Hitler, while Sonia obtained her information from the Red Orchestra, the Communist network inside Germany and Nazi-occupied Europe. Roessler refused to work through any other handler than Sissy or Taylor, and Rado never discovered his identity.

In late 1941 Roessler sent Rado Hitler's battle plans for the invasion of Russia, including the divisions involved, where they were to be located, and how the assault was to be executed. Soviet intelligence could not convince Joseph Stalin that Hitler actually meant to invade Russia. Rado continued to relay corroborating evidence to Moscow as Lucy passed it through Taylor and Sissy. What made the network so successful was Rado's policy of using Duebendorfer, Schneider, and Kuczynski as code-named cut-outs (intermediaries), thereby preventing members of the ring from meeting or knowing the identity of each other.

Extravagance Becomes Dangerous

The British SIS Ultra operation had broken the German Enigma codes and also knew when and where the Germans planned to invade Russia. SIS did not want the Russians to know they had captured an Enigma machine and tried to warn the Soviets through Foote that Germany was about to mount a massive attack against Kursk. Foote staggered Soviet intelligence when he sent the mes-

In 1943 Soviet GRU intelligence officials asked Duebendorfer for Lucy's identity. She refused to tell them.

CONFIDENTIAL.

M. I. C.,
General Headquarters,
Middle East Forces.

MIC/190.

C. I. O.,
S. I. M. E, G. H. Q., (two).

Subject: <u>Alexander RADO.</u> (Code name "LANE").

1.   This morning at approximately 0930 hours I received
a telephone message from Captain DUNKERLEY to say that Captain
BIDMEAD would be bringing down a guest for examination.

2.   Captain BIDMEAD and RADO arrived at 1005 hours.
RADO was placed in room Y.10. and Captain BIDMEAD then gave me
a short summary of the case as it was then known to him. Since
I understood that the man had come to us voluntarily and for
his own protection, and was for examination only, I decided
that the examination should proceed forthwith without the usual
formalities. I was under the impression that whether he was
to be admitted as a normal guest or not, would depend upon the
result of Captain BIDMEAD's preliminary examination.

3.   As I had to leave for G. H. Q., I asked Captain BIDMEAD
to leave me a note with the Guard Commander.

4.   RADO returned from his examination and had his lunch
at 1200 hours. His dirty plate etc. was removed at 1240 hours
at which time he was quite alright.

5.   At 1430 hours the guard went to his room to fetch
RADO for his exercise. He found the man lying on his bed
with a blanket over his head and blood dripping on the floor.
The guard informed his sergeant who in turn informed the M. I.
Room and my office. As it happened I was in "Z" block. The
medical sergeant and I arrived together at Y. 10; and found the
man in a comatose condition with a severe wound in his neck.
The medical sergeant immediately rendered first-aid and then
sent for Captain HYND. I endeavoured to get in touch with
Captain GRANT but was unable to do so.

6.   By this time RADO had partially recovered and tried
to sit up and move his head to and fro. I quietened him with
the aid of a guard and RADO said "Let me die" - "Let me die".
Captain HYND arrived and found that the man had also endeavoured to
cut both his wrists. Captain HYND thought it advisable that the
man should be taken to the 15th Scottish Hospital for expert
treatment and possible detention. I telephoned to Colonel KIRK,
who agreed that this should be done.

7.   RADO left for the 15th Scottish Hospital by ambulance
at 1545 hours accompanied by Captain HYND and two escorts.

8.   The attempted suicide was made with a Blue Gillette
razor blade which was found in the man's blankets when he sat up.

9.   On his departure this morning, Captain BIDMEAD left
word with the Guard Commander that he expected to be down to see
me this afternoon.

JGFS/RJL.
12/1/45.   (J. G. FRENCH SMITH) Captain.
                                I. O. 1/c. M. I. C.

3 enclosures.
--------- ---

Right and Opposite:

The frustration of the British at Rado's prevarication and failure to provide them with any truly worthwhile information can be seen in these documents. His failure to cooperate to their satisfaction led to the British decision to refuse to grant Rado asylum.

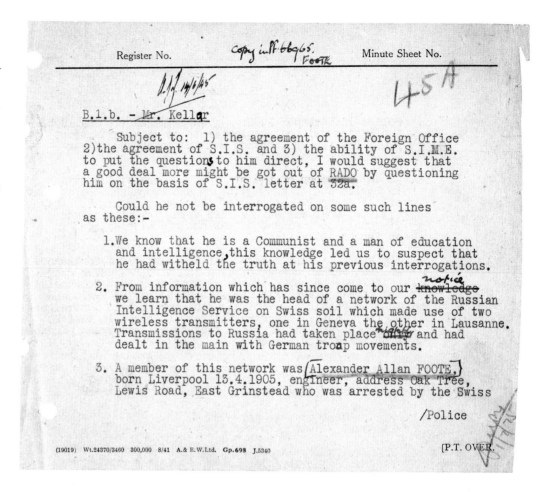

sage detailing, step by step, the German battle plan. This time Stalin reacted to the information and prepared for the attack.

Although Rado ran one of the most effective espionage networks in Europe, he developed sloppy personal habits. Because he was paid exceptionally well, he enjoyed luxuries and lavish living. While his agents worked in some of the most dangerous settings on earth, Rado relaxed with his family in an expensive lakeside villa and enjoyed all the comforts and benefits of neutral Switzerland. Two possible double agents who disliked Rado's extravagances reported the spymaster's activities to Berlin. The German government gave the Swiss government an ultimatum: dismantle Rado's network or else. Switzerland did not want to disrupt Rado's operation because they depended on Roessler to

provide them with intelligence on Germany. In October 1943, to placate Germany, Swiss counterintelligence made a token arrest of Rado's operatives. Rado panicked and told Foote he was going into deep cover. Foote took the clue, vanished into France, and joined the French resistance.

Back Together Again

A few weeks after the liberation of Paris, Foote reconnected with Rado in the city. Foote reestablished communications with the GRU, which immediately inquired why Rado deserted his network in Switzerland. Soon afterward, instructions arrived for Rado and Foote to return to Moscow.

On January 6, 1945, Rado and Foote boarded a Soviet passenger plane in Paris

Police in November 1943. I suggest that it should be insinuated, without saying it in so many words, that FOOTE has turned informer and is the source of our information against RADO.

4. As an ex-member of the staff of the Soviet Embassy in Berlin and of the Agitation and Propaganda Depar nt of the Central Committee of the German Communist Party (32a), what was RADO's wife doing in Switzerland? It should be insinuated that she was also engaged in espionage activities.

5. The story of RADO's agreement to leave Paris for Moscow and his sudden change of mind in Cairo has never rung quite true to me. It seems surprising that he should not have realised his danger before leaving Paris and that he should have talked about his work to a stranger on the plane. I wonder whether the truth is that he wanted to get out of Paris because he anticipated trouble from the French Police.

F2c
14.6.45.

H.W. Shillito

and, to avoid flying over a war zone, made an intermediate stop in Cairo. Because of mechanical problems, the plane waited two days in Cairo for repairs. Meanwhile, Rado and Foote shared the same hotel room.

Rado constantly fretted that if he returned to Moscow, he would be executed. A short time later, Rado walked out of the room and Foote never saw him again. Foote flew on to Moscow, convinced the GRU of his faithfulness, and asked for another assignment.

Shortly after Foote flew out of Cairo, Rado contacted British authorities in Cairo and attempted to defect in exchange for information. However, he attempted to hedge his bets by not betraying anything that would alienate Moscow too much. The information that Rado gave to the British was a mixture of truths, half-truths, lies, and distortions. Despite being in their custody for six months, Rado did not manage to convince the British that his defection would be worth their while and they refused to alienate the Soviets by granting him asylum. Rado returned to his second-class Cairo hotel disguised as a Red Army colonel, using the alias Itgnati Kulichev. Soviet agents soon located Rado and bundled him off to Moscow, where everyone believed he had been executed. Instead, Stalin died and Rado survived. He resurfaced in 1955, teaching cartography at his old alma mater in Budapest.

In 1972 Sandor Rado published a carefully edited autobiography about his wartime exploits, entitled *Codename Dora: The Memoirs of a Russian Spy*, that was no doubt scrutinized carefully by his Soviet censors.

REDL, ALFRED (1864–1913)

Alfred Redl had three loves in life—espionage, money, and men. He rose quickly from poverty and became a cunning spymaster whose habits led to his own destruction.

As one of 14 children supported by a poor Austrian railway official, Redl might not have had many opportunities in life had he not been bright. Though poor, Redl managed to enter Lemberg Cadet School in 1878, and after graduating in 1882 he joined the armed forces of Emperor Franz Joseph. Redl rose quickly through the grades, and in 1899 the Austrian army posted him as an observer with the Russian army.

Throughout his younger years, Redl had been fascinated with espionage and made his interests known. His boyhood dream came true in 1900 when he became an officer in General Baron von Giesel's Kundschaftsstelle, Austria's counterintelligence corps.

```
-----DOSSIER--------
Name: Alfred Redl
Code Name: None
Birth/Death: 1864-1913
Nationality: Austrian
Occupation: Austrian
Army Officer
Involvement: Austrian
Spymaster
Outcome: Committed Suicide
```

Austria's Bizarre Kundschaftsstelle Chief

Redl proved to be a quick learner. General Giesel put him in charge of counterintelligence in Vienna, and Redl set to work modernizing espionage techniques by introducing the likes of photography and fingerprinting. A hidden camera photographed persons entering his office, regardless of where they sat. He lightly coated the arms of office chairs with powder, so that he could collect the fingerprints of his visitors. A hidden microphone transmitted his conversations to a voice-recording machine. Redl also invented some novel interrogation techniques such as the "third degree": using blinding bright lights to flood the suspect's face during questioning. He provided the Austrian army with booklets describing his interrogation techniques and lectured on the subject to staff officers.

Redl also lived another life, one unknown to his superiors. He aggressively pursued relationships with men—sometimes with Austria's nobility and sometimes in the notorious fleshpots of Vienna. He lived luxuriously, but on his wages he could not afford the expense of maintaining his sensualistic lifestyle. Desperate for money, he decided to sell his country's secrets.

Moving Up in the Spy Business

Having worked beside Russian army officers in 1899, Redl traveled to St. Petersburg in 1902 and offered to sell Austria's contingency war plans. The czarist government's Okhrana (secret police) paid well for the information. In 1903 the Austrian Foreign Office realized that Russia had obtained the secret documents but could not imagine how. Counterintelligence chief Redl received instructions to find the traitor.

Redl had no trouble finding himself, so he went back to the Okhrana and asked for suggestions. Russia's military considered Redl too valuable to lose, so they gave him the names of a few minor Austrians who had been recruited to spy on Franz Joseph's army. Redl arrested the pawns and accused them of selling Austria's secrets.

Breaking the alleged spy ring cemented Redl's reputation as a spymaster. In 1907 the army promoted him to the rank of major and named him director of espionage for Austria. The promotion put Redl in direct communication with

Walther Nicolai, the kaiser's intelligence chief. From occasional meetings with Nicolai, Redl further enhanced his income by selling Germany's secrets to Russia and Austria's secrets to Germany.

In 1912 Franz Joseph promoted Redl to colonel and made him General Giesel's

Below: Redl became known as one of history's greatest traitors as his actions led to the slaughter of half a million of his countrymen.

chief of staff for the Eighth Army. By then, Redl was also selling secrets to France and Italy. The colonel moved to Giesel's headquarters in Prague and began offering secrets to almost anyone who would pay for them. Now he could truly afford to live well, and he resumed his sexual escapades with an entirely new group of participants.

The Curiosity of Maximilian Ronge

Captain Maximilian Ronge, having been trained by Redl, replaced him as Austria's director of counterintelligence in Vienna. Redl had established partial postal censorship, which Ronge expanded into the so-called Black Cabinet, a cell where every piece of mail entering or leaving the Vienna post office was inspected for content and coded messages. When Redl

moved to Prague, he forgot to provide the Black Cabinet with a forwarding address, not that it mattered.

On March 2, 1913, two letters addressed to "Nikon Nizetas" arrived at the Black Cabinet from Eydtkuhnen, a small East Prussian town on the Russian border which Ronge knew to be infested with spies. When nobody claimed the letters, Ronge sent them back. A few days later the two letters returned in a single, larger envelope from Walther Nicolai of German intelligence. The Black Cabinet opened the two smaller envelopes and found 14,000 Austrian kronen inside, together with the addresses of espionage centers in Paris and Geneva. Ronge became curious. He wanted to know the identity of the person receiving the money.

Ronge installed a special wire that linked a button in the post office and a

When Redl's personal effects were collected in 1913, agents found a list of several thousand names and addresses of men living in Vienna, Paris, Prague, Brussels, Berlin, and dozens of other towns. Wherever he went, Redl was never without sexual companionship.

bell in the nearby police station. If somebody called for the envelopes, the postal clerk would immediately press a button to alert the police. Meanwhile, two more envelopes arrived, also containing money. Ronge kept agents in the police station around the clock for 83 days.

On a Saturday afternoon in May 1913, the bell in the police station rang. Ronge went immediately to the police office and found Colonel Redl waiting for his cash. Ronge did not immediately suspect Redl of doing anything improper, but he made the colonel sign a receipt. Ronge compared the handwriting on the receipt with a handwritten list of instructions from Redl describing methods for tracking down spies and noted that the handwriting matched. Ronge did not suspect Redl of mischief, but it bothered him that the letters had been sent from Eydtkuhnen.

The Spy Who Caught Himself

Ronge simply followed Redl's instructions. When the colonel departed from the post office, one of Ronge's agents tailed him. Along the way, Redl tore his letters to pieces and spread the scraps along the street. The surveillance agent ignored the scraps and continued tailing Redl, but lost him. The agent retraced his footsteps, recovered all the scraps, and returned them to Ronge. After putting the pieces together, Ronge compared the names and addresses with a list of spies he kept in his office and concluded that Redl was, indeed, a double agent.

After informing his superiors, who were stunned by the information, Ronge managed to locate Redl in a Vienna hotel. He entered his room unannounced and found the colonel sitting at a table writing his confession. Redl told Ronge that all his activities as a double agent were documented and could be found in his apartment in Prague. Then he asked for a pistol. Ronge did not carry a weapon but sent one of his agents to obtain one. The agent returned with a loaded Browning revolver and placed it on the desk. Ronge waited in a nearby café, sending an agent to Redl's room every 30 minutes to determine whether he had committed suicide.

Finally, at 5:00 a.m., 13 hours after picking up the letters, Ronge found Alfred Redl lying on the floor, naked, with a bullet in his head. Redl had taken the only path that he thought an honorable officer could take, although in retrospect, Emperor Franz Joseph might rather have had the chance to find out what secrets the traitor had given away.

NOTES

An investigation of Redl's activities revealed that he had been in communication with the Serbian Black Hand Society, a secret nationalist federation plotting the assassination of Archduke Franz Ferdinand, which plunged Europe into World War I.

REILLY, SIDNEY GEORGE (1874?–1925?)

During World War I, Sidney Reilly became the
most innovative spy of the early twentieth century and
a man of many legends.

Born near Odessa, Russia, the illegitimate son of a Russian woman of Polish descent and a wealthy Jewish physician from Vienna, Reilly always thought of himself as a man without a name. He took the name Sigmund Georgievich Rosenblum from his father, who he never knew because his mother was actually married at the time to a Russian colonel in the court of the czar.

Part of the story of Reilly's life comes from his own embellished account. He did attend grade school and afterward taught himself everything that his brilliant mind was capable of absorbing. Thirsting for knowledge, he read continuously and taught himself to speak seven languages fluently.

How much of Reilly's life was imagined rather than true will probably never be known. According to his own account, after studying chemistry in Vienna from 1890 to 1893, he left for Brazil, where he worked on safaris, exploring the Amazon jungle.

While in Brazil, he claimed to have rescued two or three British officers, who rewarded him with a passport to England. In 1896 he obtained a job with British intelligence, changed his name to Reilly, and in 1898 married a wealthy and

```
- - - - DOSSIER - - - - - - - -
Name: Sidney George Reilly
Code Name: ST1
Birth/Death: 1874?-1925?
Nationality: Russian
Occupation: Odd Jobs
Involvement: British Spy
in Russia
Outcome: Disappeared in
Russia and Presumed
Executed in 1925
```

attractive young widow named Margaret Thomas.

It is possible that part of Reilly's background was created by British intelligence during his work for them, in order to give him a counterfeit persona. However, the one unquestioned truth about Reilly is that he became a master spy.

British Secret Agent ST1

British Naval Intelligence (NID) recruited Reilly around 1898, gave him the code name ST1, and sent him to Holland during the Boer War to monitor arms shipments to South Africa. To get the information, he wore a disguise and impersonated a Russian arms buyer. He

Left: 1915 photograph of Reilly. Shortly after the first James Bond novel, *Casino Royale*, was published in 1953, its author, the former naval intelligence officer Ian Fleming, told a colleague at the *Sunday Times* that he had created the character of James Bond after reading about Reilly's exploits in the British Intelligence Services archives during World War II.

Reilly was perceived by many of his contemporaries to be a shady character with a penchant for self-aggrandizement. His ruthless pursuit of his own aims made him unpopular with some of his colleagues.

inspected Dutch arms-producing plants and returned to London with the intelligence, even though some NID agents questioned whether Reilly ever left England.

Reilly was actually more interested in spying for whoever paid him well. He loved living in luxury and he loved womanizing. He cared no more for England than he did his native country of Russia. As a spy for hire, he dutifully fulfilled his assignments, but mainly under the auspices of British intelligence.

British Petroleum Company, Ltd.

Reilly thoroughly enjoyed the heroic endeavors that brought him notoriety. Early in his career, the NID sent Reilly to Persia (now Iran) because the shah had given Australian businessman William Knox D'Arcy permission to grant concessions for the exploitation of the country's newly discovered oil deposits. England, France, Russia, and Germany all vied for the rights.

While private discussions between representatives from the four nations were in progress, Reilly crashed the meeting dressed as a priest and asked D'Arcy for a few minutes of time in private. D'Arcy excused himself from the meeting

and listened to Reilly's plea for consideration because, the phony priest claimed, orphanages all over the British Empire were running out of money. He implored D'Arcy to give the concession to Great Britain for the sake of the children.

D'Arcy buckled to the fervent tears in Reilly's eyes and, on that day, the Anglo-Persian Oil Company was born. The oil giant became British Petroleum, or as it has become known, just plain BP.

The Triple Juggle

In 1901 the NID gave ST1 a bundle of cash and sent him with his wife to Port Arthur on the Liatung Peninsula, Russia's Far East naval base. Reilly bought into a lumber company as a cover and later became manager of a Danish company, in which he also invested. Having established himself as a businessman, Reilly proceeded to spy on the Russian warships in Port Arthur's harbor, carefully noting their nomenclature, armaments, and arrivals and departures. He sent the information back to London and sold a second copy to Colonel Motojiro Akashi of Japanese intelligence. When the Russians learned (probably from Reilly himself) that Reilly was dealing with the dangerous Japanese spy Akashi,

In 1982 a twelve-part miniseries, *Reilly: Ace of Spies*, starring Sam Neill as Reilly, was broadcast on British television.

they paid him a considerable sum to learn the Japanese plans.

No one knows exactly what Reilly may have told the Japanese or the Russians, or whether what he sold was in the best interests of England or purely in the best interests of himself. NID suspected him of becoming involved in the Japanese surprise attack on Port Arthur, which preceded the Russo-Japanese War. Knowing Russian ship movements certainly would have helped the Japanese.

Reilly also warned NID that the Manchu dynasty of China would collapse, and it did. He could have drawn that conclusion from being on site, or he may have merely expressed the opinion of Colonel Akashi, whose spies were actively undermining the Manchus. One fact trumped all: Reilly returned to England a wealthy man.

The Consummate Spy

By 1909, when Great Britain established the Secret Intelligence Service (SIS), one of the first spies hired by SIS chief Mansfield Cumming was Reilly. Concerned about the kaiser's mobilization, SIS sent Reilly to Germany to learn what kind of war weapons the Germans were building. Reilly took a job as a welder in a Krupp armaments facility. He could not get a camera into the plant's drafting office, so he volunteered for the night fire brigade. A few days later he strangled the night security foreman, knocked out another guard, broke into the drafting office, and walked out of the plant with a bulging sack of drawings. With German police hot on his trail, he boarded a train, reached the coast, and hired a ship to take him to England.

Cumming next presented Reilly with the task of investigating the kaiser's plans for strengthening the German navy. Loaded with an enormous amount of money, Reilly went to St. Petersburg and began sponsoring air races over the Baltic Sea for Russian aviators. Every plane carried a camera to shoot pictures of German warships. The low-flying sporting event to collect espionage made Reilly a great favorite in Russia.

While in St. Petersburg, Reilly met a man named Massino, the assistant to Russia's minister of marine. From Massino, whose wife Reilly seduced, he learned that the Germans were actively soliciting Russia to replace the fleet the czar lost during the recent Russo-Japanese War. With Massino's help, Reilly set up a dummy company and began feeding the German shipbuilding firm Blohm and Voss contracts to rebuild Russia's navy. Of course, before sending the German designs to Massino, Reilly photographed the specifications and forwarded them to SIS.

Probably no spy on earth ever performed so many missions as Sidney Reilly. His career stretched on for more than three decades before the double-dealing caught up with him. After spying on Russia for more than 20 years, he finally overstayed his welcome after the country became the Soviet Union. In 1925 he entered Russia on one more mission and disappeared, becoming both a legend and an enigma.

Recently released MI5 documents suggest that Reilly was executed on the instructions of Stalin.

> **NOTES**
>
> Some historians claim that when Reilly reentered the Soviet Union in 1925, he stayed because he had been a Russian spy from the beginning of his career. His wife disagreed, claiming that her husband had been a British spy and was likely executed.

REVERE, PAUL (1735-1818)

Paul Revere acted as a courier and spy during the American Revolution and earned distinction as one of the new nation's greatest patriots.

Born to Huguenot parents in Boston, Massachusetts, Paul Revere received his education and training at home. As a youth he demonstrated natural ability, a quick mind, and considerable pluck and determination. Once he reached his teens, he apprenticed to his father as a silversmith. In 1756 the 21-year-old Revere answered the call to arms and served as a colonial volunteer in the French and Indian War. When he returned from the adventure, he opened his own silversmith's shop, and during his lifetime earned recognition as one of the finest engravers and craftsmen in America.

A Man of Patriotic Views

Revere might never have become anti-British had it not been for the king's punitive taxes, which the colonists of the era called the "Intolerable Acts." He joined the patriots in 1770, and to commemorate a clash between drunken rebels and British regulars, he fashioned the famous, beautifully etched copper plate titled "Boston Massacre," from a sketch by Henry Pelham. Revere sold many copies, and with them created one of America's factually accepted myths.

In 1773 Revere became a member of the Sons of Liberty, a clandestine group of Boston revolutionaries. He joined a band of locals who disguised themselves

----DOSSIER--------

Name: Paul Revere

Code Name: None

Birth/Death: 1735-1818

Nationality: American

Occupation: Silversmith

Involvement: American Spy During the Revolution

Outcome: Died of Natural Causes

as Indians and, in an action celebrated as the Boston Tea Party, dumped tea valued at £10,000 into the harbor as a protest against British taxes. After the British closed Boston's port in reprisal, Revere jumped on his horse and rode south to rally the support of other colonies.

The Self-Appointed Spymaster

Becoming a spy in Boston required little effort because of the steady flow of leaks from British headquarters, but Revere wanted a central authority for collecting intelligence and appointed himself to the position. Using his silversmith shop as headquarters, he recruited a network composed of men, women, and youths. They strolled the streets, peddled farm products in British camps, counted soldiers, took notes on armaments and supply dumps, and observed the routines of British soldiers. Revere condensed the information and carried it to John Hancock, head of the Committee of Safety. Once, when Revere learned the British were planning to reinforce Portsmouth, New Hampshire, he jumped on his horse, rode to the city, and warned fellow patriot John Sullivan. Sullivan called out his band of New Hampshire followers, broke into the local arsenal, and stole all the guns and ammunition before the British arrived.

By 1775, Revere's spy network had expanded into the countryside and began contending with Tory (British loyalist) informants. Benjamin Church, though thought to be a friend of revolutionaries Samuel Adams, Joseph Warren, and John Hancock, was actually spying for British general Thomas Gage. Gage's Bostonian wife happened to be an informant for the colonists. The Tories were already busy outside Boston, collecting intelligence on

colonial militia activities for Gage. With so much confusion over the sources of intelligence, Revere made the right decision by having all observations and messages brought to him for analysis.

"One if by Land, Two if by Sea"

By the spring of 1775, both the British garrison in Boston and the colonial revolutionaries in the neighborhood had been primed to take action. General Gage hesitated to create another incident but

Above: A 1770s portrait of Paul Revere by John Singleton Copley. Revere's most significant contribution to the American Revolution was the alarm and messenger system that he designed and implemented before the battles of Lexington and Concord.

Henry Wadsworth Longfellow wrote a stirring poem titled "The Midnight Ride of Paul Revere." Although the poem was filled with historical inaccuracies, the public still quotes what Longfellow wrote and not what Revere actually did.

realized he must act after receiving a list from Benjamin Church detailing the location of the colonial militia's stash of hidden weapons. On April 16 Revere learned of Gage's intentions through his spies and immediately warned Hancock. He jumped on his horse and galloped through the countryside to alert the militia. On his way he stopped at the home of William Conant, who lived across the Charles River from Boston, and asked him to watch, on the night of April 18, for a lantern signal from the steeple of Old North Church—"one if by land, two if by sea"—designating the British line of march. Revere rode on to warn Samuel Adams and John Hancock's Committee of Safety. Hancock agreed to post the militia at Concord, where most of the cannon and munitions were stored, and designated

Right: Paul Revere's written commission as official messenger to the Safety Committee. He was one of a band of 30 or so formed in early 1775 to watch the movements of the British soldiers and the Tories in Boston. They took turns patrolling the streets at night in small groups of two or three.

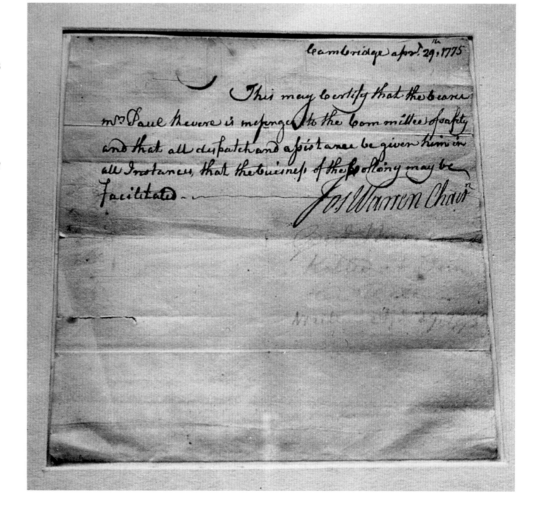

William Dawes to work with Revere in monitoring the movements of the enemy.

On the night of April 18, Revere waited in the steeple of the Old North Church with local members of the Committee of Safety. He scanned the darkened waters of the Charles River and soon spotted a flotilla of small boats crossing the river. He hung two lanterns to signal Conant, who was waiting with a cluster of patriots near Charleston. Revere turned to Dawes and told him to ride quickly through the countryside and give the alarm. Dawes departed, slipping through the fortifications on Boston Neck. Two friends in a small boat rowed Revere across the river to Charlestown. He jumped on a waiting horse and began his historic ride, shouting the alarm from the saddle as he galloped toward Lexington.

The Midnight Ride

Outside Charleston, two British sentinels grabbed the reins of Revere's horse. The silversmith kicked a soldier in the face and galloped into the night. When he reached Lexington, he found Hancock with Adams and warned them to stay hidden. A short time later Dawes, who had taken a different route, arrived with Dr. Samuel Prescott. The three men jumped back on their horses and galloped toward Concord.

After passing through Lexington, a British patrol tried to stop the night-riders. Dawes pulled up his horse, reeled about, and galloped back to Lexington. Prescott gave his horse a kick, jumped a fence, dis-

Left: Paul Revere pictured late in his life. He continued to be an icon of the American fight for independence from the British, and on his death the obituary in the *Boston Intelligence* commented: "Seldom has the tomb closed upon a life so honorable and useful."

appeared across a field, and pounded on to Concord to give the alarm. Revere was trapped and his horse confiscated. Taken before a British officer, Revere said he had been out drinking with his friends, and thinking the patrol may have been highwaymen, they chose to flee as an alternative to being robbed. The officer released Revere in the morning but kept his horse.

While walking back to Lexington, Revere heard firing coming from the village. It was "the shot heard 'round the world," though nobody ever admitted to firing it. The alarm had aroused the militia, and they gave the stunned British a humiliating defeat. Revere returned to Boston and continued to operate his espionage network, but spent most of his time designing state seals, engraving, and printing Continental currency.

As a side job, Revere made false teeth, giving rise to the story that General Washington's teeth had been made by the silversmith. However, this fable is not true.

RICHELIEU, CARDINAL (1585–1642)

Cardinal Richelieu elbowed his way into the court of King Louis XIII, and to preserve his power, he established the greatest espionage network in seventeenth-century France.

Born in 1585, Armand-Jean du Plessis came from a Parisian family of nobility and, as a teenager, became a junior member of the aristocracy. He entered the clergy early in life and in 1607, at the age of 22, became Bishop of Luçon. Seven years later he represented the clergy of his district at the last States-General summoned by King Louis XIII before the French Revolution.

Du Plessis demonstrated his political ambitions by ingratiating himself with Marie de Medici, the mother of the king, who brought him into the court and in 1616 influenced his subsequent appointment as Secretary of State for Foreign Affairs.

One year later, his career suffered a setback when Marie de Medici fell into disfavor because of her constant interference in political affairs. However, du Plessis returned to power in 1621 after gaining the support of François Leclerc du Tremblay, a Capuchin friar at court. He soon became Tremblay's most trusted adviser, which led the way for du Plessis to become cardinal in 1622 and chief minister to Louis XIII in 1624, positions that he would hold for the rest of his life.

```
-----DOSSIER--------
Name: Armand-Jean du
Plessis
Code Name: None
Birth/Death: 1585-1642
Nationality: French
Occupation: Clergyman,
Secretary of State for
Foreign Affairs
Involvement: French
Statesman and Spymaster
Outcome: Died of Natural
Causes
```

The "Day of Dupes"

Du Plessis, now known as Cardinal Richelieu, knew he had many personal enemies. To quash them before they became too troublesome, he created his own personal network of spies. He financed the effort from the king's enormous coffers, and put thousands of spies on the payroll to root out those conspiring to ruin him. Though mainly concerned about his own welfare, Richelieu did spy on the nobility to uncover conspiracies against the king. Without the king, Richelieu's power meant nothing, but with the king, the cardinal had leverage against the powerful influences plotting against him. Richelieu situated spies in every part of the kingdom, including Italy and the German states.

Left: As chief minister, Richelieu brought untold suffering to the general population of France as he fought to make it the greatest power in Europe. It was said that you either loved him or hated him; there was no in between. Days before his death he wrote to Louis XIII: "I have the consolation of leaving your kingdom in the highest degree of glory and of reputation."

One such conspiracy came from inside the court. Marie de Medici and her cadre of supporters feared that the man they had promoted as chief minister to the king had amassed enough power to usurp the throne. Through spies in the court, Richelieu became aware of the plot to unseat him, and during a private meeting to discuss the cardinal's fate, Richelieu burst into the room and confronted them.

He cleverly parried the queen mother's concerns and convinced the king that only he could guarantee the court's safety and preserve France. Louis XIII agreed, the court conspiracy ended, and Richelieu's authority remained unchallenged by the king for the rest of the cardinal's life. French historians have since dubbed the affair the "Day of Dupes."

"If you give me six lines written by the most honest man, I will find something in them to hang him."—Cardinal Richelieu

Cardinal Richelieu's espionage network relied heavily on François Leclerc du Tremblay. In European councils he became known as "Father Joseph" and Richelieu's "Gray Eminence."

Hoodwinking the Hapsburgs

Richelieu placed great faith in his Capuchin friar, François Leclerc du Tremblay, who became the cardinal's closest adviser and top undercover agent. On Richelieu's behalf, the friar traveled through the lesser states of the Holy Roman Empire spreading discontent against the Holy Roman Emperor, Ferdinand II, who was also the Hapsburg emperor of Austria and France's greatest political rival.

Richelieu and Tremblay believed that by weakening Ferdinand, the title of Holy Roman Emperor could be shifted to Louis XIII. Persistence rewarded Richelieu. A master at double-dealing his enemies, the cardinal maintained a compatible relationship with Austria while encouraging Protestant king Gustavus Adolphus of Sweden to invade the Hapsburg Empire. The Thirty Years' War (1618–48) so weakened Austria that France emerged as the strongest nation on the European continent.

Through the services of Tremblay, Richelieu continued to meddle in Austrian affairs. When the Thirty Years' War began to bog down in 1630, Richelieu concocted evidence that Tremblay passed to Ferdinand, suggesting that the defeats were being caused by extreme cautiousness on the part of the king's favorite Catholic general, Albrecht von Wallenstein. Ferdinand cashiered Wallenstein, who happened to be Austria's most efficient general. In 1632, when the Swedish army began overrunning Austrian provinces, Ferdinand restored Wallenstein to command of the army, but by then the damage had been done. The Protestant intervention, planned and financed by Richelieu, prevented the Hapsburgs from reimposing their former authority over the German states, which in turn strengthened France.

Maintaining the Equilibrium

During the seventeenth century, nobody knew the value of spies better than Richelieu. He flooded Europe with his agents. When dancing or fencing instructors went abroad, they all received extensive training in espionage and received a stipend for spying. Every kingdom, court, church, political body, or military organization contained spies on Richelieu's payroll. Richelieu made Vienna one of his important spy centers, giving the city a reputation for espionage that extended into the twentieth century.

Richeleu's methods brought glory to his nation, but by harsh means. By some accounts, Richelieu's network contained some 10,000 agents spread across the European continent from St. Petersburg, Russia, to the heel of Italy, and across the English Channel to Great Britain. Even after Richelieu's death in 1642, an equally cunning spymaster, Cardinal Mazarin, took over the network and kept it running for another generation.

Opposite: Cardinal Richelieu pictured with King Louis XIII of France at the Port of La Rochelle during their battle against the Huguenots.

RINTELEN, FRANZ VON (1885–1949)

Franz Rintelen became the first German saboteur in the United States during World War I. American authorities could not decide how to counter his activities because the United States had no statutes on the books covering espionage and sabotage.

Franz "Fritz" Rintelen grew up a member of the German Junker class aristocracy. His father had influential friends in Germany and because of interests in the United States, he was well-known in New York as a director of the Deutsche Bank. Rintelen spoke English as well as he spoke German. In 1903 he entered the German navy and rose rapidly through the grades. At the outbreak of World War I in 1914, 29-year-old Captain Rintelen was already a member of the kaiser's high command.

Quarreling Junkers

In 1915 Walther Nicolai, director of the Abwehr, sent Rintelen to the United States, which was still neutral, to sabotage merchant vessels carrying arms and ammunition to the Allies and to blow up warehouses in American harbors. Rintelen arrived in mid-April with a false Swiss passport identifying him as Emile V. Gasche. Rintelen reported to Franz von Papen, who served as military attaché in the German Consulate in New York City. Papen had organized Germany's first spy network in the United States, and his mission was to prevent American

----DOSSIER--------

Name: Franz von Rintelen

Code Names: Emile V. Gasche, E. V. Gibbons, Edward V. Gates

Birth/Death: 1885–1949

Nationality: German

Occupation: German Naval Officer

Involvement: German Spymaster and Saboteur

Outcome: Died of Natural Causes

Papen understood the meaning of neutrality and wanted nothing of a destructive nature done to turn Americans against Germany. When Rintelen told Papen that he planned to blow up American merchant ships, Papen immediately balked and tried to prevent Rintelen from creating a diplomatic crisis. Nicolai, to whom both men reported, had created the problem without considering the consequences.

The Mind of Captain Rintelen

Rintelen refused to be deterred. He had developed two bombs and proudly showed them to Papen. His ingenious watertight pipe bomb contained sulfuric acid at one end and picric acid at the other end, with a copper plate in between. When the sulfuric acid ate away the copper plate and contacted the picric acid, a massive explosion would occur. Rintelen explained how an underwater diver would affix his other bomb to a ship's propeller. The device would be set off by the thrust of the propeller's rotation, and would disable the ship and by blowing a hole in the stern. Rintelen predicted that he could sink a million tons of American supplies and ships. While Rintelen described his plans, Papen noticed that the demolition expert's "eyes blazed, and he cackled like a lunatic!"

When Nicolai sent Rintelen to New York, he also sent a demolition team of saboteurs. Though Rintelen reported to Papen, the saboteurs reported only to Rintelen. Papen found the reporting relationship bizarre and unworkable. He forbade Rintelen from conducting any sabotage in America until after he consulted with Nicolai. Rintelen snubbed him and said, "I will not take orders from you," and left to carry out his plans.

supplies from reaching England. Because America was not at war with Germany, he used passive techniques to redirect ammunition away from Britain.

Nicolai expected Rintelen, who came from the navy, and Papen, who came from the army, to make an excellent team. Rintelen understood ships and knew exactly how to blow them up.

A Maniac in America

In New York, Rintelen created a luxurious life for himself, using the Deutsche Bank as his cover. Under the alias E. V. Gibbons, he established an import-export business as a front. As another cover, he created a wine business using the alias Edward V. Gates. The Abwehr had provided him with plenty of money, and Rintelen began his work by infiltrating American labor unions at arms and weapons plants. His operatives incited strikes at a Remington arms facility and at General Electric's main plant in Schenectady, New York. The strategy worked well and even corresponded with efforts approved by Papen.

Rintelen, however, devoted his main effort to building bombs. His manufacturing site became an interned German ship in New York's harbor. His operatives made the bombs on the ship, planted them on arms-carrying freighters in the harbor, and set them to blow up somewhere in the middle of the Atlantic. Rintelen took credit for blowing up 35 ships, and from the accounts of survivors, most of them believed a torpedo had struck their ship.

Congress Sleeps

William J. Burns of the Bureau of Investigation, forerunner of the FBI, collected evidence of Rintelen's activities but found it impossible to arrest him because the United States had no statutes regarding espionage or sabotage. Nor could the bureau find a way of deterring Rintelen's import-export company from purchasing 300,000 rifles for the German army. Burns notified the British Secret Intelligence Service (SIS) in New York, and they agreed to put Rintelen under surveillance. Rintelen knew he was being followed but did not seem to care. He reported his escapades to Papen and Nicolai; in addition to sinking ships, these included the destruction of American harbor facilities and damage to the U.S. naval base at Mare Island, California.

The Noordam in Southampton

Papen's messages to Nicolai about Rintelen's recklessness brought a temporary end to sabotage activities. Papen brought Rintelen to his office and informed him that he was being recalled. The saboteur demanded proof. Papen showed him Nicolai's coded message.

A few days later, Rintelen set sail for Europe on the neutral Dutch liner *Noordam*. British intelligence had broken the German code and knew the *Noordam* would be stopping in Southhampton to disembark British passengers. Reginald Hall, head of British naval intelligence, informed MI5 and Scotland Yard. When *Noordam* pulled to the dock, British agents boarded the vessel, went straight to Rintelen's stateroom, and detained him. After a search of Rintelen's personal belongings, agents found a heap of incriminating documents in the false bottom of one of his trunks. Rintelen suspected Papen of sabotaging him.

Rintelen was held in a British jail until the United States entered the war. Extradited to America, Rintelen served two sentences totaling 30 months. President Woodrow Wilson eventually commuted his sentence, and Rintelen spent the rest of his life in England.

Opposite: Rintelen was dispatched from Berlin to New York with orders to assist Von Papen in a sabotage campaign. Within weeks of arriving he had organized a team of 80 sailors and officers and set up a bomb factory in New York's harbor. He was to be responsible for the sinking of some 35 ships that, due to the size of the explosions, were thought to have been hit by a torpedo from a submarine and not an onboard bomb.

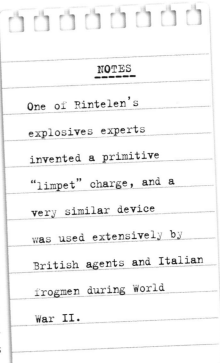

NOTES

One of Rintelen's explosives experts invented a primitive "limpet" charge, and a very similar device was used extensively by British agents and Italian frogmen during World War II.

ROESSLER, RUDOLF (1897–1958)

Code-named "Lucy," Rudolf Roessler headed the Lucy Ring, a closely interwoven group of anti-Nazis who spied for the Soviet Union through a network domiciled in Switzerland.

Born on November 22, 1897, in Kaufbeuren, Bavaria, Rudolf Roessler grew up in a strict Protestant environment not far from Munich. His father worked for the Bavarian Forestry Commission and provided a comfortable living for his family. Roessler attended school in Augsburg, at the Realgymnasium, from where he graduated during the early years of World War I.

Roessler served in the German army during the war, and afterward became a newspaper reporter in Augsburg. He was the founder of the Augsburg Literary Society, and later he moved to Berlin and became a literary critic. Two of his friends from this time, novelist Thomas Mann and poet Stefan George, were later put on Hitler's death list and their books banned.

In 1933, after the German economy recovered and Hitler rose to power, Roessler moved to Lucerne, Switzerland, where he wrote anti-Nazi articles. As a cover, prior to and during World War II, he established a publishing business and named it Vita Nova Verlag.

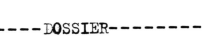

----DOSSIER--------

Name: Rudolf Roessler

Code Name: Lucy

Birth/Death: 1897–1958

Nationality: German

Occupation: Journalist

Involvement: German Spy for Allies in World War II

Outcome: Died of Natural Causes

The Mouse Who Hated Hitler

Roessler never became a Communist, but in 1933 chose to aid the Soviet Union as an alternative to fascism. He hated dictators and he hated depressions, and at the time, only the Soviet system seemed to offer a political and economic remedy to life's unendurable miseries. Roessler was not the type of person to attract attention as a spy. He had a slight physique, thinning hair, and wore thick spectacles. He fidgeted and shook, and despite being asthmatic, constantly chain-smoked.

Roessler's publishing business supplied him with enough money to travel, and he made frequent trips into Germany. Nobody knows exactly how Roessler began his career in espionage, but he connected with other anti-Nazis in the German military hierarchy who felt the same way about Hitler as he did. Roessler also made friends with Captain Hans Hausamann of Swiss intelligence, and Roger Mason, head of Swiss military intelligence; both aided and abetted his efforts to pass information to the Soviets. By 1939, Roessler had established contacts with Hans Oster, deputy director of the Abwehr, and possibly Admiral Wilhelm Canaris, who ran German intelligence. Roessler had agents working in the German high command (OKW) and in the offices of General Franz Halder, Walther von Brauchitsch, and George Thomas. All of Roessler's contacts trusted him because he never wrote anything down and kept matters of importance filed and indexed in his head. He remembered everything he read and anything someone told him if it pertained to troop movements, arms production, tank development, aircraft performance, and the details of the general staff's future planning. Superfluous information he shed as if he never heard it.

Connecting the Links

Roessler refused to disclose the proper names of the spies in his network. He knew them only by their code names,

and they knew him only as Lucy. Anna, Bill, Olga, Teddy, and Werther all worked inside the German high command. Collectively, they would become known as the Lucy Spy Ring. Only two cut-outs (intermediaries) may have known Roessler's identity: Christian Schneider, code-named Taylor, and Rachel Duebendorfer, code-named Sissy.

Below: Rudolf Roessler, left, the Soviet Union's master spy of World War II, and his Swiss contact man, Dr. Xavier Schnieper, during their trial in Lucerne, Switzerland, on November 2, 1953.

S. Form 81/rev. 1.52.

EXTRACT.

25A

S.F. 92/Czech/Switzerland/1.

Extract for File No.: P.F.123185   Name: ROESSLER @ ROSSLER.

Original in File No.:*   (ROTE KAPELLE)   Serial: Vol: Receipt Date:

Original from: B.4.D. source report   Under Ref: 15/3997   Dated: 30.4.53.

Extracted on: 12.5.53.   by: DMT   Section: B.2.D.

Copy of B.4.D. source report re ROTE KAPELLE, mentioning ROSSLER.

     Further to previous reports:

     The Hamburg weekly "Der Spiegel" of April 15th published a long article on the activities of the Rote Kapelle (see pages 21-24). It is alleged that after the war the Rote Kapelle continued its espionage activities in Switzerland and that the German born publisher Rudolf ROSSLER, recently arrested in Lucerne, was one of the Rote Kapelle agents working under the pseudonym Lucie. He and his associates, the paper states, were agents in the service of the Soviets for many years, after the war working via Prague. The paper suggests that ROSSLER was arrested by the Swiss Security authorities under pressure of the German Federal Government in Bonn which was interested to find out ROSSLER's sources of information in Germany during the war. The article then gives a picture of the war-time activities of the Rote Kapelle and their groups, "Gilbert" in France, "Kent" in

/Belgium, ...

USE WITH CAUTION

S. Form 81/rev. 1.52.

EXTRACT.

Extract for File No.:   Name:

Original in File No.:*   Serial: Vol: Receipt Date:

Original from: Under Ref: Dated:

Extracted on: by: Section:

Belgium, "Coro" in Berlin, "Hilda" in the Netherlands, and "Rado" in Switzerland. The paper also alleges that ROSSLER (who is now 56 years old, German born, former editor of the "Augsburger Allemeine Zeitung" who emigrated to Switzerland in 1936 where he is now the proprietor of the publishing company Vita-Nova) worked also for the Swiss Military Intelligence and for the British.

     "Der Spiegel" names Alexander FOOTE as source of information for the materials used in this article and states that the "Spiegel" had interviewed FOOTE in his London boarding house alleging that FOOTE was an ex-agent of the Soviets, was in contact with ROSSLER, is the author of the "Handbook for Spies" (London, Museum Press) and was now an official in the Ministry of Agriculture and Fisheries in London. "Der Spiegel" London correspondent, who obviously is the interviewer of Alexander FOOTE and the author of the enclosed article, is H. G. ALEXANDER of 56, Northend House, Fitz James, Avenue, W.14.

     Attached is a copy of "Der Spiegel".

     From an established and usually reliable source.

Ruth Kuczynski, code-named Sonia, also operated out of Switzerland, but she probably did not know the identity of Lucy because she received her orders from Sandor Rado, who headed the Soviet network.

Kuczynski brought Alexander Foote, code-named Jim, from Great Britain to handle Rado's radio transmissions to Moscow. The system worked in the following way: Anna, Bill, Olga, Teddy, and Werther sent intelligence to Taylor, who passed it Lucy, who passed it to Sissy. Sissy passed it to Rado, who gave the intelligence to Sonia, who passed it to Jim for transmission to Moscow. It is possible that Jim (Foote) was also a double agent who passed the same information to British intelligence.

At times, the intelligence that was transmitted to Moscow was difficult for Joseph Stalin to believe—it was so startlingly accurate. In August 1939, Roessler returned from Germany and informed Moscow that German forces were about to invade Poland and plunge Europe into war. Few believed him. He shocked Stalin by informing Moscow exactly where, when, and how Hitler intended to invade Russia. Stalin still refused to believe the intelligence until he received a similar report from Richard Sorge, a Soviet spy working in the German Embassy in Tokyo.

From Roessler, Stalin learned the composition of German forces on the eastern front, Hitler's overall strategy, and the exact battle plans and divisions involved—information that could only have come from Canaris or Oster at the Abwehr. Later, Roessler presented the exact battle plan of Germany's invasion of Holland, Belgium, and France months before it happened. If Foote were indeed functioning as a double agent, then British MI5 would have received the same intelligence.

Lucy Goes to Jail

Rado ran his espionage network out of Geneva, and much of the intelligence he gathered out of Germany came from spies who had no connection with Roessler. He lived luxuriously in a plush villa by the lake and did not always pay close attention to the business of espionage. In 1943 German double agents infiltrated Rado's operation and began collecting names. Hitler ordered Switzerland to shut down Rado's operation or suffer the consequences. Rado escaped to France, but many of his agents, including Roessler, Foote, and Duebendorfer, were arrested. Roessler spent a short time in a Swiss jail, but in the fall of 1944 the government released the prisoners because they could never collect enough evidence to hold them for espionage.

After the war, Roessler could no longer make money with his publishing business and tried to reconstruct a spy network to sell the Soviets intelligence on Allied occupation forces during the early stages of the cold war. He did not succeed because information was readily available in Western newspapers. Nevertheless, Swiss authorities arrested him once more for espionage, and this time he spent a year in jail.

Roessler died in 1958, without ever giving away the name of his high-placed contact in the Abwehr.

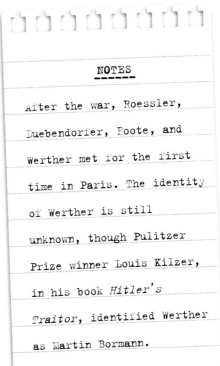

NOTES

After the war, Roessler, Duebendorfer, Foote, and Werther met for the first time in Paris. The identity of Werther is still unknown, though Pulitzer Prize winner Louis Kilzer, in his book *Hitler's Traitor*, identified Werther as Martin Bormann.

ROSENBERG, JULIUS (1918–1953) AND ETHEL (1915–1953)

Had it not been for Julius and Ethel Rosenberg, many years may have passed before the Soviet Union developed the technology to create an atomic bomb.

Both of the Rosenbergs were children of Jewish parents and born and raised in New York City. Julius attended Seward Park High School and graduated at the age of 16. He went to City College of New York and graduated with a degree in electrical engineering.

Ethel Greenglass graduated from high school during the depression and, though she set her heart on becoming an actress, dancer, and musician, she lacked the talent to become successful. Before they married, Ethel was a clerical worker and active trade unionist.

Julius and Ethel both became card-carrying members of the Communist Party. They met at a party-affiliated workers' fund-raising meeting and married in 1939.

To Serve Mother Russia

The Rosenbergs' loyalties, whether right or wrong, were clear from an early stage. In 1939 they defended

```
----DOSSIER--------
Name: Julius Rosenberg
Code Names: Antenna,
Liberal
Birth/Death: 1918-1953
Nationality: American
Occupation: Civilian U.S.
Army Inspector
Involvement: Soviet Spy
Outcome: Executed

Name: Ethel Greenglass
Rosenberg
Birth/Death: 1915-1953
Nationality: American
Occupation: Clerical Worker
Involvement: Soviet Spy
Outcome: Executed
```

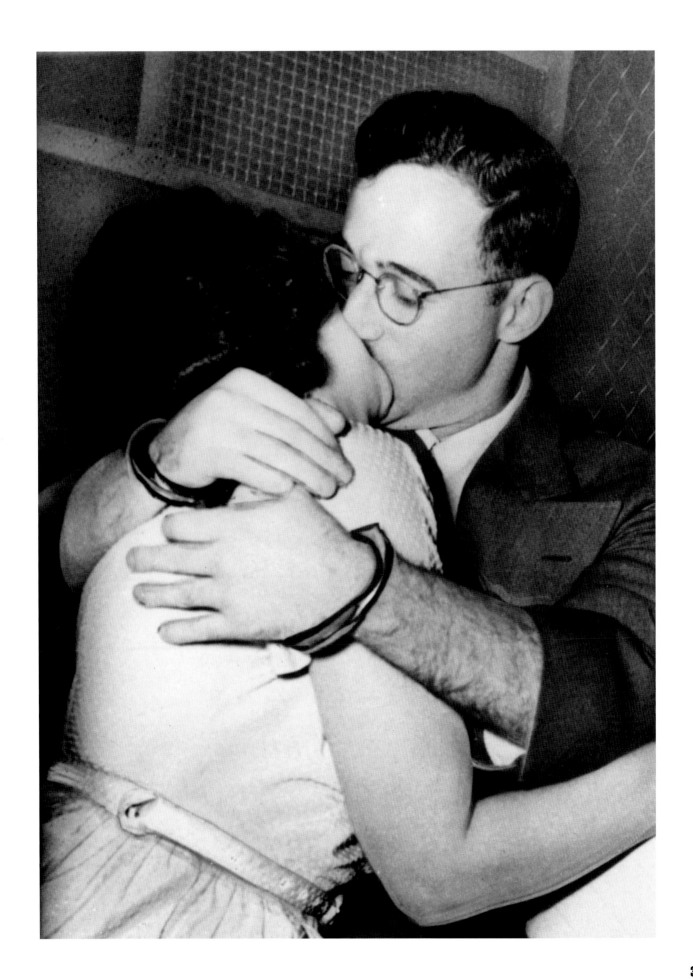

Stalin's nonaggression pact with Germany even though most Jews in Europe wanted nothing to do with the Nazi Party. When Hitler started World War II by invading Poland, the Rosenbergs lobbied for America to remain neutral. But in 1941, after Germany attacked Russia, the Rosenbergs wanted the United States to go to war immediately in defense of mother Russia.

Sometime during the late 1930s, Gaik Ovakimian, the NKVD's resident in New York City, recruited the Rosenbergs as spies. In 1940, Julius went to work as a civilian employee of the U.S. Army Signal Corps. In 1942, the same year Julius began actively spying, he attained the position of inspector. One year later, he discontinued his Communist Party affiliation in order to conceal his espionage activities for the Soviet Union. Ovakimian returned to Moscow in 1943 and Alexander Feklisov, a KGB agent attached to the Soviet Embassy in New York, became Rosenberg's new handler.

Julius Rosenberg had no involvement in the Soviet cell devoted to stealing atomic secrets until 1944, when Ethel's brother, David Greenglass, went to work as a machinist at a top-secret laboratory in Los Alamos, New Mexico, where scientists were building the first atomic

Opposite: A demonstration in Paris, attended by thousands, calling for the pardon of U.S. communists Julius and Ethel Rosenberg, following their conviction for passing atomic secrets to the Soviets.

Below: An aerial view of Sing Sing Prison in Ossining, New York, where Ethel and Julius Rosenberg were executed on June 19, 1953.

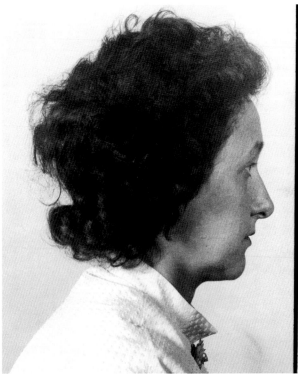
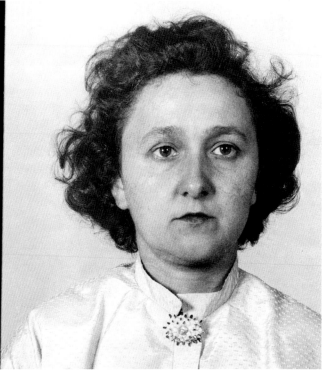

Above: Mug shots of Ethel Rosenberg. Following her and her husband's convictions for spying and passing U.S. atomic secrets to the Soviets, Judge Irving R. Kaufman remarked, "It's a sad day when American citizens lend themselves to the destruction of our country."

bomb. Anatoli Yakovlev also arrived from Moscow in 1944, with instructions to steal atomic bomb research. Hearing that Greenglass was actually working in the laboratory and that the Rosenbergs were related to Greenglass, Yakovlev sent Harry Gold (real name Golodnotsky), a Russian-born immigrant who had become a Soviet spy, to act as courier for Greenglass and Rosenberg. Gold already had one mole at Los Alamos, the physicist Klaus Fuchs, but with two, material could be corraborated.

Soon after Julius Rosenberg began working as an atomic spy, the FBI detected an increased flurry of encrypted messages passing between the Soviet

Consulate in New York and Moscow. In 1947 the messages were turned over to army cryptanalysts for decoding. What the code-breakers found was shocking. The Soviets had infiltrated the Manhattan Project, and the primary person responsible for stealing technical information was Klaus Fuchs, who had by this time returned to England.

The Domino Effect

Fuchs admitted his involvement and implicated his courier, Harry Gold. Gold gave up David Greenglass, who was promptly arrested. Greenglass claimed his sister Ethel had become involved in a spy

Julius Rosenberg's spy network was actually more involved in stealing secrets from conventional weapons companies, and his later involvement in atomic energy resulted from his relationship with David Greenglass, his brother-in-law.

Although Julius Rosenberg may not have been as deeply involved in selling atomic secrets to the Soviets as his record suggests, cryptanalysts discovered 21 cables sent to and from Moscow mentioning his code names, Antenna and Liberal.

ring run by her husband Julius. In June 1950, Rosenberg decided to flee to Moscow and obtained passport photos for himself and his family, but he didn't act soon enough. On June 17, 1950, the FBI arrested Julius Rosenberg and on August 11 they took Ethel Rosenberg into custody.

In March 1951 the Rosenbergs and Greenglass went on trial in New York City before Judge Irving Kaufman, charged with conspiracy to commit espionage. The U.S. Department of Justice recommended that Julius Rosenberg be executed and Ethel be sentenced to 30 years. The Korean War had just begun, and the judge blamed the Rosenbergs for giving the Soviets the atomic bomb, which enabled the North Koreans to start a war because their ally, the Soviet Union, also had the

Below: Mug shots of Julius Rosenberg, taken after his arrest on charges of spying and passing American atomic secrets to the Soviets.

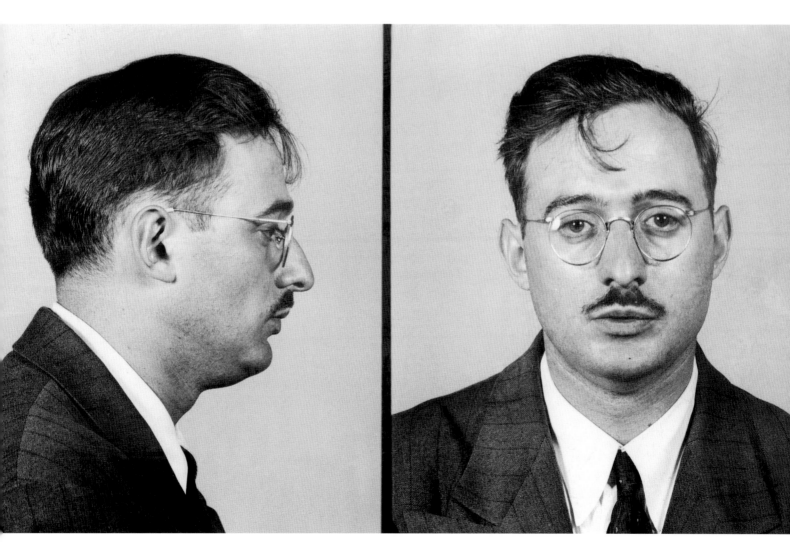

bomb. As a consequence of the judge's anger and Greenglass accusing his sister of treachery to save his wife from prison, both Rosenbergs were sentenced to death.

The Final Curtain

On June 19, 1953, the electric chair in Sing Sing Prison in Ossining, New York, ended the lives of Julius and Ethel Rosenberg. Ethel became the first woman to be executed in the United States since 1865, when Mary Surratt was hanged for her involvement in the assassination of President Lincoln.

The death sentences shocked the world. In Europe, there were suggestions of anti-Semitism; the French philosopher Jean Paul Sartre described it as "a legal lynching which smears with blood a whole nation." Even J. Edgar Hoover of the FBI considered it folly for the United States to be seen orphaning the Rosenbergs' two children.

Twenty appeals over a period of two years did not alter the fatal outcome. For 40 years, facts and fictions circulated in an effort to clear the Rosenbergs and prove them innocent—or at least less guilty. Former Soviet premier Nikita Khrushchev did not help the apologists' case when he stated in his book, *Khrushchev Remembers* (1990), how pleased Stalin's government was with the atomic intelligence that they received from the Rosenbergs.

Below: Hundreds of placard-waving demonstrators parade before the White House, asking for presidential clemency for spies Julius and Ethel Rosenberg. They are joined by two picketers with opposing sentiments: left is Glen Smiley of St. Petersburg, Florida. His friend is Tommy Flemming of Norfolk, Virginia.

The final curtain came down on the case in 1995, when the National Security Agency released the Verona cables. The cables showed that the NKVD and the KGB had indeed operated an atomic spy ring in which Julius Rosenberg, code-named both Antenna and Liberal, was deeply involved. The same cables, however, did not implicate Ethel Rosenberg, other than to portray her as an uninvolved wife, devoted to her husband's work. There is a good chance that had David Greenglass not testified against his sister to save his wife, Ethel may have served a few years in prison and lived out her life with her two children, who tried for four decades to vindicate her.

Above: Judge Irving R. Kaufman sits at his desk in federal court on March 29, 1951, before sentencing Julius and Ethel Rosenberg, who were found guilty of conspiracy to commit espionage in wartime.

SCHULMEISTER, KARL LOUIS (1770–1853)

Karl Schulmeister, a man of exceptional imagination, spied for the French during the Napoleonic wars and almost single-handedly brought down the Austrian army.

The son of an Alsatian Lutheran pastor, Karl Schulmeister grew up on the banks of the Rhine River in New Freistett, where he received his early education. He believed himself to be the son of a dashing Hungarian nobleman who had seduced his mother.

He married a local girl and decided to become a man worthy of the Legion of Honor. While he contemplated how to achieve this goal, he worked by day as a grocer and iron peddler in Strasbourg, and by night as a river smuggler. Schulmeister chatted freely with French soldiers who patronized his daytime business and learned the schedules of river patrols well enough to avoid them. Smuggling now opened doors to other pursuits.

```
----DOSSIER--------
Name: Karl Louis
Schulmeister
Code Name: None
Birth/Death: 1770-1853
Nationality: Alsatian
Occupation: Grocer,
Ironmonger, and Smuggler
Involvement: French Spy
During the Napoleonic Wars
Outcome: Died of Natural
Causes
```

The Alsatian Opportunist

Schulmeister was naturally bright. He spoke French, German, and Hungarian fluently and performed much of his smuggling business while wearing a disguise. Any prospect of making money appealed to him. His opportunity came during the French Revolution when disaffected aristocrats began filtering through Strasbourg in an attempt to escape the guillotine. He turned them over to the revolutionaries.

In 1799 René Savary, a colonel in Napoleon Bonaparte's army, met the 29-year-old Schulmeister in Alsace and enlisted him in the French intelligence service. Using his iron business to screen his activities, Schulmeister performed undercover missions into Germany and Austria, and by 1804 he had climbed the ladder to become a secret agent for Joseph Fouché, Napoleon's top spymaster.

In 1805 Napoleon summoned Schulmeister and gave him a virtually impossible mission: to infiltrate Austria's military intelligence system. He obtained the clothes of a nobleman, packed them into trunks, hired an elegant coach and servants, and rumbled into Vienna, posing as a Hungarian aristocrat exiled from France by Napoleon. Taking rooms in a fine hotel, Schulmeister began writing letters to General Karl Mack, whose troops were on the Danube at Ulm. He applied for a position in Austrian intelligence and offered to divulge all the secrets he possessed about Napoleon's Grand Army. Mack agreed to an interview and was so awestruck by Schulmeister's knowledge and sincerity that he put the Alsatian on his general staff and made him head of intelligence for the army.

The Schulmeister-Napoleon Conspiracy

Schulmeister found himself in a position with two options: he could betray Napoleon and aid Austria or betray General Mack and aid France. Since

Napoleon agreed to pay him well, Schulmeister betrayed Mack, which had been the original plan. So, in October 1805, as the day of battle approached, Schulmeister informed Mack that Napoleon's army was on the verge of mutiny because the troops had not been paid in months. The lie convinced the Austrian general to advance before Napoleon's soldiers got paid. Schulmeister then sent one of his so-called servants

Above: Schulmeister was adept at hiring secret agents and informants to garner information for his master; however, he still insisted carrying out many investigations himself. His success in this was due to his exceptional ability to adopt convincing disguises.

> Schulmeister's ruse demonstrates one of history's anomalies: an agent from one nation running an enemy's military intelligence service.

For a short period of time, Schulmeister became Napoleon's chief of police in Vienna. As one Frenchman observed, "Schulmeister inspires in the Viennese so much terror that he is by himself worth an army corps."

through the lines to inform Napoleon of Mack's battle plan.

Bonaparte orchestrated the next move. He posted troops near Mack's position at Ulm and made it appear that they were deserting. Mack now believed every word of Schulmeister's ruse and boldly led his 30,000-man army out of Ulm to pursue Napoleon's demoralized Frenchmen. Once outside his fortifications and on open ground, Mack gasped when he saw Marshal Michel Ney's French forces attacking from the front. His amazement doubled when he observed Marshal Nicolas-Jean Soult, Marshal Auguste-Frederic-Louis Marmont, Marshal Jean Lannes, and the grand cavalry under Marshal Joachim Murat converging on his flank and rear. Mack surrendered his entire army with barely a fight.

The French helped Schulmeister escape to Vienna, where he attempted to convince the Austrian and Russian monarchs that Mack had failed because he refused to take his advice. Austrian intelligence did not believe Schulmeister's explanation and was about to arrest him when Murat's cavalry appeared outside Vienna and compelled Austria to surrender. Napoleon then destroyed the balance of the Austrian army at the battle of Austerlitz, and Austrian resistance ended.

The Turbulent World of a Loyal Spy

Schulmeister continued to spy for Napoleon. In 1808 he organized a spy ring in Prussia to keep track of military plots against the French. He fought in Napoleon's battles, and often at his side. Though not a soldier, he suffered wounds and asked in return to be awarded what he always wanted most— the coveted Legion of Honor. Napoleon snubbed the request, saying such medals were only for soldiers, while a spy's reward was gold.

In 1810, Napoleon married Austrian archduchess Marie Louise, who, naturally, hated Schulmeister for having humiliated her father in 1805. At her request, Napoleon dismissed his spy. Schulmeister took his gold and purchased two large estates. When Napoleon's army collapsed in 1813, the Austrian army returned to Alsace in vengence and pulverized one of Schulmeister's two estates with their artillery. In 1815, after Napoleon's final defeat at Waterloo, the French authorities arrested Schulmeister for supporting the exiled emperor. The former spy bought his freedom by paying a ransom that consisted of his entire net worth. He returned to Strasbourg penniless and received a concession for a tobacco kiosk. Schulmeister lived another 38 years performing his new job.

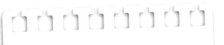

NOTES

In 1809 Schulmeister actually gained temporary military command of part of the French army. He suffered sword wounds during Napoleon's second Austrian campaign, but Bonaparte always thought of Schulmeister as a spy and not a soldier.

SORGE, RICHARD (1895–1944)

Richard Sorge became the greatest Soviet spy in the Far East, consistently sharing the plans and strategies of the Germans and the Japanese far in advance of their actual implementation.

Born on October 4, 1895, in Baku, Russia, Sorge was the son of a Russian woman and a German mining engineer. Three years later, the family moved to Berlin, where they remained during Richard's school years. During World War I, Sorge enlisted in the kaiser's army, was wounded at the eastern front, and earned the Iron Cross. During his recovery he studied Karl Marx, and after the German revolution in 1918 he joined the Communist Party. His paternal grandfather had been Marx's personal secretary and it was natural for Sorge to take an interest in Communism. After the war he attended the University of Hamburg and in 1920 graduated with a Ph.D. in political science. In 1921 Sorge married Christiane Gerlach, the ex-wife of one of his college professors, and moved to a house in Solingen.

----DOSSIER--------

Name: Richard Sorge

Code Names: William Johnson, Ramsey

Birth/Death: 1895-1944

Nationality: Russian

Occupation: Lecturer, Journalist

Involvement: Soviet Spy in Japan

Outcome: Hanged as a Spy

The Making of a Spy

In 1920, the year before his marriage, Sorge joined Russia's newly established intelligence service for the Red Army (GRU) and went to Moscow for training. Over the next 10 years, he traveled through Scandinavia, Great Britain, the United States, and Germany gathering intelligence, undercover, as a lecturer and journalist for the *Frankfurter Zeitung*. In

Above: Sorge's reputation among the experts of the espionage world is second to none. He was described by Ian Fleming as "the man whom I regard as the most formidable spy in history." Historian Arthur M. Schlesinger Jr. said of him: "The twentieth century has been the century of espionage, and Richard Sorge was probably its most fascinating exemplar—a spy of unparalleled charm, nonchalance, courage, impudence, and brilliance."

1930 the GRU sent Sorge to Shanghai to set up a spy network. Under the alias of an American named William Johnson, Sorge built a small, tightly knit network that consisted of Agnes Smedley, an American with whom he had an affair; Japanese newspaper journalists Hatsumi Ozaki and Yotoku Miyagi, who were both acquainted with the Communist underground in China; Max Klausen, a German radio operator; and Branko de Voukelich, a Yugoslav photographer.

Sorge began funneling information on nationalist leader Chiang Kai-shek and a new enterprising communist organizer, Mao Tse-tung, back to the GRU. The Chinese never suspected Sorge of being anything other than a newspaper reporter. They allowed him to travel wherever he wished, although they dis-

trusted his Japanese companions, Ozaki and Miyagi. Sorge met and befriended Chiang and wrote laudatory articles about his nationalist movement for the *Frankfurter Zeitung*.

The German Who Spied on Germans

Sorge learned that Germany was planning to discontinue its relationship with Chiang and shift political and diplomatic support to China's timeless enemy, Japan. In view of the massive Japanese military buildup, the information resulted in Sorge's recall to Moscow in 1932 for a strategy session. The GRU made the decision to send Sorge to Japan to infiltrate the German diplomatic corps and to determine whether the Japanese intended to attack the Soviet Union.

This time Sorge dropped his American persona as William Johnson and, using his father's citizenship, obtained a German passport. On September 6, 1933, Sorge arrived in Yokohama, still using his cover as a journalist, and went to work for Eugen Ott, the military attaché at the German Embassy. He also joined the up-and-coming Nazi Party. Two years later Sorge returned to Moscow to debrief the GRU and the NKVD.

The two Soviet intelligence agencies sent him back to Japan with instructions to establish a spy ring in Tokyo. He brought Klausen and Voukelich from Shanghai to Tokyo and renewed his contact with Ozaki. As a source for information, he also renewed his relationship with Ott. During 1936, Sorge was able to inform Moscow that Japan intended to attack China and not Siberia. The intelligence intrigued the GRU and the NKVD, and once again Sorge returned to Moscow for more discussions.

During his operations at the German Embassy in Japan, Sorge told GRU general Yan Karlovich Berzin, "I think I am managing to lead them all by the nose."

Sorge's Greatest Coup

In 1938 Eugen Ott became German ambassador to Tokyo. He brought his amusing and learned friend Sorge into the embassy to work on highly confidential matters regarding the political and military relationship between Germany and Japan. Aware of Sorge's connection with Ozaki, Ott depended upon Sorge to glean secrets from Ozaki, who had become well connected with Japan's Imperial General Headquarters.

Handling top-secret documents from Berlin in the German Embassy while collecting high-level Japanese intelligence from Ozaki enabled Sorge to keep Moscow informed as the stage was being set for World War II. When, in early 1941, Sorge warned Moscow that Hitler intended to invade Russia, Stalin refused to believe him. Sorge continued prepping Moscow for war with Germany, and Stalin finally conceded the intelligence was accurate when Sandor Rado's spy network, which worked out of Switzerland, provided the same information.

Sorge later notified Moscow that the Japanese were planning to send its fleet into the Pacific during the late fall of 1941 for maneuvers near the Hawaiian Islands. A few days later he added that the Japanese intended to attack the Dutch East Indies and French Indochina. This time Stalin reacted. He recalled the Red Army defending Siberia's borders to make the force available for the defense of Moscow.

The Kempi Tai Strikes Back

For several months, the Kempi Tai—Japanese intelligence—had been tracking radio transmissions but could not locate the senders. Sorge baffled the Kempi Tai by keeping his radio on a sailboat and only sending his messages while at sea. Japanese agents, however, began tracking the movements of Ozaki because of his Communist sympathies. Through Ozaki, they connected the transmissions to Sorge but did not know where to locate his radio. Instead of immediately arresting Ozaki, they apprehended Miyagi, who they discovered was also associated with Sorge. Under intense interrogation, Miyagi gave up Ozaki and Sorge. On October 14, 1941, the Kempi Tai arrested Ozaki, who told them where to find Sorge and his radio equipment.

Two days later the Japanese arrested Sorge as he returned home after dining with friends from the German Embassy. Agents searched his residence and found packets of incriminating documents. During a secret trial, a Japanese military court found Sorge guilty and sent him to prison. Guards kept him alive for two years, torturing him to confess his involvement with the Soviet Union. He finally confessed and, on November 7, 1944, he was hanged.

NOTES

Twenty years after Sorge's execution, the Soviet Union posthumously awarded him the Hero of the Soviet Union Medal.

TALLMADGE, BENJAMIN (1754–1835)

During the American Revolution, when spies were not particularly sophisticated, Benjamin Tallmadge built the New York Culper Ring, an espionage network so carefully constructed that a century passed before the public learned who belonged to it.

Born and educated in New York, Benjamin Tallmadge enrolled at Yale and graduated in 1773. He went to work in the Connecticut school system but in 1775, after the skirmishes with British regulars at Lexington and Concord, he joined the Connecticut militia and was made a lieutenant.

A few months later, his militia company became part of General George Washington's Continental Army. In 1776 Tallmadge became a captain, and in 1777 he was promoted to major. He fought in several key battles and distinguished himself at Long Island, White Plains, Brandywine, Germantown, and Monmouth. In 1778, after Washington failed to establish an effective system of espionage, he turned the problem over to Tallmadge.

Washington asked him to develop a spy ring in New York City. The task would not be easy: thousands of British regulars, commanded by Sir Henry Clinton and fresh from evacuating Philadelphia, occupied the city.

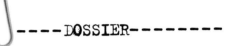

```
----DOSSIER--------
Name: Benjamin Tallmadge
Code Names: John Bolton,
721
Birth/Death: 1754-1835
Nationality: American
Occupation: Schoolteacher
Involvement: Spymaster
During the American
Revolution
Outcome: Died of Natural
Causes
```

The Culper Ring

Tallmadge put his military uniform away and returned to his hometown of New

York. The only previous spy in the New York area had been Nathan Hale, who the British captured and hanged in 1776. Washington wanted intelligent, highly placed agents who knew how to protect themselves while collecting useful information. Tallmadge gave himself the code name John Bolton and began recruiting the smartest men he could find.

He built the organization around Robert Townsend, who used the alias Samuel Culper Jr., and Abraham Woodhull, who used the alias Samuel Culper Sr. Tallmadge added Austin Roe, Caleb Brewster, and Enoch Hale (who hated the British for killing his brother Nathan). After organizing the network, he named his group after the aliases of two of his spies and called it the Culper Ring.

Only Washington, Tallmadge, Townsend, and Woodhull held the key to the codes and ciphers used by

Left: An engraving from a pencil sketch of Benjamin Tallmadge by Colonel Trumbull. In his youth, Tallmadge was reputed to have been one of the most handsome men of his time.

Townsend, who wrote the majority of his messages using invisible inks. Roe and Brewster performed a special service: Townsend gave the messages to Roe, who crossed the East River. Roe rode horseback to Setauket and delivered reports to Woodhull. In turn, Woodhull passed the reports to Brewster, who sailed across Long Island Sound, landed on the Connecticut shore, and met with Tallmadge in Fairfield. Tallmadge then carried the intelligence to Washington.

Saving the French Navy

Townsend became especially adept at judging troop movements, monitoring deliveries made by supply ships, and observing the arrival and departure of

Below: Tallmadge wrote a memoir, appropriately entitled *Memoir of Benjamin Tallmadge Prepared by Himself at the Request of His Children*, that was first published in 1858. It was a 68-page work dealing mainly with his experiences during the Revolutionary War.

warships. He and others also kept Clinton's headquarters under surveillance and were able to identify loyalists posing as patriots. The surveillance paid off in July 1780, when Admiral De Ternay planned to land Lieutenant General Count Jean Baptiste de Rochambeau and 5,000 French troops at Newport, Rhode Island. Townsend observed that the British were boarding ships to sail to Newport to stop the landing and advised Tallmadge. Tallmadge told Washington, who intentionally informed one of Clinton's undercover loyalist spies that 12,000 Continentals were on the way to attack New York. The spy promptly disappeared and informed Clinton. Sir Henry canceled his plans, recalled all the ships preparing to sail for Newport, and set to work improving his shore defenses.

The Arnold-André Incident

During the autumn of 1780, Tallmadge became involved in General Benedict Arnold's traitorous scheme to deliver West Point, New York, to the British. Had it succeeded, the colonies would have been cut in half.

Arnold wanted assurances from Clinton that if he defected, he would be handsomely rewarded and would retain his status as general in the British army. Clinton agreed and sent Major John André, who used the alias John Anderson to find Arnold and seal the deal. To meet with Arnold, André had to sail up the Hudson River in an armed British sloop and rendezvous with the general at a safe location near the American lines. Arnold feared that André might be stopped, so he wrote Tallmadge asking that if John Anderson should be detained and brought to Continental headquarters, to kindly provide him with an escort to West Point.

In Tallmadge's ciphers for his agents, he was identified as 721 and Washington as 711.

André reached the rendezvous safely, met with Arnold, and confirmed that Clinton had accepted the general's terms. As André returned to the Hudson, he realized his sloop had been driven downriver by Continental artillery. André changed into civilian clothes and tried to return to New York on horseback. Intercepted by a Continental patrol, he soon found himself in the hands of Tallmadge.

Tallmadge had André searched and found the details of the West Point plot in his boot. Meanwhile, Tallmadge received a dispatch from Townsend saying to watch out for a British spy calling himself John Anderson but who was actually Major John André, a member of Clinton's staff. Tallmadge understood what was occurring and attempted to get to West Point and arrest Arnold, but the general had already escaped on the sloop intended for André.

Tallmadge personally accompanied André to the gallows, admiring the young man's courage as he faced his fate. He later wrote: "I became so deeply attached to Major André that I can remember no instance where my affections were so fully absorbed in any man."

Immediately after the André episode, Tallmadge feared that Arnold had become aware of the Culper Ring and temporarily suspended operations. He took command of a regiment and led a victorious raid against a British position at Oyster Point. He soon realized that Arnold knew nothing about the Culper Ring and recalled his spies just in time to divert the French navy from a collision with the Royal Navy.

The War Ends

Tallmadge continued to divide his time between the Culper Ring and fighting in the battles of the Continental Army. He may have enjoyed fighting more than spying, but he recognized the importance of both. In 1783 Washington promoted his spymaster to the brevet rank of lieutenant general, but the war ended just weeks later.

Following the war, Tallmadge became a successful merchant in Litchfield, Connecticut, buying a property that is still known as Tallmadge Place. He served 16 years in Congress and remained one of Washington's strongest supporters, endorsing his policies when the general became the nation's first president.

Nobody discovered the identity of the New York members of the Culper Ring for more than a century.

After Arnold defected, he wrote to Tallmadge and invited him to defect to the British and serve with him.

THURLOE, JOHN (1616–1668)

John Thurloe, a maverick politician who disdained monarchies, served Oliver Cromwell in many administrative capacities, but none ever compared to his role as the lord protector's spymaster.

John Thurloe grew up in Sussex, England, the son of a parson in the Church of England. He abandoned his father's church, became a political rebel, and joined Oliver Cromwell in the Great Rebellion of 1642 that ousted King Charles I. Thurloe studied law and in 1645 obtained his degree and opened a practice. Six years later, Lord Protector Cromwell sent him to the Netherlands on a diplomatic mission. In 1652 he brought the diplomat back to England and named him Secretary to the Council of State. Thurloe held many titles under Cromwell, but his actual position in the government was equivalent to that of a viceroy. When Cromwell needed something done, he gave the task to Thurloe.

```
-----DOSSIER--------
Name: John Thurloe
Code Name: None
Birth/Death: 1616-1668
Nationality: English
Occupation: Lawyer,
Diplomat, Minister
Involvement: Antiroyalist
Spymaster for Oliver
Cromwell
Outcome: Died of Natural
Causes
```

Aftershock

In 1649 Cromwell engineered the execution of Charles I. The act bred immediate repercussions. Monarchists sought to place Charles II on the throne, and rallied support from those disaffected by Cromwell's methods of government. Cromwell became understandably worried and summoned Thurloe to hire spies and identify the ringleaders. He gave Thurloe and unimaginable sum of money, the modern equivalent of about nine million dollars, to

direct the effort. A superb organizer, Thurloe built the most efficient espionage network since the late sixteenth century, when Sir Francis Walsingham organized a ring of spies to protect Elizabeth I.

A Spymaster at Work

Within months, Thurloe had built a broad-based spy network that actually incorporated three distinctly different espionage operations. He formed a coun-

terintelligence network in England, a spy network in Europe, and he even sent spies to the colonies in the New World. He engaged John Wallis, an Oxford mathematician who specialized in cryptology, to break any code that Cromwell's enemies used, and he put the postal system under a massive letter intercept to prevent coded messages from being sent by mail. Most espionage information, however, came to Thurloe through his spies and not from the postal service.

Above: John Thurloe, one of the earliest and most accomplished English spymasters, died in his chambers in Lincoln's Inn. Thurloe's surviving correspondence is kept in the Bodleian Library, Oxford, and in the British Museum.

Under Cromwell, Thurloe held many posts, sometimes several at the same time—at one point or another, he was in charge of virtually every aspect of the government.

Thurloe recruited his agents from all walks of life. They included scholars, aristocrats (both wealthy and impoverished), dangerous criminals (who were promised pardons), and foreigners willing to serve as double agents. All of his spies, including those sent to foreign capitals, were expected to report once a week, if possible. One foreign ambassador admitted that while the English government seemed to know what every other government was doing, the reverse was not true.

Thurloe authorized his agents to bribe royalists for information, and sometimes he paid quite well to get the intelligence. One episode led to the complete dismantling of a royalist plot known as the "sealed knot" and the arrest of its members. On another occasion, Charles II was almost kidnapped and would have been, if one of Thurloe's men hadn't betrayed the plot hours before its planned execution. Thurloe later discovered that one of his most trusted spies, Sir George Downing, a British resident in Holland, had tipped off the exiled monarch. Downing had switched alliances because he recognized the stirrings in England for the restoration of the monarchy.

Cromwell began to enjoy several fringe benefits from Thurloe's far-reaching network. Spies began noting the sailing schedules of Spanish treasure convoys. When the British fleet captured a convoy off the Canary Islands, the credit belonged to one of Thurloe's spies in Jamaica.

A Maverick Politician Steps Down

After Cromwell died in 1658, Thurloe served his successor, Richard Cromwell, a man incapable of governing. In 1660 England soon tired of "Tumbledown Dick," and monarchists replaced him with Charles II. On May 15, 1660, Charles threw Thurloe into prison for high treason; however, he soon realized that he needed a man of Thurloe's skills and released him on the condition that he serve the Crown faithfully. Thurloe kept his word, but he never again became powerful. He spent most of his time writing profound articles on politics and international problems and became one of the king's most reliable consultants, serving in that capacity until he died on February 21, 1668.

With Thurloe gone, the king turned the intelligence service over to Secretary Morrice, but only allotted him £700 a year for intelligence. Charles never showed much interest in espionage, and the networks built by Thurloe soon vanished. However, not all the spies trained by Thurloe stopped working—some of them became agents for other countries and began spying on Charles.

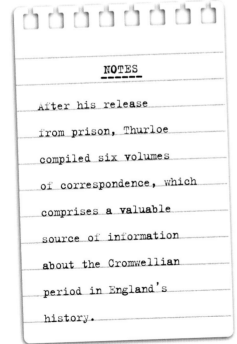

NOTES

After his release from prison, Thurloe compiled six volumes of correspondence, which comprises a valuable source of information about the Cromwellian period in England's history.

TREBITSCH, ISAAC TIMOTHY (1872–1943)

Isaac Trebitsch could never find a place in life that satisfied him, so he became a pastor, a thief, a forger, a spy, and a double-crosser without ever succeeding at anything.

Born in Paks, Hungary, to a wealthy Jewish ship-building family who lived on the Danube, Trebitsch received the finest education money could buy. He studied languages because they interested him. His parents wanted their son to become a rabbi, so he appeased them by attending the Jewish seminary in Hamburg, Germany. His secular interests soon superseded his religious studies and he became distracted by women and money. Trebitsch dropped out of school and began a life of wandering. He changed his loyalties and his politics whenever it suited his interests.

In 1896, with the police on his heels for committing petty crimes, Trebitsch departed hurriedly for England with little money in his pocket. There he met Reverend Epstein, who converted him to the Church of England. Accused of stealing small sums of money from the collection box, Trebitsch fled to Hamburg, where he joined a Methodist church and became baptized. In 1899 Trebitsch went to Canada, converted to

```
----DOSSIER--------
Name: Isaac (Ignatz) Timothy
Trebitsch
Code Names: Lincoln, Abbot
Chao Kung
Birth/Death: 1872-1943
Nationality: Hungarian
Occupation: Cleric,
Journalist, Member of
Parliament
Involvement: Hungarian Spy
for Highest Bidder
Outcome: Died Mysteriously
in China
```

Lutheranism, and studied for the ministry. He mixed seminary life with seducing a ship captain's daughter, and when confronted by her parents, he agreed to

Above: Photograph of Trebitsch from October 1919. While he tried unsuccessfully to resolve his religious life, Trebitsch kept solvent by dipping into the collections of the church.

marry the girl. On Christmas Day 1902, having switched back to the Church of England, Trebitsch was ordained an Anglican minister by the archbishop of Montreal. If Trebitsch learned nothing else from his religious experiences, he did learn how to speak several languages in a voice that attracted attention.

The Man Who Needed Money

In 1903 Trebitsch returned to England, lost interest in his religious career, and switched to business and politics. He met Quaker leader Seebohm Roundtree, a prominent member of the Liberal Party and a multimillionaire with vast holdings in the chocolate trade. Trebitsch worked for Roundtree from 1906 to 1909, which

was the longest he ever held a job. He became a naturalized British citizen in 1909 and changed his name to Lincoln so he could run for Parliament as a Radical. He conducted an impressive campaign with funds purloined from the coffers of Roundtree, though no one could ever prove the theft. To everyone's surprise, Lincoln won a seat in the House of Commons, which he abruptly lost in the next election.

Lincoln tried journalism, but the job paid too little, so he hoodwinked the gullible Roundtree into lending him enough money to go into the oil business. When the venture proved disastrous, Lincoln declared bankruptcy and became a foreign correspondent. While covering the Balkan Wars in 1912 and 1913, he realized that he could make money by selling information. Though he felt no commitment to either the Bulgarians or the Turks, he obtained a job on one side as a spy for Bulgaria, which paid him amply, and as a spy for the Turks on the other side, which also paid him well. The Bulgarian secret service caught Lincoln playing both ends against the middle, and threw him in jail in Sofia. For no apparent reason, Walther Nicolai, head of German military intelligence, arranged for Lincoln's release. The only logical conclusion would be that Lincoln had previously been hired by Nicolai to spy on Great Britain.

The Wandering Spy

Lincoln returned to London at the beginning of World War I and offered his services to MI6 (British intelligence). MI6 turned him down because they suspected him of spying for Germany, so he took a job on the Hungarian desk of British censorship. On December 29,

1914, Lincoln went to Holland, presumably to visit his ailing mother-in-law in Rotterdam, but actually to confer with Lieutenant General von Ostertag, who MI6 knew headed the Abwehr in The Hague. When Lincoln returned to London, he attempted to ingratiate himself with MI6 by offering to sell the German code used by the Abwehr. British intelligence and navy intelligence (NID) inspected the codes and concluded that Lincoln had either made them up or obtained them from Ostertag and threw them away. In 1915, knowing that he was now suspected of being a spy, Lincoln booked passage on the liner *Philadelphia* and headed for New York.

Lincoln attempted to work as a spy for the German Consulate in New York, but his reputation as a foul-up preceded him. He found work as a freelance writer for anti-British publications and spewed out his venom until London demanded his extradition for forging a check in Roundtree's name. The FBI arrested Lincoln on August 4, 1915, and sent him back to London. Tried and convicted, Lincoln spent three years in prison.

The Jubilant Days of Abbot Chao Kung

Released from prison in 1919, Lincoln returned to Hungary as Trebitsch during the brief, brutal reign of Béla Kun. Finding life unbearable, he reverted back to Lincoln and departed for Germany. He joined the Kapp Putsch effort of 1920 to overthrow the Weimar Republic and gave speeches advocating the return of the kaiser. He wandered about Europe unsuccessfully attempting to garner public interest in the return to monarchy. When that failed, he went to Italy and joined Benito Mussolini's black shirts and became involved in the assassination of Geocomo Matteotti, Mussolini's only opponent.

Nothing Lincoln attempted ever worked to his advantage, so in 1921 he turned up in China as a secret agent for Chiang Kai-shek's intelligence operation. For a while, he worked for Morris "Two Gun" Cohen, spying on warlords in provinces that were falling under the influence of Japan or Mao Tse-Tung's communists. On one occasion, he returned to England to see his son, who was about to be executed for murder, but lost all his money in a poker game and arrived too late. He hovered around Europe only long enough to buy arms for Chiang's army before returning to China.

Sometime during his years of wandering, Lincoln converted to Buddhism. In 1926 he spent part of his time in a Sri Lankan monastery, where he changed his name to Abbot Chao Kung. Returning to Shanghai in 1930, he proclaimed himself a Buddhist preacher, leader, and healer. He built a large monastery and filled it with monks and begging girls, all of who became spies for Colonel Kenji Doihara's vast Japanese espionage network. Lincoln now had plenty of money, a fanciful temple to call home, and servants to attend to his care. In October 1943, the Japanese reported the "revered Abbot Chao Kung" dead. Colonel Doihara discovered that his Hungarian spy had become a double agent for Chiang Kai-shek. A knife-wielding Japanese assassin did the rest.

NOTES

Trebitsch viewed espionage as a business proposition that would make him rich, but his sloppy efforts to always work both sides at once led to a catalog of failures.

TREPPER, LEOPOLD (1904–1982)

Leopold Trepper, who attached himself to the Communist cause as a young man, became a totally ruthless spymaster. He created the Red Orchestra and then aided its destruction to save his skin.

Born in Neumark, Poland, the son of a Jewish shopkeeper, Leopold Trepper received most of his early education at home. He attended a local school during his teens, after which he enrolled at Krakow University. Lacking funds and unable to continue his education, Trepper worked at several different jobs, and finally became a miner at Galicia.

Disgusted with hard labor and slave wages, he joined the Communist Party, and in 1925 he helped organize a huge illegal strike at Dombrova. Arrested, Trepper spent the next eight months in jail.

In 1926 he moved to Palestine, and to cement his fervor for Zionism, joined a kibbutz, or communal farm. The work soon reminded him of laboring in the mine, so he joined another Communist group and resumed life as an agitator. Expelled from Palestine by the British in 1928 for being a Communist troublemaker, Trepper returned to Europe and became involved in the Communist movement in France. At the start of the 1930s, he led elements of the Rabcors, a French organization working illegally for the Soviet Union. In 1932 French authorities broke up the Rabcors and arrested Trepper. He escaped to the Soviet Union in early 1933 and received a warm welcome in Moscow. This welcome began Trepper's new spying career.

----DOSSIER--------

Name: Leopold Trepper

Code Names: Grand Chef, Big Chief, Jean Gilbert

Birth/Death: 1904–1982

Nationality: Polish

Occupation: Miner, Farmer

Involvement: Polish Spy for the Soviets

Outcome: Died of Natural Causes

Tuning the Red Orchestra

In 1933 Trepper became a full-fledged NKVD spy and for the next six years traveled as a courier between Moscow and Paris. Six years later, he arrived in Brussels as the Soviet spymaster in Western Europe, replacing resident director Walter Krivitsky, who had defected to England because he was outraged at Stalin's increasingly ruthless policies.

Trepper's job was to rebuild and coordinate all the Soviet spy rings previously controlled by Krivitsky. He formed underground operations in Germany, Belgium, Holland, France, and Switzerland, which collectively became known as the Red Orchestra, with Trepper as the "Grand Chef" or "Big Chief." Unlike the Black Orchestra, the secret society of high-ranking anti-Hitler Germans that transmitted intelligence by music, the Red Orchestra called their transmitters "music boxes" and their radio operators "musicians." But like members of the Black Orchestra, many of the Red Orchestra's informants included high-placed members of the German government who were opposed to Hitler. The informants included aristocrats from the Junker class, intelligence officers from the German Ministry of Air, and officials from the Ministry of Economics, Ministry of Labor, Ministry of Propaganda, and the Foreign Office. The Abwehr knew all about the Red Orchestra, but virtually nothing about the informants.

Trepper established his headquarters in Brussels and from there directed all radio transmissions to Moscow. In 1940, when Germany began overrunning western Europe, Trepper set up another operation in Paris and traveled between the two cities. When German counterespionage began tracking radio broadcasts, they narrowed down transmissions to the operation in Brussels. Trepper barely escaped arrest, walking into the building containing their headquarters at the same time as Gestapo agents were apprehending Johann Wenzel, the radio operator.

Below: Former chief of the Soviet spy organization Red Orchestra during World War II, Leopold Trepper waves as he walks down the gangway after landing in London.

S. Form 81/P.G./3000/4.47.

B2B.

44ab

EXTRACT.

Extract for File No. : PF. 68258   Name : TREPPER, Otto

Original in File No. : PF. 66965 v.1.   Serial : 63a   Receipt Date : —

Original from : B.2.b.   Under Ref. : —   Dated : 20.7.47.

Extracted on : 2.12.47.   by : HFC   Section : R5

Extract from "Comments of S's 2nd interview with FOOTE", Soviet
agent working for the Rote Drei, on Sunday morning.

● ●

16.   I got F talking about the occupants of the plane in which
he left PARIS for MOSCOW in January 1945. After he had described
IVANOV to me as "plump, pink complexion, medium build, fair hair,
blue eyes, fluent French with a very queer accent", I produced the
photograph of OTTO TREPPER. F leapt at it in great contrast to
his doubtful attitude towards other photographs and said that he
was positive that this was the man. Without any suggestion from
me, he said "I am prepared to swear that that is IVANOV". I
concealed my interest and asked him what else he knew about IVANOV.
F. said that he did not think I need waste my time about this man
since he appeared to have done no work at all, but to have spent
the war in hiding. He said that IVANOV was very friendly and that
he evidently knew what F had been doing. He described IVANOV as
a man who knew his way about. On one occasion F had made some
slightly disparaging remark to MIASNIKOV (also in plane) about the
Jews. MIASNIKOV had told him to be tactful pointing out that

/IVANOV 6/12

Above and right: British secret service interview notes from the interrogation of Alexander Foote, the radio operator of the Swiss-based "Lucy Ring." Although they were both working for the Soviets, Foote was obviously unaware of who Ivanov (Trepper) was and his importance to Soviet intelligence during the war.

IVANOV was a Jew, which F had not realised. IVANOV appears to
have been a good companion to F throughout the journey to MOSCOW.
Because of some mix-up in the flight, the party arrived at MOSCOW
unheralded and F told IVANOV that he was worried about what they
should do. IVANOV apparently took things into his own hands and
"rang up the Foreign Office". Two cars then came down, one for
F and one for IVANOV. The Russian woman Major who took such a
leading part in F's interviews in Moscow arrived with the cars.
I asked whether she appeared to be on particularly friendly terms
with IVANOV and he said that in fact they came up to him together
where he was sitting at the airfield. IVANOV had also told him
beforehand that they would be put up in an hotel. During the journey
IVANOV showed an affectionate interest in his wife in RUSSIA and
went out in CAIRO to buy her a fur hat. Perhaps the most interesting
point about IVANOV was the questions which F was asked about him
in MOSCOW. He was required to give his views on IVANOV and all
he could do was to report a statement that had been made to him in
the plane. IVANOV had suggested that there was a strong possibility
of HIMMLER's seizing power in Germany and making a separate peace
with Russia. When F told his Russian interrogator this, he said
that IVANOV was a "stupid idiot".

● ●

According to one report, Trepper talked the Gestapo out of arresting him in Brussels by pretending to be a rabbit salesman.

Curtain Call for the Music Makers

By 1942 the German Gestapo had a clear idea of how the Red Orchestra operated and took advantage of the fact that they now had Wenzel. The Gestapo interrogated Wenzel and eventually he snapped, agreeing to work for German intelligence. Not knowing that they had already let Trepper slip through their fingers in Brussels, the Gestapo demanded to know the identity of the Grand Chef. Wenzel replied, "Jean Gilbert," Trepper's code name. When asked where Gilbert could be found, Wenzel replied that he was hiding in Paris. The Abwehr traced the so-called Jean Gilbert through his dentist and arrested him while he was sitting in the dental chair having a cavity filled.

In an effort to save members of his family, Trepper gave up the names of most members of the Red Orchestra, but he never mentioned Sandor Rado's operation in Switzerland. Wenzel also offered up names of colleagues. The penalty Germans paid for spying for the Red Orchestra was terrible.

Hitler took a personal interest when 14 of the accused were brought to trial. Eleven of the spies received immediate death sentences while two women received long sentences and one committed suicide. The eleven sentenced to death were strung up on meat hooks while still alive and left to hang until they died. Dissatisfied with the sentences for the women, Hitler demanded they be executed. Guards took the women outside and beheaded them.

Trepper's Last Call

Miraculously, Trepper escaped the horrors meted out by the Gestapo and joined the French resistance. After the liberation of Paris, he flew to Moscow in Stalin's personal plane. Instead of a hero's welcome, the NKVD threw him into Lubianka Prison.

Trepper told the NKVD a tall tale about how he had filled his captors' minds with disinformation and never gave up a single person. He even brought with him signed statements from the French Communist underground to validate his testimony. Trepper remained in prison while Stalin, taken aback by the documents, reconsidered his earlier decision to torture Trepper before executing him. While still considering Trepper's fate, Stalin died. Four years later the Soviets set Trepper free.

Trepper returned to Poland to resume life with his wife and three sons. He soon learned that all Jews were suffering because of rampant Soviet-induced anti-Semitism. He filed for visas to move his family to Israel, but neither Poland nor the KGB would permit him to leave. Trepper defied the government, lobbied the international press to intercede, and finally moved to Israel in 1974. He died there eight years later at the age of 87.

NOTES

When six Abwehr agents accosted Trepper, exclaiming, "You are under arrest," the spymaster replied in perfect German, "You did a fine job."

T.6.

TREPPER, Leopold or Liebeh.

ALIAS:

TREPER, Leiba ben Zeharya
MIKLER, Adam   (cover in Belgium 1939-40)
GILBERT, Jean   (cover in France, 1940-42)
IVANOWSKI, Vladislav Ivanovitch (for travel
                  from Paris to Moscow, 1945)
de WINTER
SOMMER
Grand Chef
Le General
L'Oncle
Onkel Otto

TOP SECRET

ESPIONAGE:

A full account of TREPPER's functions and activities as a director of Red Army Intelligence in Western Europe from 1936 until 1945 is contained in the report to which this biography is attached. His movements are given below under "History".

In spite of the calamities which overtook TREPPER's organisation and its agents during the German occupation of France and the Low Countries, it has been shown that TREPPER probably played a skilful triple-cross game against his captors during 1943, and he must be regarded as potentially an extremely dangerous and useful R.U. agent, who may well be posted again to an office of vital importance to the R.U. It is, however, perhaps unlikely that so distinctive a figure would ever return to the territories of Western Europe, in which he became so well-known, and he may in future direct R.U. operations from within the bounds of the Soviet Union.

ADDRESSES:

March, 1939   198, avenue Richard Neyberg, Brussels.
        1941   rue de Gentilhomme, Paris
                  94, rue Varennes, Paris.
                  6, rue Fortuny, Paris.
Autumn 1943   9, allee de la Pepiniere, Suresnes.

VAN LEW, ELIZABETH (1817–1900)

Born in Richmond, Elizabeth Van Lew became one of the most revered women among captured Union soldiers, and one of the most hated women in the Confederacy.

Born in 1817 to a wealthy hardware store owner in Richmond, Virginia, Elizabeth Van Lew lived a pampered life and received much of her education in Philadelphia. Her father came from New York and her mother from Pennsylvania, which, with her Northern education, probably accounts for her abolitionist views.

Before the Civil War, the Van Lews freed all their slaves, although many of them continued to work for the family and received wages. In April 1861, after Fort Sumter fell to South Carolina's militia and Virginia seceded from the Union, Van Lew dressed only in black. She openly declared herself an abolitionist and defiantly walked the streets with her servants.

The public sneered as she passed, sometimes calling her "witch" or "traitor." Her neighbors called her "Crazy Bet." None of the slurs troubled her in the least, because 44-year-old Elizabeth Van Lew had her own agenda.

The Van Lews lived in an elegant mansion on Church Hill, built atop the highest of Richmond's seven hills. The home consisted of three stories, all with large rooms and a stable below. On the third floor, over the front portico, was a secret room where Van Lew hid up to 50 escaping Union soldiers at a time. Because the neighbors shunned her, they never noticed all the nocturnal activity occurring at the Van Lew mansion.

----DOSSIER--------

Name: Elizabeth Van Lew

Code Name: Crazy Bet

Birth/Death: 1817–1900

Nationality: American

Occupation: Housekeeper

Involvement: Union Spy in the Civil War

Outcome: Died of Natural Causes

Getting Started in Espionage

Although the people of the city knew that Crazy Bet was a Union sympathizer, no one stopped her when she rode to Libby Prison to distribute small baskets of fruit to starving federal prisoners. Even the Confederate provost marshal, General John H. Winder, considered her a harmless eccentric and allowed her to visit the prison with her food, and the hospital to distribute books, delicacies, and to do whatever she thought good.

Early in the war she received a request from an unnamed federal agent asking if she would spy for the Union. Van Lew agreed, and a short time later a courier arrived from General George Henry Sharpe with a cipher written on a two-inch piece of green paper. She tucked the cipher into a large watch that she carried on her person at all times. Then she went to work.

Infiltrating the Confederate Government

Van Lew picked her spies from among the servants who knew and trusted her. She used her influence to place Mary Elizabeth Bowser, an ex-slave whom she had personally educated, in the Confederate White House, where president Jefferson Davis lived. Within months, Bowser was providing Van Lew with discarded drafts of Confederate domestic and diplomatic strategies, military movements, supply problems, command changes, treasury problems, and other abstracts from President Davis's wastebasket.

Van Lew did her own spying while visiting the Union troops in hospitals. Whenever Confederate physicians tried to drive her away, she complained to General Winder. He rebuked most anyone who denied her access to her prisoners, mainly because he believed that all her activities were humane. She brought in custards, homemade breads, and cookies, and spent endless hours writing letters home for the wounded.

Crazy Bet also collected fresh information on Confederate activities in the field and slipped notes into the false bottom of a French plate warmer. After arriving home, she passed the documents to her servants, who carried them to ex-slaves acting as couriers along a route that stretched to Washington and eventually led to either Allan Pinkerton or General Lafayette Baker.

But by 1862 Winder began to suspect that Van Lew was much more than an eccentric middle-aged woman. After being tipped off by a friendly Confederate captain, Van Lew became more cautious. When a bedraggled soldier came to her home asking for a place to sleep, she suspected he was a plant and turned him away. She made the right decision and changed her routine.

In her own words, Van Lew said, "I am naturally fond of adventure, a little ambitious, and a good deal romantic—but patriotism was the true secret of my success."

> Neighbors believed that Van Lew had lost her mind. She messed up her hair and tried to appear insane. When she passed children on the street, they would cackle, "Crazy Bet, Crazy Bet, lives in a mansion with no rooms to let."

"Old Bet's Gone Crazy"

Van Lew continued to give sanctuary to escaped Union prisoners. Because she had stabled her horse in the library instead of the stable, people believed she had gone berserk and paid little attention to activities in the mansion. When 109 Union prisoners dug a tunnel and escaped from Libby Prison, 49 of them went straight to Van Lew's mansion. She had shown the men where to dig their way out of prison and provided them with instructions to her home. Aided by Van Lew's couriers, every man made it safely to Union lines.

During the summer of 1864, when General Ulysses S. Grant put Richmond and Petersburg under siege, Van Lew sent him daily messages on conditions in the Confederate capital. She set up five relay stations run by ex-slaves. An old man trudged through Confederate picket lines every day with messages hidden between the soles of his brogans for the general. He sometimes carried a small bundle of flowers, fresh from the spy's garden, that made their way to Grant's dinner table at City Point, in Virginia.

After Grant entered Richmond at the end of the war, he went directly to Van Lew's mansion to personally express his thanks for her services. He later stated, "You have sent me the most valuable information received from Richmond during the war." After he became president, he named her postmistress of Richmond with a salary of $4,000 a year, which she held from 1869 to 1877. However, her wartime alliances had made her an outcast from her society: "No one will go with us anywhere; and it grows worse and worse as the years roll on."

Van Lew was never cut out to be a postmistress. After failing to have her position renewed, Captain Paul Revere provided her with a yearly annuity. He had been one of the escapees from Libby Prison whom she had hidden during the Civil War. When Van Lew died in 1900, a 2,000-pound bronze plaque from the Revere family in Massachusetts arrived to mark her grave at Shockhoe Cemetery. The plaque read: *Elizabeth Van Lew 1818–1900. She risked everything that is dear to man—friends, fortune, comfort, health, life itself, all for the one absorbing desire of her heart—that slavery be abolished and the Union be preserved.*

By then, everybody knew that Crazy Bet was not so crazy after all.

NOTES

After the war, Van Lew wrote her memoirs, titled *Nurse and Spy in the Union Army*, a story filled with pathos, suspense, and daring.

VASSALL, WILLIAM JOHN (1924–1996)

John Vassall, who never used his first name, was blackmailed into becoming a KGB spy because of his homosexuality. When he discovered how much espionage paid, he continued in the trade for six years before being caught.

The son of a Church of England clergyman, William Vassall received his education in a public school. He left school in 1940 at the age of 16 to become a clerk in a bank. Finding the work boring, he applied to the civil service and obtained a job as a temporary grade-3 clerk with the Admiralty.

After shuffling papers for two years, he enlisted in the Royal Air Force. Rejecting him as a pilot, the RAF trained him as a photographer, and Vassall served in that capacity until after the war. In 1946 he returned to the Admiralty as a clerical officer, but because of his poor work habits and lackadaisical performance, he was repeatedly skipped over for promotion. Nevertheless, in 1954 the Admiralty posted him as an assistant to the naval attaché in the British Embassy in Moscow.

The KGB's Recruiting Guidelines

Despite his performance problems, the Admiralty sent Vassall to Moscow to read,

----DOSSIER--------

Name: William John Christopher Vassall

Code Name: Vera

Birth/Death: 1924–1996

Nationality: British

Occupation: Banker, Clerk

Involvement: British Spy for the Soviet Union

Outcome: Died of Natural Causes

process, file, and write confidential documents flowing between the British Embassy and the Admiralty. As soon as Vassall arrived in Moscow, KGB agents began to follow him. They sent young men to seduce him, photographed their sexual encounters, and exploited him by using the photos as blackmail. The KGB had no fear of being exposed by Vassall because, by doing so, Vassall would simply be exposing his sexual preferences to his embassy employers, and homosexuality was considered unacceptable at that time. Vassall received a weekly salary of £15, and the KGB's promise of greater rewards provided him with a strong inducement to spy.

In September 1955, Vassall, using the code name Vera, began his nefarious work by "borrowing" secret documents from the naval attaché's office, handing them to a KGB operative for photographing, and then returning them to the office before they would be missed. This exchange went on until July 1956, when Vassall was posted back to London. The job change might have ended Vassall's career as a spy had he not been reassigned to the Admiralty's Naval Intelligence Division (NID).

A Life of Lavish Living

Vassall stepped up in the world when the NID cleared him for access to classified atomic energy documents and top-secret defense information. The KGB paid well for this information—so well, in fact, that Vassall moved into an expensive apartment in the exclusive Dolphin Square district in London, and furnished his bungalow with fine antiques. He made a few friends, and to those who asked about his newly acquired wealth, Vassall merely replied that he had received small legacies from two deceased aunts.

Using skills he acquired in the RAF, Vassall now photographed borrowed documents with his own equipment and hand-delivered the microfilm to Soviet contact Nikolai Borisovich Rodin (alias Korovin) at prearranged drop-offs in

London. British intelligence remained lax to the point that nobody questioned Vassall's sudden opulence. By 1959, he was peddling details of British innovations in radar, antisubmarine devices, naval tactics, fleet operational orders, and communications. To his credit, Vassall conducted his personal security—except for living in style on a small income—with prudence.

Below: A tribunal was held to investigate the failure of the British secret service to detect Vassal's traitorous ways. The tribunal exonerated the government, enabling them to refute claims of incompetence that had been made by the British press.

> John Vassall possessed no particular intellectual talents, but because he managed to accumulate seniority with the Admiralty, the Naval Intelligence Division shuffled him into positions where he had access to top secrets.

In 1961, when the Portland spy case broke and Scotland Yard arrested Gordon Lonsdale, Ethel Gee, Harry Houghton, and Peter and Helen Kroger, Soviet handlers told Vassall to cease operations for a spell. Vassall waited a few months before the KGB gave him the green light to continue his activities. He had never been suspected of spying, and most of the blame for the peddling of secrets pointed to the Portland ring.

British Intelligence Investigates Itself

In addition to shutting down the Portland ring, British intelligence had also arrested George Blake (Behar), an MI6 double agent selling secrets to the Soviets. After a double dose of embarrassment, MI5, MI6, and NID began looking more critically at the methods they used to monitor the activities of employees working in departments handling secret documents. Oddly enough, they knew that Vassall was a homosexual, and while that did not necessarily mean that he was a spy, MI5 did know that homosexuals were especially good targets for KGB recruiters because of their vulnerability to being blackmailed.

The Invincible Mistake

During the early 1960s, the Soviet Union initiated plans to build the helicopter carriers *Moskva* and *Leningrad*. During the same period, the Admiralty planned to begin construction on the new Invincible-class carriers. It seemed that the Soviets could never build anything without first stealing secrets from someone else. Vassall dutifully borrowed the plans for the Invincible carriers, photographed the designs, and delivered the film to his handler.

In 1962 MI5 learned through the British Embassy in Moscow that the Soviets had the plans for the navy's new carriers. The information could only have come directly from the Admiralty office in London. Several persons came under surveillance, and the search narrowed down to Vassall. Agents from Scotland Yard's Special Branch entered Vassall's apartment and found 176 classified documents and photographic equipment hidden in a secret drawer.

That same year Vassall went to trial at the Old Bailey and admitted stealing, photographing, and returning more than 1,000 classified documents. The court sentenced Vassall to 18 years in prison. He was released on parole in 1973. Years later, a former MI5 agent speculated that the KGB might have given up Vassall to distract attention away from a far more important mole in the Ministry of Defense.

NOTES
_____

Like so many spies during the cold war era, Vassall wrote his memoirs, *The Autobiography of a Spy*, after being released from prison, which chronicled his life from youth to imprisonment.

WALKER, JOHN ANTHONY JR. (1937–)

A retired naval officer, John Anthony Walker Jr. operated a spy ring that included his son, Michael; his brother, Lieutenant Commander Arthur J. Walker; and his friend, Senior Chief Radioman Jerry Whitworth.

Born in Scranton, Pennsylvania, on July 28, 1937, John Walker performed poorly in school and regularly found himself in trouble with the law. He dropped out of school and committed a number of petty thefts. In 1955 he was about to go to jail when his older brother Arthur came to his rescue and talked the judge into letting John go into the navy instead of prison.

To everyone's surprise, Walker did well in the navy and received exemplary appraisals from superiors for his technical skills. He became an excellent radioman, completed submarine training in Groton, Connecticut, and received top security clearance for submarine duty. In 1957 Walker married Barbara Crowley of Boston and they had three daughters and one son. By 1967 Walker's assignments had included duty in two nuclear-powered strategic missile submarines. His lengthy sea duty, however, led to a separation from his wife, and he became a flamboyant, hard-drinking womanizer.

----DOSSIER--------

Name: John Anthony Walker Jr.

Code Name: Jaws

Birth/Death: 1937–

Nationality: American

Occupation: Chief Warrant Officer in the U.S. Navy

Involvement: Spied for the Soviets

Outcome: Serving a Life Term in Prison

Formation of the Walker Spy Ring

In the mid-1960s, Walker bought a bar in South Carolina, with which he racked up a massive debt. By 1967, he badly needed money, and having "top secret-cryptographic" clearances, he walked into

Walker claimed he had been selling the Soviets "yellow" sheets ever since 1962, which were continuous teletype printouts of moderate value that sometimes contained pearls of top-secret information.

the Soviet Embassy in Washington, D.C., and sold a radio cipher card for a few thousand dollars. In exchange for promises of KGB cash, he agreed to steal more intelligence about the navy's most guarded secrets. Now in the spy business,

Walker decided he needed other agents and recruited his brother Arthur, a navy lieutenant commander.

The next accomplice turned up in 1969, after the navy put Walker in charge of training recruits at the radioman school in San Diego. Because there was not much intelligence to be gathered at radioman school, the Soviets dropped Walker's stipend of $4,000 a month to $2,000. Walker sought ways to revive his income and recruited Senior Chief Radioman Jerry Whitworth, who had access to highly classified communications data. He knew Whitworth was scheduled for sea duty and made arrangements to pick up intelligence wherever he docked. In the meantime, Walker also went to sea as chief radioman. He photographed cryptographic material from data-spewing code machines, and once again began pocketing $4,000 a month. One consequence of Walker's dealings with the Soviets was the USS *Pueblo* incident, which enabled North Korea to capture the navy communications surveillance ship.

Retirement Planning for a Spy

Reassigned to Norfolk, Virginia, Walker continued to collect his own intelligence along with any passed to him by Whitworth or his brother. Using the bottom of trash bags, he made regular weekly drops of microfilm in Virginia and Maryland, always careful to put nothing in the bag that would attract animals.

Later, he went to another letter-drop area to pick up his cash, along with new instructions from his KGB handler.

Walker retired from the navy in 1975, but he didn't retire from spying. Whitworth had become an officer involved in satellite communications and continued to supply Walker with intelligence. As a cover, Walker set up two businesses in Norfolk, a general detective agency called Confidential Reports, Inc., and a firm for removing "bugs" called Electronic Counter-Spy, Inc. Walker's compensation from the KGB, however, depended almost entirely on Whitworth, who began talking about retirement. Walker convinced his handlers that the satellite information was worth a lump sum payment of $200,000. He shared half the money with Whitworth, who agreed to reenlist and continue funneling top-secret information to Walker.

The Head of the Family

Soon after reenlisting, Whitworth was transferred to a post devoid of secret information. With his sources drying up along with his cash, Walker attempted to enlist his daughter, Laura Walker Snyder, who was pregnant and in the army, but planning to give up her job. Laura refused. She was later to testify that: "He told me I was stupid for [quitting] the army, that I had no hope for the future, that I would never amount to anything. I was an idiot."

Walker then contacted his son, Michael Lance Walker, who joined the navy in 1982 at the age of 20, with every intention of working for his father as a spy. Walker trained his son in camera work, and soon Michael had the good fortune of being assigned to the USS *Nimitz*, one of the most technologically advanced aircraft carriers in the world. Whenever the ship docked, Walker rendezvoused with his son, picked up the film, and paid him $1,000.

Indignant over her father's callousness, Laura Walker confided her contempt to her mother, Barbara. Walker's ex-wife had also grown weary of years of her ex-husband's refusal to pay alimony so, on November 29, 1984, she met with an FBI agent at her home and told her story. Because she had been drinking, the agent listened, departed, and reported that the interview was useless and should be ignored.

Joseph Wolfinger, an agent in Norfolk who was well aware of Walker's extravagances, somehow managed to see the report and decided to do his own investigation. He began with an interview of Laura Walker in Buffalo, New York, and gradually pulled facts together through subsequent investigations. At the same time, Whitworth, annoyed because his cash flow from Walker had been discontinued, tried to get even by writing anonymous letters to the FBI incriminating his former partner.

In May 1985, the FBI closed in on Walker and arrested the entire spy ring. The four men were tried and convicted of espionage. John Walker went to prison for life. Michael Walker received a reduced sentence by turning in evidence against his father. Lieutenant Commander Arthur Walker received three life terms, and Whitworth was sentenced to 365 years in prison. None of them, except Michael, ever demonstrated any remorse for selling secrets to the Soviets.

Opposite: John A. Walker Jr., left, is escorted by a U.S. federal marshal as he leaves the Montgomery County Detention Center in Rockville, Maryland, for federal court on October 28, 1985. Walker had just pleaded guilty to running a spy ring that sold sensitive codes to the Soviets, allowing them to read over a million classified Navy cables.

NOTES

The FBI attempted to estimate how much money Walker collected from the Soviets over a 20-year span and stopped counting when the amount reached one million dollars.

WALSINGHAM, SIR FRANCIS (1532?–1590)

Francis Walsingham was the unappreciated spymaster of Queen Elizabeth I. He conspired with her to liquidate Mary Stuart, Queen of Scots, and was instrumental in saving her crown when it was threatened by Spanish intervention.

The son of a Norfolk lawyer who served King Henry VIII, Francis Walsingham grew up in a Protestant family of means and graduated from Cambridge in 1552 with a degree in law. When Mary Tudor came to the throne, Walsingham spent five years living on the Continent in protest of the queen's Catholic policies. While living in Italy, he became interested in master codes, ciphers, and the art of secret writing that came into existence during the early Renaissance.

In 1558, when Queen Elizabeth I assumed the throne, Walsingham returned to England. He joined the Protestant movement to persecute Catholics, and in 1563, with the patronage of the queen's adviser, William Cecil (later Lord Burghley), Walsingham entered Parliament. In 1573 he joined the Privy Council, and in 1577 was knighted. During those years, Walsingham remained a loyal supporter of Elizabeth and her unbending anti-Catholic policies.

```
----DOSSIER--------
Name: Sir Francis
Walsingham
Code Name: None
Birth/Death: 1532?-1590
Nationality: English
Occupation: Lawyer,
Parliamentarian
Involvement: Director of
Intelligence for Queen
Elizabeth I
Outcome: Died of Natural
Causes
```

Every Queen Needs a Spymaster

During the Protestant Reformation, English Catholics plotted to restore the old beloved religion. Catholic ambassadors from the Continent were automatically viewed as spies. They found a leader in Mary Stuart, queen of Scotland and heiress to the English throne by her own dynastic claim. Because Elizabeth had no children, Catholics throughout Europe extolled Mary as England's only hope. When Protestant reformers moved into Scotland, Mary became vulnerable to the plots of assassins. Elizabeth cunningly offered her sanctuary in England and then betrayed and imprisoned her. To deter rescue attempts, Elizabeth moved Mary from place to place for security, and London became a hotbed for espionage and counter-espionage.

Walsingham had already established the most extensive spy network in Europe. In 1573, after organizing a secret service in London, he had branched into Europe. He placed secret agents in the courts of Spain, Italy, and France to ferret out Catholic plots against Elizabeth. He considered it his number-one duty to see that none of the pro-Mary schemes succeeded. Some Catholic conspirators were working hard to inveigle Philip II of Spain to send an invading army to England to dethrone Elizabeth in the name of Catholicism. Walsingham would not let that happen.

What to Do about Mary

Mary became the lightning rod for the Catholics, and Elizabeth wanted the menace removed. She conspired with Walsingham to compromise Mary, who had become the solitary hope of the powerful and determined Catholic conspirators in Europe. The only way to defuse the time bomb was to eliminate Mary, and the queen expected Walsingham to work out the details.

Walsingham used popular writers as spies, one of whom was Christopher Marlowe. He sent Marlowe to Rheims to study at the Catholic seminary. The seminary, however, had become the center for hatching plots against Elizabeth, and Walsingham wanted an undercover agent embedded to somehow implicate Mary in an open conspiracy against Elizabeth. It is said that Marlowe became involved in a

Below: Despite the nature of his work, Walsingham believed that the end justified the means: "I call God to witness that as a private person I have done nothing unbeseeming an honest man, nor . . . have I done anything unworthy of my place."

SPIES & ESPIONAGE: A DIRECTORY

After Walsingham's death, Thomas Phelippes founded England's first private detective agency, one that catered mainly to the kingdom's gentry.

tavern brawl and mysteriously disappeared. Some of the so-called plots against Elizabeth were Walsingham's own inventions, and some believed that he had also arranged for Marlowe to disappear.

Walsingham also sent Anthony Munday to the English College in Rome to investigate papal plots. Munday succeeded in exposing a number of anti-Elizabeth plotters in London. Walsingham made the necessary arrests, but he also hatched cases against many innocent people simply to increase the queen's dependence on him for protection. However, one real plot developed in 1586 when William Babington conspired to release Mary from the Tower of London and topple Elizabeth. Walsingham's spies unearthed the plot, rounded up Babington and his plotters, and sent them to the executioner.

In London, Walsingham employed John Dee, Thomas Phelippes, and Gilbert Gifford, all scholars of ancient ciphers and codes, to study and decipher Mary's mail. Dee and Gifford claimed to have decoded one letter implicating Mary in Babington's plot. It is likely that Walsingham conspired with Dee or Gifford, and possibly with Elizabeth, to concoct the forgery that enabled the queen to sign Mary's death warrant.

In 1587 Mary Stuart, Queen of Scots, went to her death on the block.

Walsingham's Reward

Mary's execution infuriated King Philip of Spain. He branded Elizabeth a regicide, sought revenge, and used gold from the New World to build a huge armada. He vowed to sail to England, invade the island, sweep Elizabeth from the throne, and reestablish Catholicism.

Walsingham sent Anthony Standen and a collection of his best spies to the coast of Spain and France to watch for the armada. Standen embedded a spy on the staff of the Marquis of Santa Cruz, admiral of the Spanish fleet. Standen not only communicated the armada's sailing times, he knew every detail about the Spanish fleet, from the number of troops assigned to transports to the very construction and armament of the ships involved. When the Spanish armada sailed on July 12, 1588, Lord Howard of Effingham and Sir Francis Drake knew all the particulars of Spain's plans. With the help of a hurricane that damaged part of the Spanish fleet, the English captains destroyed the remainder.

Walsingham had become quite powerful, and the queen feared that someday he might implicate her in the conspiracy to eliminate Queen Mary. In 1588, soon after the destruction of the Spanish fleet, she removed him from office. Walsingham lived penniless for the remaining two years of his life. Despite many petitions to Elizabeth, she never replied personally.

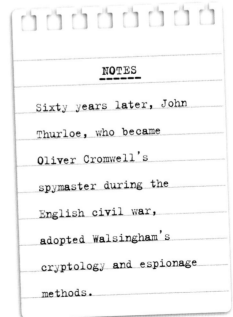

NOTES

Sixty years later, John Thurloe, who became Oliver Cromwell's spymaster during the English civil war, adopted Walsingham's cryptology and espionage methods.

WRIGHT, PETER (1916–1995)

Peter Wright began a witch hunt for moles in British counterintelligence and made unsupported allegations that provoked the wrath of the government.

One might say that Peter Wright was born to follow in his father's footsteps. At the time of Peter's birth, Maurice G. M. Wright headed research at the Marconi Company, and during World War I he also served as a British intelligence (MI6) agent for Reginald Hall and the Secret Intelligence Service (SIS).

Wright attended Oxford University, and during World War II worked in the Admiralty Research Office. In 1949 Sir Frederick Brundrett recruited Wright, who was then in charge of research in a private firm, as part-time scientific advisor for British counterintelligence (MI5). In 1955 Wright joined MI5 as a full-time deputy director handling the technical aspects of counterintelligence during the cold war. At the time, MI5 had been suffering a lapse in the department's ability to track Soviet spies within Great Britain, and had been understandably embarrassed by the treachery of Guy Burgess, who had worked in intelligence, and Donald Maclean, who had worked in the Foreign Office.

```
----DOSSIER--------
Name: Peter Wright
Code Name: None
Birth/Death: 1916-1995
Nationality: British
Occupation: Scientific
Researcher
Involvement: Deputy
Director of British
Counterintelligence
Outcome: Died of Natural
Causes
```

The Deputy Director

A deputy director in MI5 served as a department head. Wright was less concerned with the day-to-day operation of the department and more directly involved in improving the technical capabilities of MI5. He designed and improved wiretapping devices, direction-finding instruments for locating illegal radio transmitters, and other devices to pinpoint Soviet espionage activity. He had helped to identify Burgess and Maclean before becoming deputy director, and after joining MI5 as deputy director, he helped to identify Harold Philby, the third man of the Cambridge Spy Ring, and later Anthony Blunt, the fourth man. In 1962 he also helped expose the Portland Spy Ring run by Gordon Lonsdale and supported by Peter and Helen Kroger and two employees of the Royal Navy's Underwater Weapons Establishment. His track record with MI5 showed promise.

The Case of Sir Roger Hollis

Because the Cambridge Spy Ring had infiltrated British intelligence, Wright became obsessed with the idea that MI5 still had spies working on the inside. In his book *Spy Catcher* (1987), he accused Sir Roger Hollis, the former head of MI5, of being the notorious fifth man of the Cambridge Spy Ring.

Wright built his public case against Hollis years after the former MI5 director had retired and died. Wright had also put Anthony Blunt through six years of debriefing trying to pinpoint the fifth man without success. His case against Hollis actually began when the latter was

posted in MI5 before the beginning of World War II. Wright conceived the theory that Hollis had been recruited as a double agent while serving in Shanghai, where Soviet spymaster George Sorge operated a network that paid extremely well. Wright's allegations resulted in two investigations. An exhaustive check of records showed no connection between Hollis and Sorge, nor were any leaks discovered in Hollis's pursuit of members of the Cambridge Spy Ring, the Portland Spy Ring, or George Blake, all of which Hollis handled expediently and professionally.

The Persistence of Peter Wright

In 1969, four years after Hollis retired, MI5 agents questioned him in an undisclosed location to investigate the charge without directly accusing him. MI5 agents and Wright listened to the testimony from another room. Hollis never revealed anything incriminating, and MI5 closed the file. The matter might have been dropped had Wright not spoken with James J. Angleton, head of CIA intelligence—a man as obsessed with moles in the CIA as was Wright in MI5. Angleton had no evidence to share about Hollis, but he convinced Wright of the worthiness of his campaign, and to pursue his gut feelings. When the CIA's new director, William Colby, pressured Angleton into resigning, Wright failed to realize that his friend's sudden departure was because he had paralyzed the CIA with his witch hunts. In

In *Spy Catcher*, Wright wrote: "By the beginning of 1964, both Arthur Martin, a senior MI5 officer and I were convinced that Hollis . . . was the most likely suspect for the spy we were certain had been active inside MI5 at a high level."

January 1976, Wright knew he would never be promoted, so he resigned and moved to a farm in Australia.

The Spy Catcher Unveiled

Wright remained in contact with friends in London who were responsible for security matters. Through their urging, he decided to write a book about his years with MI5 and the hunt for the fifth man of the Cambridge Spy Ring, which Wright still insisted was the now-deceased Sir Roger Hollis. In addition to having his say about Hollis, his autobiogrpahy also spoke of an MI5 cabal to run a "black propaganda" campaign against Labor prime minister Harold Wilson by labeling him a Communist sympathizer. Wright also intensely disliked J. Edgar Hoover's autocratic and bullying traits and castigated the FBI director mercilessly.

The revelations in Wright's autobiography so rattled Conservative prime minister Margaret Thatcher that she initiated a two-year campaign to ban the book and prevent newspapers from publishing reviews. The British government even filed suit in an attempt to prevent the publication of the book in Australia. J. Edgar Hoover also waged an attack against the book in the United States.

Seven of the 20 principal British newspapers ignored Thatcher's efforts to restrict the freedom of the press. Despite Thatcher's ban, thousands of copies of *Spy Catcher* were ferreted into the United Kingdom.

NOTES

Conspiracy theories follow dramatic events. Lord Victor Rothschild had been one of the men who encouraged Wright to write *Spy Catcher*. People claimed that he wanted Hollis publicly pegged as the traitor to deflect attention away from himself, the real mole.

Yeo-Thomas sought an adventurous life, but when he joined British Special Operations to help organize the French resistance, he had not planned to be captured by the German Gestapo.

Though born in London, Forest Frederick Edward Yeo-Thomas spent most of his youth in Paris, where his father owned a lucrative business. He received part of his education in England and part in France, and could speak both languages fluently. Having developed a natural penchant for adventure, Yeo-Thomas joined the French army while still in his teens and fought in World War I. After Germany surrendered, he looked for more excitement and went to Poland in 1919 to help turn back Bolshevik invaders. Captured by the Russians, he escaped during the Bolshevik retreat and returned to Paris.

With help from his father, Yeo-Thomas opened a successful Parisian women's fashion house and operated it until the outbreak of World War II. In 1939 he joined the RAF and served as an interpreter for British forces in France. When France collapsed in 1940, Yeo-Thomas evacuated and returned to England where, in 1940, he was assigned as an interpreter to the Free French forces led by General Charles de Gaulle.

----DOSSIER--------

Name: F. F. E. Yeo-Thomas

Code Name: White Rabbit

Birth/Death: 1901-1964

Nationality: British

Occupation: Proprietor of Fashion House

Involvement: British Spy in World War II

Outcome: Died of Natural Causes

The Emergence of White Rabbit
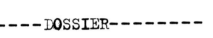

From London, de Gaulle operated a Free French intelligence service (BCRA) in France in conjunction with Britain's Special Operations Executive (SOE). Both organizations aided espionage/sabotage

De Gaulle was delighted when Yeo-Thomas told him that the underground looked to him for leadership. He tried to award Yeo-Thomas the Croix de Guerre with palms, but the RAF forbade Yeo-Thomas from accepting the medal because de Gaulle was not the recognized head of France.

Below: Wing Commander Edward Yeo-Thomas, seen here in civilian clothes in the RAF Demobilization Center.

efforts by underground resistance fighters in Nazi-occupied countries. In 1942 Wing Commander Yeo-Thomas joined the ranks of British Special Operations as liaison officer between the SOE and Colonel André Dewavrin of the BCRA. In 1943, using the code name White Rabbit, Yeo-Thomas and Dewavrin parachuted into France to design strategy and to unify underground efforts against the Germans. The two men rendezvoused with Major Pierre Brosselette and the trio visited the numerous clusters of widely scattered resistance organizations, imploring them to concentrate more on the collection of intelligence and less on the commission of sabotage. While traveling through France, Yeo-Thomas also met groups calling themselves the Maquis—bands of young guerrilla fighters who had gone into the hills to escape Nazi labor conscription. Jean Moulin, de Gaulle's

REMEMBER IN FUTURE YOU MAY HAVE TO USE COUPONS – CHOOSE WISELY

PLEASE DO NOT HURRY IN YOUR CHOICE

P.O.W. Card

YEO-THOMAS, Forest Frederick Edward   Allied French Section

Born: 17.6.1901 at London

Acting S/Ldr R.A.F., 89215

Alias: DODKIN, GAONACH, sHELLEY, VILLARS, CHEVAL, CHEVALIER,
        CHANCELIER, TIRELLI, THIERRY

Sent: from U.K. 24.2.44

Last heard of in Buchenwald Concentration Camp

SRL A814/815   PRIORITY EMERGENCY   FOR 122155B
FROM WATERMARK
TO HOLE UPPERMOST   WORDS 160

MUS 369 FORRE BROOK FROM CD
    615 INSUL FOR ROWLANDSON FROM CD
FOLLOWING IS DECODED VERSION OF MESSAGE RECEIVED FROM ASYMPTOTE
QUOTE INVALUABLE DOCUMENTS CONCERNING LATEST RESEARCH AND
DISCOVERIES BACTERIOLOGICAL WARFARE ALSO PLANS SECRET
UNDERGROUND DUMPS AND FACTORIES KEPT HERE AT BUCHENWALD STOP
ALL PREPARED TO SECURE THEM BUT CAN SUCCEED ONLY PROVIDING RAPID
ASSISTANCE ARRIVES JUST BEFORE OR IMMEDIATELY UPON GERMAN
CAPITULATION AS CAMP OFFICIALS WILL TRY DESTROY ALL DASH VALUE
OF DOCUMENTS WARRANTS EVERY EFFORT STOP SPEEDY ARRIVAL AIRBORNE
OR PARATROOPS ESSENTIAL WILL FIND ORGANISED ASSISTANCE WITHIN
CAMP BUT I HAVE NO ARMS DASH BEARER THIS MESSAGE TRUSTWORTHY
AND KNOWS EVERYTHING AWAITS REPLY AND INSTRUCTIONS STOP
ACKNOWLEDGE BY IODOFORM DU MOINEAU AU LAPIN STOP HAVE
EVERYTHING UNDER CONTROL AND HOPE FOR EARLY VICTORY STOP
VINGT CINQ SEPTEMBRE STOP ALL MY LOVE BARBARA TOMMY STOP
CHEERIO DIZZY ASYMPTOTE UNQUOTE THIS MESSAGE ENCODED IN LOW
GRADE CIPHER WHICH EASILY BROKEN BY ENEMY IF IT HAS BEEN
INTERCEPTED STOP OUR COMMENTS FOLLOW 121045B

TP 121019Z MT AS
KKK
INT WDS 162
WORDS 162
R PW
PLS 121020Z MT++

Above and Left: SOE card regarding Yeo-Thomas's incarceration at Buchenwald, above. At left is a deciphered version of a coded message he sent with details of the atrocities being committed at the camp. The dignified and dispassionate evidence that Yeo-Thomas gave at the Nuremburg Trials helped to convict, among others, the camp commandant of Buchenwald.

Above: Yeo-Thomas's SOE history sheet. As well as the bravery that Yeo-Thomas displayed, he also possessed a high degree of fair-mindedness. He gave evidence at Nuremburg in defense of the German commando Otto Skorzeny, whom he considered an honorable foe.

special emissary, was also trying to unify the underground effort, but locating and organizing the independent Maquis bands had always been a problem.

A Conversation with Winston Churchill

In late 1943, de Gaulle learned that the Gestapo had captured Moulin and other key leaders of the French resistance. He sent Brosselette to France to replace Moulin, and Yeo-Thomas went with him. The Gestapo had decimated the underground organization through the efforts of double agents recruited by the Abwehr. The entire underground operation had to be reorganized and reunified, and Yeo-Thomas set out with Brosselette to put it back together again. While making the rounds, Yeo-Thomas discovered how poorly equipped the underground groups were, especially the Maquis guerrillas who lived in small pockets in the hills.

After eight weeks in France, Yeo-Thomas was picked up and flown back to London. The SOE operative went directly to 10 Downing Street to speak with the prime minister, Winston Churchill.

Churchill agreed to give him five minutes. The prime minister was impressed with Yeo-Thomas's description of the work being performed by French resistance fighters and their desperate need for arms and ammunition. Thirty minutes passed before Churchill terminated the discussion. He promised to send planes, with weapons and supplies, as soon as arrangements could be made for air drops.

The Final Ordeal

While in London, Yeo-Thomas learned that Brosselette had been captured and thrown into Rennes Prison. He parachuted into France to free the BCRA resistance leader and pulled together a small force of underground volunteers to raid the prison. The day before the rescue, Yeo-Thomas's courier gave him up to the Gestapo. Before he could swallow a cyanide tablet, the SS agents grabbed him and took him to Gestapo headquarters. Then the torture began. With his hands cuffed behind him, the thugs beat

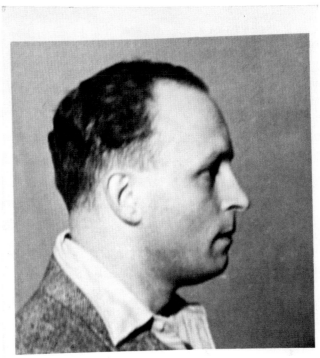

him unconscious. After he refused to say anything and passed out, they threw him in a tub of ice-cold water to wake him up and beat him again. They pounded his face with gloved fists, kicked him in the stomach and groin, whipped his back and torso with leather thongs and steel rods, and continued the torture for 12 hours, day in and day out. When they concluded that Yeo-Thomas would not disclose information, they threw him in a cell. Meanwhile, Brosselette committed suicide by jumping out of a window, but Yeo-Thomas did not learn his friend had died until later.

Yeo-Thomas spent several months in Fresnes Prison, at times awakened from sleep for more interrogation. The Gestapo finally gave up and sent him to Buchenwald to be tortured and starved until he died. Somehow, Yeo-Thomas, though not a large man or particularly muscular, tolerated the punishment with an iron will and survived. He gathered his strength and tried to escape, only to be caught and subjected to more torture. A German guard admired Yeo-

Thomas's resilience. Just before he was due to be executed, the guard arranged a switch of identities with a man who had died of typhus, and the SOE agent escaped again. This time he made it to the lines of advancing American troops, who picked him up more dead than alive.

In 1947 Yeo-Thomas testified against the war criminals at Buchenwald, helping to send 22 to the gallows. With the war behind him, he went back to Paris and returned to his business as a designer of women's clothes. However, the punishment inflicted on him by the Gestapo had permanently damaged his health, and Yeo-Thomas died in 1964.

Yeo-Thomas never wrote a book about himself, but in 1960 Bruce Marshall published *The White Rabbit*, taken directly from personal interviews with the former SOE officer.

Above: Mug shots of Yeo-Thomas. At a memorial service held on April 30, 1964, Yeo-Thomas was described by Sir James Hutchison as "a giant in courage, in fortitude, in loyalty, in resoursefulness, and in patriotism."

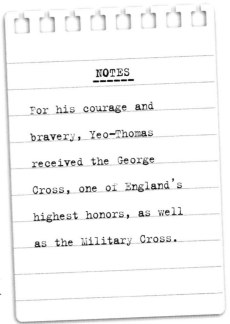

NOTES

For his courage and bravery, Yeo-Thomas received the George Cross, one of England's highest honors, as well as the Military Cross.

ZACHARIAS, ELLIS M. (1890–1961)

Ellis Zacharias spent most of his career in the U.S. Navy as an intelligence officer. His missions before World War II paint a grim picture of Japanese treachery.

Ellis Zacharias grew up in Jacksonville, Florida, and as a teenager, set his sights on a career in the U.S. Navy. In 1908, with the help of his district congressman and excellent grades in high school, Zacharias received an appointment to the U.S. Naval Academy in Annapolis, Maryland, and graduated in 1912. The navy noticed Zacharias's ability in languages and sent him to Tokyo in 1920 to study Japanese. He remained in Japan for four years, but returned to the United States for a few months in 1921 to participate in the Washington Naval Conference, where the United States, Great Britain, Japan, France, and Italy placed restrictions on the tonnages of ships and the sizes and number of armaments. Even in the 1920s, the U.S. Navy was keeping an eye on Japan.

The Intelligence Gatherer

Prior to the Washington Naval Conference, Herbert Yardley had broken the Japanese diplomatic code, which gave the U.S. Navy insight into Japan's goals.

```
----DOSSIER--------

Name: Ellis M. Zacharias

Code Name: None

Birth/Death: 1890-1961

Nationality: American

Occupation: Naval Officer

Involvement: Intelligence

Officer for the U.S. Navy

Outcome: Died of Natural

Causes
```

Instead of sending Zacharias immediately back to Japan, the Office of Naval Intelligence (ONI) assigned him to tracking Commander Yoshitake Uyeda, the Japanese naval attaché in Washington. Zacharias discovered that Uyeda was having an affair with a secretary in the Navy Department. ONI decided to not interfere with the affair but to use the secretary to

Above: Aboard America's oldest heavy cruiser in service, the *Salt Lake City*. Captain Ellis Zacharias, right, looks on as crewmen try on a suit they created themselves for protection from steam.

locate Uyeda's Red Navy codebook. Zacharias soon learned that Uyeda kept the codebook in his quarters outside the Japanese Embassy. Agents raided the building, stole the codebook, and gave it to the navy. Zacharias returned to Japan to continue his language studies and mingle with members of the Japanese navy while keeping watch on the movements of warships in Tokyo's harbor.

The ONI had other missions in mind for their language expert. In October 1926 the navy transferred Zacharias to command the destroyer *McCormick*, which had been fitted with sophisticated radio equipment especially designed to monitor Japanese dispatch traffic. After

sailing into the Yellow Sea, Zacharias left the ship in 1927 and spent the next few months traveling from one port to another in the Far East and the Pacific Islands, upgrading navy communication systems to the new radio technology. When he learned that the Japanese navy intended to perform war games with 170 warships in the middle of the Pacific, he went onboard the USS *Marblehead* and stationed the destroyer in close radio proximity, but well below the horizon. He noted how the Japanese used aircraft carriers, as well as carrier craft tactics, to great advantage. When he reached Kobi, he passed the intelligence to ONI.

During World War II, Zacharias commanded a number of ships, including the light cruiser *Salt Lake City* and the battleship *New Mexico*.

The Search for Colonel X

Lieutenant Colonel Earl H. "Pete" Ellis was one of the most brilliant and eccentric spies to ever wear a Marine uniform. After World War I he began lecturing on the role of the Marine Corps in the next war; in 1920, he personally believed it would be against Japan. In 1921 he put together a 50,000-word island-hopping strategy for attacking Japan's bases in the Pacific, which included stepping through the Marshall, Caroline, Gilbert, Mariana, Palau, and the Ryukyu (Okinawa) islands to Japan. The navy reviewed the recommendation and filed it away as "Plan Orange" without realizing that, with few alterations, it would be the key warfighting strategy applied by the navy against Japan from 1943 to 1945.

In 1922 Ellis was living in Yokohama posing as a businessman at the same time that Zacharias was serving as assistant naval attaché in Tokyo. Ellis had a drinking problem, so Zacharias closely monitored his colleague's behavior. Ellis was never an effective spy, but he had been sent to Japan to find the best way, if war should come, to gain quick control of Japan's Pacific islands. In 1923 Ellis, code-named Colonel X, departed from Yokohama on his tour of the southern Pacific islands. He never returned. After a lengthy search, Zacharias learned that Ellis had died under mysterious circumstances on Koror, an island in the Carolines.

At Zacharias's request, Captain V. R. Webb dispatched Chief Pharmacist Lawrence Zembsch to the Carolines to retrieve Ellis's remains. When Zembsch returned to Tokyo, Zacharias found him huddled in a cabin in what resembled a drunken stupor and clutching a white box containing the cremated remains of Ellis. Zembsch looked like he had not shaved, eaten, or bathed for weeks. He remained unable to communicate for five days. When he was finally able to speak, he remembered nothing, as though his memory had been completely erased. Zacharias attempted to trace Ellis's steps and came to the conclusion that the Japanese had made the colonel quite comfortable all the way to Jaluit and at some point introduced lethal drugs into his drinks. Zacharias assumed that a different mind-blanking drug may have been used on Zembsch to render him unable to relate anything he may have learned while probing Ellis's death.

In 1942 Zacharias became the deputy director of ONI and was given his first battleship command. Much of his active service during the World War II was participating in the island-hopping campaign designed by Ellis in 1921. Zacharias retired from the navy in 1946 but continued to study the psychology of the Japanese, and never really considered his life of information-gathering over until he died on June 27, 1961.

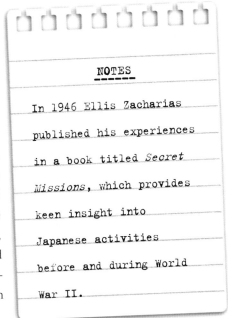

NOTES

In 1946 Ellis Zacharias published his experiences in a book titled *Secret Missions*, which provides keen insight into Japanese activities before and during World War II.

GLOSSARY OF ORGANIZATIONS

ABWEHR: German intelligence (1866–1945)
BBC: British Broadcasting Corporation
BCRA: Free French intelligence service in World War II
Cheka: Soviet secret state police (1917–1922)
CIA: U.S. Central Intelligence Agency (established 1947)
DORA: Code name for the Soviet GRU espionage network
FBI: U.S. Federal Bureau of Investigation (established 1924)
GPU: Soviet secret police and intelligence service (1922–1923)
GRU: Soviet intelligence headquarters for the Red Army (1920–present)
KGB: Soviet secret police and intelligence service (established 1954 to succeed the MVD). Dissolved into three new branches in 1991, with the SVR section designated for foreign intelligence.
MI5: British counterintelligence (established 1909)
MI6: British intelligence, also SIS (established 1911)
MVD: Soviet secret police and intelligence service (1946–1954)
NATO: North Atlantic Treaty Organization (established 1949)

NID: British Naval Intelligence Department
NIS: U.S. Naval Investigative Service
NKVD: Soviet secret police and intelligence service (1934–1946)
NSA: U.S. National Security Agency (established 1952)
OGPU: Soviet secret police and intelligence service (1923–1939)
ONI: U.S. Office of Naval Intelligence (1882–present)
OSS: U.S. Office of Strategic Services (1940–1946)
SD: Nazi party intelligence organization (1931–1945)
SIGENT: U.S. signals intelligence gathering system (1943–present)
SIGINT: British signals intelligence gathering system (1943–present)
SIS: British Secret Intelligence Service (1909, becomes MI6 in 1911)
SMERSH: Soviet assassination agency (1943–1946)
SO: Special Operations of OSS
SOE: UK Special Operations Executive for espionage in Nazi-occupied Europe (1940–1941)
SS: Security police for the Gestapo and SD (1925–1945)
SVR: Russian Foreign Intelligence Service (1991–present)
UDT: U.S. underwater demolition team

BIBLIOGRAPHY

Ashley, Maurice. *Oliver Cromwell and His World.* New York and London, 1972.

Baden-Powell, Robert. *My Adventures as a Spy.* London, 1915.

Bakeless, John. *Spies of the Confederacy.* Philadelphia, 1970.

Bartz, Karl. *Downfall of the German Secret Service.* London, 1956.

Bazna, Eleyza. *I Was Cicero.* New York, 1962.

Belloc, Hillaire. *Richelieu.* Philadelphia, 1929.

Bergamini, David. *Japan's Imperial Conspiracy.* New York, 1971.

Blake, George. *No Other Choice.* New York, 1990.

Boyle, Andrew. *The Last Man.* New York, 1979.

Brodie, Fawn M. *The Devil Drives: A Life of Sir Richard Burton.* London, 1967.

Brook-Shepherd, Gordon. *The Stormy Petrels.* New York, 1982.

Bulloch, John, and Henry Miller. *Spy Ring: The Story of the Naval Secrets Case.* London, 1961.

Bushong, Millard K. *General Turner Ashby and Stonewall's Valley Campaign.* Verona, Virginia, 1980.

Chambers, Whittaker. *Witness.* New York, 1952.

Connolly, Cyril. *The Missing Diplomats.* London. 1952.

Cookridge, E. H. (pseud.) *Inside SOE.* London, 1966.

———. *The Third Man.* London, 1974.

Coulson, Thomas. *Mata Hari: Courtesan and Spy.* London, 1930.

Cox, Cynthia. *The Enigma of the Age: The Strange Story of the Chevalier d'Eon.* New York, 1966.

Crawford, Iain. *The Profumo Affair: A Crisis in Contemporary Society.* London, 1963.

Dallin, David J. *Soviet Espionage.* New Haven, Conn., 1955.

Dank, Milton. *The French Against the French: Collaboration and Resistance.* London, 1978.

Deacon, Richard. *A History of the British Secret Service.* London, 1980.

———. *A History of the Russian Secret Service.* London, 1972.

Deakin, F. W. D. and G. R. Storry. *The Case of Richard Sorge.* New York, 1967.

Dukes, Paul. *Red Dusk and the Morrow.* London, 1932.

———. *The Story of "ST25": Adventure and Romance in the Secret Intelligence Service in Red Russia.* London, 1939.

Edmonds, Sara Emma. *Nurse and Spy in the Union Army.* Hartford, Conn., 1865.

Fisher, David. *Operation Lucy: The Most Secret Spy Ring of the Second World War.* New York, 1981.

Flexner, James T. *The Traitor and the Spy.* New York, 1953.

Forbes, Esther. *Paul Revere and the World He Lived In.* New York, 1941.

Ford, Corey. *A Peculiar Service.* Boston, 1965.

Giskes, Hermann J. *London Calling North Pole.* London, 1953.

Gouzenko, Igor. *The Iron Curtain.* New York, 1948.

Haukelid, Knut. *Skiis Against the Atom*. London, 1954.

Hayward, F. H. *Alfred the Great*. London, 1936.

Hiss, Alger. *In the Court of Public Opinion*. New York, 1957.

Höhne, Heinz. *Codeword: Direktor: The Story of the Red Orchestra*. New York, 1971.

Houghton, Harry. *Operation Portland: The Autobiography of a Spy*. London, 1972.

Hyde, H. Montgomery. *The Atom Bomb Spies*. New York, 1980.

Hynd, Alan. *Betrayal from the East: The Inside Story of Japanese Spies*. New York, 1943.

Ivanov, Yevgeny, with Gennady Sokolov. *The Naked Spy*. London, 1992.

Kahn, David. *Hitler's Spies: German Military Intelligence in World War II*. New York, 1978.

Kaufman, Louis, and Barbara Fitzgerald, et al. *Moe Berg: Athlete, Scholar, Spy*. New York, 1974.

Khokhlov, Nicolai. *In the Name of Conscience*. New York, 1959.

Khrushchev, Nikita. *Khrushchev Remembers*. Boston, 1970.

Kilzer, Louis. *Hitler's Traitor: Martin Bormann and the Defeat of the Third Reich*. Novato, Calif., 2000.

Kinchen, Oscar A. *Women Who Spied for the Blue and the Gray*. New York, 1972.

Klein, Alexander. *The Counterfeit Traitor*. New York, 1958.

Knight, Amy. *Beria: Stalin's First Lieutenant*. Princeton, N.J., 1993.

Krivitsky, Walter G. *In Stalin's Secret Service*. New York, 1939.

Lampe, David, and Szenasi Laszlo. *The Self-Made Villain: A Biography of I. T. Trebitsch-Lincoln*. London, 1961.

Lewis, David. *Prisoners of Honor: The Dreyfus Affair*. New York, 1973.

Lewis, Leslie. *Connoisseurs and Secret Agents*. London, 1961.

Lindsey, Robert. *The Falcon and the Snowman: The True Story of Friendship and Espionage*. New York, 1979.

Lucas, Norman. *The Great Spy Ring*. London, 1966.

Maclean, Fitzroy. *Take Nine Spies*. New York, 1978.

Masterman, John Cecil. *The Double-Cross System in the War of 1939–45*. New Haven, Conn., 1972.

Marshall, Bruce. *The White Rabbit: From the Story Told to Him by Wing Commander F. F. E. Yeo-Thomas*. London, 1952.

Maugham, W. Somerset. *The Summing Up*. London, 1938.

McAleavy, Henry. *A Dream of Tartary*. London, 1963.

Newman, Bernard. *Epics of Espionage*. New York, 1951.

————. *Spy and Counter-Spy: The Story of the British Secret Service*. New York, 1970.

Nicolaievsky, Boris. *Aseff, the Russian Judas*. New York, 1934.

Orlov, Alexander. (Leon Lazerevik Feldbin) *The Secret History of Stalin's Crimes*. New York, 1953.

Overton-Fuller, Jean. *Madeleine*. London, 1952.

Papen, Franz von. *Memoirs*. London, 1952.

Penkovsky, Oleg. *The Penkovsky Papers*. Garden City, N.Y., 1965.

Pennypacker, Morton. *The Two Spies*. New York, 1932.

Petrov, Vladimir, and Evdokia Petrov. *Empire of Fear*. New York, 1956.

Pilat, Oliver. *The Atomic Spies*. New York, 1952.

Pinkerton, Allan. *The Spy of the Rebellion*. New York, 1877.

Powers, Gary Francis, with Curt Gentry. *Operation Overflight: The U-2 Spy Pilot Tells His Story for the First Time*. New York, 1970.

Pugh, Marshall. *Frogman: Commander Crabb's Story*. London, 1956.

Raphael, Frederic. *W. Somerset Maugham and His World*. London, 1976.

Read, Anthony, and David Fisher. *Operation Lucy: Most Secret Spy Ring of the Second World War*. London, 1980.

Read, Conyers. *Mr. Secretary Walsingham and the Policy of Queen Elizabeth*. Cambridge, Mass., 1925.

Reilly, Sidney George. *Britain's Master Spy: His Own Story*. New York, 1985.

Rintelen, Franz von. *Memoirs*. London, 1952.

Ronge, Maximilian. *The Treachery of Colonel Redl*. London, 1921.

Rowan, R. W. *Spy and Counter-Spy*. New York, 1928.

Seth, Ronald. *The Executioners*. London, 1967.

————. *Forty Years of Soviet Spying*. London, 1965.

————. *Secret Servants: A Story of Japanese Espionage*. New York, 1957.

————. *Unmasked: The Story of Soviet Espionage*. New York, 1965.

Sutherland, Douglas. *The Great Betrayal: The Definitive Story of Blunt, Philby, Burgess, and Maclean*. London, 1981.

————. *The Fourth Man*. London, 1980.

Tanenhaus, Sam. *Whittaker Chambers: A Biography*. New York, 1997.

Thomson, Sir Basil. *My Experiences at Scotland Yard*. London, 1935.

Trepper, Leopold. *The Great Game: Memoirs of the Spy Hitler Couldn't Silence*. London, 1977.

Van Doren, Carl. *Secret History of the American Revolution*. New York, 1941.

Vassall, John. *Vassall: The Autobiography of a Spy*. London, 1975.

West, Nigel, ed. *The Faber Book of Espionage*. London, 1993.

West, Rebecca. *The Vassall Affair*. London, 1963.

White, John Baker. *The Soviet Spy System*. London, 1948.

Wright, Peter. *Spycatcher*. New York, 1987.

Zacharias, Ellis M. *Secret Missions: The Story of an Intelligence Officer*. New York, 1946.

Zweig, Stefan. *Life of Joseph Fouché*. London, 1930.

7 Sergei Gunayev/Time Life Pictures/Getty Images; 8 Sergey Zhukov/AFT/Getty Images; 11 Bettmann/CORBIS; 12 Time Life Pictures/Getty Images; 13 Bettmann/CORBIS; 14 Bettmann/CORBIS; 23 Spencer Arnold/Getty Images; 24 Bettmann/CORBIS; 27 Markowitz Jeffrey/CORBIS SYGMA; 28 Jeffrey Markowitz/CORBIS SYGMA; 29 CORBIS SGYMA; 30 Richard A Bloom/CORBIS; 31 Markowitz Jeffrey/CORBIS SYGMA; 32 Markowitz Jeffrey/CORBIS SYGMA; 33 left Markowitz Jeffrey/CORBIS SYGMA; 33 right Markowitz Jeffrey/CORBIS SYGMA; 35 Hulton Archive/Getty Images; 36 Hulton Archive/Getty Images; 38 Time Life Pictures/Getty Images; 44 Hulton Archive/Getty Images; 45 MPI/Getty Images; 46 LOC LC-USZ62-40505; 47 LOC LC-USZ62-68483; 49 CORBIS; 52 Hulton Archive/Getty Images; 55 Bettmann/CORBIS; 56 Hulton Archive/Getty Images; 59 Medford Historical Society Collection/CORBIS; 70 The National Archives, ref. KV6-8 Cicero 19B; 73 Michael Nicholson/CORBIS; 74 Imagno/Austrian Archives/Getty Images; 77 Keystone/Getty Images; 78 Bettmann/CORBIS; 79 Thomas D. Mcavoy/Time Life Pictures/Getty Images; 80 Bettmann/CORBIS; 82 Thomas D. Mcavoy/Time Life Pictures/Getty Images; 85 Bettmann/CORBIS; 86 Bettmann/CORBIS; 89 Hulton Archive/Getty images; 90 Dimitri Baltermants/The D. Baltermants Collection/CORBIS; 93 Keystone/Getty Images; 98 Fox Photos/Getty Images; 101 Keystone/Hulton Archive/Getty Images; 102 Keystone/Hulton Archive/Getty Images; 105 Bettmann/CORBIS; 106 Bettmann/CORBIS; 109 LOC, LC-DIG-CWPBH-01988; 110 LOC, LOC-DIG-CWPBH-01991; 113 Express/Express/Getty Images; 116 Bettmann/CORBIS; 117 Hulton-Deutsch Collection/CORBIS; 119 top The National Archives, ref. FO371-47341; 119 bottom The National Archives, ref. FO371-47341; 120 Keystone/Getty Images; 123 Keystone/Hulton Archive/Getty Images; 124 The National Archives, ref. KV2-934; 125 The National Archives, ref. KV2-934; 126 The National Archives, ref. KV2-933; 128 The National Archives, ref. KV2-933; 129 The National Archives, ref. KV2-934; 131 Bettmann/CORBIS; 132 Bettmann/CORBIS; 134 Bettmann/CORBIS; 135 Hank Walker/Time Life Pictures/Getty Images; 137 The National Archives, ref. KV2-462; 138 The National Archives, ref. KV2-461; 139 The National Archives, ref. KV2-461; 139 bottom right The National Archives, ref. KV2-461; 140 The National Archives, ref. KV2-462; 142-143 The National Archives, ref. KV2-462; 145 Hulton-Deutsch/CORBIS; 146 Arthur Aidala/Bettmann/CORBIS; 150 Hulton-Deutsch Collection/CORBIS; 152 Bettmann/CORBIS; 155 Hulton Archive/Getty Images; 159 Hulton Archive/Getty Images; 162 Hulton Archives/Getty Images; 163 Time Life Pictures/Mansell/Time Life Pictures/Getty Images; 165 Carl Mydans/Time Life Pictures/Getty Images; 167 Carl Mydans/Time Life Pictures/Getty Images; 169 Hulton-Deutsch Collection/CORBIS; 170 Bettmann/CORBIS; 179 State Archives of Michigan; 180 State Archives of Michigan; 186 AP/EMPICS; 189 The National Archives, ref. KV2/1612; 190 The National Archives, ref. KV2/1612; 191 The National Archives, ref. KV2/1612; 192 The National Archives, ref. KV2/1612; 195 Getty Images; 199 EMPICS; 200 The National Archives, ref. KV2-1258; 201 CORBIS; 202 AP/EMPICS; 203 The National Archives, ref. KV2-1253; 204 The National Archives, ref. KV2-1263; 205 Keystone/Getty Images; 210 AP/EMPICS; 211 The National Archives, ref. KV2-564; 212 The National Archives, ref. KV2-564; 213 The National Archives, ref. KV2-564; 215 The National Archives, ref. KV2-963; 216 The National Archives, ref. KV2-963; 217 The National Archives, ref. KV2-961; 218 The National Archives, ref. KV2-961; 221 The National Archives, ref. KV2-1424; 222 The National Archives, ref. KV2-1419; 223 The National Archives, ref. KV2-1421; 224 AP/EMPICS; 226 EMPICS; 227 Bettmann/CORBIS; 229 LOC, LC-DIG–CWPBH-04849; 232 MPI/Getty Images; 233 MPI/Getty Images; 234 Bettmann/CORBIS; 237 The National Archives, ref. HS9 676-4; 238 The National Archives, ref. HS9 676-4; 239 The National Archives, ref. HS9 676-4; 240 The National Archives, ref. HS9 676-4; 241 AP/EMPICS; 243 William Bond/Keystone/Getty Images; 244 Thomas D. Mcavoy/Time Life Pictures/Getty Images; 245 James Whitmore/Time Life Pictures/Getty Images; 246 Herbert Gehr/Time Life Pictures/Getty Images; 247 left The National Archives, ref. FO 371; 247 right The National Archives, ref. FO 371; 248 AFP/AFP/Getty Images; 249 Helaye Seidman/AFP/Getty Images; 251 AP/EMPICS; 254 The National Archives, ref. KV2-1384; 255 The National Archives, ref. KV2-1384; 256 The National Archives, ref. KV2-1384; 259 F.A. Swaine/Hulton Archive/Getty Images; 262 The National Archives, ref. HS9 836; 263 top The National Archives, ref. HS9 836-5; 263 bottom The National Archives, ref. HS9 836-5; 264 top left The National Archives, ref. HS9 836-5; 264 bottom right The National Archives, ref. HS9 836-5; 265 The National Archives, ref. HS(836-5; 267 Carly Mydans/Time Life Pictures/Getty Images; 268 Carly Mydans/Time Life Pictures/Getty Images; 270 AP/EMPICS; 273 The National Archives, ref. KV2 803-1; 275 EMPICS; 276 McCabe/Express/Getty Images; 277 Keystone/Getty Images; 278 Hulton-Deutsch Collection/CORBIS; 281 Illustrated London News/Getty Images; 282 Fox Photos/Getty Images; 283 Hulton Archive/Getty Images; 285 Keystone/Getty Images; 288 Keystone/Getty Images; 291 Bettmann/CORBIS; 292 The National Archives, ref. KV2-1; 293 The National Archives, ref. MEP 03-2444; 294 The National Archives, ref. MEP 03-2444; 295 Hulton Archives/Getty Images; 296 Hulton Archives/Getty Images; 297 The National Archives, ref. MEP 03-2444; 299 Hulton Archive/Getty Images; 302 Bettmann/CORBIS; 305 Keystone/Getty Images; 306 The National Archives, ref. HS9 1070-6; 307 The National Archives, ref. HS9 1070-6; 308 The National Archives, ref. HS9 1070-6; 311 The National Archives, ref. KV2 280; 312 The National Archives, ref. KV2 1279; 313 The National Archives, ref. KV2 1280; 314 The National Archives, ref. KV2 279; 317 Walter Daran/Time Life Pictures/Getty Images; 320 Imagno/Schostal Archiv/Getty Images; 321 AP/EMPICS; 322 Imagno/Austrian Archives/Getty Images; 323 Time Life Pictures/Getty Images; 325 Stuzhin & Cheredintez/Keystone/Hulton Archive/Getty Images; 326 Keystone/Getty Images; 329 Keystone/Hulton Archive/Getty Images; 330 Central Press/Hulton Archive/Getty Images; 333 Keystone/Getty Images; 334 Terry Ashe/Time Life Pictures/Getty Images; 335 Harold Clements/Express/Getty Images; 337 LOC, LC-USZ62-117576; 338 LOC, LC-DIG-CWPB-04326; 339 LOC, LC-DIG-CWPB-03855; 341 AP/EMPICS; 342 David Silverman/Getty Images; 343 Alex Wong/Getty Images; 345 John Domninis/Time Life Pictures/Getty Images; 346 Keystone/Getty Images; 347 Keystone/Getty Images; 348 Carl Mydans/Time Life Pictures/Getty Images; 349 AP/EMPICS; 351 Hulton-Deutsch Collection/CORBIS; 354 Topical Press Agency/Getty Images; 355 keystone/Getty Images; 356 Keystone Getty Images; 357 EMPICS; 359 The National Archives, ref. KV2 1647; 361 The National Archives, ref. KV2 1649; 362 The National Archives, ref. KV2 1647; 363 The National Archives, ref. KV2 1647; 365 Hulton Archive/Getty Images; 366 Imagno/Getty Images; 369 Hulton Archive/Getty Images; 373 John Singleton Copley/Hulton Archive/Getty Images; 374 Francis Miller/Time Life Pictures/Getty Images; 377 Hulton Archive/Getty Images; 378 Time Life Pictures/Mansell/Time Life Pictures/Getty Images; 381 General Photographic Agency/Getty Images; 382 Topical Press Agency/Getty Images; 385 AP/EMPICS 386 top The National Archives, ref. KV2 1627; 386 bottom The National Archives, ref. KV2 1627; 389 Hulton Archive/Getty Images; 390 Keystone/Getty Images; 391 AFP/AFP/Getty Images; 392 Hulton Archive; Getty Images; 393 Hulton Archive/Getty Images; 394 Bettmann/CORBIS; 395 Bettmann/CORBIS; 397 Hulton Archive/Getty Images; 400 AP/EMPICS; 403 Hulton Archive/Getty Images; 404 Hulton Archive/Getty Images; 407 Archive Photos/Getty Images; 410 Topical Press Agency/Getty Images; 413 AP/EMPICS; 414 top The National Archives, ref. KV2 2074; 414 bottom The National Archives, ref. KV2 2074; 416 The National Archives, ref. KV2 2074; 421 EMPICS; 424 AP/EMPICS; 427 Hulton Archive/Getty Images; 431 Patrick Riviere/Getty Images; 434 Central Press/Getty Images; 435 top The National Archives, ref. HS9 1458; 435 bottom The National Archives, ref. HS9 1458; 436 The National Archives, ref. HS9 1458; 437 The National Archives, ref. HS9 1458; 439 Bettmann/CORBIS; 440 Bob Landry/Time Life Pictures/Getty Images